# HISTORY OF BANKING

# HISTORY OF BANKING

*Edited by*

FORREST H. CAPIE

VOLUME I

*General Introduction*
*Money*

LONDON
WILLIAM PICKERING
1993

*Published by Pickering & Chatto (Publishers) Limited*
*17 Pall Mall, London, SW1Y 5NB*



British Library Cataloguing in Publication Data
History of Banking 1650–1850 – Vol. I:
Money
I. Capie, Forrest
332.109
Set ISBN 1 85196 126–7
This volume ISBN 1 85196 127–5

*Printed and bound in Great Britain by*
*Antony Rowe Limited*
*Chippenham*

VOLUME I

# CONTENTS

VOLUME II

# CONTENTS

VOLUME III

# CONTENTS

VOLUME IV

## CONTENTS

VOLUME V

# CONTENTS

VOLUME VI

# CONTENTS

VOLUME VII

# CONTENTS

VOLUME VIII

## CONTENTS

VOLUME IX

# CONTENTS

VOLUME X

# CONTENTS

# PREFACE

As the introductory essay tries to make clear, this collection of material is intended to provide a guide to the history of banking in England from the late seventeenth century until the middle of the nineteenth century as reflected in the contemporary literature. Other topics than banking strictly defined, of necessity, require some comment. The range of material available is enormous but this collection aims at being representative and capturing the essence of the major issues, debates, and developments. In an ambitious project of this kind there are bound to be differences of view and judgement on what, and how much, should be included. Each specialist will doubtless find fault when it comes to his/her own area, but it is hoped that overall it will prove to be both a valuable primary source and a reference collection that will provide easy access to the most important contributions to this literature.

I have been fortunate in being able to call on the two most distinguished monetary historians in the country, Leslie Pressnell and Keith Horsefield, and I should like to acknowledge their kind help and guidance. Leslie Pressnell and Keith Horsefield know just about all there is to know on these subjects. The know too many of the problems to embark on such a project as this themselves. It is only the bold who proceed. But they have been more than generous in providing ideas and correction. They are wholly absolved from all the remaining blemishes.

I should also like to acknowledge the generous assistance of the Goldsmiths' Library at the University of London Library and the House of Lords Record Office.

*City University Business School*
*May 1993*

FORREST CAPIE

# INTRODUCTION

## THE EVOLUTION OF MODERN BANKING IN BRITAIN, 1650–1850

Following the establishment of parliamentary government in England in the last quarter of the seventeenth century, there were substantial changes in the financial system. That pace of change was rapid until around 1720. Thereafter, while the system continued to evolve, it did so at a declining rate of change for much of the next century. The changes in money and banking in the century 1660–1760 were enormous and they were followed for another century by industrial and economic change on a substantial scale, all of which resulted in Britain becoming, by the mid-nineteenth century, the world's foremost economic power with a highly developed financial system. Britain was to remain at the heart of the world economy at least until the outbreak of the first world war. The collection of pamphlets and other material presented here are taken from the two centuries of financial and economic change that ended in 1850, and illustrate vividly the evolution of the modern banking system in all its forms in England, and its relationship with policy and the real economy.

The period covered is, in Dennis Robertson's (Professor of Economics at Cambridge in the 1950s) words, one in which we see in the seventeenth century, 'the London goldsmiths discovering that they could, in the most literal sense, make money by lending out their own promises to pay, and so filching from the Crown its immemorial right to determine, subject always to the vicissitudes of foreign trade, the volume of the country's money supply'. And it goes through until just after the 1844 Act when Robert Peel tried, 'to recapture the right of the Crown by giving a virtual monopoly of note issue to the Bank of England. ... But alas, or rather perhaps fortunately, the banks had already invented a dodge even neater than the note, namely the cheque, which enabled them to escape from Peel's net...' ('The Credit Squeeze' March, 1956. Reprinted in Dennison and Presley p. 59)

As might be imagined, there is a huge literature from which to select from. The purpose of bringing some of it together in this collection is to provide a representative sample that reflects the major issues and the tenor of debate that took place, and thereby to show how the banking sector evolved. The choice of items is a reflection in part of the extent of the activity under discussion. So, for example, the great flurry of activity on several fronts in the 1690s is reflected in the number of items presented. By comparison the middle years of the eighteenth century were relatively quiet. Then again the period from 1790–1815 was full of incident and a parallel literature, thus a correspondingly large number of entries appears for these years. (If there is a slightly disproportionate amount of room given to the seventeenth-century material, the justification would be that this material is generally much less accessible than, for instance, the early nineteenth-century material.)

The items chosen are in the main self-contained, but where they were contributions to a debate it has not always proved possible to include all the exchanges. An attempt has been made to include the most important contributions, though of course on occasions this is a matter of judgement. In some cases where well-known and easily accessible material is available it is given only minimal coverage here and sometimes simply a mention. Its relative importance will be commented on in this introduction.

*Money*

Money is both the starting point for a discussion of banking and at the centre of any such discussion. Banks are of interest primarily because they have a role to play in the provision of money services and in the creation of money. On several occasions, including the present day, there have been proposals that fractional reserve banking should be abandoned and 100 per cent reserves insisted on. This would turn banks into 'cloakrooms' simply charging fees for their services and remove the key element that makes them interesting. It is their ability to create and destroy money that generates excitement and necessitates some preliminary discussion on the nature of money and the forms it has taken.

The idea of money and the use of money have been around for thousands of years, but the nature and extent of use have changed enormously over time. So too has the impact of different kinds of channels of transmission. Money is essentially whatever people are content to use as money. In its earliest use (primitive money) it took many forms: animals, furs, tobacco and other products have all been used as money at different times. Shells, particularly cowrie shells, being small and of relatively consistent sizes, and easily transportable, have also proved popular, and are still in use in some parts of the world today. In its ideal form money will provide three basic functions: medium of exchange, store of value, and unit of account.

## GENERAL INTRODUCTION

In the development of a monetary economy the search for more suitable forms of money gave rise to metals. Copper and tin coins were used for transactions of small denomination. Silver became quite widely used in the late medieval period, and gold has also had an important role to play in the higher denomination transactions. Gradually paper money based on metals emerged. In the period covered by the literature in this collection, we move from the middle of the seventeenth century when metallic currency was in widespread use, and predominated in the money supply, through to the second half of the nineteenth century when paper money and bank deposits predominated in the total stock of money. This is not to say, however, that barter ever entirely disappeared, and it is still in use today in limited forms. In the eighteenth century it was still quite widespread. Adam Smith discusses some of the types of exchange that existed in Scotland in the late eighteenth century – one of the most advanced economies and with one of the most efficient monetary systems in the world at that time.

Discussion has seldom faded on the respective beneficial and adverse effects of money, and hence, by implication of banks. The introduction of money to an economy raises economic welfare, by removing the inefficiency of individuals having to search for coincident wants. The use of money and its smooth transmission helps promote efficient production and consumption. That much is positive. On the negative side there can be an excess of money in relation to output, and the consequent inflation introduces inequities in debtor/creditor relationships. All that has been known for a long time though some of the niceties of the process continue to be debated.

Heads of state have invariably used money for their own ends. In England the Tudor inflation was in part attributable to the debasement of the currency, the practice being to produce coins with a lower metallic content than their face value intimated. Governments everywhere have been unable to resist the temptation to produce too much money and hence subject the population to the inflation tax – a tax that is impossible to avoid and one that even the weakest government can impose.

If the quantity of money grows faster than the rate of growth of output there will be a rise in the long-run price level. This was clearly set out in the eighteenth century by David Hume and expanded on by Thornton at the beginning of the nineteenth century. (No collection of this kind would be complete without reference to Hume but his work is so widely available that we have included only one item here.) Even today there is still disagreement over the nature of money and the extent of its effects, be they beneficial or adverse. Not surprisingly it is a topic of continuous discussion throughout the period covered here.

*Usury*

Any discussion of money leads soon to discussion of the rate of interest. The rate of interest is the opportunity cost of holding money. The outcome of the relative strengths of the demand for money, and the supply of money, will be reflected in changes in the rate of interest. When the price level is not constant there is an important distinction to be made between the real rate of interest and the nominal rate. Real interest rates are what matter to investors. Nominal interest rates are the rates over which governments have some influence, and governments have always been keen to influence the rate at which they borrow. In periods of relatively stable prices, nominal rates should stay close to real rates.

From at least as early as medieval times there have been notions of fairness in matters concerning money and the price charged for borrowing. The term usury was originally an innocuous one which meant the taking of payments for the 'use' (or loan) of a sum of money. To charge 'too much' for a loan came to be referred to as usurious. In 1571 a Usury act was passed, which allowed interest rates of ten per cent per annum to be charged. That may seem high but it was, of course, in the middle of the great Tudor inflation when prices were rising at annual rates of around five or six per cent. As inflation eased somewhat in the 1620s the legal maximum was reduced to eight per cent (1624). Roseveare comments on this rate that, 'only the Crown's privilege and power enabled it to enforce this inadequate rate for its extensive borrowing and tardy repayments' (*The Financial Revolution, 1660–1760* 1991 p. 9). In 1660 the legal rate of interest was set at six per cent. Later, the parliaments of Charles II interfered by authorising preferential rates of interest (of seven per cent in 1670 and eight per cent 1677–9) on the borrowing of the crown.

The history of usury clearly predates our period but a great debate on usury ran through the early part of the period. There were many pamphleteers and distinguished contributors, such as John Locke and Josiah Child, participated. The issue never went away entirely and it was 1825 before the usury laws were repealed.

*Financial revolution*

The most dramatic innovations in banking came at an early stage. The scale and pace of change in financial innovation that was particularly concentrated in the decade of the 1690s constituted what surely can truly be called a revolution. The word revolution has been overused in historical studies, but this occasion does seem to be one where it is appropriate. How far outside that decade the term could be taken to apply is more problematic. Clearly there were several essential conditions laid down in the preceding decades, and the ramifications of the 1690s' changes carried on through the first few decades of the eighteenth century. When the subject was first set out with such clarity first by Horsefield (1960) and then by Dickson (1967) the whole period of financial change carried the dates 1650–1710 and 1688–1756 respectively. In the most recent view (Roseveare, 1991) the dating has been extended somewhat to 1660–1760, and the emphasis placed on smoothing over the sharper discontinuities that had previously obtained.

The background to the financial revolution was the change that had taken place in the nature of the state (importantly the sovereign parliament's control of finance). The responses in banking and finance were remarkable. There followed the well-known institutional innovations in the founding of the Bank of England and the origins of the National Debt. It was also at this point that the stock market proper emerged.

The military defeat at the hands of the Dutch in the 1660s was related to the financial inadequacies of government and was undoubtedly behind the recognition of the need for change. The changes then came and, by 1760, Britain had been transformed indisputably into the world's leading financial power. Her financial strength rested on a complex set of factors many of them intangible such as the confidence and trust that were the necessary pre-requisites for good credit.

A host of factors could be arrayed as part of the necessary background to the changes that came in the late seventeenth century, but high on that list, and probably crucial, was the initiative of 1665 to facilitate the government's wartime borrowing. Parliament was able to insist on knowing the purpose for which money given was to be used. In exchange for loans lenders were given official receipts which could be traded. This was the beginning of the gilt-edged security and it also marked the beginning of accountability.

The system was not of course reformed at a stroke. Bankers continued to earn huge profits and public opprobrium, and since one ambition of the 1665 initiative had been to allow government to borrow directly from the public further measures were introduced. Certificates called Treasury Orders were created in the years 1667–71 when Sir George Downing was Secretary to the Treasury. Downing had a reputation for efficiency and is seen as an important figure in shaping the modern relationship between the Treasury and parliament. He later gave his name to Downing Street and the fortune he left financed Downing College, Cambridge.

When, in December 1671, Charles II decided to defer repayments of debts (the 'stop' on the Exchequer) the beginning of another financial innovation was made. The debt that was frozen was owed in the main to the less than popular goldsmith bankers which undoubtedly mitigated the effects of the action at the time. Nevertheless, the King had irreparably damaged the Crown's credit and at the same time destroyed a generation of bankers. The solution to the problem which came in 1677 was the creation of annuities. The bankers were reimbursed in part. About half of the debt was repaid; but there was an obligation on them to repay their depositors. The annuities became the first long-term investment instruments and an active secondary market in these developed in the 1680s.

As far as the Crown was concerned a number of other sources of funds was still available to it, especially the large joint stock companies such as the East India Company. But the Crown was of diminishing importance: the basis of the nation's financial strength lay in the development of the Treasury as a powerful department of state, and in the parliamentary control of finance. It was the revolution of 1688 that saw the Treasury emerge as a public department.

The decade of the 1690s is however where most of the interesting action took place. It was a decade of extraordinary financial changes. The great achievements of the decade in financial terms were: the establishment of long-term borrowing, the founding of the Bank of England, the recoinage of the metallic currency, and the circulation of paper money (based on the credit of the issuer). Progress rested on acceptable government finance; indeed was underpinned by such finance.

Most of the decade was taken up with the war of the League of Augsburg (1689–97). The increased spending that that involved and the need for many of the funds to be spent abroad meant a number of different fiscal measures were also advanced and employed. But as is also usual these did not cover the costs, and borrowing was resorted to at an early point. Short-term loans were raised but at ever rising interest rates and by 1692 the situation was critical. Three new techniques were then employed: lotteries, tontines, and annuities. The latter two were long-term instruments and mark the beginning of deliberate long-term borrowing. But these were all dwarfed by the borrowing organised in the foundation of the Bank of England.

### *Recoinage*

The state of currency and credit in the late seventeenth century, were such that they gave rise to calls for changes. In the seventeenth century the currency was made up of a large number of metallic coins. There were gold coins of 20s, 10s and 5s, and silver coins of 5s, 2/6, 1/–, 2d, 1d and 1/2d. The state had minted copper farthings since 1644 but the great bulk of small transactions were taken care of by the mass of tokens put into circulation by private individuals (Berry).

Credit was extended by a variety of means. There were Exchequer orders from 1667 until the 'stop' of 1672. Exchequer Bills provided some and commercial credit instruments increasingly came into use. There were inland (as opposed to international) bills of exchange from about 1650 and, while they did pass from hand to hand, that use was limited by virtue of the size of the bills (often in the region of £100 and more) and because the transferability of bills of exchange was not complete until 1699. There were also promissory notes, much like bills but with inferior legal status. But it was the currency that presented problems. The particularly serious problem of the period, and indeed one that was for ever arising with the kind of metallic currency system in use, was that one metal would become over-valued in terms of the other – the mint and market ratios differed. Also in the last quarter of the seventeenth century there was the great deterioration in the quality of the silver coinage. Coins had become worn and also shaved or clipped. By 1695 the condition was so bad that the government decided there had to be a recoinage, known as 'the great recoinage'. In 1696 all silver coins were demonetised and gold coins revalued. All the existing coins were reminted at public expense. There was a lot of debate but most of it centred on whether the coins should have been devalued – what became known as the 'Locke–Lowndes' controversy.

Out of these debates and the associated crises at the end of the century a climate developed that provided the right kind of opening for advocates of extra credit facilities. For example, the emerging banks were attempting to attract deposits and this was stimulated by the opportunities that existed for culling out heavy-weight coins. The deposits made enabled the banks to lend – to the crown up to 1672, and further afield after that. They gave 'accountable notes' for deposits and these notes began to pass from hand to hand. It was a short step from there to making loans in notes even where there was no corresponding deposit. Thus the development of banking was given a considerable fillip from the poor state of the currency.

It is not surprising that these developments prompted many exponents to advance views of rival forms of banking. For example, there were the Lumbard banks where credit was based on goods. There are no modern survivors of these, though the pawnbroker is the nearest equivalent. There were also plans to capitalise government revenues and it was these that led to the establishment of the Bank of England. A third group was based on commercial obligations, the source of modern commercial banking. Then there were those proposals where credit was based on land. Present day building societies are the lineal descendants of such institutions.

## *Banks*

### *Land banks*

Following the growth of the needs of finance in the 1690s, the principal interest then settled on a variety of banking schemes. In modern times there has seldom been a period free from the desire to increase the purchasing power available. This has often arisen from perfectly good intentions. The ambition has been to use the available assets of the community more effectively. One of the more popular schemes over several centuries has been to use land as the backing for currency. The argument has been of the form, why should short-term liabilities of commercial undertakings be regarded as ideal investments for banks when mortgages are not?

Some of the earliest proposals in England can be found in the 1660s, and in their most basic forms these banks were designed as institutions whose assets were titles to land, notably Sir William Petty's scheme of the early 1660s. The motives were mostly entirely honourable. For example, one of the most commonly discussed aims was the need to improve the ease, convenience, and safety in the movement of funds. Frequently these aims were proposed as a means of raising purchasing power and thus exhibited some desire to help the poor. That was thought of as improving the facilities of manufacturing which, by extension, would benefit those in need.

It was in the last decade of the century though that proposals of all kinds being advanced and prominent among them were those for land banks. In 1689 Dr Hugh Chamberlen put forward one of his many schemes to issue interest bearing bills on the security of land. Chamberlen is today the best known of the unorthodox writers on banking in the period. Other members of his family had made other banking proposals. Chamberlen had been Physician to King Charles II and although by the 1690s his career in the medical world had faltered, he was still an eminent and respected figure.

John Briscoe was, next to Chamberlen, the most prolific exponent of land banks. Indeed he may have taken his ideas from Chamberlen. Other important contributors to the discussion were Asgill and Barbon, and there were a number of minor proposals from people such as Brewster and Murray, though none of the latter was successful. They were all part of that persistent urge to find ways of increasing purchasing power. Much of the pamphlet literature of the decade was an exchange of views on the relative merits of these various proposals. Various flaws were exposed and some criticisms were answered.

The proposals came from people from a variety of backgrounds and there were no well-established principles of banking at the time. This activity was all part of the search for new means of financial intermediation. Horsefield has provided a succinct summary of the arguments contained in these views: 'the best basis of trade is credit; the best basis of credit is land; therefore the best basis of trade is land-credit' (1960, p. 159). The inescapable problem in this kind of arrangement of course was that all assets were locked up in long-term, non-self-liquidating assets – mortgages, when the liabilities were of a much shorter duration.

This collection concentrates on banking but it should already be clear that it is necessary to consider the borders of money and related topics in the discussion. The central consideration in bringing this literature together is to illustrate how theory and practice developed and how institutions emerged and responded to the changing demands in the economy.

## *Commercial banks*

The precise origins of modern banking are still the subject of debate. A number of possible claimants compete for the source – scriveners, goldsmiths, and the older state financiers – but what is clear is that by the beginning of the period covered here the practice of deposit banking was established. Private banks prospered especially in London, while joint stock banks were prohibited by law. Country banks were the product of, and the contributors to, the process of industrialisation in the provinces and in the main were established at a later date. They developed a close and profitable business with the London private banks. Joint stock banking had to wait the change in public perceptions of the Bank that came in the nineteenth century, and the gradual erosion of the Bank of England's monopoly.

Forms of deposit banking had existed on continental Europe from medieval times, but English deposit banking had its beginnings in the middle of the seventeenth century. Deposit banking was different from what was commonly regarded by contemporaries as banking. Contemporaries saw banks as money lenders and brokers rather than the more modern concept of institutions making money by the creation and use of deposits.

The earliest explanation of the origins of deposit banking – and one that went unchallenged for almost two centuries) was that the goldsmiths, sometime in the seventeenth century, began to act as cashiers.

When they later began to hold cash (or deposits) they paid interest on them. A natural next step was that they loaned these reserves out at higher rates of interest than they paid to their depositors. Tawney (Professor of Economic History at the LSE in the 1940s and 1950s) was one of those who took issue with the view that the goldsmiths were the source. He showed that the Elizabethan scriveners took deposits from graziers and lent them out at a profit. The real authority on the origins of banking is Richards who provided a more eclectic view. He held that the state bankers' experience was transmitted to the goldsmith bankers, and that neither should be excluded in a full account.

Scriveners, brokers, and goldsmiths had long performed some of the functions associated with banking and made their profits from the fees they charged for their services. But they had stopped short of the key function of modern banking: the creation of deposits. Evidence is not easy to assemble but it is clear that that practice, albeit in nascent form, was developing in the course of the seventeenth century. Sir Robert Clayton whose origins were with the scriveners, was one of the first such bankers – holding deposits of almost £2 million in the mid 1660s; and at that time goldsmith bankers were also making loans with their clients' money. It has become clear that the scale of the monetary transactions at this time was a multiple of the stock of 'base' money.

This then is where the origins of the London private banks lie. There were around thirty of them in the early eighteenth century and most of them were to survive for a long time. In fact their numbers grew modestly in the course of the eighteenth century. There were fifty in 1750 and seventy by 1800. Some still exist – names such as Hoare's and Child's. These latter were 'West End' banks as opposed to the City banks. The former dealt with wealthy clients usually in the aristocracy and specialised in mortgages while the latter's balance sheets were biased to trade bills and stock exchange securities. The City private banks also played a significant part in channelling the funds of the provincial private banks into the London money market. Note issue was never of any significance to the London private banks and by the 1790s the practice had died out altogether.

## *Country banking*

The real growth in country banking had to wait until the second half of the eighteenth century. Provincial, or country, banks grew up in tandem with the economic changes that took place in the provinces in the course of the century. They were clearly an important part of the industrialisation process. Their origins can be found in a number of different kinds of businesses from manufacturing to retailing and service firms. Thus there were brewers and distillers, drapers, tax collectors and solicitors all prominent for slightly different reasons. Once confidence in them was established and there were opportunities for remitting to London they were able to put the idle balances that they had to work. There were perhaps twelve of these country banks in 1750 and that had grown to 120 by the 1780s and even more dramatically to almost 400 by the end of the century and as many as 800 by 1810. Precision is not possible since definition is not straightforward. These banks provided a remittance business in bills on London (dealing with the private London City banks). They created credit and the circulating medium for their local communities by issuing notes, and once they had built up the necessary confidence they were trusted with deposits and their contribution to deposit banking began.

### *Joint stock banks*

A number of factors lie behind the change in legislation that allowed the emergence and great growth of the modern joint stock banks. There was considerable antipathy to the Bank of England at the beginning of the nineteenth century with public opinion strongly opposed to the Bank's monopoly position. Further, the collapse of scores of banks in the recession that came at the end of the Napoleonic wars persuaded many that there was a need for institutions with a stronger capital base and that the restrictions on size were in need of revision. (Banks had been restricted to a maximum of six partners.) Also, the growth of the economy and the increasing size of some enterprises undoubtedly added more weight to this argument.

In 1826, following another burst of failures in the famous financial crisis of the previous year, legislation was enacted that finally allowed joint stock banking. There was not complete freedom, however. The new banks were institutions with unlimited liability but more importantly they could only operate outside a distance of sixty-five miles from London and they were thus denied access to some of the most lucrative business in the country. Legislation of the mid 1820s also encouraged the Bank of England to establish branches in the provinces to export good practice and to provide competition for the anticipated new joint stock banks. Several banks were formed in the next few years.

In 1833 a further act was passed allowing joint stock banks to operate in London for all kind of banking business except the issue of notes, which was to remain the preserve of the Bank of England. In the years following that Act a large number of banks formed, some of them the great joint stock banks that are still in existence today.

A controversy had developed at the turn of the century concerning the role that banks played in the determination of monetary and real variables. That controversy never entirely died out and indeed was vigorous in the 1820s and 1830s. The nature of the argument that prevailed for the rest of the decade after the act (1833–40) and into the 1840s was the extent to which the note issue was responsible for price and output movements in the short run. One group, the Currency School, held the view that the Bank of England should be constrained and that the notes issued should be strictly tied to gold. Their opponents in the Banking School felt that the note issue could be left safely to the discretion of the Bank. But the Bank Charter Act of 1844 provided more of a victory for the Currency than the Banking School. The Act divided the Bank into two departments – an Issue and a Banking department. And apart from a fiat issue of 14 million, note issue was to be concentrated in the Bank of England and tied to gold reserves. Banks were no longer allowed new issues of notes and when merging gave up their right of note issue. By around 1870 there was no significant private note issue.

The growth in personal banking, more or less until the end of our period, largely accommodated the middle classes. However, there is another development that should be noted. By the end of the eighteenth century, the possibilities for catering for working-class savings began to emerge. Wages of even a few shillings per week did at that time allow some little scope for saving. At the same time the means for protecting money and valuables were often limited. Ideas on friendly societies and similar institutions including some form of savings banks were being discussed from the early nineteenth century. These discussions often took the form of the middle classes encouraging thrift among the poor. It was a Mrs Priscilla Wakefield of Tottenham who is usually cited as the originator of the savings bank. Mrs Wakefield had a burning passion for social work. In 1798 she started a Female Benefit Club offering pensions to the over 65s. She went on to establish one of the first savings banks. However, Dr Henry Duncan is still thought of as the real father of the movement. The Rev. Duncan was from Dumfreisshire in Scotland, and like many early nineteenth century reformers was concerned with moral progress and was convinced of the character improving powers of thrift. He first carried out an experiment in savings in a country parish before establishing the Ruthwell Savings Bank in 1810, and it is this that is usually cited as the first real savings bank. Bentham and Malthus were enthusiastic supporters of the early developments and after the act of 1817 a large number of banks appeared in the following few years. This continued in the second quarter of the century, such that by 1860 there were scores of savings banks scattered across the whole country. Even so their significance must be kept in perspective, for even by mid-century their total assets amounted to £30 million, a small fraction of other commercial bank assets.

The nineteenth century also witnessed the emergence of many other kinds of banks and similar institutions. To take just two, for example, there were the merchant banks which in the main, and by virtue of their origins, were engaged in the finance of international trade; and the overseas banks which pursued banking business abroad. These did not have their origins in British domestic banking. And coming towards the end of the period dealt with here – the 1830s and 1840s – they can really be seen as another part of the development of the capital markets.

### *Central banking*

The phrase central banking probably has its origins in the twentieth century but there is no doubt that there were central banks in the modern sense long before they acquired that description. They were certainly present in the nineteenth century and possibly even in the eighteenth century. The reason we say that is that the essential element, almost the definition, of central banking is the function of last resort lending. The phrase is found in its earliest form in Francis Baring's *Observations* ... (1797), where he talks of the 'dernier resort'. (Sir Francis Baring was the founder of the firm Baring Brothers, the famous London merchant bank.)

But what exactly is meant by the lender of last resort? There is no widespread agreement. There are those who regard the lender of last resort function as being the ability of the central bank to come to the rescue of the financial markets in a very specific sense – to come to the rescue even to the point of bailing out an individual institution that has found itself in difficulties. Against that there are those who adhere to a more classical definition, one that insists that the lender of last resort provides liquidity to the market as a whole and *not* to individual institutions. Of course individual institutions present bills for discounting, but the point to be stressed is that the central bank should not concern itself with the solvency or liquidity of individual institutions, but simply discount good quality paper. When liquidity pressures develop in the market there will be poorly run and essentially insolvent banks which will fail. They should be allowed to fail. There will also be well-run institutions and the central bank should ensure that there is sufficient liquidity in the market as a whole to cater for their needs. The central bank should stand ready to discount all good commercial paper that is brought to it for discount. This is the proper behaviour of the lender of last resort but it requires another feature and that is what is currently called pre-commitment. That is they should make it known in advance that they will always come to the rescue of the market in this fashion. When the liquidity crisis has passed it is the job of the lender of last resort to withdraw the excess liquidity from the market. Henry Thornton's classic text was the first to set out this doctrine clearly and unambiguously.

'To limit the amount of paper issued, and to resort for this purpose, whenever the temptation to borrow is strong, to some effectual principle of restriction; in no case, however, materially to diminish the sum in circulation, but to let it vibrate only within certain limits; to afford a slow and cautious extension of it, as the general trade of the kingdom enlarges itself; to allow of some special, though temporary, increase in the event of any extraordinary alarm or difficulty, as the best means of preventing a great demand at home for guineas; and to lean to the side of diminution, in the case of gold going abroad, and of the general exchanges continuing long unfavourable; this seems to be the true policy of the directors of an institution circumstanced like that of the Bank of England. To suffer either the solicitations of merchants, or the wishes of government, to determine the measure of the bank issues, is unquestionably to adopt a very false principle of conduct.' (*Paper Credit*, p. 259)

There were liquidity crises in the eighteenth century and the Bank of England did come to the rescue of the market, but it did not always do so and it was not always clear that it would. Such behaviour had to wait until the closing decades of the nineteenth century following, and in part undoubtedly as a result of, the writings of Walter Bagehot, editor of the *Economist* in the 1860s and 1870s. Bagehot made it clear that the Bank had a public responsibility to protect the nation's cash reserves. His particular suggestion was that this should be done by the Bank making it clear that it would always be there to supply the necessary funds in a crisis. In other words it should commit itself in advance. This was not the mischievous policy that Hankey of the Bank called it but the only sensible way to proceed.

'Theory suggests, and experience proves, that in a panic the holders of the ultimate Bank reserve (whether one bank or many) should lend to all who bring good securities quickly, freely, and readily. By that policy they allay a panic; by every other policy they intensify it. *The public have a right to know whether the Bank of England – the holder of our ultimate bank reserve – acknowledge this duty, and are ready to perform it.* But this is now very uncertain.
(italics added) (*Lombard Street*, p. 165)

In recent years the big issue that has come to be discussed in relation to central banks is the need for independence from government. The argument is that if central banks are dependent on governments they will be obliged to provide cash needs for ever greedy coffers and inflation is likely to prevail and indeed worsen. An independent central bank with obligations to produce price stability will therefore be a superior institution. This has been particularly true in recent years when the world has been on fiat money and there has been no discipline from a commodity standard. However, this was not the issue when the first central banks were born. The Bank of England for example, was established as a joint stock company completely separated from government and certainly without the obligation to meet cash needs on demand. When central banks are discussed they are usually referred to as being the government's bank and in addition the bankers' bank. They do indeed fulfil these functions though the precise nature needs to be carefully specified.

None of these issues was being discussed when the Bank was in the process of being set up and neither did it crop up as a subject of serious discussion until the nineteenth century. On its foundation the Bank lent to the government and to a host of private customers and enjoyed a monopoly of joint stock banking until the second quarter of the nineteenth century. The evolutionary path to its modern form took a long time and its full functioning had to await some other developments in the financial markets. The directors of the Bank resisted for a very long time the idea that they could influence the price level. They were still clinging to the notion that they could not even in the period of the inconvertibility of its notes, 1797–1821.

### *Free banking*

Free banking is essentially *laissez-faire* in money. An entirely free system would be one in which there was completely free entry and exit and an absence of stipulated capital requirements and so on. Anyone would be free to open a bank and issue their own currency. And there would be no central bank, since competition would provide the necessary discipline.

Recently there has developed a fresh interest in the success or otherwise of what is known as free banking. The reason is obvious, with banks performing poorly and when banking services have become heavily circumscribed there is understandable curiosity about alternative regimes. Over several centuries some banking systems have become highly regulated. Nowhere was this more true than in the United States. Every time that a bank or a banking system ran into any sort of difficulty there would be calls for further or tighter regulation. However, in recent decades in line with other economic thinking on regulation this has been questioned and in some countries deregulation has flourished. The question is how far should such deregulation be taken? What happens when there are no regulations?

It is this that has prompted investigations of previous instances of relatively unregulated systems.

The practice of free banking can be found in a variety of countries from the late seventeenth century through until the middle of the nineteenth century. The classic case though was that of Scotland. From around the last decade or so of the seventeenth century when banks were established in Scotland until the state brought it to an end in 1845 there was a system that closely approximated *laissez-faire*. There were many banks all issuing their own notes and there was no central bank. (The view that the Bank of England was the lender of last resort to the Scottish system does not really hold up as will be evident from some of the discussion given in this introduction.) In other words it was a competitive system and competition or market forces provided the discipline. The system prospered as indeed did Scotland for around a century and a half. The criticisms that are generally made of such a system are that the note issuers will be motivated by short-term considerations and will over-issue their notes, will be unable to redeem them and will consequently fail (especially in the absence of a central bank). It is also asserted that in such a system counterfeits would flourish. But the record from the Scottish experience certainly does not bear any of this out. (Lawrence White)

Other countries too allowed these freedoms at least for limited periods. Sweden, for example, more or less imitated the Scottish system throughout most of the nineteenth century and successful it seems to have been. The French allowed the same kind of freedoms in the 1790s and beyond. There was wild inflation in France at that time and the unregulated banks were accused of being the cause. Eugene White (1991) has shown that this was not the case and neither were there serious problems of counterfeiting. The cause of the inflation was the issue of excess paper money (the assignats) by the central government. Similarly, in the United States there were episodes of free banking in several different states in the first half of the nineteenth century. It is from that experience that the term 'wildcat banking' derives but again Rockoff (1991) has defended the greater number of these episodes as being successful. And so the story could go on.

Why then did these free banking episodes come to an end? The answer invariably is that the State has stepped in in order to secure a monopoly of the note issue and gain seignorage. This is frequently tied to the notion of sovereignty.

The issues surrounding free banking were all hotly debated topics in the nineteenth century. In England in the 1820s, 1830s, and into the 1840s free banking was the third strand (with the Currency School and the Banking School being the other two) in the debate over the causes of economic fluctuations. The advocates of free banking were particularly critical of the Bank of England for over-expansion and over-contraction, regarding the Bank as being the cause and principal driving force in those fluctuations. They wanted to see the system made self-regulating. The writers belonging to this school of thought produced a host of pamphlets and articles in this period some of which have been included here.

### *'Restriction'*

In 1797, under the strains of war, Britain's attachment to gold was severed. That is to say the free convertibility of paper money into gold was suspended indefinitely. Convertibility was restored in 1821. The period 1797–1821 is variously known as the period of suspension, or inconvertibility, or restriction (of cash payments). Britain was at war from 1793–1815 (on a large scale), also in the middle of great industrial change, and undergoing continuing financial change. All of this led to widespread discussion of the behaviour of macroeconomic variables, both monetary and real, and the period is seen correctly, as the birthplace of modern monetary economics.

Britain was the first industrial nation. Sometime in the course of the eighteenth century the pace of economic change began to accelerate and the composition of output shifted to a growing concentration on industrial goods. The dating of the industrial revolution used to be given with both confidence and precision. For example T S Ashton's little book *The Industrial Revolution, 1760–1830 implicitly dated it precisely*. (Ashton was Professor of Economic History at LSE in the 1960s) Later Walt Rostow (Professor of Economic History at MIT in the 1950s and 1960s) identified Britain's take-off into modern and sustainable economic growth as the year 1783. Modern scholars are unhappy with such precise dating and the implicit suggestion of a major discontinuity. A preference has developed for pushing the beginnings of the change back, or to talk in terms of evolution rather than revolution. However it is viewed by historians, it is clear that those living at the time were conscious of living in a rapidly changing society. The question relating to money and banking and economic change was: what was cause and what effect?

In the process of industrialisation a great growth of banking took place. As we have seen banking is much older than industrialisation, but in the course of the eighteenth century there was an enormous expansion of the banking sector, particularly in the provinces – the country banks. These banks were generally small and local. They were prevented by legislation from having more than six partners and so their capital base was necessarily limited. They could, however, issue their own notes though they tended to hold Bank of England notes as cover for their own. They also developed quickly into fractional reserve banking, and were therefore more than providers of funds, they were creators of money. By the end of the eighteenth century, as we have noted, there were many hundreds of these banks. They too were to become the focus of charges that their overissue or other misdemeanours were responsible for, or at least contributed to, the great turmoil of the period.

The Bank of England was also at the centre of the storm. It had few friends and in the years of the restriction it too was accused of overissue and of abuse of its monopoly position, particularly distasteful in a time of national crisis such as the war with France.

The war with France broke out in 1793 and it proved to be expensive. Britain supported her allies in Europe with both loans and grants, and had to borrow at home and abroad in order to do this. In addition new forms of taxation were introduced. But also, as just mentioned, the Bank printed money – a favourite technique of finance in time of war. The situation was confused since there were also big changes taking place in real variables. The wars brought particular problems for the external accounts. British exports were dampened by the loss of customers and the switch to wartime production. This was compounded by a series of bad harvests in the late 1790s which necessitated a large increase in grain imports. The consequence was a severe deterioration in the current account of the balance of payments. Thus in both parts of the external accounts there were unfavourable pressures that resulted in a deteriorating exchange rate.

The period of 'restriction' was then one of considerable disruption in both the real economy and in the financial markets. There was monetary expansion and inflation and there were large changes in output and in employment. Real and nominal variables were changing for a variety of reasons, making for difficulties in debate. Was the cause of disturbance real or nominal? Were the 1790s different from the later period? What role did the Bank and the banks have to play?

It was into this melee that Henry Thornton stepped in 1802 with his book, *An Enquiry into the nature and effects of paper credit in Great Britain*, so well known now that the title *Paper credit* is sufficient to identify it. Thornton was born in 1760 into a well-established banking family. Both his father and his grandfather had been directors of the Bank of England. In the course of his life he worked in his family's private bank (Down, Thornton, and Frere), was himself a director of the Bank of England, and was an MP for thirty years. He was therefore well qualified by background and experience to expatiate on money and banking.

*Paper credit* is probably the greatest work on monetary theory in the nineteenth century. The distinguished historian of economic thought, Schumpeter (1954), referred to it as 'an amazing performance', and one that 'outdistances all others so far as width of comprehension and analytic power are concerned' (p. 689). *Paper credit* was also a great work of monetary practice – not surprising given Thornton's background. However, since it was published in 1802 just before some of the greatest changes in money and banking practice took place, much of the book was more of historical interest than practical application. The excerpt from *Paper Credit* that is reproduced here is a long one the justification for which should be obvious. Thornton's contribution was just one, albeit a central one, in what became a huge pamphlet literature.

## *Summary*

By the middle of the nineteenth century there was in place a modern banking system which, with only some modification, was to last for over a century. The Bank of England stood at the head of this system and was poised to accept its full public responsibility as keeper of the nation's ultimate reserve of cash; and it behaved as protector of the system by means of acting as lender of last resort. Then there were the banks, London and Provincial, and joint stock banks and private banks, with the joint stock banks coming to dominate and, significantly, establishing branch networks. These latter were to become important in providing greater stability to the system. There had also grown up in the nineteenth century alongside the joint stock banks discount brokers who played an important role as the buffer between the banks and the Bank of England. In the 1830s they were simply brokers, but by the 1870s they had acquired sufficient capital base to run their own portfolios. In addition there were other parts to the system such as the emergence of the merchant banks. They were important in the finance of overseas trade and in the growing acceptance business.

The banking system became increasingly concentrated in the late nineteenth century but the structure of the system that had evolved by the mid-nineteenth century was very much the one that was still there in the middle and even the late twentieth century. That was inspite of all the great upheavals of war and depression, exchange rate disruption and a considerably changed economy. Indeed some would argue that the structure that had evolved by the third quarter of the nineteenth century was what enabled such stability to follow.

The collection of material gathered in these volumes is arranged largely in chronological order but that corresponds closely to the themes treated. They appear therefore in the same order as that discussed in this introduction: usury, financial revolution, recoinage, land banks, commercial banks, country banks, joint stock banks, free banking, central banking and inconvertibility of paper money. It should be obvious that the history and development of some of these topics is not covered adequately here. It is not meant to have been. For instance the subject of usury has a history that goes back many centuries before the start of this period. But some discussion of it was warranted by virtue of the associated discussion and the inclusion of some material on it also seemed sensible.

The emphasis of the collection is on the domestic and commercial banking sector in particular. That, of course, requires setting in the wider context of financial and economic development and the collection therefore reflects the discussion that surrounded these developments. It seeks to give the flavour of the debates that ran through these two centuries which were of such significance for the emergence of banking. It supplements the contributions made by the major participants with selected pieces of legislation that continued to reflect and provide for the changing institutional arrangements. And, of course, it also provides some of the most important raw material – the primary sources – for any investigation of the subject. It should provide a route into all the major issues in banking in the period and at the same time be the basis for any understanding of the modern world of banking.

# BIBLIOGRAPHY


Ashton, T. S. *Economic Fluctuations in England, 1700–1800* (Oxford: Clarendon Press, 1959).

Ashton, T. S. and Sayers, R. S. (eds) *Papers in English Monetary History* (Oxford: Clarendon Press, 1953).

Ashton, T. S. *The Industrial Revolution, 1760–1830* (London, 1968).

Bagehot, Walter *Lombard Street* (London: John Murray, 1922).

Berry, George *Seventeenth Century England: Traders and their Tokens* (London: Seaby, 1988).

Capie, Forrest H. and Wood, G. E. (eds) *Unregulated Banking, Chaos or Order* (London: Macmillan, 1991).

Checkland, S. G. *Scottish Banking A History, 1695–1973* (London: Collins, 1975).

Clapham, Sir John *The Bank of England: A History* (Cambridge: Cambridge University Press, 1944).

Clay, Christopher *Public Finance and Private Wealth* (Oxford: Oxford University Press, 1978).

Coleman, D. C. 'Sir John Banks, Financier: An essay on Government Borrowing under the later Stuarts', Fisher F. J. (ed) *Essays in the Economic and Social History of Tudor and Stuart England* (Cambridge: Cambridge University Press, 1961).

Collins, Michael (ed) *Central Banking in History* 3 Vols (Edward Elgar, 1992).

Collins, Michael *Money and Banking in the UK: A History* (London: Croom Helm, 1988).

Dennison, S. R. and Presley, John R. (eds) *Robertson on Economic Policy* (London: Macmillan, 1992).

Dickson, P. G. M. *The Financial Revolution in England: A Study in the Development of Public Credit 1688–1756* (London: Macmillan, 1967).

Feaveryear, A. E. *The Pound Sterling* (Oxford: Oxford University Press, 1931).

Fetter, F. W. *Development of British Monetary Orthodoxy, 1797–1875* (Cambridge, Mass.: Harvard University Press, 1965).

Goodhart, C. A. E. *The Evolution of Central Banks* (Cambridge, Mass.: MIT Press, 1988).

GREGORY, T. E. *Select Statutes Documents and Reports Relating to British Banking, 1832–1928* (Oxford: Oxford University Press, 1929).

HABAKKUK, H. J. 'The Long-term Rate of Interest and the Price of Land in the Seventeenth Century' *Economic History Review* (1952).

HOPPIT, JULIAN *Risk and Failure in English Business, 1700–1800* (Cambridge: Cambridge University Press, 1987).

HORNE, H. O. *A History of Savings Banks* (Oxford: Oxford University Press, 1947).

HORSEFIELD, J. KEITH *British Monetary Experiments 1650–1710* (London: G. Bell & Sons, 1960).

HORSEFIELD, J. KEITH 'The 'Stop of the Exchequer Revisited' *Economic History Review* (November 1982).

JUDGES, A. V. 'The Origins of English Banking' *Economic History Review* (1931).

KERRIDGE, ERIC *Trade and Banking in Early Modern England* (Manchester: Manchester University Press, 1988).

MATHIAS, P. 'Capital, Credit and Enterprise in the Industrial Revolution' *Journal of European Economic History* (1973).

MCCULLOCH, J. R. *A Select Collection of Early English Tracts on Commerce* (1856).

MUNN, CHARLES W. *The Scottish Provincial Banking Companies* (Edinburgh: John Donald, 1981).

NEAL, LARRY *The Rise of Financial Capitalism* (Cambridge: Cambridge University Press, 1990).

PRESSNELL, L. S. *Country Banking in the Industrial Revolution* (Oxford: Clarendon Press, 1956).

PRESSNELL, L. S. (ed) *Studies in the Industrial Revolution* (London, 1960).

RICHARDS, R. D. 'Early English Banking Schemes' *Journal of Economic and Business History* (1928).

RICHARDS, R. D. *The Early History of Banking in England* (1929).

ROBERTSON, DENNIS 'The Credit Squeeze' (March 1956) in Dennison and Presley (eds).

ROCKOFF, HUGH 'Lessons from The American Experience with Free Banking' Capie and Wood, *Unregulated Banking* (London: Macmillan, 1991).

ROSEVEARE, HENRY *The Treasury, 1660–1870: The Foundations of Control* (London: George Allen & Unwin, 1973).

ROSEVEARE, HENRY *The Financial Revolution, 1660–1760* (London: Longman, 1991).

SCHUMPETER, JOSEPH A. *A History of Economic Analysis* (London: George Allen & Unwin, 1954).

SCHUMPETER, E. B. 'English Prices and Public Finance, 1660–1823' *Review of Economic Statistics* (1938).
SCOTT, W. R. *Constitution and Finance of English, Scottish and Irish Joint Stock Companies* (1912, reprinted 1951).
SHAW, W. A. *Select Tracts and Documents Illustrative of English Monetary History, 1626–1730* (1896, reprinted 1935).
SMITH, ADAM *The Wealth of Nations Bk II* (1776).
SUPPLE, B. E. 'Currency and Commerce in the Early Seventeenth Century' *Economic History Review* (1957).
THORNTON, HENRY *An Enquiry into the Nature and Effects of the Paper Credit of Great Britain* with an Introduction by F. A. von Hayek (London: George Allen & Unwin, 1939).
WHITE, EUGENE 'Experiments with Free Banking during the French Revolution' Capie and Wood, *Unregulated Banking* (London: Macmillan, 1991).
WHITE, LAWRENCE *Free Banking in Britain, Theory experience and debate, 1800–1845* (Cambridge: Cambridge University Press, 1984).

THE

# Mystery of the New Fashioned GOLDSMITHS OR BANKERS.

THEIR

Rise, Growth, State, and Decay,

Discovered in a

Merchant's Letter

To a

Country Gent.

Who desired to bind his Son Apprentice to a

GOLDSMITH.

Printed in Year 1676.

1, 1676. Anon., *The Mystery of the New Fashioned Goldsmiths or Bankers. Their Rise, Growth, State, and Decay, Discovered in a Merchant's Letter to a County Gent. . . .*, London.

# The Myſtery of the New Faſhioned GOLDSMITHS, &c.

*SIR*,

SInce you are pleaſed to demand my advice in the diſpoſal of your Son to the *Goldſmiths* Trade, and my opinion of the Trade it ſelf; I muſt trouble you more than I was willing to ſet down what I have obſerved of the *Goldſmiths* ſince I have Traded, and the ſteps of their Riſe and Progreſs, and leave the judgment of the whole to your Self; tis but fit that a Son ſhould owe the good choice of his imployment and way to his fortunes to the prudence and love of his Father.

If I could now diſcourſe you, I ought to be ſatisfied whether you have thoughts to put your Son to a *Goldſmith* of the Old or New Faſhion, thoſe of that profeſſion having of late years wholly changed their way of Trading. In my time their whole imployment was to make and ſell Plate, to buy forreign Coyns and Gold and Silver imported to melt and cull them, and cauſe ſome to be coyned at the *Mint*, and with the reſt to furniſh the *Refiners*, *Plate-makers*, and *Merchants*, as they found the price of gold and ſilver to vary, and as the Merchants had occaſion for Forreign Coyns.

But about Thirty years ſince, the Civil Wars giving opportunity to Apprentices to leave their Maſters at will, and the old way having been for Merchants to truſt their Caſh in one of their Servants cuſtody, many ſuch Caſhiers left their Maſters in the lurch and went to the Army; and Merchants knew not how to confide in their Apprentices; then did ſome Merchants begin to put their Caſh into *Goldſmiths* hands to receive and pay for them, (thinking it more ſecure) and the trade of Plate being then but little worth, moſt of the Nobility and Gentry, and others melting down their old Plate rather then buying new, and few daring to uſe or own Plate, the *Goldſmiths* ſought to be the *Merchants* Caſh-keepers to receive and pay for nothing, few obſerving or conjecturing their profit they had for their pains.

It

It happened about that time that the then Parliament had coyned out of Plate, and otherwise seven Millions in Half-Crowns, and no Mills being then used in the *Mint*, the Money was of a very unequal weight, sometimes two pence or three pence in an ounce difference, & the *French* and others then changing the value of their Coins often, which made silver and gold of much greater value abroad then at our *English Mint*: The *Goldsmiths* found a new Mischeivous trade to send all the money trusted in their hands into their Cocklofts, where they had Scales and various Weights adapted for their pourpose, and servants constantly weighed every half-crown (at least) and sorted them to melt for Two pence or three pence, or sometimes less gain by the ounce, and sometimes their advantage being greater by the accidents of the rise or fall of the exchange, those heaviest Coins were sent way in specie, several *French* men and other Merchants making it their whole and only business weekly to transport the gold and silver so culled, either melted down or in specie; and from hence the *Goldsmiths* set up another new Trade of buying the old English gold coin at a rate much above its Lawful coyned value, buying and selling it at five, seven, eight and ten pounds in the hundred more then it was coyned for, still sending it away so fast, or supplying those with it whose business was to Transport it, that by a modest computation eight parts of ten of the coyn'd Gold was suddenly consumed, and two shillings a piece was commonly given for gold, when a penny a piece was often given before to exchange gold into silver; the Seven Millions also of silver new Coyned, was apparantly reduced to less then one Million; and the people so abused in their money, that there was little Coin passed in trade but overworn, washed, and clipt, to the great vexation and loss of the Traders.

These unlawful practices and profits of the *Goldsmiths*, made them greedy to ingross all the Cash they could, and to combine with all mens servants who continued to keep any Cash, to bring their moneys to them to be culled, and to remain with them at four pence the day interest *per centum* without the Masters privity: And having thus got Money into their hands, they presumed upon some to come as fast as others was paid away; and upon that confidence of a running Cash (as they call it) they begun to accommodate men with moneys for Weeks and Moneths upon extraordinary gratuities, and supply all necessitous Merchants that over traded their Stock, with present Money for their Bills of Exchange, discounting somtimes double, perhaps treble interest for the time as they found the Merchant more or less pinched.

Profit

Profit arising by this Trade, some of them who had the highest Credit, undertook to receive Gentlemens Rents as they were returned to Town, and indeed any Man's money, and to allow them some intrest for it though it lay for a month only, or less, the Owners calling for it by a hundred or fifty pounds at a time as their occasions and expences wanted it; this new practice giving hopes to every body to make Profit of their money until the hour they spent it, and the conveniency as they thought, to command their money when they pleased, which they could not do when lent at intrest upon personal or reall Security; These hopes I say, drew a great Cash into these new *Goldsmiths* hands, and some of them stuck to their old Trade, but every of them that had friends and credit, aspired to this new Mystery to become *Bankers* or *Casheers*, and when *Cromwell* usurped the Government, the greatest of them began do deal with him to supply his wants of Money upon great Advantages especially after they had bought those Dollers whereof he robb'd the *Spaniards* to about the value of 300000 l.

After the King's return he wanting money, some of these Bankers undertook to lend him not their own but other mens money, taking barefaced of Him ten pound for the hundred, and by private contracts many Bills, Orders, Tallies, and Debts of the King's, above twenty, and somtimes thirty in the hundred, to the great dishonor of the Government.

This Prodigious unlawful Gain induced all of them that could be credited with moneys at intrest to become lenders to the King to anticipate all the Revenue, to take every Grant of the *Parliament* into pawn as soon as it was given, I had almost said, before the *Act* was passed for it, and to outvie each other in buying and taking to pawn, Bills, Orders, and Tallies, in effect, all the King's revenue passed their hands, and if *Solomon* be in the right, *that the Borrower is a Slave to the Lender*, the King and Kingdom became Slaves to these *Bankers*, and the Kingdom gave no small share of their Taxes to them, paying double and treble Intrest, as if they had not been able to raise Money for the publick Service at the times it was requisite:

But the number of these *Bankers* increased so fast, and the money at Interest come so much into their hands, that the King and His Farmers, and all Tallies of Anticipation and Orders, could not secure all the money they had to lend Hereupon they sought out according to their several natural wits and capacities, how to dispose of money for more then lawful

lawful Intrest, either upon Pawns or Bottom, Reason or unreasonable discounts of Intrest for Bills, or upon notorious usurious Contracts, or upon personal Securities from Heirs whose Estates are in expectancy, or by sudden advance of money to Projectors, who drawn into Projects many Responsible Men to the ruin of their Families; These *Goldsmiths* however getting 10l. or 15l. *per Centum*, and sometimes more, only for the present advance of the money, besides the future Intrest, These and a hundred other practices they have used and do still continue in contempt of Law and Justice, whereof they are so conscious to themselves, that most of them do once a year (at least) sue out their general Pardon to avoid the penalty of those wholsom Laws made to prevent such Frauds, Oppressions, contempt of Government, and mischeives to the Publick as they are dayly guilty of: Tis also suspected that their original Trade of culling the heavy Money is not deserted by some of them; also how come all clipt and washt money to pass so currant at their Shops, and so little appearance in payments of all the new coyned Money since the King's return, so many 100000 ls. of the *Parliaments* Coin, besides *Bullion* imported having been new coyned, and how comes *Guinies* also to be bought and sold by them so much above the Coynage rate, that upon their account only, and by their means, they pass currant in payments for more then they are really worth from some of their Shops; I am sure some Merchants are supplyed with Gold and Silver *English* Coyn, to transport upon the advantage of the exchange, or making their present Bargains in *France* and elswhere, for importing Prohibited Goods.

SIR,

I *Have given you my Remarques upon the Rise and growth of these new kind of* Goldsmiths, *and I take them to have been in their highest Ascendant or State about the time that our Ships were burnt at* Chatham *by the* Dutch: *that cold Storm of the Peoples fears that their money was not safe in the* Bankers *hands blighted them, and since being in their declension, the Famous stop upon the* Exchequer *almost blasted their very root, men being unwilling to trust money in their hands to lend his Majesty, so long as they hear the deplorable Cryes of the Widdow and the Fatherless, whose money they say at Feasts, they lent the King, and cannot repay them, no not their Intrest to buy them Bread.*

Now

Now admitting that all the Creditors of the *Bankers* can no more think it safe that their money should be lent to the King; since Tallies, Orders, and the Great Seal it self, are found to be no security, I cannot imagine how Bread should be got by their trade of borrowing money upon lawful Intrest to lend upon unlawful to private persons; though they can silence their consciences and forget Christianity, and neither regard their neighbors welfare, nor the good of the whole Kingdom, but seek by Usurious unlawful Bargains, and oppressive Exactions from the needy and men in streights, and by hook and by crook to make the most of their Cash.

I dare take it for granted that the men now of that Trade are not men of greater natural Abilities nor acquired parts, then other Tradesmen of their age and degree, nor are they better instructed then others to imploy greater Stocks in an advantagious Trade, nor have they greater Stocks of their own to hazzard to remote places, from whence most profit may be hoped for; Neither have these men greater skill in Law then other Citizens, to judg of Securities to be taken for Money, nor have they more knowledg of Men to guess at the value of their Bonds; how then should they be able to make more Intrest of money then other Traders; yet the profit that may satisfy other Traders, cannot be sufficient for them to keep open their Shops; they must have a great dead stock of Cash to answer all Payments, and be always ready occasionally to advance great Summs; their Servants and Shops must be maintained for no use but Payments and Receipts, and deducting dead Stock and Charges, if they do not take nine *per Cent.* Intrest for what they Lend and dispose of, they cannot make one of one, much less subsist. Besides there must be allowance for Charges to defend themselves against Informers for their usurious Contracts, and procuring frequent Pardons, and for hazard of loss of their Money lent upon unlawful Intrest, every borrower having it in his power to plead their usury against them in lue of their Debts. All these things, and many more being duly considered, I suppose people will suddenly come to their wits, and begin to examine why a *Goldsmith-banker* should be better Security then another man, or fitter to be trusted for ten times more then he is worth: They give only personal Security, and many times their Notes for 500 l. 1000l. or more, when they owe before they give that Note, twenty times the value of their own Estates, and yet these free Lenders will scarce be satisfied with two or three Mens Bonds for 1000 l. that are known to be worth 5000 l. a Man; doubtless I say, People will think at last that a

*Banker*

*Banker* ought to give as good Security for money he borrows as another man, especially since he runs the greatest hazards in his disposing of Money for excessive Gain or intrest.

I leave it then to your self to jugd whether *Banking* be like to continue half your Son's Apprenticeship, and whether all the Arts that they can teach him can be worth one of the 200 l. you design to give with him; I presume upon your Pardon for my plainness and tediousness; Yet I am prompted to say somthing more in point of Conscience, doubting whether it be Lawful to exercise any Trade in a constant avowed breach of the Laws of the Kingdom, as all *Bankers* do, these Laws being made for the good of the Society, to which the Scripture commands obedience for Conscience sake, *where they are not contrary to the Laws of God.*

Perhaps it is worth the inquiry upon that account, whether any man that hath exercised the Mystery of *Banking*, hath living or dying, gone off the Stage with a clear good Estate, all his Creditors being paid, fully paid. But I judg no Man. *I submit these thoughts and my Self to Your Prudent Censure, and remain,*

*Sir,*

Your Humble Servant

*J. R.*

**FINIS.**

# A DISCOURSE ON THE Late FUNDS of the *Million-Act*, *Lottery-Act*, and *Bank of* England.

SHEWING,

That they are Injurious to the Nobility and Gentry, and Ruinous to the Trade of the Nation.

Together with

PROPOSALS for the Supplying their Majesties with Money on easy Terms, Exempting the Nobility, Gentry, &c. from Taxes, Enlarging their Yearly Estates, and Enriching all the Subjects in the Kingdom.

---

Humbly offered and submitted to the Consideration of the Lords Spiritual and Temporal, and Commons in Parliament assembled,

By *J. B.*

---

*London*, Printed in the Year MDCXCIV.

2, 1694. John Briscoe, *A Discourse on the Late Funds of the Million-Act, Lottery Act, and Bank of England. Shewing that they are Injurious to the Nobility and Gentry, and Ruinous to the Trade of the Nation. ...*, London.

TO THE

# KING & QUEENS

## Most Excellent Majesties.

*May it please your Majesties* ;

THE present Enjoyment of our Religion and Liberty being wholly owing, under Heaven, to your Majesties; and the Preservation of them having engaged your Majesties in an expensive War with the most powerful Enemy to the Religion and Prosperity of this Nation; It is become the Duty of every particular Person (as well as of the whole Body of the People) to contribute his Endeavour for securing and perpetuating those inestimable Blessings. This Consideration engaged me upon those Thoughts which I have digested in the following Treatise, and

and now most humbly present to your Majesties: Wherein I principally aim'd to furnish your Majesties with the Hearts and Purses of your Subjects, by proposing such a Method for the Supply of your Majesties, that it shall be their very Interest to support your Majesties and the Government, whether in Peace or War.

It is the peculiar Felicity of our Constitution that makes this Design practicable only in *England*, (for no People under an Absolute or Arbitrary Government is capable of it;) and if my Zeal does not blind my Judgment, I think I have laid a Foundation for this Nation's Greatness and Riches, which none of our Neighbours are capable of disturbing, or arriving to themselves.

That your Majesties may long enjoy the Fruits of it, and the Nation long enjoy the Happiness of your Government, is the hearty Prayer of

Your Majesties most obedient, and

most faithful Subject and Servant,

*J. BRISCOE.*

# THE
# PREFACE.

*WE generally ſuſpect that Perſon to be in a declining Condition who pays extravagant Intereſt for Money to ſupport his Credit, or whoſe Bills or Notes under his Hand are refuſed to be diſcounted by monied Men, unleſs for more than an ordinary* Premium *or Conſideration; and it cannot but trouble every true Engliſh Man (who hath any Eſteem for his Country) to ſee the Nation (not inferiour in Riches to any in* Europe*) treated like a Bankrupt, the Nation's Bills (if I may ſo call Exchequer Tallies, Debenters and Sea-mens Tickets) ſign'd by their Majeſties Commiſſioners, being leſs eſteem'd than a Note under the Hand of an ordinary Tradeſman, to the no ſmall Diminution of the Honour of the Nation, and the great Diſcouragement of our Engliſh Sea-men, who hazard their Lives in Defence of their Country: and their Majeſties are obliged to pay Extortion for almoſt every thing they buy; and none for that Reaſon will truſt the Publick but upon the Proſpect of moſt extravagant Profit and Advantage.*

*And if we would enter into the Account of it, do not theſe Loſſes fall upon the Nation? If their Majeſties muſt pay three Millions for what might be bought with ready Money for two Millions, muſt not the Nation pay one Million in three extraordinary, out of their Eſtates, more than is neceſſary, for want of taking other and better Meaſures? The War it ſelf muſt needs be very expenſive; and ought we not then to exerciſe all the good Husbandry we can to make the Taxes as eaſy as may be to the Subject? Was there ever ſo great a Complaint of the Scarcity of Money as now there is? It would be endleſs to ſhow the many Hardſhips and Preſſures which many of the Subjects labour under, all which is charg'd to the Account of the Government, as if their Majeſties were the Occaſion of them, when the real Cauſes proceed from our ſelves, as will appear in the*

*the ensuing Treatise. A most unworthy and disingenuous Requital to their Majesties, who have been the Instruments (under God) to restore our expiring Liberties, when we had scarce any thing left of our antient Rights.*

*I must confess I do not delight to think of these things, but heartily wish all were buried in Oblivion, could it be, and we not forget who were our Restorers. It is therefore my Duty to do their Majesties that Right, as to let the Subjects know where a great part of the Money goes which they pay for the Use of their Majesties, and that their Majesties have the least part of it to carry on the War: And therefore if any of the Subjects be grieved; it is fit they should be acquainted, that their Pressures (if any are upon them) proceed not so much from the Taxes as from other Causes, which (if not removed) will in a few Years ruin the Kingdom.*

*I have, it's true, declared my Opinion against the Manner of raising Money upon the late Funds, I mean of the Million-Act, Lottery-Act, and Bank of* England; *and I believe (when my Arguments are well weighed) it will appear not to be without Reason. I doubt few have entred into the Account of it; but whoever lives but a few Years, will find them (if some other Methods are not taken to prevent it) like a Canker, which will eat up the Gentlemens Estates in Land, and beggar the Trading Part of the Nation, and bring all the Subjects in* England *to be the monied Mens Vassals.*

*Some probably may think I am for destroying the Settlements made on those Funds wherein the Parliament have been pleased to invest the several Contributors with a Property: whereas I am not for destroying them, but for preventing their destroying others; and am content that they continue till Time wears them out, so that a Stop be put to the raising more Money after the like manner, so pernicious to the whole Nation: and therefore I hope none need to be offended if I lay before the Great Council of the Kingdom the many Evils that of Necessity do and will attend the great Encouragements given those who advanced Money on the said Funds, which are already too visible: nor that it will be look'd upon as a Presumption in me, if I humbly propose to their great Judgments other Methods of raising Money for the future; so far from being grievous, that they will be for the Ease, Satisfaction, and Advantage of the Subject.*

*It*

*It is likely that some may wonder that the Parliament should pass the said Acts, seeing they ever had a very great Regard to keep up the Value of their Lands, and for the sake of which they were pleased to prohibit the importing of Irish Cattel, which (some are of Opinion) was no small Advantage to the trading Part of the Nation; whereas (if it be well examin'd) it will appear that the Encouragement given to Persons to advance Money on the said Funds, will be more ruinous to Gentlemens Estates, than would have been the bringing in Irish Cattel for a thousand Years; and will certainly (if not remedied) bring Lands to less than fourteen Years Purchase; Land-Security (formerly reputed the best Fund or Security in the Nation) being now disregarded, and Gentlemen of Estates, how great soever are their Necessities, cannot without very great Difficulty raise Money on Land-Security; while some Mens Bills, on a less substantial Fund, pass currant in Payment as so much Money. What may be said to solve this Riddle is, That there was a Necessity for Money to carry on the War, and no better way was then thought of for raising it, and the Parliament chose rather to supply their Majesties by giving Encouragement to all those who would advance Money on the said Funds, though thereby they impaired the Value of their own Estates, than to subject their Lives, Liberties, Religion, and all that is dearest to them, to the Will of the French Monarch: however I am not without Hopes, if the Methods I have laid down shall be approved of, and put in Practice, that it will set us all again upon a right* Basis; *their Majesties will be enabled to carry on the War with a yet greater Vigour than ever, being so plentifully supplied with Money; the Subjects will be easy under their Taxes; Trade will encrease and flourish; the Value of Lands will be inhanced, and (what may seem at first a* Paradox) *the more Money any Persons shall advance to their Majesties, the more they will have; and the longer the War shall continue, the richer will be the Subject.*

*I am not unsensible that by my writing on this Subject I shall create my self many Enemies, such who propose to raise their Estates by making Merchandize of the Government, and who care not if they hazard the Kingdom, or ruin their Fellow-Subjects, so they can enrich themselves.*

*I doubt not in the leaſt but there are very many who have advanced Money on the late Funds, who are Perſons of publick Spirits; and if their Majeſties can be ſupplied with Money a better way, and the Subject eaſed, they will be as forward as any to encourage it. And this Method I have propoſed will not only ſupply their Majeſties, and eaſe the Subject, but it will enable all the Nobility, Gentry, and others in the Kingdom, who have any Encumbrances upon their Eſtates, (and who are even ground to pieces between their Creditors and the Taxes) to clear their Eſtates, to raiſe Portions for their Children, and to lend their Majeſties Money at eaſy Intereſt: And as it lies in the Parliament's Power to help all the Freeholders in the Kingdom who are under any pinching Straits or Exigencies, ſo Providence ſeems to concur in their Deliverance, in making it the very Intereſt of the whole Nation to relieve them.*

---

AL.

ALL Kingdoms and States being more or leſs opulent and potent, as Trade and Induſtry is promoted and encouraged by them; and no Nation being better ſituated for Trade than this Kingdom of *England*, it is certain that nothing can hinder our being the moſt flouriſhing People in the Univerſe, if our own Endeavours are not wanting to promote it. Trade therefore being the only *Medium* whereby Riches can be conveyed to us, we ought to exert the utmoſt of our Abilities to encourage it, and to take care that nothing be done which may prove injurious, much leſs deſtructive to it.

Now there having been greater Sums of Money required to carry on the War againſt *France*, than could be raiſed on Lands, Houſes, Perſonal Eſtates, Poll-Money, *&c.* the Parliament have been neceſſitated (for the enabling their Majeſties to proſecute the ſame) to raiſe Money by ſuch new Methods as they thought would be leaſt burdenſom to Trade, and moſt eaſy to the Subject, ſuch as are the Funds of the Million-Act, Lottery-Act, and Bank of *England*; but though the Duties upon which ſuch Funds are ſettled may not be very prejudicial to Trade, yet it is to be feared that the great Encouragement given to thoſe who advanced Money on theſe Funds will be very detrimental to Trade, and injurious to the greateſt Part of the Nation. And becauſe it may be reaſonably ſuppoſed that thoſe who have taſted the Sweetneſs of high Intereſt, and other the like Advantages, will endeavour the next Seſſions of Parliament to promote the raiſing more Money by the ſame Methods; I think my ſelf obliged in Duty to their Majeſties, and for the preſerving many Gentlemen and poor induſtrious Traders and their Families from Ruin, occaſion'd by the Scarcity of Money and high Intereſt, to repreſent the many Evils that will unavoidably enſue the great Encouragements given ſuch who advanced Money on the late Funds, and then humbly to propoſe Ways by which the Parliament (if they ſhall think fit) may not only plentifully ſupply their Majeſties with

with Money, but how they may enrich the Subjects, by the very Taxes which ſhall be raiſed upon them. But before I enter upon it, it may not be improper to make ſome few Remarks upon the aforeſaid Acts.

The Million-Act ſettles a Fund for ninety nine Years, to pay an hundred Thouſand Pound *per annum*, for the firſt ſeven Years, and ſeventy Thouſand Pound *per annum* for the Reſidue of the ninety nine Years, free of all Taxes, to the Contributors of a Million of Money, or their Nominees, with Benefit of Survivorſhip, until there ſhall be but ſeven Nominees living, after which there ſhall be no more Benefit of Survivorſhip; but upon the Death of any of the ſaid Nominees, ſuch Nominees ſeventh Part ſhall revert to their Majeſties, their Heirs or Succeſſors: but in caſe the whole Million of Money were not advanced before the firſt Day of *May*, 1693. upon Survivorſhip, then any Perſon after the ſaid firſt Day of *May*, until the twenty ninth Day of *September* following, ſhould have fourteen Pound *per Cent. per annum*, free of all Taxes for every hundred Pound paid in by him or her during the Life of ſuch Nominee.

The Lottery-Act ſettles a Fund to pay an hundred and forty Thouſand Pound *per annum*, free of all Taxes to the Contributors of one Million of Money for ſixteen Years, to be divided among them according to their ſeveral Lots or Adventures.

The Act for the Bank of *England* ſettles a Fund to pay an hundred Thouſand Pounds *per annum* for ever, free of all Taxes, to the Subſcribers of twelve hundred Thouſand Pound, with this Reſervation, that if the twelve hundred Thouſand Pound ſhall be repaid them at any time after the firſt Day of *Auguſt*, *Anno Dom.* 1705. the yearly Payments of one hundred Thouſand Pounds *per annum*, from thence forward ſhall ceaſe and determine.

Now that it may appear upon what Diſadvantages to the Nation their Majeſties are ſupplied with Money on theſe Funds, I have hereunto ſubjoined exact Tables, calculated (for the more Exactneſs) to the *20th* part of a Farthing, ſhowing in what term of Years the ſeveral Contributors or Adventurers will be repaid their whole Principal, and Intereſt, with Intereſt upon Intereſt, after the rate

rate of five Pound *per Cent. per annum*, on which Terms any Man might have had Money upon good Security, before this unhappy way of raising Money on these Funds took place; and also how much the Nation must pay over and above after they shall have fully paid and satisfied the advanced Money, and Interest, and Interest upon Interest.

And herein I have no Regard to what any particular Person may receive, by reason of Survivorship, or as fortunate or unfortunate, but only what the Nation *(bona fide)* must pay, among all those who advanced their Money on the said Funds: And as I have computed the advanced Money at five Pound *per cent. per annum* Interest, with Interest upon Interest; so I have cast up the Money payable yearly out of these Funds, at five Pound *per cent. per annum* Interest, with Interest upon Interest, but with this Advantage to the Contributors, that although their Majesties pay the Money, arising by some of these Funds weekly, I have cast it up as if it was paid to the Contributors at every Year's End only, as will more plainly appear upon Examination of the following Tables.

## *A* TABLE *of the Million Act.*

| *Paid their Majesties by the Contributors.* | | | | | *Terms* | *Annual Fund paid to the Contributors.* | | | | |
|---|---|---|---|---|---|---|---|---|---|---|
| *l.* | *s.* | *d.* | *q.* | 20 | | *l.* | *s.* | *d.* | *q.* | 20 |
| 1000000 | | | | | | | | | | |
| 50000 | | | | | | | | | | |
| 1050000 | | | | | 1 | 100000 | | | | |
| 52500 | | | | | | 5000 | | | | |
| | | | | | | 100000 | | | | |
| 1102500 | | | | | 2 | 205000 | | | | |
| 55125 | | | | | | 10250 | | | | |
| | | | | | | 100000 | | | | |
| 1157625 | | | | | 3 | 315250 | | | | |
| 57881 | 05 | 00 | 0 | 00 | | 15762 | 10 | 00 | 0 | 00 |
| | | | | | | 100000 | | | | |
| 1215506 | 05 | 00 | 0 | 00 | 4 | 431012 | 10 | 00 | 0 | 00 |
| 60775 | 06 | 03 | 0 | 00 | | 21550 | 12 | 06 | 0 | 00 |
| | | | | | | 100000 | | | | |
| 1276281 | 11 | 03 | 0 | 00 | 5 | 552563 | 02 | 06 | 0 | 00 |
| 63814 | 01 | 06 | 3 | 00 | | 27628 | 03 | 01 | 2 | 00 |
| | | | | | | 100000 | | | | |
| 1340095 | 12 | 09 | 3 | 00 | 6 | 680191 | 05 | 07 | 2 | 00 |
| 67004 | 15 | 07 | 2 | 15 | | 34009 | 11 | 03 | 1 | 10 |
| | | | | | | 100000 | | | | |
| 1407100 | 08 | 05 | 1 | 15 | 7 | 814200 | 16 | 10 | 3 | 10 |

| *Paid their Majesties by the Contributors.* | | | | | *Terms* | *Annual Funds paid to the Contributors.* | | | | |
|---|---|---|---|---|---|---|---|---|---|---|
| *l.* | *s.* | *d.* | *q.* | 20 | | *l.* | *s.* | *d.* | *q.* | 20 |
| 1407100 | 08 | 05 | 1 | 15 | 7 | 814200 | 16 | 10 | 3 | 10 |
| 70355 | 00 | 05 | 0 | 05 | | 40710 | 00 | 10 | 0 | 11 |
| | | | | | | 70000 | | | | |
| 1477455 | 08 | 10 | 2 | 00 | 8 | 924910 | 17 | 09 | 0 | 01 |
| 73872 | 15 | 05 | 1 | 00 | | 46245 | 10 | 10 | 2 | 12 |
| | | | | | | 70000 | | | | |
| 1551328 | 04 | 03 | 3 | 05 | 9 | 1041156 | 08 | 07 | 2 | 13 |
| 77566 | 08 | 02 | 2 | 07 | | 52057 | 16 | 05 | 0 | 14 |
| | | | | | | 70000 | | | | |
| 1628894 | 12 | 06 | 1 | 13 | 10 | 1163214 | 05 | 00 | 3 | 07 |
| 81444 | 14 | 07 | 2 | 01 | | 58160 | 14 | 03 | 0 | 03 |
| | | | | | | 70000 | | | | |
| 1710339 | 07 | 01 | 3 | 14 | 11 | 1291374 | 19 | 03 | 3 | 10 |
| 85516 | 19 | 01 | 1 | 03 | | 64568 | 14 | 11 | 2 | 07 |
| | | | | | | 70000 | | | | |
| 1795856 | 06 | 06 | 0 | 17 | 12 | 1425943 | 14 | 03 | 1 | 19 |
| 89792 | 16 | 03 | 3 | 12 | | 71297 | 03 | 08 | 2 | 05 |
| | | | | | | 70000 | | | | |
| 1885649 | 02 | 10 | 0 | 09 | 13 | 1567240 | 18 | 00 | 0 | 02 |
| 94282 | 09 | 01 | 2 | 16 | | 78362 | 00 | 10 | 3 | 04 |
| | | | | | | 70000 | | | | |
| 1979931 | 11 | 11 | 3 | 05 | 14 | 1715602 | 18 | 10 | 2 | 06 |

| Paid their Majesties by the Contributors. l. | s. | d. | q. | 20 | Years | Annual Fund paid to the Contributors. l. | s. | d. | q. | 20 |
|---|---|---|---|---|---|---|---|---|---|---|
| 1979931 | 11 | 11 | 3 | 05 | 14 | 1715602 | 18 | 10 | 3 | 06 |
| 98996 | 11 | 07 | 0 | 15 | | 85780 | 02 | 11 | 1 | 07 |
| | | | | | | 70000 | | | | |
| 2078928 | 03 | 07 | 0 | 00 | 15 | 1871383 | 01 | 10 | 0 | 13 |
| 103946 | 08 | 02 | 0 | 12 | | 93569 | 03 | 01 | 0 | 08 |
| | | | | | | 70000 | | | | |
| 2182874 | 11 | 09 | 0 | 12 | 16 | 2034952 | 04 | 11 | 1 | 01 |
| 109143 | 14 | 07 | 0 | 04 | | 101747 | 12 | 02 | 3 | 17 |
| | | | | | | 70000 | | | | |
| 2292018 | 06 | 04 | 0 | 16 | 17 | 2206699 | 17 | 02 | 0 | 18 |
| 114600 | 18 | 03 | 3 | 04 | | 110334 | 19 | 10 | 1 | 04 |
| | | | | | | 70000 | | | | |
| 2406619 | 04 | 08 | 0 | 00 | 18 | 2387034 | 17 | 00 | 2 | 02 |
| 120330 | 19 | 02 | 3 | 04 | | 119351 | 14 | 10 | 0 | 18 |
| | | | | | | 70000 | | | | |
| 2526950 | 03 | 10 | 3 | 04 | 19 | 2576386 | 11 | 10 | 3 | 00 |
| 126347 | 10 | 02 | 1 | 07 | | 128819 | 06 | 07 | 0 | 11 |
| | | | | | | 70000 | | | | |
| 2653297 | 14 | 01 | 0 | 11 | 20 | 2775205 | 18 | 05 | 3 | 11 |
| 132664 | 17 | 08 | 1 | 11 | | 138760 | 05 | 11 | 0 | 07 |
| | | | | | | 70000 | | | | |
| 2785962 | 11 | 09 | 2 | 07 | 21 | 2983966 | 04 | 04 | 3 | 18 |
| 139298 | 02 | 07 | 0 | 06 | | 149198 | 06 | 02 | 2 | 11 |
| | | | | | | 70000 | | | | |
| 2925260 | 14 | 04 | 2 | 13 | 22 | 3203164 | 10 | 07 | 2 | 09 |
| 146263 | 00 | 08 | 2 | 10 | | 160158 | 04 | 06 | 1 | 10 |
| | | | | | | 70000 | | | | |
| 3071523 | 15 | 01 | 1 | 03 | 23 | 3433322 | 15 | 01 | 3 | 19 |
| 153576 | 03 | 09 | 0 | 03 | | 171666 | 02 | 09 | 0 | 07 |
| | | | | | | 70000 | | | | |
| 3225099 | 18 | 10 | 1 | 08 | 24 | 3674988 | 17 | 11 | 0 | 06 |
| 161254 | 19 | 11 | 1 | 05 | | 183749 | 08 | 10 | 3 | 00 |
| | | | | | | 70000 | | | | |
| 3386354 | 18 | 09 | 2 | 13 | 25 | 3928738 | 06 | 09 | 3 | 06 |
| 169317 | 14 | 11 | 1 | 02 | | 196436 | 18 | 04 | 0 | 07 |
| | | | | | | 70000 | | | | |
| 3555672 | 13 | 08 | 3 | 15 | 26 | 4195175 | 05 | 01 | 3 | 13 |
| 177783 | 12 | 08 | 0 | 19 | | 209758 | 15 | 03 | 0 | 07 |
| | | | | | | 70000 | | | | |
| 3733456 | 06 | 05 | 0 | 14 | 27 | 4474934 | 00 | 05 | 0 | 00 |
| 186672 | 16 | 03 | 3 | 08 | | 223746 | 14 | 00 | 1 | 00 |
| | | | | | | 70000 | | | | |
| 3920129 | 02 | 09 | 0 | 02 | 28 | 4768680 | 14 | 05 | 1 | 00 |
| 196006 | 09 | 01 | 2 | 12 | | 238434 | 00 | 08 | 2 | 13 |
| | | | | | | 70000 | | | | |
| 4116135 | 11 | 10 | 2 | 14 | 29 | 5077114 | 15 | 01 | 3 | 1 |
| 205806 | 15 | 07 | 0 | 10 | | 253855 | 14 | 09 | 00 | 7 |
| | | | | | | 70000 | | | | |
| 4321942 | 07 | 05 | 3 | 04 | 30 | 5400970 | 09 | 11 | 0 | [illegible] |
| 216097 | 02 | 04 | 1 | 19 | | 270048 | 10 | 05 | 3 | [illegible] |
| | | | | | | 70000 | | | | |
| 4538039 | 09 | 10 | 1 | 03 | 31 | 5741019 | 00 | 04 | 3 | 16 |
| 226901 | 19 | 05 | 3 | 13 | | 287050 | 19 | 00 | 0 | 19 |
| | | | | | | 70000 | | | | |
| 4764941 | 09 | 04 | 0 | 16 | 32 | 6098069 | 19 | 05 | 0 | 15 |

| Paid their Majesties by the Contributors. l. | s. | d. | q. | 20 | Years | Annual Fund paid to the Contributors. l. | s. | d. | q. | 20 |
|---|---|---|---|---|---|---|---|---|---|---|
| 4764941 | 09 | 04 | 0 | 16 | 32 | 6098069 | 19 | 05 | 0 | 15 |
| 238247 | 01 | 05 | 2 | 08 | | 304903 | 09 | 11 | 2 | 12 |
| | | | | | | 70000 | | | | |
| 5003188 | 10 | 09 | 3 | 04 | 33 | 6472973 | 09 | 04 | 3 | 07 |
| 250159 | 08 | 06 | 1 | 19 | | 323648 | 13 | 05 | 2 | 11 |
| | | | | | | 70000 | | | | |
| 5253347 | 19 | 04 | 1 | 03 | 34 | 6866622 | 02 | 10 | 1 | 18 |
| 262667 | 07 | 11 | 2 | 09 | | 343331 | 02 | 01 | 2 | 17 |
| | | | | | | 70000 | | | | |
| 5516015 | 07 | 03 | 3 | 12 | 35 | 7279953 | 05 | 00 | 0 | 15 |
| 275800 | 15 | 04 | 1 | 11 | | 363997 | 13 | 03 | 0 | 00 |
| | | | | | | 70000 | | | | |
| 5791816 | 02 | 08 | 1 | 03 | 36 | 7713950 | 18 | 03 | 0 | 15 |
| 289590 | 16 | 01 | 2 | 09 | | 385697 | 10 | 10 | 3 | 16 |
| | | | | | | 70000 | | | | |
| 6081406 | 18 | 09 | 3 | 12 | 37 | 8169648 | 09 | 02 | 0 | 11 |
| 304070 | 06 | 11 | 1 | 03 | | 408482 | 08 | 05 | 2 | 00 |
| | | | | | | 70000 | | | | |
| 6385477 | 05 | 09 | 0 | 15 | 38 | 8648130 | 17 | 07 | 2 | 11 |
| 319273 | 17 | 03 | 1 | 16 | | 432406 | 10 | 10 | 2 | 06 |
| | | | | | | 70000 | | | | |
| 6704751 | 03 | 00 | 2 | 11 | 39 | 9150537 | 08 | 06 | 0 | 17 |
| 335237 | 11 | 01 | 3 | 06 | | 457526 | 17 | 05 | 0 | 08 |
| | | | | | | 70000 | | | | |
| 7039988 | 14 | 02 | 1 | 17 | 40 | 9678064 | 05 | 11 | 1 | 05 |
| 351999 | 08 | 08 | 2 | 01 | | 483903 | 04 | 03 | 2 | 05 |
| | | | | | | 70000 | | | | |
| 7391988 | 02 | 10 | 3 | 18 | 41 | 10231967 | 10 | 02 | 3 | 10 |
| 369599 | 08 | 01 | 2 | 19 | | 511598 | 07 | 06 | 0 | 11 |
| | | | | | | 70000 | | | | |
| 7761587 | 11 | 00 | 2 | 17 | 42 | 10813565 | 17 | 09 | 0 | 01 |
| 388079 | 07 | 06 | 2 | 10 | | 540678 | 05 | 10 | 2 | 12 |
| | | | | | | 70000 | | | | |
| 8149666 | 18 | 07 | 1 | 07 | 43 | 11424244 | 03 | 07 | 2 | 13 |
| 407483 | 06 | 11 | 0 | 13 | | 571212 | 04 | 02 | 0 | 14 |
| | | | | | | 70000 | | | | |
| 8557150 | 05 | 06 | 2 | 00 | 44 | 12065456 | 07 | 09 | 3 | 07 |
| 427857 | 10 | 03 | 1 | [illegible] | | 603272 | 16 | 04 | 2 | 15 |
| | | | | | | 70000 | | | | |
| 8985007 | 15 | 09 | 3 | 06 | 45 | 12738729 | 04 | 02 | 2 | 02 |
| 449250 | 07 | 09 | 1 | 19 | | 636936 | 09 | 02 | 2 | 02 |
| | | | | | | 70000 | | | | |
| 9434258 | 03 | 07 | 1 | 05 | 46 | 13435665 | 13 | 05 | 0 | 04 |
| 471712 | 18 | 02 | 0 | 13 | | 672283 | 05 | 08 | 0 | [illegible] |
| | | | | | | 70000 | | | | |
| 9905971 | 01 | 09 | 1 | 18 | 47 | 14187948 | 19 | 01 | 0 | 08 |
| 495298 | 11 | 01 | 0 | 05 | | 709397 | 08 | 11 | 1 | 10 |
| | | | | | | 70000 | | | | |
| 10401269 | 12 | 10 | 2 | 03 | 48 | 14967346 | 08 | 00 | 2 | 04 |
| 520063 | 09 | 07 | 2 | 18 | | 748367 | 06 | 04 | 3 | 06 |
| | | | | | | 70000 | | | | |
| 10921333 | 02 | 06 | 1 | 01 | 49 | 15785713 | [illegible] | 05 | 1 | 10 |
| 546066 | 13 | 01 | 2 | 01 | | 789285 | 13 | 08 | 2 | 13 |
| | | | | | | 70000 | | | | |
| 11467399 | 15 | 07 | 3 | 02 | 50 | 16644999 | 03 | 02 | 0 | [illegible] |

| Paid their Majesties by the Contributors. l. | s. | d. | q. | 20 | Years. | Annual Fund paid to the Contributors. l. | s. | d. | q. | 20 |
|---|---|---|---|---|---|---|---|---|---|---|
| 11467399 | 15 | 07 | 3 | 02 | 50 | 16644999 | 08 | 02 | 0 | 03 |
| 573369 | 19 | 09 | 1 | 11 | | 832249 | 19 | 04 | 3 | 12 |
| | | | | | | 70000 | | | | |
| 12040769 | 15 | 05 | 0 | 13 | 51 | 17547249 | 07 | 06 | 3 | 15 |
| 602038 | 09 | 09 | 1 | 00 | | 877362 | 09 | 04 | 2 | 03 |
| | | | | | | 70000 | | | | |
| 12642808 | 05 | 02 | 1 | 13 | 52 | 18494611 | 16 | 11 | 1 | 18 |
| 632140 | 08 | 03 | 0 | 09 | | 924730 | 11 | 10 | 0 | 13 |
| | | | | | | 70000 | | | | |
| 13274948 | 13 | 05 | 2 | 02 | 53 | 19489342 | 08 | 09 | 2 | 11 |
| 663747 | 08 | 08 | 0 | 06 | | 974467 | 02 | 05 | 1 | 02 |
| | | | | | | 70000 | | | | |
| 13938696 | 02 | 01 | 2 | 08 | 54 | 20533809 | 11 | 02 | 3 | 13 |
| 696934 | 16 | 01 | 1 | 02 | | 1026690 | 09 | 06 | 2 | 19 |
| | | | | | | 70000 | | | | |
| 14635630 | 18 | 02 | 3 | 10 | 55 | 21630500 | 00 | 09 | 2 | 12 |
| 731781 | 10 | 10 | 3 | 15 | | 1081525 | 00 | 00 | 1 | 18 |
| | | | | | | 70000 | | | | |
| 15367412 | 09 | 01 | 3 | 05 | 56 | 22781025 | 00 | 10 | 0 | 10 |
| 768370 | 12 | 05 | 1 | 19 | | 1139101 | 05 | 00 | 2 | 00 |
| | | | | | | 70000 | | | | |
| 16135783 | 01 | 07 | 1 | 04 | 57 | 23991126 | 05 | 10 | 2 | 10 |
| 806789 | 03 | 00 | 3 | 17 | | 1199556 | 06 | 03 | 2 | 02 |
| | | | | | | 70000 | | | | |
| 16942572 | 04 | 08 | 1 | 01 | 58 | 25260682 | 12 | 02 | 0 | 12 |
| 847128 | 12 | 02 | 3 | 05 | | 1263034 | 02 | 07 | 1 | 04 |
| | | | | | | 70000 | | | | |
| 17789700 | 16 | 11 | 0 | 06 | 59 | 26593716 | 14 | 09 | 1 | 16 |
| 889485 | 00 | 10 | 0 | 12 | | 1329685 | 16 | 03 | 3 | 09 |
| | | | | | | 70000 | | | | |
| 18679185 | 17 | 09 | 0 | 18 | 60 | 27993402 | 11 | 06 | 1 | 05 |

## The Table of the Lottery-Act

| Paid their Majesties by the Contributors. l. | s. | d. | q. | 20 | Years. | Annual Fund paid to the Contributors. l. | s. | d. | q. | 20 |
|---|---|---|---|---|---|---|---|---|---|---|
| 1000000 | | | | | | | | | | |
| 50000 | | | | | | | | | | |
| 1050000 | | | | | 1 | 140000 | | | | |
| 52500 | | | | | | 7000 | | | | |
| | | | | | | 140000 | | | | |
| 1102500 | | | | | 2 | 287000 | | | | |
| 55125 | | | | | | 14350 | | | | |
| | | | | | | 140000 | | | | |
| 1157625 | | | | | 3 | 441350 | | | | |
| 57881 | 05 | | | | | 22067 | 10 | | | |
| | | | | | | 140000 | | | | |
| 1215506 | 05 | | | | 4 | 603417 | 10 | | | |
| 60775 | 06 | 03 | | | | 30170 | 17 | 05 | | |
| | | | | | | 140000 | | | | |
| 1276281 | 11 | 03 | | | 5 | 773588 | 07 | 05 | | |
| 63814 | 01 | 05 | 3 | | | 38679 | 08 | 04 | 2 | |
| | | | | | | 140000 | | | | |
| 1340095 | 12 | 09 | 3 | 00 | 6 | 952267 | 15 | 10 | 2 | |
| 67004 | 15 | 07 | 2 | 15 | | 47613 | 07 | 09 | 2 | 02 |
| | | | | | | 140000 | | | | |
| 1407100 | 08 | 05 | 1 | 15 | 7 | 1139881 | 03 | 08 | 0 | 02 |
| 70355 | 00 | 05 | 0 | 05 | | 56994 | 01 | 02 | 0 | 16 |
| | | | | | | 140000 | | | | |
| 1477455 | 08 | 10 | 2 | 00 | 8 | 1336875 | 04 | 10 | 0 | 18 |
| 73872 | 15 | 05 | 1 | 06 | | 66843 | 15 | 02 | 3 | 12 |
| | | | | | | 140000 | | | | |
| 1551328 | 04 | 03 | 3 | 06 | 9 | 1543719 | 00 | 01 | 0 | 10 |
| 77566 | 08 | 02 | 2 | 07 | | 77185 | 19 | 00 | 0 | 04 |
| | | | | | | 140000 | | | | |
| 1628894 | 12 | 05 | 1 | 13 | 10 | 1760904 | 19 | 01 | 0 | 14 |
| 81444 | 14 | 07 | 2 | 01 | | 88045 | 04 | 11 | 1 | 16 |
| | | | | | | 140000 | | | | |
| 1710339 | 07 | 01 | 3 | 14 | 11 | 1988950 | 04 | 00 | 2 | 10 |
| 85516 | 19 | 04 | 1 | 03 | | 99447 | 10 | 02 | 1 | 14 |
| | | | | | | 140000 | | | | |
| 1795856 | 06 | 05 | 0 | 17 | 12 | 2228397 | 14 | 05 | 0 | 04 |
| 89792 | 16 | 03 | 3 | 12 | | 111419 | 17 | 08 | 2 | 04 |
| | | | | | | 140000 | | | | |
| 1885649 | 02 | 10 | 0 | 09 | 13 | 2479817 | 11 | 11 | 2 | 08 |
| 94282 | 07 | 01 | 2 | 16 | | 123990 | 17 | 07 | 0 | 14 |
| | | | | | | 140000 | | | | |
| 1979931 | 11 | 11 | 3 | 0 | 14 | 2743808 | 09 | 06 | 3 | 02 |
| 98996 | 11 | 07 | 0 | 15 | | 137190 | 08 | 05 | 2 | 19 |
| | | | | | | 140000 | | | | |
| 2078928 | 03 | 07 | 0 | 00 | 15 | 3020998 | 18 | 00 | 2 | 01 |
| 103946 | 08 | 02 | 0 | 12 | | 151049 | 18 | 10 | 3 | 04 |
| | | | | | | 140000 | | | | |
| 2182874 | 11 | 09 | 0 | 12 | 16 | 3312048 | 16 | 11 | 1 | 05 |

# The Table of the Bank of *England*.

| *Paid their Majesties by the Contributors.* l. | s. | d. | q. | 20 | *Years.* | *Annual Fund paid to the Contributors.* l. | s. | d. | q. | 20 |
|---|---|---|---|---|---|---|---|---|---|---|
| 1200000 | | | | | | | | | | |
| 60000 | | | | | | | | | | |
| 1260000 | | | | | 1 | 100000 | | | | |
| 63000 | | | | | | 5000 | | | | |
| | | | | | | 100000 | | | | |
| 1323000 | | | | | 2 | 205000 | | | | |
| 66150 | | | | | | 10250 | | | | |
| | | | | | | 100000 | | | | |
| 1389150 | | | | | 3 | 315250 | | | | |
| 69457 | 10 | | | | | 15762 | 10 | | | |
| | | | | | | 100000 | | | | |
| 1458607 | 10 | | | | 4 | 431012 | 10 | | | |
| 72930 | 07 | 06 | | | | 21550 | 12 | 06 | | |
| | | | | | | 100000 | | | | |
| 1531537 | 17 | 06 | | | 5 | 552563 | 02 | 06 | | |
| 76576 | 17 | 10 | 2 | | | 27628 | 03 | 01 | 2 | |
| | | | | | | 100000 | | | | |
| 1608114 | 15 | 04 | 2 | | 6 | 680191 | 05 | 07 | 2 | |
| 80405 | 14 | 09 | 0 | 18 | | 34009 | 11 | 03 | 1 | 10 |
| | | | | | | 100000 | | | | |
| 1688520 | 10 | 01 | 2 | 18 | 7 | 814200 | 16 | 10 | 3 | 10 |
| 84426 | 00 | 06 | 0 | 06 | | 40710 | | 10 | 0 | 11 |
| | | | | | | 100000 | | | | |
| 1772946 | 10 | 07 | 3 | 04 | 8 | 954910 | 17 | 09 | 0 | 01 |
| 88647 | 06 | 06 | 1 | 11 | | 47745 | 10 | 10 | 2 | 12 |
| | | | | | | 100000 | | | | |
| 1861593 | 17 | 02 | 0 | 15 | 9 | 1102656 | 08 | 07 | 2 | 13 |
| 93079 | 13 | 10 | 1 | 04 | | 55132 | 16 | 05 | 0 | 14 |
| | | | | | | 100000 | | | | |
| 1954673 | 11 | 00 | 1 | 19 | 10 | 1257789 | 05 | 00 | 3 | 07 |
| 97733 | 13 | 06 | 2 | 09 | | 62889 | 09 | 03 | 0 | 03 |
| | | | | | | 100000 | | | | |
| 2052407 | 04 | 07 | 0 | 08 | 11 | 1420678 | 14 | 03 | 3 | 10 |
| 102620 | 07 | 02 | 3 | 00 | | 71033 | 18 | 08 | 2 | 07 |
| | | | | | | 100000 | | | | |
| 2155027 | 11 | 09 | 3 | 08 | 12 | 1591712 | 13 | 00 | 1 | 17 |
| 107751 | 07 | 07 | 0 | 07 | | 79585 | 12 | 07 | 3 | 05 |
| | | | | | | 100000 | | | | |
| 2262778 | 19 | 04 | 3 | 15 | 13 | 1771298 | 05 | 08 | 1 | 02 |
| 113138 | 18 | 11 | 2 | 11 | | 88564 | 18 | 03 | 1 | 13 |
| | | | | | | 100000 | | | | |
| 2375917 | 18 | 04 | 2 | 06 | 14 | 1959863 | 03 | 11 | 2 | 15 |
| 118795 | 17 | 11 | 0 | 02 | | 97993 | 03 | 02 | 1 | 10 |
| | | | | | | 100000 | | | | |
| 2494713 | 16 | 03 | 2 | 08 | 15 | 2157856 | 07 | 02 | 0 | 05 |
| 124735 | 13 | 09 | 3 | 02 | | 107892 | 16 | 04 | 1 | 04 |
| | | | | | | 100000 | | | | |
| 2619449 | 10 | 01 | 1 | 10 | 16 | 2365749 | 03 | 06 | 1 | 09 |

| *Paid their Majesties by the Contributors.* l. | s. | d. | q. | 20 | *Years.* | *Annual Fund paid to the Contributors.* l. | s. | d. | q. | 20 |
|---|---|---|---|---|---|---|---|---|---|---|
| 2619449 | 10 | 01 | 1 | 10 | 16 | 2365749 | 03 | 06 | 1 | 09 |
| 130972 | 09 | 06 | 0 | 05 | | 118287 | 09 | 02 | 0 | 09 |
| | | | | | | 100000 | | | | |
| 2750421 | 19 | 07 | 1 | 15 | 17 | 2584036 | 12 | 08 | 1 | 18 |
| 137521 | 01 | 11 | 3 | 01 | | 129201 | 16 | 07 | 2 | 09 |
| | | | | | | 100000 | | | | |
| 2887943 | 01 | 07 | 0 | 16 | 18 | 2813238 | 09 | 04 | 0 | 07 |
| 144397 | 03 | 00 | 3 | 16 | | 140661 | 18 | 05 | 2 | 08 |
| | | | | | | 100000 | | | | |
| 3032340 | 04 | 08 | 0 | 12 | 19 | 3053900 | 07 | 09 | 2 | 15 |
| 151617 | 00 | 02 | 3 | 04 | | 152695 | 00 | 04 | 2 | 14 |
| | | | | | | 100000 | | | | |
| 3183957 | 04 | 10 | 3 | 16 | 20 | 3306595 | 08 | 02 | 1 | 09 |
| 159197 | 17 | 02 | 3 | 15 | | 165329 | 15 | 04 | 3 | 13 |
| | | | | | | 100000 | | | | |
| 3343155 | 02 | 01 | 3 | 11 | 21 | 3571925 | 03 | 07 | 1 | 02 |
| 167157 | 15 | 01 | 1 | 03 | | 178596 | 05 | 02 | 0 | 13 |
| | | | | | | 100000 | | | | |
| 3510312 | 17 | 03 | 0 | 14 | 22 | 3850521 | 08 | 09 | 1 | 15 |
| 175515 | 12 | 10 | 1 | 08 | | 192526 | 01 | 05 | 1 | 01 |
| | | | | | | 100000 | | | | |
| 3685828 | 10 | 01 | 2 | 02 | 23 | 4143047 | 10 | 02 | 2 | 16 |
| 184291 | 08 | 06 | 0 | 06 | | 207152 | 07 | 06 | 0 | 10 |
| | | | | | | 100000 | | | | |
| 3870119 | 18 | 07 | 2 | 08 | 24 | 4450199 | 17 | 08 | 3 | 06 |
| 193505 | 19 | 11 | 0 | 14 | | 222509 | 19 | 10 | 2 | 11 |
| | | | | | | 100000 | | | | |
| 4063625 | 18 | 06 | 3 | 02 | 25 | 4772709 | 17 | 07 | 1 | 17 |
| 203181 | 05 | 11 | 0 | 11 | | 238635 | 09 | 10 | 2 | 05 |
| | | | | | | 100000 | | | | |
| 4266807 | 04 | 05 | 3 | 13 | 26 | 5111345 | 07 | 06 | 0 | 02 |
| 213340 | 07 | 02 | 2 | 15 | | 255567 | 05 | 04 | 2 | 00 |
| | | | | | | 100000 | | | | |
| 4480147 | 11 | 08 | 2 | 08 | 27 | 5466912 | 12 | 10 | 2 | 02 |
| 224007 | 07 | 07 | 0 | 02 | | 273345 | 12 | 07 | 2 | 18 |
| | | | | | | 100000 | | | | |
| 4704154 | 19 | 03 | 2 | 10 | 28 | 5840258 | 05 | 06 | 1 | 00 |
| 235207 | 14 | 11 | 2 | 06 | | 292012 | 18 | 03 | 1 | 05 |
| | | | | | | 100000 | | | | |
| 4939362 | 14 | 03 | 0 | 16 | 29 | 6232271 | 03 | 09 | 2 | 05 |
| 246968 | 02 | 08 | 2 | 04 | | 311613 | 11 | 02 | 1 | 2 |
| | | | | | | 100000 | | | | |
| 5186330 | 16 | 11 | 3 | 00 | 30 | 6643884 | 14 | 11 | 3 | 07 |
| 259316 | 10 | 10 | 0 | 15 | | 332194 | 04 | 08 | 3 | 19 |
| | | | | | | 100000 | | | | |
| 5445647 | 07 | 09 | 3 | 15 | 31 | 7076078 | 19 | 08 | 3 | 06 |
| 272282 | 07 | 04 | 2 | 15 | | 353803 | 18 | 11 | 3 | 07 |
| | | | | | | 100000 | | | | |
| 5717929 | 15 | 02 | 2 | 10 | 32 | 7529882 | 18 | 08 | 2 | 13 |

| Paid their Majesties by the Contributors. | | | | | Years | Annual Fund paid to the Contributors. | | | | |
|---|---|---|---|---|---|---|---|---|---|---|
| *l.* | *s.* | *d.* | *q.* | 20 | | *l.* | *s.* | *d.* | *q.* | 20 |
| 5717929 | 15 | 02 | 2 | 10 | 32 | 7529882 | 18 | 08 | 2 | 13 |
| 285896 | 09 | 09 | 0 | 10 | | 376494 | 02 | 11 | 0 | 18 |
| | | | | | | 100000 | | | | |
| 6003826 | 04 | 11 | 3 | 00 | 33 | 8006377 | 01 | 07 | 3 | 11 |
| 300191 | 06 | 02 | 3 | 19 | | 400318 | 17 | 00 | 3 | 19 |
| | | | | | | 100000 | | | | |
| 6304017 | 11 | 02 | 2 | 19 | 34 | 8506695 | 18 | 08 | 3 | 10 |
| 315200 | 17 | 06 | 2 | 18 | | 425334 | 15 | 11 | 0 | 19 |
| | | | | | | 100000 | | | | |
| 6619218 | 08 | 09 | 1 | 17 | 35 | 9032030 | 14 | 08 | 0 | 09 |
| 330960 | 18 | 05 | 1 | 01 | | 451601 | 10 | 08 | 3 | 04 |
| | | | | | | 100000 | | | | |
| 6950179 | 07 | 02 | 2 | 18 | 36 | 9583632 | 05 | 04 | 3 | 13 |
| 347508 | 19 | 04 | 1 | 06 | | 479181 | 12 | 03 | 0 | 19 |
| | | | | | | 100000 | | | | |
| 7297688 | 06 | 07 | 0 | 04 | 37 | 10162813 | 17 | 08 | 0 | 12 |
| 364884 | 08 | 03 | 3 | 16 | | 508140 | 13 | 10 | 2 | 08 |
| | | | | | | 100000 | | | | |
| 7662572 | 14 | 11 | 0 | 00 | 38 | 10770954 | 11 | 06 | 3 | 00 |
| 383128 | 12 | 08 | 3 | 16 | | 538547 | 14 | 06 | 3 | 15 |
| | | | | | | 100000 | | | | |
| 8045701 | 07 | 07 | 3 | 16 | 39 | 11409502 | 06 | 01 | 2 | 15 |
| 402285 | 01 | 04 | 2 | 07 | | 570475 | 02 | 03 | 2 | 14 |
| | | | | | | 100000 | | | | |
| 8447986 | 09 | 00 | 2 | 03 | 40 | 12079977 | 08 | 05 | 1 | 09 |
| 422399 | 06 | 05 | 1 | 14 | | 603998 | 17 | 05 | 0 | 05 |
| | | | | | | 100000 | | | | |
| 8870385 | 15 | 05 | 3 | 17 | 41 | 12783976 | 05 | 10 | 1 | 14 |
| 443519 | 05 | 09 | 1 | 03 | | 639198 | 16 | 03 | 2 | 01 |
| | | | | | | 100000 | | | | |
| 9313905 | 01 | 03 | 1 | 00 | 42 | 13523175 | 02 | 01 | 3 | 15 |
| 465695 | 05 | 00 | 3 | 01 | | 676158 | 15 | 01 | 1 | 03 |
| | | | | | | 100000 | | | | |
| 9779600 | 06 | 04 | 0 | 01 | 43 | 14299333 | 17 | 03 | 0 | 18 |
| 488980 | 00 | 03 | 3 | 04 | | 714966 | 13 | 10 | 1 | 08 |
| | | | | | | 100000 | | | | |
| 10268580 | 06 | 07 | 3 | 05 | 44 | 15114300 | 11 | 01 | 2 | 05 |
| 513429 | 00 | 03 | 3 | 19 | | 755715 | 00 | 06 | 2 | 14 |
| | | | | | | 100000 | | | | |
| 10782009 | 06 | 11 | 3 | 04 | 45 | 15970015 | 11 | 08 | 1 | 00 |
| 539100 | 09 | 04 | 0 | 15 | | 798500 | 15 | 07 | 0 | 01 |
| | | | | | | 100000 | | | | |
| 11321109 | 16 | 03 | 3 | 19 | 46 | 16868516 | 07 | 03 | 1 | 01 |

| Paid their Majesties by the Contributors. | | | | | Years | Annual Funds paid to the Contributors. | | | | |
|---|---|---|---|---|---|---|---|---|---|---|
| *l.* | *s.* | *d.* | *q.* | 20 | | *l* | *s.* | *d.* | *q.* | 20 |
| 11321109 | 16 | 03 | 3 | 19 | 46 | 16868516 | 07 | 03 | 1 | 01 |
| 566055 | 09 | 09 | 3 | 03 | | 843425 | 16 | 04 | 1 | 09 |
| | | | | | | 100000 | | | | |
| 11887165 | 06 | 01 | 3 | 02 | 47 | 17811942 | 03 | 07 | 2 | 10 |
| 594358 | 05 | 03 | 2 | 15 | | 890597 | 02 | 02 | 0 | 14 |
| | | | | | | 100000 | | | | |
| 12481523 | 11 | 05 | 1 | 17 | 48 | 18802539 | 05 | 09 | 3 | 04 |
| 624076 | 03 | 05 | 3 | 07 | | 940126 | 19 | 03 | 1 | 19 |
| | | | | | | 100000 | | | | |
| 13105599 | 15 | 00 | 1 | 06 | 49 | 19842666 | 05 | 01 | 1 | 03 |
| 655279 | 19 | 09 | 0 | 01 | | 992133 | 06 | 03 | 0 | 05 |
| | | | | | | 100000 | | | | |
| 13760879 | 14 | 09 | 1 | 07 | 50 | 20934799 | 11 | 04 | 1 | 08 |
| 688043 | 19 | 08 | 3 | 07 | | 1046739 | 19 | 06 | 3 | 05 |
| | | | | | | 100000 | | | | |
| 14448923 | 14 | 05 | 0 | 16 | 51 | 22081539 | 10 | 11 | 0 | 13 |
| 722446 | 03 | 08 | 2 | 16 | | 1104076 | 19 | 06 | 2 | 04 |
| | | | | | | 100000 | | | | |
| 15171369 | 18 | 02 | 03 | 12 | 52 | 23285616 | 10 | 05 | 2 | 17 |
| 758568 | 07 | 10 | 03 | 15 | | 1164280 | 16 | 06 | 1 | 02 |
| | | | | | | 100000 | | | | |
| 15929938 | 08 | 01 | 3 | 07 | 53 | 24549897 | 06 | 11 | 3 | 19 |
| 796496 | 18 | 04 | 3 | 11 | | 1227494 | 17 | 04 | 0 | 15 |
| | | | | | | 100000 | | | | |
| 16726435 | 06 | 06 | 2 | 18 | 54 | 25877392 | 04 | 04 | 0 | 14 |
| 836321 | 15 | 03 | 3 | 14 | | 1293869 | 12 | 02 | 2 | 08 |
| | | | | | | 100000 | | | | |
| 17562757 | 01 | 10 | 2 | 12 | 55 | 27271261 | 16 | 06 | 3 | 02 |
| 878137 | 17 | 01 | 0 | 10 | | 1363563 | 01 | 09 | 3 | 15 |
| | | | | | | 100000 | | | | |
| 18440894 | 18 | 11 | 3 | 02 | 56 | 28734824 | 18 | 04 | 2 | 17 |
| 922044 | 14 | 11 | 1 | 11 | | 1436741 | 04 | 11 | 0 | 02 |
| | | | | | | 100000 | | | | |
| 19362939 | 13 | 11 | 0 | 13 | 57 | 30271566 | 03 | 03 | 2 | 19 |
| 968146 | 19 | 08 | 1 | 08 | | 1513578 | 06 | 01 | 3 | 18 |
| | | | | | | 100000 | | | | |
| 20331086 | 13 | 07 | 2 | 01 | 58 | 31885144 | 09 | 05 | 2 | 17 |
| 1016554 | 06 | 08 | 0 | 14 | | 1594257 | 04 | 05 | 2 | 14 |
| | | | | | | 100000 | | | | |
| 21347641 | 00 | 03 | 2 | 15 | 59 | 33579401 | 13 | 11 | 1 | 11 |
| 1067382 | 01 | 00 | 0 | 14 | | 1678970 | 01 | 08 | 1 | 09 |
| | | | | | | 100000 | | | | |
| 22415023 | 01 | 03 | 3 | 09 | 60 | 35358371 | 15 | 07 | 3 | 00 |

*To*

Had the Million-Act been fill'd up with Annuities, and admitting that upon each Nominee's Life, one with another, there had been 500 *l.* advanced, there would have been in the whole 2000 Nominees, among whom (ſuppoſing there were ſeveral Children and young People) it is very probable that 7 of the 2000 Nominees would be living ſixty Years after the Commencement of the Act; and ſo long as ſeven ſhall be living, the whole yearly Fund of ſeventy thouſand Pounds *per annum* muſt be paid to the Survivors. Now the whole Million advanced, and Intereſt, with Intereſt upon Intereſt, being over-paid (as appears in the Table) in 19 Years, the Nation muſt pay 70000 *l. per annum* to the Survivors, for 41 Years after the Principal and Intereſt, and Intereſt upon Intereſt ſhall be paid, which comes to 9314216 *l.* 13 *s.* 9 *d.*

The Annuity on the Lottery-Act is not ſo diſadvantageous to the Nation, becauſe it is of a ſhorter Continuance; yet the whole Million advanced being paid in about nine Years time, with Intereſt and Intereſt upon Intereſt, the 140000 *l. per annum* muſt notwithſtanding be continued to be paid for ſeven Years longer, after the Contributors ſhall be repaid the whole advanced Million, with Intereſt, and Intereſt upon Intereſt, as aforeſaid, which amounts to 1129174 *l.* 5 *s.* 2 *d.* ſo much being given for an Encouragement to advance one Million of Money for 16 Years.

The Bank of *England* (if not redeemed by Parliament at the 1 Years end) will be the moſt detrimental of all the three, as hereafter will more plainly appear: For ſuppoſing the Contributors t the Bank ſhould pay the whole 1200000 Pounds they have ſubſcribed in to the Bank, they will be repaid the whole 1200000 and Intereſt, with Intereſt upon Intereſt, in leſs than ninetee Years, and then the Nation muſt notwithſtanding pay the 100000 *l. per annum* for ever, although the full Principal and Intereſt, with Intereſt upon Intereſt, is paid: However, we will ſuppoſe it were to terminate at 60 Years End, (for ſo far I have trac it) the Contributors will receive almoſt 14 Millions more than the

Pri

Principal and Intereſt, with Intereſt upon Intereſt; a moſt prodigious Sum for advancing 1200000 Pounds, beſides thoſe many Advantages in diſcounting Merchants Bills, Exchequer-Tallies, *&c.*

Having thus ſhewn the Advantages the Contributors will receive for advancing their Money on theſe Funds, I now come to ſhew the many Evils that unavoidably attend the raiſing Money by thoſe Methods.

And here I might take notice how the monied Men are enrich'd by the Ruines of the poor and induſtrious Traders, how Gentlemen (whoſe Eſtates are in Land) are preſſed with Taxes, while the monied Men are in a manner Tax-free; the Landed-man paying more Taxes to their Majeſties out of an Eſtate of 100*l. per annum*, than the monied Men do for 10000*l.* in Money, (what they advance on thoſe Funds being excuſed from Taxes by Act of Parliament) notwithſtanding they receive more Profit by 1000 Pounds in Money than a Gentleman can receive out of an Eſtate in Land worth 3000 Pounds, as I doubt not but to make appear.

I might alſo have ſhown how landed Gentlemen and the poor induſtrious Tradeſmen raiſe Money not only to carry on the War, but to enrich thoſe who advance Money on theſe Funds, they having no ſmall Part of the Money raiſed, as appears by the foregoing Tables.

I might alſo take notice of the extraordinary Advantages given to monied Men; ſuch as putting a Perſon into a Capacity for 500*l.* or leſs, to receive from 100*l. per annum*, to 10000*l. per annum* Annuity, as in the Million-Act; and for 10 Pounds, to have from 10 Pounds *per annum*, to 1000 Pounds *per annum*, as in the Lottery-Act: But I ſhall wave theſe, becauſe if this had been all the Grievance, the Evil had been the leſs, in regard the Nation would have been never the poorer, but only one Subject enrich'd by the Spoils of another; but I will prove, that this new Method of raiſing Money endangers the Nation it ſelf, and that in divers Reſpects.

*Firſt*; It will moſt certainly ruine our Trade, without which the Nation cannot long ſubſiſt, much leſs be able to maintain a War.

*Secondly*; It will be a Means to carry out our Wealth, and thereby will impoveriſh the Kingdom.

*Thirdly*; It will ruine many Gentlemen of Eſtates, and bring Land to 12 or 14 Years Purchaſe.

That

That these Funds will ruine our Trade, I prove by these Arguments. Whatsoever draws the Money out of Trade, or impairs the Credit of Traders, must necessarily be very injurious, if not destructive to Trade, because no Trade can be managed without Money or Credit: but these Funds do draw the Money out of Trade, and impair the Credit of Traders, and consequently are very injurious, if not destructive to Trade.

My first Proposition all Men must grant; I shall therefore apply my self to prove the second Proposition, *viz.* That these Funds draw the Money out of Trade, and impair the Credit of Traders.

To prove which I shall consider Traders as trading with their own Stocks, or borrowing Money at Interest, to drive their Trades. To begin therefore with such who trade with their own Stocks: Before these Encouragements were given to those who advanced Money on these late Funds, our Merchants, and considerable Traders, if they could get 12 or 14 *per cent. per annum* clear for every 100 Pounds they had in Stock, were well contented, thinking themselves sufficiently rewarded for their Pains and Industry, not knowing any other way, wherein to employ their Money to the like Advantage: but these late Funds have diverted that Humour, and turn'd their *Genius* from Trade, quite another way; for whereas formerly a great Part of their Time was taken up in contriving how to improve their Money to the best Advantage in the way of their Trade, and to provide for their Families, by an honest Industry; now almost their whole Discourse is of Lottery-Tickets, Annuities, Bank-Bills, *&c.* and in contriving how they may draw their Money out of Trade, to put it in upon some of these late Funds, upon the Prospect of the great Advantages they are capable of receiving thereby, beyond what they can expect to gain by their Trade, and that also free from Taxes. Now although their Majesties have been supplied with Money by these Means, yet the greatest Part of the Money so advanced being drawn out of Trade, must necessarily impair and lessen the Trade of the Nation, for want of sufficient Stock to carry it on: which will more plainly appear, if we cast our Eye upon the poor industrious Traders, who not having Stock enough of their own, wherewith to drive their Trades,

Trades, having been forc'd to borrow Money at Intereſt, to ſupply that Defect; their Creditors who formerly (not being able otherwiſe to diſpoſe of their Money) courted them to take their Money at eaſy Intereſt, knowing them to be Honeſt and Careful in their Buſineſs; now call in their Money, alledging they can make 10, 15, or 20 *l. per Cent. per annum*, by lending it to the Government, or by paying it in upon theſe Funds: which ſudden Demands, the poor Tradeſmen being unable to comply with, they are forc'd to pacify their Creditors, with Promiſes of larger Intereſt. But the poor Men, not being able to drive their Trades on ſuch diſadvantageous Terms, and to provide for their Families, are forc'd to leave off their Trades, and get in their Money to pay off their Creditors, and betake themſelves to ſome other Employments for their Livelyhoods, or elſe they ſink under their Burdens, being no longer able to bear the Preſſures of them.

I come now to ſhow how Injurious theſe Funds are to our Foreign Trade, the Preſervation whereof is of no ſmall Import to the Nation; for that being once Loſt, is not eaſily Regained: and that theſe Funds are Injurious to our Foreign Trade, I prove by theſe Arguments. Thoſe Merchants who can ſell their Commodities cheapeſt at any Foreign Markets, may Engroſs to themſelves the Trade of thoſe Foreign Parts; thoſe who pay a leſs Intereſt for Money, as ſuppoſing 3 or 4 *per Cent. per Annum*, can ſell their Commodities cheaper, than thoſe who pay a greater Intereſt, *viz.* 8 or 10 *per Cent. per Annum:* but ſome of our Neighbours pay no more than 3 or 4 *per Cent. per Annum* for Intereſt, and our Engliſh Merchants muſt pay 8 or 10 *per Cent. per Annum* for Intereſt; and conſequently thoſe our Neighbours may Engroſs to themſelves the Trade of thoſe Foreign Parts.

The Truth of theſe Propoſitions are ſo obvious, that I need not bring any Proof to corroborate them, but I ſhall only illuſtrate them by one plain Inſtance, *viz.* I ſuppoſe none will deny, that Intereſt of Money in *Holland*, is not above 3, or at higheſt 4 *per Cent. per Annum*, and any Dutch Merchants may have what Money they pleaſe on thoſe Terms; now how is it poſſible for our Engliſh Merchants, who muſt pay almoſt 3 times the Intereſt for Money,

Money, to ſell their Commodities ſo cheap as the Dutch Merchants? for ſuppoſe a Dutch Merchant takes up Money at Intereſt, and therewith trades to *Turkey*, or to any other Part, where our Engliſh Merchants trade, if the Dutch Merchant makes 20 or 25 *per Cent.* Profit of his Money, and hath his Returns in a Year or too, he is well ſatisfied with his Gain, and continues on his Trade, having 12 or 14 or 16 *per Cent.* Profit, more than his Intereſt; but if our Engliſh Merchant makes but 20 or 25 *per Cent.* Profit in the like time, the great Intereſt he muſt pay, will ſwallow up almoſt his whole Profit, leaving him little or nothing for his Adventure. Now this in proceſs of Time, will diſhearten our Merchants, diſcourage Navigation, ruin our Trade, and will leave it in the Hand of thoſe who can trade with leſs Diſadvantages than we can, and who having once got the Trade in their Hand, will not eaſily part with it.

Object. *If any Object, that there is not ſuch ſcarcity of Money among Merchants, or Traders, as I have ſet forth; neither do they give ſuch high Intereſt for Money as* 8 *or* 10 per Cent. per Annum.

*Anſw.* I Anſwer, the ſcarcity of Money, and the great Complaints of all ſorts of Traders for want of Money, (ſince it hath been drawn out of Trade, to advance on the late Funds) is a Truth too well known, to be denied; and that our Merchants, and other Traders, muſt pay 8 or 10 *per Cent. per Annum* Intereſt for Money (if they want it) is as demonſtrable; for admit a Trader muſt take up Money at Intereſt, can it be reaſonably ſuppoſed, that any Man will lend his Money for 5 or 6 *per Cent. per Annum*, when he can make 8 or 10 *per Cent. per Annum*, by advancing it on theſe Funds? or can it be thought, that Perſons wil continue their Money in Tradeſmens hands at the uſual Intereſt when they can have almoſt double the Intereſt, by lending it to the Government; eſpecially when they come to be well ſatisfied that what they advance on the ſaid Funds, is ſafe and ſecure?

Object. *But a great part of the Money was advanced by ſuch who had plenty of Money, and did not employ it in Trade, and not by Tradeſmen.*

*Anſw*

*Answ.* That very many Traders paid in large Sums of Money from 1000 to 10000 *l.* apiece, cannot be denied by any, who have seen the Lists of the Names of the Contributors to the several Funds; and the Money advanced by those who had no Trade, was notwithstanding taken out of Trade, as being drawn out of Tradesmens hands, to whom such Money was lent, as hath been already set forth.

Object. *But many of our Merchants trade with their own Stocks, and have no occasion to take up Money at Interest.*

*Answ.* This amounts to one and the same thing; for if our Merchants can get as much by advancing their Money on these Funds, as they can by Trading abroad, can we think they will be so imprudent, to venture their Estates to Foreign Parts out of their Reach, and subject to so many Risques, as Dishonesty or Insolvency of Factors, hazard of the Sea, and danger of the Enemy? At the best, it cannot be supposed they will employ so much of their Estates in Trade, as they would have done, had they not had this Opportunity of making such considerable Advantages of their Money at home, by paying it in on these Funds; and no doubt when they have found the Sweet of it, they will draw the remainder of their Estates out of Trade, in expectation of the like opportunity, if the Parliament shall think fit to raise more Money by the like Methods.

I come in the next place to show, that the great Encouragements given to Persons to advance Money on the late Funds, will be a means to carry out our Wealth, and thereby will impoverish the Kingdom. I need not form any Arguments to prove this Assertion: those who know what high Interest is, must acknowledg it is generally destructive to those who pay it, but is a certain Profit to such who receive it; and there being leave given to all Foreigners to advance Money on the said Funds, and very considerable Sums (as I have been inform'd) being remitted from Foreign Parts, and paid in by Foreigners for that purpose, it cannot be expected but the Interest of such Money, must be sent out of the Nation every Year, as it grows due, which in 16 Years, will be above 330 *l.* for every 100 *l.* advanced by them on the Lottery Act, and

and above 3000 *l.* for every 100 in 60 Years time, for all they pay into the Bank of *England*; beſides their Parts or Shares in the great Advantages, that will be made by diſcounting Bills, Exchequer-Tallies, *&c.* And if that *Maxim* holds true, as it muſt and does in this preſent caſe, *That the Wealth of a Nation is greater or leſſer in Proportion, according as its Imports and Exports do more or leſs exceed each other*; I am ſure, the great Sums that muſt be ſent over yearly for the Intereſt of Money advanced by Foreigners from abroad, muſt in time beggar the Nation; ſince we receive nothing again in return for what is ſo ſent out: and if it be an Evil (as it really is) to enrich a few of our own Subjects, by the ruin of the far greater Part, I am ſure, *à fortiori*, it is a much greater Miſchief for us to enrich Foreigners by the Spoils of our Engliſh Subjects: and therefore whatſoever value any Perſon may put upon the bringing great Sums of Money into the Nation from abroad; it is plain it is not for the Nation's Intereſt to encourage it.

I come now to ſhow, that the great Encouragments given tc thoſe who advanced Money on the late Funds, fall no leſs heavy on Gentlemen whoſe Eſtates are in Land, the value of which al-ways bears ſome proportion with the Intereſt of Money, theſe being pincht both ways: for as the Taxes (neceſſarily laid on Lands) make Land leſs eſteemed, and conſequently leſs valuable than formerly; ſo this Encouragment given to the Contributors t the late Funds (which is in effect a creating a new ſort of Pur-chaſes much more advantageous than Land) will certainly brin Land to 12 or 14 Years purchaſe, if not leſs. For Men will hard-ly be prevailed with to keep, much leſs to purchaſe Eſtates i Land, by which they cannot have 4 *l. per Cent. per Annum* for thei Money, when they can buy a perpetual Rent-charge on the Crowı (as in the Bank of *England*) which will bring them in abov 8 *l. per Cent. per Annum*, clear of all Taxes, beſides the other propo-ſed Advantages. For admit any Perſon hath 50 *l. per Annu* Eſtate in Land, the Taxes of 4 *s.* in the Pound, Charges fo finding Arms, Trophy-Money, *&c.* ſwallow up 11 or 12 *l. p Annum*, by which means the Owner hath not above 38 or 39 *per Annum* at moſt, clear to himſelf; if therefore he ſells l

Laı

Land but at 12 Years purchaſe, it will yield him *600 l.* with which he may purchaſe *50 l. per Annum* in the Bank free of all Taxes, which is 11 or 12 *l. per Annum* more than he could receive out of his Eſtate during the War, and as much as his Eſtate will bring him in in time of Peace, beſides his Intereſt in the aforementioned Advantages.

And who will not chooſe to have the Bank-Bills rather than Land at 20 Years Purchaſe, if they go current, with *3 l. per cent. per annum* Intereſt? which is almoſt as much as his Lands will bring him in; the Bank-Bills being ſo much more preferable than Land, as they are always as ſo much ready Money by a Man to anſwer any preſent Occaſions; while the Land, like a Drug, lies on his Hands, upon which he is not able to raiſe half the Value, unleſs he ſells it out-right, which he cannot do without great Expence of Time and Money, in examining Titles, drawing Conveyances, levying Fines, *&c.* Far better had it been for the Gentlemen whoſe Eſtates are in Land, to have paid half their yearly Incomes in Taxes, ſince that would have pinch'd them only for the preſent, during the War; and by retrenching their Expences, they might have preſerv'd their Eſtates; which, if notwithſtanding they had been neceſſitated to ſell, they might have had as many Years Purchaſe within a Year or two, as they could have had before the Taxes were laid upon them, the Purchaſers knowing theſe Taxes will not laſt always. But now perpetual Rent-Charges (if I may ſo call them) being to be bought, ſo far more advantageous than Land, and the Bank-Bills being ſo profitable, and (for the Reaſons aforeſaid) more eligible than Land, it cannot be expected if the War were ended, that Land ſhould ſell for 18, much leſs for 20 Years Purchaſe, when a Man at the ſame time may buy a perpetual Income from the Crown, free from Taxes, for 12 Years Purchaſe.

Object. *But it may be objected, that there are not any Eſtates in Land to be ſold at ſuch low Rates as 12 or 14 Years Purchaſe, as hath been ſuggeſted.*

*Anſw.* I grant it, for tho there are many Eſtates to be ſold, and never more than at this time, thoſe who have lent Money upon Gentlemens Eſtates calling it in to advance upon ſome of theſe late Funds; yet

yet Perſons are very loth to part with their Eſtates at an Undervalue, tho part with them they muſt, ſuch whoſe Eſtates are in Mortgage: and if they cannot ſell their Eſtates for what they would, they muſt ſell them for what they can get, or elſe muſt expect to be ejected, or barr'd of the Equity of Redemption. Beſides, theſe Funds being as yet but Novelties, every one is not ready to embarque in them; but when People once find that when they go to the Exchequer, or to the Bank, they have their Annuities or Intereſt-Money paid them punctually every half Year, upon Demand, without any farther Trouble or Defalcation for Taxes, it will quickly cauſe them to diſeſteem Land, with which they meet with ſo much Trouble, and upon which are ſo many Taxes; and therefore it is not rational to take our Meaſures from the preſent Value of Lands, but rather from the Value we may reaſonably ſuppoſe Lands will come to be ſold for, when Gentlemen whoſe Eſtates are mortgaged, are under a Force and abſolute Neceſſity of ſelling their Eſtates, and when Perſons are a little better acquainted with, and reconciled to theſe new ſorts of Purchaſes.

Object. *I ſhall anſwer one Objection more, no leſs frivolous than common,* viz. *That the Money paid in on theſe Funds will circulate.*

*Anſw.* I grant it does circulate; for Money is made to paſs from one to another in Payment, but does it circulate into the Tradeſman's Stock again, out of which it was taken, ſo as to enable him to drive as great a Trade as formerly, before he leſſen'd his Stock, by advancing his Money upon theſe Funds? Is the poor Trader relieved thereby, who was forc'd to draw his Money out of his Trade to ſatisfy his Creditors? Is the Gentleman whoſe Eſtate is mortgaged, any thing the better for this Circulation? or is the Intereſt of Money lower'd thereby? or does it not rather in time circulate into the Pockets it came out of? as I have already ſhown it does.

Much might be ſaid of the Bank of *England* in particular, as they are a Body of Men incorporated by their Majeſties, and confirm'd by Parliament. And I cannot but take notice of the prudent Foreſight of our Legiſlators, who wiſely provided againſt the Danger of creating ſo great a Body, without fit Bounds and Limitations

ons, and did therefore prohibit the Bank, to buy, ſell, or trade in any Goods or Merchandize, that ſo the Subject might not be oppreſs'd by their monopolizing with their commanding Stock; but yet I find they are enabled to purchaſe and enjoy to them and their Succeſſors, Lands, Rents, Tenements and Hereditaments, of what Nature or Quality ſoever (Crown-Lands excepted) without any ſuch Limitation, as is uſual in other Charters: and if by the Statute of *Mortmain*, 15 *Rich.* 2. all petty Corporations of Cities, Towns, or Boroughs, which have a perpetual Commonalty, were prohibited to purchaſe Lands, becauſe they have perpetual Succeſſion, I doubt not but the Parliament (if they ſhall think fit to continue the Corporation of the Bank for a longer time than eleven Years) will be pleaſed to put them under ſome Limitations, in reſpect of Purchaſes. For ſuppoſe this Bank have never no other Fund or Revenue ſettled upon them, upon their advancing more Money to their Majeſties, (which without doubt they have an eye to, and thoſe who enter not into the Account of it, may think it will be no ſmall Advantage to their Majeſties and the Kingdom, to have ſuch a Bank ready at any time to aſſiſt their Majeſties with Money upon any extraordinary occaſions) the Bank (with the 100000 *l. per Annum* already ſettled upon them, if it be continued to them and their Succeſſors for 60 Years) may divide 5 *l. per Cent. per Annum*, every Year among them, and may have above fourteen Millions (being more than all the Money ſuppoſed to be in the Kingdom) in their hands: So that (in ſuch caſe) all Perſons muſt in time come to them for Money if they want it, and muſt give them what *Premium*, or Conſideration they ſhall think fit, for the Loan of it; and being once Maſters of the whole Caſh of the Nation, what ſhall hinder them of being (in time) Maſters of the Land too, ſince there will be indigent Perſons to the End of the World, that will ſell their Eſtates? And if the Directors of the Bank manage their Buſineſs as they may, none elſe having Money, there can be no Buyers but themſelves; and conſequently they may have Gentlemens Eſtates at their own rates, and will be Maſters of the Eſtates as well as the Caſh of the Nation: and what ſhall hinder them, but they may in time make the Nation it ſelf pay what they pleaſe for the Loan of Money, if they

they ſhall ſtand in need of it? And tho I doubt not, but many may make a Jeſt of this my Suggeſtion; yet nothing is more plain than that it may be ſo, if they are continued a Corporation for 60 Years, (the time I have ſuppoſed) againſt which we have no other Security, but the Gentlemens good Nature, that they will not be ſo unkind to their Prince, nor ſo ſevere to their fellow-Subjects: for if it be granted, that there be not 12 Millions of Money in the Nation (whereas ſome compute, that there are not 8 Millions in the Kingdom) and the Governour and Directors of the Bank are not obliged to make Dividends but when they pleaſe, as I do not find by the Act they are, they may have all the Money in the Nation three times over in 60 Years.

Obj. *But ſome may ſay, that all this Buſineſs which I make ſuch a Scarecrow of, is but* 3 l. per Cent. per Annum *extraordinary Intereſt, paid to ſuch who advance Money to their Majeſties; and the Nation muſt be in a very ſorry Condition, if the paying* 3 l. per Cent. per Annum *extraordinary Intereſt, will ruin it.*

*Anſw.* Thoſe who make a Butt of 3 *l. per Cent. per Annum*, know not what they ſay; they may as well ſay, it is but 30000*l. per Annum* extraordinary for a Million of Money, and that in 60 Years time comes to above 11 Millions, at 5 *l. per Cent. per Annum* Intereſt, with Intereſt upon Intereſt, upon one Million of Money only; and what loſs muſt it be then to the Nation, if we ſhould take up many Millions at the ſame Terms? And yet this is the leaſt of the Nation's Loſs, for it occaſions the loſs of our Trade, the ruin of Families, and the deſtruction of Gentlemens Eſtates, as hath been already ſhown: ſo that nothing is more obvious, than that the raiſing Money on Funds, by the late Methods, will ruin Trade, diſcourage our Navigation, leſſen their Majeſties Cuſtoms, impoveriſh the Subjects, abate the value of Lands to 12 or 14 Years Purchaſe; and if the War ſhoud continue a few Years longer, I cannot foreſee which way the Parliament can raiſe Money, to enable their Majeſtics to proſecute the War, or how they will be able to ſettle Funds ſufficient, whereon to raiſe Money for the ſupply of their Majeſties, if they purſue the ſame Methods of raiſing it.

Having

Having thus ſhown, upon what diſadvantageous Terms both to their Majeſties and the Kingdom, their Majeſties are ſupplied with Money on the ſaid Funds; I now come to ſhow, how their Majeſties may be plentifully ſupplied with Money, and the Subjects enrich'd by the Taxes raiſed on them.

# PROPOSALS.

*Firſt*, That it be enacted, that any Perſon who hath an Eſtate in Fee, of Free-hold, or Copy-hold Land, may ſettle ſuch their Eſtate upon twenty Commiſſioners, *viz.* four Commiſſioners to be appointed by their Majeſties, their Heirs or Succeſſors; ſix Commiſſioners by the Houſe of Lords, and ten Commiſſioners by the Houſe of Commons, in Truſt for a Security, to make good all Bills, as ſhall be iſſued out upon the Credit of ſuch their Eſtates, to be ſettled for ſuch Purpoſes.

*Secondly*, That there ſhall be a general Regiſter kept in *London*, and a particular Regiſter in the chief City or Town in each County, where ſhall be entred all the Eſtates intended to be ſettled.

*Thirdly*, That none ſhall be permitted to ſettle his or her Eſtate, until he or ſhe ſhall have entered in the General Regiſter in *London*, and in the Particular Regiſter in the County, where ſuch Eſtate lies, his or her Chriſtian Name, Sirname, Profeſſion, Place of Abode, the Particulars of, and his or her Title to ſuch Eſtate, which he or ſhe deſire to ſettle for the ſpace of ſix Months; in which time, if no Claim be laid to, nor *Caveat* enter'd againſt the ſettling of ſuch Eſtate, the ſaid Eſtate ſhall be ſettled, and Bills of Credit (not exceeding the value of 20 Years Purchaſe) ſhall be iſſued out upon the Security of ſuch Eſtate, as the preſent yearly Value of ſuch Eſtate ſhall appear to be upon Examination to be made by the Commiſſioners, and by the Oaths of two or more credible Witneſſes.

*Fourthly*, That the Commiſſioners ſhall appoint three or more under-

understanding Men in each County, who ſhall make a ſtrict Enquiry in the ſeveral Counties, after the Value, Titles, Proprietors, Occupiers, or Tenants of each and every Eſtate, entred in the County-Regiſters in order to be ſettled, and ſhall tranſmit their ſeveral Informations to the Commiſſioners.

*Fifthly*, That the Commiſſioners ſhall appoint twenty able Counſel, to examine the Titles of all Eſtates which ſhall be ſettled, and no Eſtate ſhall be ſettled but upon the Approbation of three or more of the ſaid Counſel, to be ſignified under their Hands.

*Sixthly*, That no Eſtate ſhall be ſettled, againſt the Settlement whereof any *Caveat* ſhall be entred, or where the Counſel are not clear in their Opinion, that the Title is good, until ſuch Title ſhall be cleared.

*Seventhly*, If any Perſon ſhall make an undue Settlement of an Eſtate he hath no right to, the Party (whoſe Eſtate it ſhall appear to be) ſhall (upon good Proof thereof) be intituled to the Eſtate and all the Profits ariſing, or that ſhall or may ariſe by ſuch Settlement, and ſhall have his Remedy at Law, againſt the Perſon who made ſuch undue ſettlement of his Eſtate, for all the Bills of Credit or Profits he ſhall have received by virtue of ſuch Settlement; and may ſue for, and recover treble Damages, with coſt of Suit, to the Party aggrieved by ſuch undue Settlement; to be recovered by Action of Debt, Bill, Plaint or Information, in any of their Majeſties Courts at *Weſtminſter*, &c. *prout* in other Acts.

*Eighthly*, That any Perſon may ſettle his mortgaged Eſtate, giving the Mortgagee three Months notice in Writing of ſuch his intended Settlement; but no Mortgager ſhall receive any Profit or Advantage thereby, without the conſent of the Mortgagee, until ſuch time that the Mortgagee ſhall be fully paid his Principal, Intereſt, and all reaſonable Charges by the ſaid Mortgagee expended or laid out upon ſuch mortgaged Eſtate, or for or by reaſon of ſuch Mortgage, before and until ſuch time of notice given in Writing, by the Mortgager to the Mortgagee, of ſuch intended Settlement.

*Ninthly*

*Ninthly*, The ſaid Bills of Credit ſhall be current in payment, by Indorſment *toties quoties*, from the Party delivering, or paying, to the Party receiving the ſame, as the lawful Coin of the Kingdom.

*Tenthly*, That all thoſe Perſons, who ſhall ſettle their Eſtates may and ſhall chooſe 25 Directors once in every three Years, in the Month of *September*, by the Majority of Votes, to be brought or ſent in writing, the Commiſſioners giving publick Notice in three ſeveral Gazetts, a Month at leaſt before every ſuch Election or Elections: any three or more of which Directors, together with any two or more of the Commiſſioners, may prepare Bills of Credit, to be iſſued out upon the Security of any Eſtate, or Eſtates.

*Eleventhly*, That upon the Death or other Vacancy of any Commiſſioner to be appointed by their Majeſties, their Heirs or Succeſſors, their Majeſties, their Heirs or Succeſſors, may fill up ſuch, and every ſuch Vacancy.

That upon the Death, or other Vacancy, of any one or more of the Commiſſioners to be appointed by the Houſe of Lords, the ſurviving or remaining Commiſſioners, of the Houſe of Lords, ſhall nominate and appoint one or more Perſons, to ſupply ſuch, and every ſuch Vacancy, who ſhall have full Power, and Authority, to act as a Commiſſioner, or Commiſſioners, and ſhall be deemed, and taken to be ſuch, to all Intents and Purpoſes; and ſo ſhall continue to act (by virtue of ſuch Commiſſion received from the ſaid Commiſſioners) until he, or they, or until ſome other Perſon, or Perſons, ſhall be choſen and appointed by the Houſe of Lords, and no longer.

That upon the like Death, or Vacancy, of any one or more of the Commiſſioners to be appointed by the Houſe of Commons, the ſurviving or remaining Commiſſioners of the Houſe of Commons, ſhall nominate and appoint one or more Perſons to ſupply ſuch, and every ſuch Vacancy, who ſhall have full Power and Authority to act as a Commiſſioner or Commiſſioners; and ſhall be deem'd, eſteem'd, and taken to be ſuch, to all Intents and Purpoſes; and ſo ſhall continue to act (by virtue of ſuch Commiſſion, received from the ſaid Com-

Commiſſioners) until he or they, or until ſome other Perſon or Perſons, ſhall be choſen and appointed by the Houſe of Commons, and no longer: It being hereby intended, that there ſhall never be any Vacancy of the Commiſſioners; but that there ſhall be conſtantly four Commiſſioners for their Majeſties, ſix Commiſſioners for the Houſe of Lords, and ten Commiſſioners for the Houſe of Commons.

*Twelfthly*, That their Majeſties ſhall and may allow each and every of the Commiſſioners, 1000 *l. per annum*, and no more.

*Thirteenthly*, That no Commiſſioner ſhall be diſplaced, but by Authority of Parliament.

*Fourteenthly*, That there ſhall be fifteen Commiſſioners, and twenty Directors preſent, and conſenting to the iſſuing out all Bills of Credit to be advanced to their Majeſties, upon any Parliamentary Fund.

*Fifteenthly*, That their Majeſties may allow 1000 *l. per Annum*, and no more, to the Commiſſioners and Directors, for their Charge in iſſuing out, and renewing the Bills of Credit, for each Million value in Bills advanced to their Majeſties, upon any Parliamentary Fund; and for the Salaries of Book-keepers, Accomptants, Clerks, and inferiour Officers, and all other Charges whatſoever, until the Bills of Credit iſſued out for ſuch Money, ſhall be paid and cancell'd.

*Sixteenthly*, That their Majeſties, their Heirs and Succeſſors, ſhal and may pay the Commiſſioners and Directors, out of any Fund ſettled by Parliament for that Purpoſe, 3 *l. per cent. per annum*, and no more, for Intereſt of all Bills of Credit, they ſhall advance to their Majeſties.

*Seventeenthly*, That the Commiſſioners and Directors ſhall pay the ſaid 3 *l. per cent. per annum*, to the Perſons, upon the Security of whoſe Eſtates ſuch Bills were iſſued out, every Year at two equal Payments, without any Gratuity or Reward; and if the Commiſſioners or Directors, ſhall refuſe or neglect to pay the ſaid 3 *l. per cent. per annum*, or any part of it, to the ſaid Perſons to whom it ſhall be due and payable, (provided the Commiſſioners and Directors ſhall have received the ſame) ſuch Commiſſioners and Directors ſhal ſhall forfeit and pay to each and every Perſon aggrieved by ſuch Non-payment, treble Damage, *&c.*

*Eighteenthly*, That their Majeſties, their Heirs and Succeſſors, ſhall and may pay to the ſaid Commiſſioners and Directors, for all the Bills of Credit hereafter to be iſſued out and advanced to their Majeſties upon the Credit of any Fund ſettled, or to be ſettled by Parliament for the Payment of any Annuity, in lieu of, or in recompence for ſuch Bills of Credit, by them iſſued out, and advanced to their Majeſties upon the Credit of ſuch Funds, the ſeveral Rates and Annuities, according to the ſeveral Terms, or Number of Years herein after particularly ſet down and expreſs'd, *viz.*

| | | *l. s.* | |
|---|---|---|---|
| For an Annuity of | 100 Years | 3.10. | *per Cent. per Annum.* |
| | 66. 8 Months | 4.--- | |
| | 50 Years | 4.10. | |
| | 40 Years | 5.---. | |
| | 33. 4 Months | 5.10. | |
| | 25 Years | 6.10. | |
| | 20 Years | 7.10. | |
| | 16 Years | 8.15. | |
| | 13. 4 Months | 10.--- | |
| | 10 Years | 12.10. | |

and no more, for each and every 100 *l.* value, in Bills of Credit, iſſued out to their Majeſties upon the Credit of any ſuch Fund or Funds, by the ſaid Commiſſioners and Directors as aforeſaid.

*Nineteenthly*, That the Commiſſioners and Directors ſhall pay, or cauſe to be paid to the Perſons upon the Credit of whoſe Eſtates ſuch Bills were iſſued out, 2 *l.* 10 *s. per cent. per annum*, for each 100 *l.* Pound value in Bills of Credit, advanced to their Majeſties, in like manner as is appointed for the Payment of the 3 *l. per cent. per annum* Intereſt, and upon the like Penalties or Forfeitures for Non-payment; and with the whole Reſidue of ſuch Annuities, they are to diſcharge, and cancel every Year part of the Bills of Credit: by which means, all the Bills of Credit will be paid, and cancell'd cancell'd in the determined Term of Years, for which the Payment of ſuch Annuity or Annuities, were ſettled.

*Twentieth*, That every Perſon who ſhall iſſue out, and advance Bills of Credit upon the Security of his or their Eſtate, for the Uſe of their Majeſties, ſhall be exempted from Taxes to their Majeſties, for ſuch Part of their Eſtates ſettled for thoſe Purpoſes, and advanced for their Majeſties Service: and any three of the Commiſſioners ſhall give a Certificate of the ſame; and each Certificate ſhall be entred down in a Book or Books, to be kept by the Commiſſioners and Directors for that Purpoſe.

*21ſt.* That all Eſtates ſhall be ſettled; and Bills of Credit advanced upon the Security of them, in order as they were entred in the General Regiſter, without preference or otherwiſe.

*22d.* That any Perſon or Perſons (after their Eſtate or Eſtates ſhall be ſettled ſix Months) may have what Bills of Credit they pleaſe for their own proper Uſe or Uſes, not exceeding 20 Years purchaſe, of the preſent Yearly value of their Eſtates; paying the Commiſſioners and Directors for each 100*l.* value in Bills of Credit, to be kept for their own proper Uſe or Uſes, 10 *s. per Annum* for the Charges which the ſaid Commiſſioners and Directors muſt neceſſarily be at in iſſuing out, and renewing the Bills of Credit; and towards the Payment of Salaries to Servants, and all other their Charges whatſoever.

*23d.* That any Perſon or Perſons (after their Eſtate or Eſtates ſhall have been ſettled ſix Months) may have what Bills of Credit they pleaſe on their own proper Accounts, not exceeding 20 Years purchaſe, of the preſent Yearly value of their Eſtates; paying the Commiſſioners and Directors any of the following Annuities according to the ſeveral Terms of Years, next and immediately herein after ſet down: That is to ſay,

For

For an Annuity of

| | *l. s.* | |
|---|---|---|
| 50 Years — | 2.10.— | |
| 40 Years — | 3.— — | |
| 33. 4 Months | 3.10.— | |
| 25 Years — | 4.10.— | |
| 20 Years — | 5.10.— | *per Cent. per Annum.* |
| 16 Years — | 6.15.— | |
| 13. 4 Months | 8.— — | |
| 10 Years — | 10.10.— | |

and no more, for each, and every 100 *l.* value in Bills of Credit, iſſued out by the Commiſſioners and Directors, to him or them, for his or their own proper Uſe or Uſes; 10 *s. per cent. per annum* (part of the ſaid Annuities) to be paid to the ſaid Commiſſioners and Directors, for their Charges, to be equally divided among them; and with the Remainder, or Reſidue of the ſaid Annuities, the ſaid Commiſſioners and Directors ſhall diſcharge, and cancel Bills of Credit, for part of the Principal, until all, and every part of the Principal, ſhall be paid, and the Bills of Credit iſſued out thereupon cancelled.

*24th.* That any Perſon or Perſons, who ſhall have or receive any of the ſaid Bills of Credit, may renew them once in every Calendar-Month, without Fee or Reward.

*25th.* That any Perſon or Perſons, who ſhall renew any Bill or Bills of Credit, may have as many Bills of Credit as they pleaſe for any Bill of Credit of the like value; but no Bill of Credit is to be made for a leſs value than 5 *l.*

*26th.* That any Commiſſioner or Director, who ſhall, directly or indirectly, take any greater *Premium*, Conſideration or Reward, for doing their Duties enjoined them by this Act, he or they ſhall be ſuſpended from their Place or Places, until the next Seſſion of Parliament.

*27th.* That the Commiſſioners and Directors ſhall cauſe a compleat Ballance of their Books, to be drawn up every Year, in the Month of *Auguſt*, unto the firſt Day of the ſaid Month, to be ſubject to the Inſpection of a Committee or Committees of the Lords or Commons in Parliament.

*28th*

28*th*. That every Commiſſioner or Director, who ſhall iſſue out Bills of Credit, upon the Security of any Eſtate, to a greater value than 20 Years purchaſe of ſuch Eſtate, as the ſame ſhall be ſworn to be worth by two or more credible Witneſſes; or ſhall iſſue out Bills of Credit, for the Security of which, no Eſtate ſhall be firſt ſettled; or ſhall lend, or advance to their Majeſties, any Bills of Credit, otherwiſe than upon a Parliamentary Fund, and by the Conſent and Authority of Parliament, ſhall incur, and ſuffer the Pains and Penalties of High-Treaſon.

29*th*. That it ſhall be High-Treaſon to counterfeit any of the ſaid Bills, or to offer them in Payment, knowing the ſame to be counterfeited.

Having thus finiſhed my Propoſals, I ſhall mention ſomething of thoſe many great Advantages which their Majeſties and the whole Nation will reap by this propoſed Method.

Firſt; Their Majeſties will be plentifully ſupplied with Money on much eaſier Terms, and far greater Sums might have been raiſed on the Million-Act, Lottery-Act, and Bank of *England*, by this propoſed Method, than were raiſed by the ſaid Funds by the late Methods; and the like may be done on any future Fund: and the more Money any Fund raiſes, the fewer Funds will need to be ſettled, and conſequently the Nation will be leſs burdened.

Secondly; It will certainly unite their Majeſties and the People, and engage them inſeparately in each other's Intereſt.

Thirdly; Theſe propoſed Bills of Credit being a new Species of Money, and to all Intents and Purpoſes as uſeful as Money, it will be (as it were) an introducing of ſo many more freſh monied Men into the Kingdom, with ſeveral Millions of Money more than was before, for the Supply of their Majeſties; and will anſwer all Occaſions, as the bringing in ſo many Millions of Money into the Nation would or could have done.

Fourthly; Money naturally begetting Money, every Million value in theſe Bills of Credit will produce as much Profit as a Million of Money; and if employed in Trade, and but 6 *l. per cent. per annum*

*annum* got by it, each Million value in Bills of Credit issued out upon the Security of Gentlemens Estates, will bring in 60000 *l. per annum* Profit every Year to the Nation.

Fifthly; It will keep great Sums in the Nation, that otherwise will be sent out of the Nation for Interest; and will enable us to lend, who are now forced to borrow of others.

Sixthly; It will animate our Merchants, and set them upon the same Level, in respect of Trade, with our Neighbours.

Seventhly; It will encourage all Artificers and Handicrafts, and bring new Manufactures into the Kingdom; which cannot now be wrought here by reason of high Interest; and set all our Poor at work, many Thousands of whom are now in a starving Condition for want of Employment: and it will turn the Genius of the Subjects into the right Channel again, by putting them upon the improving their Money in Trade.

Eighthly; It will ease all the Nobility and Gentry from Taxes, who shall advance Bills of Credit to their Majesties upon the Security of their Estates, and will add 50 or 60 *l. per annum* to every 100 *l. per annum* of their present Estates.

Ninthly; Gentlemen will have an Opportunity of improving their Estates by building, repairing, planting, draining or watering their Lands; who are not now able to do it, by reason of Scarcity of Money, and high Interest: by which means many thousand People, who are now chargeable to the Parishes, will be employed in all the several Parts of this Kingdom.

Tenthly; It will enable all such whose Estates are mortgaged, or otherwise engaged, to clear their Estates from Incumbrances: and those may have Bills of Credit upon the Security of their own Estates for 10 *s. per Cent. per annum*, as in Proposal 22. who now pay 5, 6 or 7 *l. per Cent. per annum*; or else by paying a small Annuity, as in Proposal 23. they may by Degrees, and upon easy Terms, pay off Principal as well as Interest.

Eleventhly; They may with Ease raise Portions for their Children, without parting with their Freeholds.

Twelfthly; It will put all People, who have Money, upon buying Land; and will in all probability, raise the Value of Land to 40 or 50 Years Purchase.

But

But becauſe Examples are the beſt for Illuſtration, I have hereunto ſubjoined Tables with the Explanations of them drawn up purſuant to my Propoſals, which will fully demonſtrate, and plainly make appear, the moſt unſpeakable Advantages this propoſed Method will be to the whole Kingdom in general.

A TABLE ſhowing the Value in Bills of Credit any Perſon may take up upon an Eſtate of 100 *l. per Annum*; the Annuity he muſt pay for any Term of Years he ſhall ſettle his Eſtate in diſcharge of Principal and Intereſt; what is to be paid every Year to diſcharge the Principal; and what is to be paid to the Commiſſioners and Directors.

| *Eſtate ſettled.* | *Bills of Credit.* | *Term of Years.* | *Intereſt or Annuity.* per Annum. | *To pay the Principal.* per Annum. | *To pay the Commiſſioners and Directors.* |
|---|---|---|---|---|---|
| 100*l*. p. Annum. | 2000 *l*. | Perpetual. | 10 *l*. | | 10 *l*. p. Annum. |
| | | 50 Years, | 50 | 40 *l*. | |
| | | 40 Years, | 60 | 50 | |
| | | 33.4 Months, | 70 | 60 | |
| | | 25 Years, | 90 | 80 | |
| | | 20 Years, | 110 | 100 | |
| | | 16 Years, | 135 | 125 | |
| | | 13.4 Months, | 160 | 150 | |
| | | 10 Years, | 210 | 200 | |

A TA-

A Table ſhewing what Sum any Nobleman, Gentleman, or other Perſon may take up upon any Eſtate, from 5 *l. per Annum*, to an Eſtate of 5000 *l. per Annum*: What he muſt pay for Intereſt, or for an Annuity for any Term of Years, in diſcharge of Principal and Intereſt; and what he muſt now pay for Intereſt, only after the Rate of 6 *per Cent. per Annum.*

| *Eſtates to be ſettled.* | *Bills of Credit.* | *Perpetual.* | | *50 Years.* | | *40 Yrs.* | *33 Years 4 Months.* | | *25 Years.* | | *20 Years.* | | *Intereſt at 6 per Cent.* |
|---|---|---|---|---|---|---|---|---|---|---|---|---|---|
| *l.* per Annum. | *l.* | *l.* per Annum. | *s.* | *l.* per Annum. | *s.* | *l.* per Annum. | *l.* per Annum. | *s.* | *l.* per Annum. | *s.* | *l.* per Annum. | *s.* | *l.* per Annum. |
| 5 | 100 | 0 | 10 | 2 | 10 | 3 | 3 | 10 | 4 | 10 | 5 | 10 | 6 |
| 10 | 200 | 1 | | 5 | | 6 | 7 | | 9 | | 11 | | 12 |
| 20 | 400 | 2 | | 10 | | 12 | 14 | | 18 | | 22 | | 24 |
| 30 | 600 | 3 | | 15 | | 18 | 21 | | 27 | | 33 | | 36 |
| 40 | 800 | 4 | | 20 | | 24 | 28 | | 36 | | 44 | | 48 |
| 50 | 1000 | 5 | | 25 | | 30 | 35 | | 45 | | 55 | | 60 |
| 100 | 2000 | 10 | | 50 | | 60 | 70 | | 90 | | 110 | | 120 |
| 150 | 3000 | 15 | | 75 | | 90 | 105 | | 135 | | 165 | | 180 |
| 200 | 4000 | 20 | | 100 | | 120 | 140 | | 180 | | 220 | | 240 |
| 250 | 5000 | 25 | | 125 | | 150 | 175 | | 225 | | 275 | | 300 |
| 300 | 6000 | 30 | | 150 | | 180 | 210 | | 270 | | 330 | | 360 |
| 350 | 7000 | 35 | | 175 | | 210 | 245 | | 315 | | 385 | | 420 |
| 400 | 8000 | 40 | | 200 | | 240 | 280 | | 360 | | 440 | | 480 |
| 450 | 9000 | 45 | | 225 | | 270 | 315 | | 405 | | 495 | | 540 |
| 500 | 10000 | 50 | | 250 | | 300 | 350 | | 450 | | 550 | | 600 |
| 750 | 15000 | 75 | | 375 | | 450 | 525 | | 675 | | 825 | | 900 |
| 1000 | 20000 | 100 | | 500 | | 600 | 700 | | 900 | | 1100 | | 1200 |
| 1500 | 30000 | 150 | | 750 | | 900 | 1050 | | 1350 | | 1650 | | 1800 |
| 2000 | 40000 | 200 | | 1000 | | 1200 | 1400 | | 1800 | | 2200 | | 2400 |
| 2500 | 50000 | 250 | | 1250 | | 1500 | 1750 | | 2250 | | 2750 | | 3000 |
| 3000 | 60000 | 300 | | 1500 | | 1800 | 2100 | | 2700 | | 3300 | | 3600 |
| 3500 | 70000 | 350 | | 1750 | | 2100 | 2450 | | 3150 | | 3850 | | 4200 |
| 4000 | 80000 | 400 | | 2000 | | 2400 | 2800 | | 3600 | | 4400 | | 4800 |
| 4500 | 90000 | 450 | | 2250 | | 2700 | 3150 | | 4050 | | 4950 | | 5400 |
| 5000 | 100000 | 500 | | 2500 | | 3000 | 3500 | | 4500 | | 5500 | | 6000 |

A

A Table ſhowing how much Money may be raiſed by this propoſed Method, upon 100000 *l. per An.* ſettled for paiment of Intereſt, or an Annuity for any Term of Years: What Intereſt or Annuities muſt be paid: The yearly Value of the Eſtates to be ſettled for the Security of Bills of Credit: What muſt be paid every Year to ſuch who ſettle their Eſtates; and what muſt be paid off every Year by the Commiſſioners and Directors in diſcharge of the Principal.

| *Annual Fund.* (per Annum.) | | *Term of Years.* | *Intereſt or Annuity.* (per Annum.) | | *Sums Advanced.* | | | *Eſtates ſettled* (per Annum.) | | | *To pay thoſe who ſettle their Eſtates.* (per Annum.) | | *To pay off the Principal.* (per Annum.) | |
|---|---|---|---|---|---|---|---|---|---|---|---|---|---|---|
| *l.* | *s.* | | *l.* | *s.* | *l.* | *s.* | *d.* | *l.* | *s.* | *d.* | *l.* | *s.* | *l.* | *s.* |
| 100000 | | Perpetual. | 3 | 00 | 3333333 | 06 | 08 | 166666 | 13 | 04 | 100000 | | | |
| 100002 | | 100 Years. | 3 | 10 | 2857200 | | | 142860 | | | 71430 | | 28572 | |
| 100000 | | 66.8 Months. | 4 | 00 | 2500000 | | | 125000 | | | 62500 | | 37500 | |
| 100098 | | 50 Years. | 4 | 10 | 2222400 | | | 111120 | | | 55560 | | 44448 | |
| 100000 | | 40 Years. | 5 | 00 | 2000000 | | | 100000 | | | 50000 | | 50000 | |
| 100001 | | 33.4 Months. | 5 | 10 | 1818200 | | | 90910 | | | 45455 | | 54546 | |
| 100002 | 10 | 25 Years. | 6 | 10 | 1538500 | | | 76930 | | | 38462 | 10 | 61540 | |
| 100005 | | 20 Years. | 7 | 10 | 1333400 | | | 66670 | | | 33335 | | 66670 | |
| 100003 | 15 | 16 Years. | 8 | 15 | 1142900 | | | 57145 | | | 28572 | 10 | 71431·5 | |
| 100000 | | 13.4 Months. | 10 | 00 | 1000000 | | | 50000 | | | 25000 | | 75000 | |
| 100000 | | 10 Years. | 12 | 10 | 800000 | | | 40000 | | | 20000 | | 80000 | |

A Table ſhowing how much *per Annum* is to be ſettled by Parliament for a Fund to be paid yearly for each Million Value in Bills of Credit to be advanced to their Majeſties at Intereſt, or for the paiment of an Annuity for a Term of Years: What yearly Value in Land is to be ſettled for the Security of the Million Value in Bills of Credit: What is to be paid yearly to ſuch whoſe Eſtates ſhall be ſettled for the Security of ſuch Bills of Credit; and what is to be paid every Year towards the Diſcharge of the Principal.

| *Sum Advanced.* | *Term.* | *Intereſt or Annuity.* (per Cent. per Annum.) | | *Annual Fund.* (per Annum.) | *Eſtates ſettled.* (per Annum.) | *Paid thoſe who ſettle their Eſtates.* (per Annum.) | *To pay off the Principal.* (per Annum.) |
|---|---|---|---|---|---|---|---|
| | | *l.* | *s.* | *l* | *l.* | *l.* | *l.* |
| A Million | Perpetual. | 03 | 00 | 30000 | —— | 30000 | |
| | 100 Years. | 03 | 10 | 35000 | | | 10000 |
| | 66.8 Months. | 04 | 00 | 40000 | | | 15000 |
| | 50 Years. | 04 | 10 | 45000 | | | 20000 |
| | 40 Years. | 05 | 00 | 50000 | 50000 | 25000 | 25000 |
| | 33.4 Months. | 05 | 10 | 55000 | | | 30000 |
| | 25 Years. | 06 | 10 | 65000 | | | 40000 |
| | 20 Years. | 07 | 10 | 75000 | | | 50000 |
| | 16 Years. | 08 | 15 | 87500 | | | 62500 |
| | 13.4 Months. | 10 | 00 | 100000 | | | 75000 |
| | 10 Years. | 12 | 10 | 125000 | | | 100000 |

The

## *The Use of the first and second Tables, applied to the Proposals.*

ADmit a Gentleman hath barely 100 *l. per Annum* Estate to live on, and hath a Wife and four Children to provide for: This Person, supposing no Taxes were upon his Estate, must be a great Husband to be able to keep his Charge, but cannot think of laying up any thing to place out his Children in the World: but according to this proposed Method, he may give his Children 500 *l.* a-piece, and have 90 *l. per annum* left for himself and his Wife to live upon; the which he may also leave to such of his Children as he pleases after his and his Wife's Decease: For first having settled his Estate of 100 *l. per annum*, as in Proposals 1, 3. he may have Bills of Credit for 2000 *l.* for his own proper Use, for 10 *s. per cent. per annum*, as in Proposal 22. which is but 10 *l. per annum* for the 2000 *l.* which being deducted out of his Estate of 100 *l. per annum*, there remains 90 *l. per annum* clear to himself.

But suppose this Gentleman hath mortgaged his Estate for 1000 *l.* for which he pays 60 *l. per annum* Interest, he hath but 40 *l. per annum* left, which will hardly keep his Wife and Children from starving, especially if he pays 20 *l. per annum* Taxes out of that small Pittance; having settled his Estate in Land, and taken up 2000 *l.* Bills of Credit upon it, he may pay off his 1000 *l.* Mortgage, and give his Children 250 *l.* a-piece, and have 50 *l. per annum* more than he now hath left him to live upon.

But admit a Gentleman hath 1000 *l. per annum*; upon which we will suppose he owes 10000 *l.* at 6 *l. per cent. per annum* Interest, (not to mention Procuration and Continuation) the bare Interest comes to 600 *l. per annum*, the Taxes of 4 *s.* in the Pound to their Majesties comes to 200 *l. per annum* more; reckoning Repairs, Militia-rate, Trophy-Money, *&c.* he hath not 200 *l. per annum* left him to maintain himself and Family.

If

If this Gentleman ſettles his Eſtate as in Propoſals 1, 2. he may have Bills of Credit for 20000 *l.* as in Propoſal 22. with this he may pay off his 10000 *l.* Mortgage: for which 10000 *l.* he muſt pay 10 *s. per cent.* which is 50 *l. per annum* to the Commiſſioners and Directors; he may lend the other 10000 *l.* to their Majeſties, for which he ſhall have 3 *l. per cent. per annum*, as in Propoſal 16. which comes to 300 *l. per annum*; and be exempted from half the Taxes upon account of the 10000 *l.* lent their Majeſties, as in Propoſal 20. So that this Gentleman who has not now 200 *l. per annnum* clear, will have almoſt 1150 *l. per annum* coming in; as appears by the following Parallel.

*The Gentleman's preſent Circumſtances.*

| | *l.* | |
|---|---|---|
| Intereſt of 10000 *l.* | 600 | *per annum.* |
| Taxes of 4 *s.* in the Pound | 200 | |
| Remaining for himſelf, not reckoning Militia-rate, *&c.* | 200 | |
| | 1000 | |

*His Circumſtances by my Method.*

| | *l.* | |
|---|---|---|
| His Eſtate | 1000 | *per annum.* |
| Intereſt of 10000 *l.* lent to their Majeſties | 300 | |
| | 1300 | |
| Paid the Commiſſio. and Direct. for 10000 *l.* Bills — 50 *l. per annum.* Taxes — 100 *l. per annum.* | 150 | |
| Remains to the Gentleman | 1150 | |

And his 10000 *l.* Mortgage paid off.

But if this Gentleman hath any Children, he may give them 10000 *l.* among them, and have 700 *l. per annum* left, *viz.*

| | | |
|---|---|---|
| Paid the Commiſſioners and Directors for 20000 *l.* Bills of Credit | 100 *l.* | *per annum.* |
| Paid Taxes at 4 *s.* in the Pound | 200 | |
| Remains to the Gentleman | 700 | |
| | 1000 | |

So here is 10000 *l.* Mortgage paid, 10000 *l.* given among his Children, 200 *l. per annum* to their Majeſties for Taxes, and 700 *per annum* the Gentleman will have to live upon.

But

But ſuppoſe the Gentleman who owes 10000 *l.* upon his Eſtate of 1000 *l. per annum,* hath a mind to pay it off gradually by a ſmall Annuity for a Term of Years, he ſhall have 10000 *l.* Bills of Credit to pay off his 10000 *l.* (for which he muſt now pay 600 *l. per annum* for Intereſt, and not a Farthing of the Principal paid) upon the Payment of 250 *l. per annum* for 50 Years, and never pay the Principal; or if the Gentleman deſires to pay it in a leſs time, he may have 10000 *l.* Bills of Credit for 550 *l. per annum* Annuity for 20 Years, and his Eſtate then cleared; which is leſs by 50 *l. per annum* than he muſt now pay for ſimple Intereſt only; and at the 20 Years end he will ſtill owe the whole 10000 *l.* Principal. Or does any Gentleman owe greater Sum upon his Eſtate, ſuppoſe 50000 *l.* he muſt pay 3000 *l.* for the bare Intereſt; whereas by this Method, he ſhall pay no more than 250 *l. per annum* for 50000 *l.* which is 2750 *l. per annum* ſaved to him out of 3000 *l. per annum.*

Inſtances of this Nature are numerous: I ſhall now ſhow that it is no leſs advantageous to the publick, than it is to private Perſons.

---

## *The Uſe of the third Table.*

If the Parliament had raiſed Money by this Method upon the Fund of 100000 *l. per annum* ſettled on the Bank of *England,* they might have had 3333333 *l.* 6 *s.* 8 *d.* which is 2133333 *l.* 6 *s.* 8 *d.* more than was raiſed upon it; and the Gentlemen who ſettled their Eſtates for Security of the Bills of Credit, would have been excuſed from Taxes, and have had 60 *l. per annum* added to every 100 *l. per annum* preſent Eſtate they now have: So that whereas the Parliament upon a Fund of 200000 *l. per annum,* is not able to raiſe above 2400000 *l.* which is not the half of one Year's Taxes; the Parliament may raiſe by my Method almoſt ſeven Millions upon a Fund of 200000 *l. per annum,* and oblige the Gentlemen of *England* into the Bargain by an Exemption from Taxes, and a conſiderable Augmentation of their yearly Eſtates: But if the Parliament had ſettled the ſaid Fund of 100000 *l. per annum* only for a certain number

number of Years, when the ſame ſhould have expired, and the Nation eaſed of the Fund; if the Parliament (inſtead of a Perpetuity) had ſettled it but for 66 Years and 8 Months, they might have raiſed 2500000 *l.* which is more by 1300000 *l.* than they have for a Perpetuity; and the Gentlemen of *England* would have had 62500 *l. per annum*, part of the ſaid Fund, in Augmentation of their Eſtates.

Or admit they had raiſed a Million of Money, as in the Lottery-Act, they might have had a Million for 100000 *l. per annum* for 13.4 Months; whereas they gave 140000 *l.* for 16 Years.

---

## *The Uſe of the fourth Table.*

ADmit the Parliament had raiſed 1200000 *l.* by my propoſed Methods, they might have had it for 36000 *l. per annum*; which is 64000 *l. per annum* leſs than is paid to the Bank of *England:* or they might have raiſed a Million upon the Payment of 87500 *l. per annum* Annuity for 16 Years, which is leſs by 52500 *l. per annum* than is paid on the Lottery-Act; or elſe upon the 140000 *l. per annum* Fund paid on the Lottery-Act, might have been raiſed 1600000 *l.* the Gentlemen muſt have ſettled 80000 *l. per annum* in Land for the Security of the Bills of Credit; for which they ſhould have 40000 *l. per annum* paid them out of the Parliamentary Fund, and the remaining 100000 *l. per annum* ſhould have paid off the 1600000 *l.* in 16 Years.

So that by theſe Means the Nation is not only ſerved on much eaſier Terms, but Gentlemen will be exempted from Taxes, and have a conſiderable Addition to their Yearly Eſtates.

I now come to conſider what Objections may be raiſed againſt theſe Propoſals, and ſhall endeavour to anſwer them, and that as briefly as I can.

Obj. *You propoſe in Propoſal 22. that any Man, who ſhall ſettle his Eſtate for the Security of Bills of Credit, may have what Bills of Credi-*

*dit he pleases to the present value of his Estate for his own proper Use: now admit a Man settles an Estate to which he hath no Right, and takes up all the Bills of Credit on his own proper Account, and buys Goods or Merchandize with the said Bills, and goes beyond Sea, what must the Person do who hath the lawful Right and Title to such Estate? for the Estate being settled in due form, as in Proposal 3. the right Owner is left remediless, if the Person who made such undue Settlement be out of his reach.*

*Answ.* 1. No Man can settle an Estate, who may not as well now sell the same Estate: for in regard no Estate can be settled but where 3 able Counsel shall give it under their hands, that the Person who settles such Estate hath a good Title to it, as Proposal 5. so any Person who can show so fair a Title to an Estate as to deceive 3 Counsel, he may as well now sell the said Estate, and go beyond Sea with the Money: and tho the Person whose Estate it really is, will not be injured, yet the Purchaser will lose his Money; and it is no less evil for the one to lose his Money, than it would be for the other to lose his Land.

*Answ.* 2. If such undue Settlement should be made, and twenty Years Purchase of the Estate received in Bills of Credit, the remaining Part of the Estate will be more worth to him who hath the legal Right to the Estate than the whole will be worth if no Settlements be made: but for brevity sake I refer my Reader for a further Answer to Proposal 7. and to Queries 14, 15, 16, 17, 18, 19, 20.

Obj. *But you have proposed 3 l.* per Cent. per Annum *for Interest, and 2 l. 10 s.* per Cent. per Annum *for Annuities, to such who shall settle their Estates for the security of Bills of Credit, to be issued out and advanced to their Majesties upon any Parliamentary Fund, as in Proposals 16, 17, 18, 19. now what Man in his Senses will settle and encumber an Estate of 2000 l. Value, for so inconsiderable an Advantage as 50 or 60 l.* per Annum, *for the payment of which he hath no other Security than a Revenue payable out of the Exchequer: and if the payment of that Annual Fund should be stopt, he will be in a sorry Condition, his Estate being notwithstanding obliged to make good the Bills of Credit issued out upon the Security of it.*

*Answ*

*Answ.* 1. None who have read what Advantages a Gentleman of a real Estate will reap by this Settlement, will call his Prudence in question, for setling his Estate in order to partake of those many Advantages, but will rather doubt of his Judgment, if he should not do it: pick out the most Profitable of the late Funds, and I will compare with it. For 2000 *l.* in Money, a Man may have 166 *l.* 13 *s.* 4 *d.* in the Bank, being 12 Years Purchase; on this we will suppose he may take up 1500 *l.* or more, at an hour's warning, at 5 or 6 *l. per Cent. per Annum*, and pay it in again when he pleases; besides he will have part of other Advantages of discounting Merchants Bills, Exchequer-Tallies, *&c.* Suppose now that I had 2000 *l.* by me: I would lay it out in Land, (upon an assurance that this proposed Method would meet with Encouragement) for which 2000 *l.* I may buy 100 *l. per Annum:* this Estate I would settle for 2000 *l.* Bills of Credit, which being lent their Majesties, will bring me in 60 *l. per Annum*, as in Proposals 16, 17. so that I should have 160 *l. per Annum*, for my 2000 *l.* and if 20 *l.* saved be 20 *l.* got, he who hath now 100 *l. per Annum*, must pay 20 *l. per Annum* Taxes, which will be saved, if he advances his Bills of Credit to their Majesties, as in Proposal 20. And then as to other Advantages, mine will be far superiour to his, for I can have 2000 *l.* upon my 100 *l. per Annum*, after the Estate is settled, on as short a warning as he can have his 1500 *l.* and need pay no more than 10 *s. per Cent. per Annum*, as in Proposal 22. when he must pay ten times 10 *s. per Cent. per Annum:* or I can give 2000 *l.* among my Children, and have 90 *l. per Annum* left; or if I have a mind to sell my Estate, I may in probability sell that for 5000 *l.* that cost me but 2000 *l.* *vide* Query 17.

*Answ.* 2. As to the Security of the Parliamentary Fund, I cannot doubt that the Parliament will take less care of the Free-holders of *England*, than they have done of the monied Men.

*Answ.* 3. As to the Annuities for which Gentlemen have but 2 10 *s. per cent. per annum*, they are rather better than the 3 *l. per cent. per annum* Interest, in regard that he who settles his Estate for 2000 *l.* Bills of Credit, to advance them to their Majesties

*comm*

*communibus annis*, ſtands engaged but for a 1000 *l*. only, in that the Annuity being paid every Year, the Sum for which their Eſtates ſtood engaged, becomes thereby leſſen'd, and conſequently the Security ſtrengthened. *Vide* Propoſals 18, 19.

Object. *But you oppoſe the monied Men making Advantages of their Money, and propoſe greater Advantages to Gentlemen of real Eſtates.*

*Anſw.* I confeſs I do, and that for ſeveral Reaſons.

*Firſt*, Gentlemen of yearly Eſtates have born the burden of the Taxes, while the monied Men have paid little or nothing for the carring on the War, or ſupport of the Government, but on the contrary many of them have enrich'd themſelves by it.

*Secondly*, None can poſſeſs or enjoy Lands but the Subjects of this Realm; but monied Men are of all ſorts, Foreigners as well as our own Subjects: and if an Advantage be to be made, it ought to be to our own Subjects rather than to Foreigners.

*Thirdly*, It is leſs hazardous to truſt the Riches of the Nation in the Hands of our own Subjects, who are ſettled here with their Families, than with thoſe who being born in Foreign Parts may, and in all likelyhood ( when they have got our Money ) will carry it out of the Nation.

*Fourthly*, The Landed Gentlemen will deſerve this Encouragement, in that they will raiſe above double the Sum of Money upon any Fund by this propoſed Method, more than was raiſed by the late Methods.

*Fifthly*, This propoſed Method encreaſes Trade, enriches the Subjects, and will raiſe the Price of Land: the late Method deſtroys Trade, impoveriſhes the Subject, and depretiates Land.

Obj. *But in a little time the Bank of* England *will be in great Repute, and they will iſſue out their Bank-Bills, which will go for Money; and theſe Bills the Directors will lend Gentlemen upon the Security of their Eſtates for* 6 l. per cent. per annum *Intereſt, and alſo to Merchants at the ſame rate, upon depoſite of Wares or Merchandize in the Cuſtody of the Bank for a Security.*

*Anſw.*

*Answ*. If Land be a Security, why may not Gentlemen be enabled by this proposed Method, to issue out Bills of Credit upon a Fund of Land settled out of their own Estates, as well as these Gentlemen Bank-Bills upon a Fund settled on the Excise? Is not 100000 *l. per Annum* in Land a better and more valuable Fund than 100000 *l. per Annum* payable out of the Excise? I am sure it was esteemed so formerly, and it is in the Power of the Parliament to make it so still if they please; and yet the Gentlemen with 100000 *l. per Annum* in Land (if they want Money) must be glad to accept of the Bank-Bills for half the Value of their Estates, for which their whole Estates must be engaged, and must give them 6 *l. per Cent. per Annum* into the Bargain, when the Security such have who take these Bank-Bills, is not near so good a Security as these Gentlemens Estates are, who yet must be forced to mortgage them for those Bank-Bills: to which I can make no fitter a Comparison, than for a Man to pawn a Guinea for a Counter, or a Diamond for a *Bristol*-Stone; and therefore I confess I can see no reason why Gentlemen should give 6 *l. per Cent. per Annum* for Bank-Bills, when they may have Bills of Credit upon their own Estates, which are better Securities, for 10 Shillings *per Cent. per Annum*.

Object. *But it is not consistent with the Wisdom or Justice of the Nation, to grant the Gentlemen of the Bank an Act for their Establishment, and to repeal it next Sessions; for the Parliament may as well repeal the Act, as to enact that Lands shall pass for Money, which is in effect to set up another Bank, or rather so many several Banks as there are landed Men in the Nation, who then need not come to the Bank to borrow Money upon their Estates, but will be able to lend Money to others.*

*Answ*. It is not material what some Gentlemen of the Bank might propose to themselves, but what the Parliament granted them which was better than 8 *l. per Cent. per Annum* for 11 Years, and longer, if it were not injurious to the Nation: and since it appears to be so already in so eminent a degree, it shows rather the great Justice of the Parliament in continuing them for 11 Years, and paying them 100000 *l. per Annum*, to the great Prejudice of their own Estates, when they may have the same Sum of 1200000 *l.* for

36000

36000 *l. per Annum*, and their Estates considerably augmented thereby.

Object. *But you propose to force the Subject to take pieces of Paper for Money which have no intrinsick Value in them, which will never be allowed of by an English Parliament, who, tho they made the Bank-Bills assignable, yet they compelled no Person to take them.*

*Answ.* 1. I grant there ought to be no force on the Subject to take any thing in Payment which has not an intrinsick Value in it self, or which conveys not an intrinsick Value along with it, whereby the Receiver may be no loser: and therefore it was not without good reason that the Parliament did not oblige the Subject to take the Bank-Bills, because the Bank hath a Fund for the Security of 1200000 *l.* only; and they may issue out Bills for as many Millions as they please, for which there is no Security but the Members of the Bank, which is but a Personal Security.

*Answ.* 2. These proposed Bills of Credit convey an intrinsick Value with them, there being a Fund of Land proposed to be settled for their Security before they are issued out, to the full value of the Bills of Credit issued out thereupon, and also a Fund settled by Parliament for all Bills of Credit advanced to their Majesties upon the Payment of any Annuity; which tho but a collateral Security for the Bills of Credit, yet it may reasonably be supposed it will be as good a Security as the Fund of the Excise. The Bills of Credit being therefore settled on the Security of private Mens Estates as well as a Parliamentary Fund, are of an intrinsick Value, as they will convey above double their Value along with them, *viz.* a Fund of Land and a Parliamentary Fund; and therefore for so publick a Good, where all will be benefited and none can be losers, I know no reason can be assigned why the Subject should not be obliged to take them: besides, this is no new thing for Land to pass for Money; for if a Man mortgages his Estate for 1000 *l.* if the Mortgagee owes 1000 *l.* to another, may he not pay him this 1000 *l.* by assigning over this Mortgage, and the Assignee to a third, and so *toties quoties ad infinitum?* Is not this passing Land up and down for Money as much as by my proposed Method? All the difference is, I have proposed for the conveniency of the Subject, to divide the

1000 *l.*

1000 *l.* into 100 or 200 parts, which by the usual way is past in Payment in one intire Sum; and yet if the Title of the Estate be good, need any Man complain for taking a Skin of Parchment for 1000 *l.* which conveys an Estate of 1000 *l.* value along with it?

*Answ.* 3. Gold and Silver (to which, when coined, we give the Name of Money) was made the *Medium* of Trade and Commerce by reason of its portability, and carrying an intrinsick Value along with it; the Government (for that reason) bearing the Charge of the Coinage, because the intrinsick Value should not be lessened by the Charge bestowed upon it, to turn it into Money, and by the Coinage-Act 18 *Car.* 2. an Imposition was laid upon Wine, Vinegar, *&c.* to bear the Charges of the Mint; and whosoever brought any Gold or Silver into the Mint, was to have the same Weight out again coined without any Charge or Deduction; and whatsoever was formerly sold, he who received his Money for what he sold, had the full value of the Sum he was to receive, in Gold or Silver; the Money (if melted down) being worth the Value for which he received it: and Persons were so careful that the Money which they received was of an intrinsick Value, that they usually carried small Weights and Scales in their Pockets to weigh any piece of Money which they suspected was too light, and if they found any piece too light they refused it. I am sure, should we try our Money now, we might write *Mene Tekel* upon 99 Shillings in every 5 Pounds, many of the Half-Crowns we take not having 12 penny worth of Silver in them, and Shillings and Six-pences as light in proportion; and therefore since our Money hath been so abused by clipping, it hath lost that essential Quality which did at first recommend it, *viz.* its intrinsick Value, the Stamp serving now to show what it was, not what it is worth; scarce 100 *l.* we receive being worth 50 *l.* intrinsick Value: and what Fund or Security is there to make good the other 50 *l.* clipt off? and yet take it we must, or else we must go without our Money, which is a Coertion with witness; but yet People quietly receive it, because they know they can pass it away again for the same Value for which they took it and I make no question but 100 *l.* *pecuniis numeratis* of such Money as is generally now passable, will be allowed by our Judges and Juries

Juries too to be a good and lawful Tender, and a good Plea in Bar of any Action that ſhall be brought againſt a Perſon for the ſaid Sum after ſuch Tender made; and if they ſhould not, I know not how any Tender can be made in what we may call *good and lawful Money of* England, unleſs we pick 100 *l.* out of 3 or 4000 *l.* and yet, as if Money had acquired a greater Excellency by being clipp'd, the Conſideration for the Loan of it is raiſed to almoſt double the Value which it was a few Years ſince, tho it was then much weightier, and conſequently better than now it is: and therefore why it ſhould be look'd upon as a Hardſhip to oblige the Subject to take Bills of Credit, which convey far more than the intrinſick Value of the Sum therein mentioned along with them, when at the ſame time they take in Payment Money which is not more than half the intrinſick Value, and Bank-Bills, for which there is no certain Fund, for my part I know not, but ſhall be obliged to any Perſon who can give a Reaſon for it.

Object. *But ſhall we not have too many of theſe Bills of Credit?*

*Anſw.* 1. Theſe Bills being a new Species of Money, and to all Intents and Purpoſes anſwering the End of Money; we may as well fear that we ſhall have too much Money in the Nation, which no wiſe Man will complain of.

*Anſw.* 2. I do not find that this was objected or conſider'd in the Conſtitution of the Bank of *England*; there is no Limitation to them, but they may coin Bank-Bills for as many Millions as they pleaſe, to an unlimited Sum; and all the Security the Subjects have for the Bank Bills, iſſued out for above the Value of 1200000 *l.* is but only a Perſonal Security, many of whom are Foreigners: And if the Members for the Time being, and not the Subſcribers, are bound, we know not who are our Bondſmen, by reaſon of the daily Transferrences: And why ſhould we be afraid of having too many Bills of Credit, more than of having too many Bank Bills, when the Nation may be Loſers by the Bank Bills? But it is impoſſible for any Man to be a Loſer by Bills of Credit, ſince no Bill of Credit may be iſſued out before a real Security out of ſome Gentleman's private Eſtate or Freehold, ſhall be firſt ſettled for the Security of ſuch Bill or Bills.

So

So that if the Nation muſt have a great Number of Bills circulating, I doubt not but every one will concur with me, that the Bills of Credit are preferable to the Bank Bills, ſo far as a Real Security is to be valued before a Perſonal Security; *vide* Propoſal 3.

*Anſw.* 3. None can be injured by our having great Numbers of theſe Bills of Credit: but ſeveral hundred thouſand Families will be relieved by theſe propoſed Bills; and almoſt as many Families will be ruin'd and undone, if ſome ſuch Method be not taken to help them. How many Gentlemen are there who pay 50, 60, or 70 *l. per Annum*, for Intereſt Money out of 100 *l. per Annum*; muſt notwithſtanding pay 20 *l. per Annum* more for Taxes, out of the little they have left to buy their Children Bread; while he who hath the Eſtate in his Clutches, and receives one half or two thirds of the Gentleman's yearly Income for Intereſt, pays not a Penny towards the Charge of the War, or Support of the Government: And therefore unleſs it can be proved, that a greater Number of the Subjects will ſuffer, than will be relieved by theſe Bills of Credit; I think if the great Plenty of the ſaid Bills ſhould be an Inconvenience, (whereas it plainly appears to the contrary, that they will be for the Eaſe and Advantage, both of their Majeſties and all the Subjects in general) I think a greater Good ought to be preferr'd before a Leſſer, and a leſſer Evil choſe before a Greater.

Much more might be ſaid, which, for brevity-ſake, I omit, and ſhall only preſent thoſe Gentlemen with the following Queries, who doubt of the Practicability or Reaſonableneſs of my Propoſals.

---

# *QUERIES.*

*Q.* 1. WHether any Perſon who hath an Eſtate, in Fee of Free-hold, or Copy-hold Land, can make a good Security out of ſuch his Eſtate, to any Perſon who ſhall lend him Money upon a Mortgage of ſuch his Eſtate? *Vide* Query 8.

*Q.* 2

*Q.* 2. Whether the Person who shall pay the Morgagee the Money by him lent upon any Estate, and have thereupon an Assignment of such Mortgage from the Mortgagee, hath not as good a Security for his Money as the Mortgagee had before such Assignment?

*Q.* 3. Whether the Assignee of such Assignee, and every subsequent Assignee that shall have any mortgaged Estate assigned over to them, upon their paiment of Principal and Interest due from the Mortgager to the several Persons assigning, have not (by virtue of such Assignments) as good a Security as the Mortgagee or first Assignee had before they assigned over their Interest in, and Title unto the mortgaged Estate?

*Q.* 4. If 1000 *l.* be lent upon the Security of an Estate of 100 *l. per Annum*; and if the Morgagee, or Assignee, shall owe twenty Persons 50 *l.* apiece, whether such Mortgagee, or Assignee, cannot assign over the said Estate to any one or more Person, or Persons, in trust for the said twenty Persons? and whether every one of the said twenty Persons may not in such case, be as secure for their several 50 pounds as the Mortgagee, or Assignee, might or could be for the whole 1000 *l.*?

*Q.* 5. Whether a Person can make as good a Security out of his Estate, unto Commissioners to be appointed by the King, House of Lords, and House of Commons, in Trust for private Persons, as he can or may do to any one or more private Persons in Trust for others? *Vide* Proposal 1.

*Q.* 6. If the Parliament should Enact, that all Mortgages, and Assignments of Mortgages, shall be currant in paiment, (by Indorsment, *toties quoties*) as the lawful Coin of the Kingdom, whether every Person who shall receive such Mortgages, or Assignments in paiment, will not be as much intituled to such Estates, as any Mortgagee or Assignee now is? *Vide* Proposal. 9.

*Q.* 7. Since I have proposed that all Persons may settle their Estates who have good Titles, and that none may be permitted to settle their Estates, who have no good Titles to such their Estates till their Titles are cleared: And since 20, or more, of the Ablest Counsel in the Kingdom, are likewise proposed to be employed, to to peruſe and examine the Titles of all the Eſtates propoſed to be ſettled upon the Commiſſioners; beſides 3 or more underſtanding Men in each County to take care of the Regiſters, and to examine and make Enquiry after the Titles, Owners, Occupiers, and Particulars of all and every the Eſtates that ſhall be entred in the County Regiſters, in order to a Settlement: Whether Three, Four, or upon occaſion all the ſaid Counſel, by peruſing the Writings, and examining the Titles of any Eſtate that ſhall be propoſed to be ſettled; together with what Information they ſhall receive from the propoſed Agents, in the County where ſuch Eſtate lies, may not be as well able to judg, whether the Title of any Eſtate, which is propoſed to be ſettled be a good Title, as well as any one Counſel in *England* can judg whether the Title of any Eſtate is Good, that is made over for a Security from a private Perſon borrowing, to another private Perſon lending Money upon the Security of ſuch Eſtate? *Vide* Propoſals 4, 5, 6.

*Q.* 8. If a Gentleman's Eſtate can be a Security to any Man who ſhall lend Money upon ſuch Eſtate, Whether it may not be made by Parliament, as good a Security for Bills of Credit to be iſſued out upon the Credit or Security of ſuch Eſtate; and whether every Perſon who ſhall receive ſuch Bills of Credit by Indorſment *toties quoties*, may not be as ſecure as the now Mortgagees or Aſſignees are or can be? *Vide* Query 1. Propoſal 9.

*Q.* 9. If a Gentleman's Eſtate may be made a good Security for Bills of Credit that ſhall be iſſued out upon the Credit of his Eſtate, why ſhould he pay 6 *l. per Cent. per Annum* Intereſt for Money taken up upon his Eſtate, when he may be ſupplied with Bills of Credit upon the Security of his Eſtate for 10 Shillings *per Cent. per Annum*, or for a ſmall Annuity, as 4 *l.* 10 *s per Cent. per Annum*, for 25 Years, or 5 *l.* 10 *s. per Cent. per Annum* for 20 Years, and never pay the Principal? *Vide* Propoſals 22, 23

*Q.* 10. If a Perſonal Security be thought ſufficient by the Parliament for the Creditors of the Bank, who ſhall take the Bank Bills for more than 1200000 *l.* each Member of the Bank being anſwerable for no more than their Proportions of ſuch Debts according to their Intereſts, or Subſcriptions; whether Gentlemens Eſtate

Eſtates in Land ſettled for the Security of Bills of Credit, iſſued out upon the Credit of ſuch Eſtates, be not a better Security for ſuch Bills of Credit than the Subjects have for the Bank-Bills? the one being a real, the other but a perſonal Security: among whom are many Foreigners and others, who upon any Failure will doubtleſs think it high time to ſhift for themſelves.

*Q.* 11. The Stock of the Bank being transferrable, and to be bought and ſold, what Security hath the Nation that the Stock may not be bought by ſuch, who, having choſe what Directors they pleaſe, may carry away all the Gold and Silver they can get together out of the Kingdom, and leave the Members and Creditors of the Bank to help themſelves as well as they can?

*Q.* 12. Whether it will not be more ſafe and reputable for the Kingdom to have the Riches of the Nation in the Hands of 20 Commiſſioners appointed by their Majeſties, the Houſe of Lords and the Houſe of Commons, and 25 Directors to be choſen once in every three Years by the Nobility and Gentry of the whole Kingdom, rather than in the Hands of a few private Perſons, who may ſell and transfer their Intereſt, and conſequently the great Truſt repoſed in them, to Foreigners, or to Perſons diſſaffected, if not perfect Enemies to their Majeſties and the Kingdom? *Vide* Propoſals 1, 10, 11, 13, 14, 27, 28.

*Q.* 13. If Gentlemen advance the Bills of Credit, which are iſſued out upon the Credit of their Eſtates, to their Majeſties upon a Parliamentary Fund, ſettled for the Payment of an Annuity every Year towards the diſcharging and cancelling ſuch Bills of Credit, till the Whole ſhall be paid and cancell'd; whether (ſuch Security being ſtrengthned every Year by paying off part of the Bills of Credit, for which ſuch Eſtates are engag'd) it doth not render Gentlemens Eſtates in Land a far better Security, than the Fund ſettled on the Bank of *England*; which will always have the full Value of 1200000 *l.* due and owing, upon the Security of it? *Vide* Propoſals 18, 19.

*Q.* 14. Suppoſing there were 10 or 12 Millions of Money in the Kingdom, whether the Subjects, ſooner or later, muſt not loſe 5 or 6 Millions by clip'd and counterfeit Money, if ever our Money be brought to its right Standard? And whether the Council to be ap-pointed

pointed by the Commissioners to examine the Titles of Estates proposed to be settled, must not be extreamly negligent and blame-worthy, if all the Subjects in the Kingdom be injured to the Value of 500000 *l.* by undue Settlements? *Vide* Query 19.

*Q.* 15. If we were certain that several of the Subjects in the Nation would be injured to the Value of a Million by undue Settlements, whether that Consideration ought to be any Hindrance to the Settlement of Estates by my proposed Method, which I will prove will be above 100 Millions in value Advantage to the Estates of the Kingdom? And whether the Nation had not better make good the Loss of such particular Persons, (if any should be) than to lose those great Advantages, that will arise by these proposed Settlements *Vide* Queries 17, 18.

*Q.* 16. If the Money advanced on the late Funds had been raised by my proposed Method, whether the Subjects would not have saved much more than can be lost by undue Settlements? *Vide* the Tables and their Uses, in *pag.* 32, to 40.

*Q.* 17. If a Man can (at any time) take up the Value of 20 Year[s] Purchase in Bills of Credit upon his Estate, and may therewith clea[r] his Estate, and provide for his Children, and sink but one tent[h] Part of his Yearly Income for the Use and Benefit of the same: or i[f] a Man can advance such Bills of Credit to their Majesties upon th[e] Security of a Parliamentary Fund, and be exempted from Taxes and have 50 or 60 *l. per annum* added to every 100 *l. per annum* Estate he hath, whether Estates in Land will not be worth 40 o[r] 50 Years Purchase? *Vide* Proposals 17, 19, 20, 22, 23. and the Ta[-]bles in *pag.* 32, to 37.

*Q.* 18. If a Man can buy a perpetual Rent-Charge of the Crow[n] free from Taxes, for 12 Years Purchase, and can take up any Su[m] less than the Capital, or purchase Money, at an Hour's warning, f[or] 5 or 6 *l. per cent. per annum* Interest, and pay it in again whensoev[er] he pleases; or if he can have 60 *l.* 16 *s.* 8 *d. per annum* Interest f[or] 2000 *l.* value in Bank-Bills, and have in effect 2000 *l.* always lyi[ng] by him; whether any Man will give 20 Years Purchase for La[nd] loaded every Year with Taxes, and upon which he cannot wit[h]out great Charge, loss of Time and Difficulty, take up one half the Purchase-Money paid by him for his Estate? *Q.* 1

*Q.* 19. If any Perſon ſhould ſettle an Eſtate to which he hath no Right, and ſhall take Bills of Credit to the Value of 20 Years Purchaſe upon the Credit of ſuch Eſtate, whether the remaining Part or Fee of the Eſtate will not be worth much more to the Right-owner, than the whole Eſtate will be worth, if no ſuch Settlement be made? *Vide* Query 17. Propoſal 7.

*Q.* 20. Whether a Truſtee, or Guardian, who is not now able to ſell, will be able to ſettle the Eſtate of any Orphan, or other Perſon of whom he hath the Care or Guardianſhip, if an Act of Parliament ſhould paſs for theſe Settlements? And whether ſuch Truſtee or Guardian will not be as accountable for his Truſt in caſe this Act ſhould paſs, as he now is before the paſſing ſuch Act? *Vide* Prop. 7.

*Q.* 21. Whether the Ruining our Trade, the Impoveriſhing the Nobility and Gentry, the Burdening the Subjects with Funds, the Bringing Land to 14 Years Purchaſe, the Flinging the Money and the Eſtates of the Kingdom into a few, or into unſafe Hands, the Carrying the Money out of the Kingdom to pay the Intereſt for Money advanced by Foreigners on the late Funds, will not be of far worſe conſequence, and more miſchievous to their Majeſties and the Kingdom, than can be all the undue Settlements which we can reaſonably imagin, or ſuppoſe may poſſibly be made?

*Q.* 22. Whether the exempting the Nobility and Gentry from Taxes, and making their Eſtates much more valuable; enlarging their Yearly Incomes, enabling them to clear their Eſtates, and to raiſe Portions for their Children; the encreaſing Trade, Navigation, and Building of Ships; the ſetting to work Handicrafts, Artificers, and all the idle Hands in the Kingdom; the bringing new Manufactures into the Nation, the burdening the Subjects with fewer Funds; will not be an Eaſe to the Subjects, enrich the Nobility and Gentry, and make the Nation vaſtly rich by our great Trade to foreign Parts, and be a moſt unſpeakable Obligation to the Nobility and Gentry, and all the Subjects in the Kingdom? And whether it will not rivet them not only in Intereſt, but in Affection to their Majeſties? *Vide* the Tables and their Uſes, *pag.* 32, to 40.

*POST-*

# POSTSCRIPT.

SOmetime after I had drawn up my Propofals in order to prefent them to the Parliament, which is now about three Months ago; and fince I have been printing them, I have been feveral times caution'd not to publifh or propofe any thing to the Parliament that might be oppofite to the Intereft of the Bank of *England*; for if I did I muft not expect to fucceed, becaufe the Gentlemen of the Bank had a very great Intereft in the Parliament, and would be too hard for me: And another told me that they would certainly crofs-bite me; to which I replied, that it was no hard matter to foil me, but that the Controverfy (if any were) would not be between the Bank and me, but between the Nobility, Gentry and Free-holders of *England*, who were almoft ruin'd with thofe Funds, and the Bank; and therefore I was not follicitous about it, having alfo fuch an Opinion of many Members of the Bank, that I did not doubt but they would have preferr'd the publick Good of the Kingdom before any little narrow Intereft of their own; infomuch, that the Perfon whom I firft pitch'd upon to fhow my Scheme to for his Approbation, is one of the Members of the Bank, and none of the meaneft of them, but he being at a confiderable diftance in the Country prevented me. And fometime fince a Friend of mine, whofe Name I fhall not mention, propofed to bring the Deputy-Governour of the Bank and me together, telling me I was a thinking Man, and that it might be for my advantage to be acquainted with the Deputy-Governour: I thank'd my Friend, but altho I have a great Refpect for the Deputy-Governour, as being a very deferving Perfon, yet (for fome Reafons) did not clofe with his Offer: however, they have (as they call it) crofs-bit me; and I refolve to let the Parliament and the Gentlemen of the Kingdom know fo, and that thefe Acts of Grace lately publifh'd by the Directors of the Bank were not defign'd in kindnefs to them, but to render ineffectua effectual what I had to propose to the Parliament: for having in the Preface to my Discourse on the late Funds, mentioned how destructive these Funds are to Trade, and that Exchequer-Tallies, Debenters and Sea-mens Tickets sign'd by their Majesties Commissioners were less esteemed than a Note under the Hand of an ordinary Tradesman, to the great diminution of the Honour of the Nation; these Gentlemen publish'd an Order in the *Gazette* dated the *3d* and *10th* of *September* last, " That all Persons who have " Tallies and Orders on Funds, *&c.* which are not remote, may " have Money for them without any Allowance; together with all " past Interest to the day on which they were brought: and that " Foreign Bills of Exchange will be discounted after the rate of " 4 *l.* 10 *s. per Cent. per Annum.*

This was but a small Bite; but whereas in *Pag.* 18,19,20. and in several parts of my Treatise I set forth the sad Condition of the Gentlemen, as well as the trading part of the Nation, occasion'd by the late Funds, and that Gentlemen whose Estates are in Mortgage are called upon for the Money, and know not how to raise it, and are therefore ejected out of their Estates, and barr'd of the Equity of Redemption; and in my Manuscript had introduced the Gentlemen, laying these their Grievances before the Parliament, which I omitted printing for fear of being too tedious: The Directors of the Bank being conscious of the Truth of what I had writ, and supposing it might put the Parliament out of Humour with them, to cross-bite me (for I shall not forget that Expression) publish'd the following Order in the *Gazette* of the first Instant.

" The Court of the Directors of the Bank of *England* give no- " tice, That after the first day of *January* next (when they have " paid into the Exchequer the Remainder of the 1200000 *l.* sub- " scribed) they will lend Money on Mortgages and real Securities " at 5 *l. per Cent. per Annum.*

And I doubt not but they will publish the same in Monday's *Gazette* again, being the day before the Parliament meets; for there is nothing like to timing of Business, especially when they know so dangerous a thing as my Treatise and Proposals is to come before the Parliament.

And

And I hope they will bite me again, and offer the Parliament when they meet, to furnish their Majesties with their Bank-Bills for 5 *l. per Cent.* too.

But that which is one of their Master-pieces, is one of their Bylaws concluded yesterday, *Novem.* the 2*d.* at a General Court. Which because every one may not understand the meaning of, I shall unfold it.

The Gentlemen of the Bank knowing my Proposals to be so just and reasonable, and for the great Advantage not only of their Majesties but of all the Subjects in the Kingdom, they feared that the Parliament would be ready to receive my Proposals, which they supposed would endanger the Bank; this it seems put them upon considering how to baffle my Design. They could not object against my proposed Fund, for that would have brought an old House upon their Heads, to maintain that a Fund payable out of the Excise, is more valuable than a Fund settled upon the security of Gentlemens Freehold Estates; nor could they therefore maintain that any Man might be injured by taking these proposed Bills of Credit, secured by such a Fund: it was also no less evident that it is better for the Nation to have their Majesties supplied with Money, at 3 *l. per cent. per annum,* who do now pay the Bank above 8 *l. per cent. per annum,* and that there would be occasion for fewer Funds, and that it must needs be a great Ease and Satisfaction to the Nobility and Gentry to be excused from Taxes, and to have a considerable Addition to their yearly Estates: nor can they deny but many a poor Soul would be relieved by this proposed Method, whose Estates are intangled, and who between the Taxes and Interest-Money, are reduced to such straits that they even want Bread for their Families: nor is it less obvious that there are many who are pinch'd in their Fortunes, and cannot spare their Children any thing while they live, but are forc'd to turn them adrift into the World without a penny to help themseves, that by my proposed Method, would be enabled to provide for their Children plentifully with a very small dimunition of their yearly Estates: and they must be forc'd to acknowledg, that it will be a great encouragement for Merchants and Traders to have Money to trade

trade with at 3 *l. per cent. per annum*; and that the Trade of the Kingdom would be very much enlarged thereby. Well, what Arguments will they uſe with the Parliament againſt my Propoſals? why, ſay they, we will acquaint the Parliament that theſe Propoſals are not practicable, for the Nation will be ſo peſter'd with theſe Bills of Credit, that we ſhall have more of them than we know what to do with: but this ſay they he hath unluckily anſwered, (which I ſhall give in the words of my Manuſcript, having varied ſome thing from it in my printed Book) *viz.* The Bank of *England* is not limited to any Sum, but may iſſue out Bank-Bills for 50 Millions, (if they pleaſe) for which the Nation hath only a perſonal Security, of whom ſeveral are Foreigners, and conſequently the Subjects may be loſers; whereas no Bills of Credit can be iſſued out until a ſufficient Security out of Gentlemens real Eſtates be firſt ſettled. Yes ſay they, but there we have croſs-bit him again by our Order or By-law, at the laſt General Court, held at Grocers-Hall, the 2*d* of this Inſtant *November*, viz. *That the Governour, Deputy Governour, and Directors; ſhall not borrow under the Common Seal any Sum exceeding in the whole* 1200000 l. *upon the Penalty of* 1000 l. *&c.*

And now I hope I have unriddled and ſhown the meaning of that Order or By-law, which doubtleſs made many thinking Men at a ſtand to know the meaning of it: ſo that our mighty Bank, that is to help their Majeſties with I know not what great Sums, and to furniſh all the Gentlemen in *England* with Money, upon the Security of their Eſtates, at 5 *l. per cent. per annum*, and to ſet up a Lumber to lend Merchants and Tradeſmen, Money upon their Goods, and to perform I know not what other extraordinary Feats, and ſupply the defect of many Millions of Money, for to ſerve a turn and to croſs-bite me, are contented to dwindle for the preſent into a little diminutive Bank of 1200000 *l.*

Well Gentlemen, but cannot thoſe who made thoſe Orders when their turn is ſerved, and that they have thereby baffled my Propoſals, break thoſe Orders again, for great and weighty Reaſons? but I hope the Parliament will not ſuffer themſelves and the Nation to be croſs-bit, tho the Gentlemen may uſe their pleaſure with me. What

I

I have propoſed, is for the good of the whole Kingdom: it lies in the Parliaments Power, if they pleaſe (and I cannot but hope they will) to make this the moſt flouriſhing Kingdom, and the Subjects the moſt happy People in the Univerſe; to whoſe great Wiſdom, I have humbly ſubmitted my Propoſals, and withal this as an undoubted Maxim, *That nothing can be more Fatal to any Government, than to diſcountenance and croſs-bite thoſe who make it their Study to promote the Good and Welfare of it.* But I am well ſatisfied. I ſhall meet with no ſuch evil Treatment from their Majeſties or the Parliament.

*FINIS.*

# THE VILLAINY OF Stock-Jobbers DETECTED,

## And the Causes of the Late RUN UPON THE BANK and BANKERS Discovered and Considered.

*LONDON,*
Printed in the Year MDCCI.

3, 1701. Daniel Defoe, *The Villainy of Stock-Jobbers Detected and the Causes of the Late Run upon the Bank and Bankers Discovered and Considered*, London.

IT has more then once been foretold that Stock Jobbers and Brokers wou'd Ruine the Trade, and ſeveral Times they have bid fair for the Performance.

But never was a greater Wound given to the Trade in General, than now; Never ſo unhappily Tim'd to the Diſadvantage both of the Publick Revenue and the Current Credit of the Nation, nor never was there ſo much Bare fac'd Villany acted, in the Affairs of Publick Trade as their is now.

Trade in general is Built upon, and ſupported by two eſſential and principal Foundations, *Viz.* Money and Credit, as the Sun and Moon in their *Diurnal Motion* alternately *Enlighten* and *Envigorate* the World, ſo theſe two Eſſentials maintain and preſerve our Trade; they are the Life and Soul of Trade, and they are the ſupport of one another too. Money raiſes Credit, and Credit in its turn is an Equivalent to Money.

From hence it follows, That Trade always bears a proportion to Money and Credit; and conſequently, they who by any methods Diminiſh the Stock of Caſh or Credit, equally injure our Trade.

Tho' it would ſeem needleſs to go back to particular Caſes for the proof of this Aſſertion, yet

yet it may not be amiſs to ſee a little from whence it comes to paſs, That our Trade is leſs now the War is over, than it was before it began.

The calling in our Coin viſibly put a ſtop to Trade, becauſe *the Stream which drove the Mill, the Oil that mov'd the Wheel*, was ceas'd. The prodigious Paper-Credit which paſt in *Lombard-ſtreet*, and which ſupply'd more than twice the Quantity of the Coin, equally ſupported Trade with the Money, and ſunk at once with the Coin.

The Merchants finding the ſenſible loſs to Trade, for want both of that Money and Credit, put their Invention on the tenters; and found out the Expedient of a Bank. The Exchequer alſo feeling the loſs of the Coin ſupplied with an imaginary Species in Exchequer-Bills, and yet both theſe fail'd in the Performance. So impoſſible it is to force Credit without Caſh. For till the ready Money began to appear again, the Brokers and Jobbers made a prey of all Mankind in the matter of Bills; and in ſpight of the endeavours of the Bank or the Exchequer, they bought and ſold their Notes at the ſhameful Diſcount of 10, to 16 and 20 *l. per Cent.*

I ſhall not think it needful to view the ill effect this had upon our Trade; how the needy Trades-men, who ſold their Goods at common

rates

rates, were fain to Difcount more than their profit to get their Money. How the Exchequer-Notes defign'd for a currency in Payments were Jobb'd about the Town; and by the Policy of thefe Gentlemen put upon the Trades-men, in order to be bought again at high Difcounts, and then Engroffed again by the Money'd Men, who obtain'd the Difcount as a *Premio* added to the Intereft upon the Originals.

I could fill a large Volume with the relation of fuch Particulars, and eafily make out the dammage that befell our Trade in General; but I have inftanc't this only to prove how fatal the finking of Paper-Credit has been to the Nation.

The fupply of new Money from the Mint, and the recovery of the Bank has reviv'd our Trade; and with our Money-Credit alfo began to revive: For Credit always follows plenty of Cafh, as naturally as the effect does the caufe.

But, as if fome ill Fate attended the Publick affairs, and we were not to recover our former magnitude in Trade; but always to be Sacrifiz'd to the Follies and Interefts of particular Men; here is another General blow given to the Publick Credit, and a ftop to the Currency of Bills. That it will have a more Fatal effect than yet appears,

I

I believe every Body expects; but I shall not so much predict the Consequences, as endeavour to Detect the Causes.

Any one might have foreseen, That the Strife and Contention of our two Rival *East-India Companies* would produce some more than ordinary Effect; and that the raising stock, of all sorts to a Value so much above the *Intrinsick*, must have some fatal Issue, and would fall some where at last so heavy as to be felt by the whole body of Trade.

But besides this, Twas easy to see that the Different Interest of Parties would lay open the Publick to be Injur'd by both of them.

Perhaps 'tis easier to Demonstrate, That this mischief is the contrivance of Persons and Parties, than it is to discover the Persons and prove the Fact. But on the other Hand 'tis not very difficult neither to Trace it back to its Original, and Detect the very Persons.

The design of this Paper is not an Invective at any particular Person or Party, nor is it wrote to court or please either side; but if any thing be said which touches or exposes the Guilty, 'tis that they, if they please, may see their Errors; and if not, the Nation may take care not to be further injured by them.

If that new *Mistery* or *Machine* of Trade we

call *Stock-Jobbing*, be firſt prov'd to be at the bottom of all this miſchief; I hope the Great Repreſentative of the Nation, the *Parliament*, will need very few Arguments to ſatisfie them of its being a Publick Grievance.

The Old *Eaſt-India* Stock by the arts of theſe unaccountable People, has within 10 Years or thereabouts, without any material difference in the Intrinſick value, been Sold from 300 *l. per Cent.* to 37 *l. per Cent.* from thence with fluxes and refluxes, as frequent as the Tides, it has been up at 150 *l. per Cent.* again; during all which differences, It would puzzle a very good Artiſt to prove, That their real Stock (*if they have any*) ſet loſs and gain together, can have varied above 10 *per Cent.* upon the whole; nor can any Reaſons for the riſe and fall of it be ſhown, but the Politick management of the Stock-Jobbing Brokers; whereby, according to the Number of Buyers and Sellers, which 'tis alſo in their Power to make and manage at will, the Price ſhall dance attendance on their deſigns, and riſe and fall as they pleaſe, without any regard to the Intrinſick worth of the Stock.

The New *Company*, the Bank of *England*, the *Exchequer*, the whole Nation, as has been lately well obſerv'd by the Author of *The Free-Holders-Plea*

*Plea against Stock-Jobbing, Elections of Parliament Mne* is, or is in a ſair way to be ſubjected to the ſame management.

To bring it home to the Caſe in hand, The apparent deſign of ſome People to ruin the Credit of the Nation by way of revenge, on a party who had oppoſed them in other deſigns, ſeems ſo clear, that it hardly needs to be further explained.

As ſoon as the Election of Parliament Men for the City of *London* was over, or ſo far over as that it plainly appeared on which ſide it enclin'd, a certain Party prepar'd their meaſures to bring about the very Deſign, which now we ſee ſo broke out upon us.

And that any obſerving People may recollect themſelves in the matter, it may be taken Notice of,

*First*, That the old *Company* has ever ſince, and ſome time before, been amaſſing to themſelves all the ready Money they could poſſibly get, in order to form the Deſign, and make a general ſcarcity of Caſh, at the ſame time ſtopping their hands as to Payments and Exports as much as they could; and ſome People pretend to ſay, they have a Million of Money by them in Specie.

From

From whence I only make two ſhort obſervations.

First, *That we may ſee the Nations Enemies are Maſters of their meaſures, and know the directeſt way to ruin us: For nothing cou'd be more Fatal to Trade and the publick Credit, than engroſſing the current Caſh, and keeping it from the Circulation, which is the Life of our Trade.* But this is not the only thing in which the Old Company have injured our General Intereſt of Trade,

Secondly, *'Tis a ſign they do not live under a* French *Governmemt; and 'tis well for them they do not, tho' themſelves have been ſo fond of that Intereſt; for a King of* France *might have ſent them Word,* That Money being made to Circulate, if they did not know how to employ it, he did; *and command them to lend it him, at* 3 per Cent.

All the while the Old *Company* were laying up the Caſh, and dreining the Town of their ready Money, Guinea's eſpecially; another ſett of Men who are known to be in the ſame Intereſt, and to have concerted meaſures together, laid up in the ſame proportion, all the Bank-Bills they could lay Hands on. It

It is impoſſible to imagine that two or three Men ſhould lay by Bank-Notes to the Tune of 300000 Pounds, which had no running Intereſt upon them, and have no deſign in it; they are known to be Men who underſtand their own Advantages better than ſo, and have not rais'd ſuch vaſt Fortunes as they poſſeſs from ſuch blind methods; but the veſting all their running Caſh in Bank-Bills, the Old *Company* at the ſame time ſecuring all the ready Money, was the firſt Preliminary of the deſign which now broke out.

Things thus prepar'd, the next ſtroke at the Publick currency of Caſh, was a report Politickly rais'd and induſtriouſly ſpread abroad, that by a complaint from the Mint, *which was nonſence in it ſelf too*, the Government was moved to cry down the *French* Piſtoles to 17 *s.* 1 *d.* and the Proclamation was in the Preſs forſooth every day; tho' neither Government nor Mint had then done any thing in the matter,

Thus the Town was prepar'd, the Guinea's was utterly vaniſh'd, the Silver Money ſo leſſen'd as to make a viſible ſcarcity; a ſtorm gathered for the Bank, Piſtoles made dubious; the next thing was the improving the approaching Seſſions of Parliament, and the proſpect of a War in *Europe*; to run down the Price of Stock; and when

when this was done, and all ripe for execution, the parties fall to Work; and firſt they began with the Bank, and running hard upon them with Sums of ſuch magnitude, as eaſily diſcovered the deſign; allarum'd the Bank, who to return them their own kind, puſh'd at their Capital Banker, and run him down preſently; and thus the Fight is begun.

But leaſt the Bank ſhould be reliev'd from the Exchequer, they forme an attack there too; where about Fifty Thouſand Pounds in Exchequer-Bills preſent themſelves for Payment at once.

This alarum'd the Exchequer too, on which a new Subſcription is call'd for by the Lords, for the exchanging Exchequer-Notes, and making them current; which Subſcription we find goes on well, and if it comes to be finiſhed, and the Bank weathers this ſtorm, as 'tis not doubted it will; all this Hurricane may yet fall on themſelves; and it were only to be wiſh'd that the fall of Stocks wou'd effect none but ſuch as have encourag'd this deſtructive *Hydra*; this new *Corporation* of *Hell*, *Stock-Jobbing*.

But ſince there are a great many honeſt Gentlemen, and Trades-men concern'd, whoſe Families and Fortunes arelike to ſuffer for it; 'tis worth while to examine whether an Evil of ſo Fatal a Nature to the Pub-

Publick, ſo Deſtructive to Trade, and ſo ruinous to the Publick Credit, ought not Effectually to be ſuppreſt.

I cannot however forbear to blame the *Bank* of *England*, for Publiſhing at ſuch a Juncture as this, their willingneſs to allow an Intereſt on their Seal'd Notes; which ſeems too plain to diſcover their fears of the Party, and is a downright begging of Credit. I ſhall ask leave here to tell a ſhort Story, ſomthing alluſive to this, and which will explain what I mean; whether the Reader pleaſe to take it for a Parable or a Hiſtory, 'tis all one to me, and will ſerve my turn as well one way as another.

A certain Trades-Man in *London* had borrowed a Thouſand Pounds of a Scrivener at 6 *per Cent.* Intereſt, and had kept it in his Hands ſome time; but loſſes coming upon him, and particularly one which ſtrook his Foundation; he began to apprehend, that if it came to the Ears of that Creditor. the Scrivener, he would call in his Money, and at that juncture, ſuch a Demand would entirely ruin him.

To go to the Scrivener and give him a Bribe, to promiſe the continuing the Money; tho' he knew that ſort of People willing enough to take Money, yet he thought it lookt like leſſening him-

himſelf, and would injure his Reputation, and poſſibly only ſerve to make that certain, which yet was but doubtful, and put him upon calling for the Money ſooner than otherwiſe; upon which he reſolv'd on a quite contrary method.

He goes to the Scrivener, and tells him he had borrow'd ſuch a Sum of Money on him, and paid him Intereſt for it; but he found the Intereſt of Money run high, and 'twas a hard thing for a Trades-Man to pay it, that 'twas but working for other Folks; for he found Trade was dull, and he gave long Credit and the like, and therefore in ſhort, he deſired him to take in the Money again, for he was uneaſie to be ſo deeply in Debt.

The Scrivener ask'd him when he wou'd pay it, he told him that Afternoon, if he would ſend the Bond to his Houſe, he had order'd his Man to Tell up the Money.

The Scrivener told him, it was hard to put the Money on them without Warning, and wou'd be a Loſs to his Client to oblige him to take it in before he was provided to put it out again, that if he had call'd it in, he wou'd a given him Three Months time to pay it in, and ſo much Notice he expected.

Aye,

*Aye, but ſays the Trades-Man, that will be a Loſs to me too, for I muſt keep it by me, or elſe it may not be ready at the time.* But, *pray Sir*, ſaid the Scrivener, *keep the Money, Trade may mend; a Man that has a Thouſand Pound by him, meets with Opportunities that he did not think on.*

The Trades-man finding his Deſign take, anſwers coldly *No*, and ſo they parted; at next Meeting, the Scrivener ſtill preſſing him too keep the Money, he tells him; *Look ye Sir, you deſire me to keep this Money, if your Client will abate me* 1 per Cent. *of Intereſt, I'll keep it longer:* The Scrivener agrees, and the Trades-man anſwer'd his End, whereas had he gone and offer'd him 1 *per Cent* more for Intereſt or Continuance, 'tis Ten to One but they had call'd for their Money.

I leave any body to apply this Story to the Bank of *England*, offering double Intereſt at a time, when a Storm threatned them, they indeed are the beſt judges of their own Affairs; but if they had ſtood their Ground boldly without it, I am of Opinion with ſubmiſſion, their Credit had ſtood clearer.

The Credit of the Bank of *England* does not immediately conſiſt in the reality of their Foundation

dation: Sir, ſure it does originally depend upon the Goodneſs of their Bottom, but the more immediate Credit of their Proceeding, depends upon the currency of their Bills, and the currency of their Bills depends upon their immediate Pay; *the Bank has no Advantage of the meaneſt Goldſmith as to their current Bills*, for no longer than their Payments continue punctual and free, no longer will any Man take their Bills, or give them Credit for Money.

All the Credit which remains to the Bank after their Payment comes to ſtop, *if ever ſuch a time ſhall be*, is that People have a Satisfaction; that at long run their Principle is ſafe, and their Bottom will pay their Debts: this is the Credit of their Stock, but the Credit of their Caſh ends, if ever they baulk but one Bill.

To ask the World to ſtay for their Money and take Intereſt, is to weaken the Credit of their Caſh, and transfer themſelves to the Credit of their Stock which no body doubts to be good.

I know therefore nothing the Bank could have done more to injure the Credit of their running Caſh, than to make ſuch a Propoſal of Intereſt upon thair Bills, which formerly they publickly refuſed.

I

I queſtion not but the Bank will out live the Deſign of all the Sir *C——s*. and Sir *L——s*. in *England*; and if they do anſwer all the Demands which now run upon them without ſtopping Payments, their Enemies will receive a particular Mortification: but I am of the Opinion at the ſame time, they will be ſenſible that the offer of doubling the Intereſt on their Bills, really rather injur'd them, then anſwered the End they propoſed.

From theſe particular Inſtances, I proceed to examine whether theſe People who have carryed on theſe Meaſures, have not anſwer'd two Deſigns together; and at one Blow attempted to wound their oppoſite Party and the Government alſo.

Whoever wounds the publick Credit, wounds the whole Nation and the Government, the giving a blow to the Currency of proper Credit, is robbing the Nation of ſo much Stock; for Credit is the ſecond branch of Stock, and Trade muſt decline accordingly; by leſſening our Stock and Trade, we are weakned in the main ſtrength of the Kingdom; the Government is weaken'd, Aids and Taxes muſt fall ſhort, eſpecially where Trade is to pay them, and Loans and Anticipia-

tions

tions, which are Advancements made for the immediate Service of the Government, will be stopt.

If it be in the power of Mercenary Brokers and Companies to engross the Current Cash, so as to make a Scarcity of Money, it must consequently be in their Power, whenever they are pleased to show their Dis-esteem to the Government, to prevent the advancement of any Sum of Money for the publick Service.

And this Experiment may be a Tryal of their Skill, to let us see what they are able to do, if the City does not take Care to oblige them by choosing Magistrates or Representatives to their Mind or out of their Party.

'Tis very hard, that this sort of Men by the Power of their Money, and the Influence they have in the Stocks of Companies, should have it in their Hands to put a general stop to Credit, Cash, Banks, and even the Exchequer it self.

'Tis known, their Affection to the Government, and some Interest of the King and Kingdom, is but very indifferent, and that generally speaking, both those two great Men we have mention'd, and almost the whole Party, who espouse the Old Companies Quarrel, have put themselves in a direct Opposition to the Friends of the Government, and always run retrograde to the King and the Nations Interest.

That

That they have design'd ill, is manifest by the Event, because they have done what lay in their Power to ruin the Nations Credit, in order to affect the general Trade, as well as the Persons.

I shall now examine a little the reason of this Combustion, and I cannot but reflect that there seems to be several Causes to which it may be assign'd; all of which seem but to expose the Temper of the People we speak of, and to make both them and their Cause odious to Mankind.

First, *from Ambition* to show the City that they are Persons whom it is Dangerous to disoblige, and that they are able to show their Resentments in a Method which they ought to be affraid of to let them see that they knew not what they did, when they Poll'd against Men of such Power and Influence as they, and that they ought to have a Care of affronting Men, in whose Power it lay so much to check the most essential point of the Cities prosperity, *their Trade*; and to let the Government see too, that they are Men of such Figures and Authority in the Nation, and can at their Pleasure so manage the Cash and Trade of the Town, that they can stop our Credit, break our Goldsmiths, sink our Stocks, embarrass the Bank, and ruine Trade at their Will and Pleasure.

*So*

*So far as this is a good Reaſon, ſo far with Submiſſion the Government is concern'd, to take Care that their Influence and Power be ſo reſtrain=ed by wholſome Laws, as that the whole Command of the Nations Caſh and Credit may not be in the Hands of Companies and Stock=jobbers.*

Another original Cauſe of the preſent Diſturbance, is theſe Men Exerting the Power I have been ſpeaking of by way of Reſentment:

1. *At the Cittizens, in the Slur they thought put upon them by the Livery, for oppoſing their Election.*
2. *At the New Company, for Reaſons drawn from the Different Intereſts of both the ſaid Companies.*

I ſhall not examin here whether the *Eaſt=India* Trade be a real prejudice to the General Stock of the Kingdom, but I muſt be excuſed to be poſſitive in this, That the two Rival Companies are certainly a prejudice to the *Eaſt=India* Trade.

And I may ſafely add, That *Jobbing* their Stocks about, raiſing and ſinking them at the Pleaſure of Parties and private Intereſts, is more prejudicial to Trade

Trade in General, than both the Companies can make amends for.

There is hardly a private Trades-man in the Town, but one way or other feel the effects of the least stop to the currency of Cash, and Goldsmiths Bills; and it seems to be *a Grievance to be punished by the Judge*, That the General head of Trade in a City, so dependant upon Trade as this is, should be liable to the Clandestine Management of Parties, and suffer for the petty Quarrels and Disputes of two *East-India* Companies that have nothing to do with them.

As to the Disputes between the two Companies being prejudicial both to themselves, and to every Body else; 'tis plain by what has been said, they are prejudicial to Trade in General, by how much their private Disputes affect the value of other Peoples Estates, raising and sinking of Stocks, which have no relation to them, and influencing publick Credit.

They are and will be certainly Destructive to the *East-India* Trade in General, by glutting the Nation so with Goods, as to prejudice the Manufacture of *England*, and disgust as well as injure the Poor; and by reducing the Prices of their own Goods to out do and under-sell one another; which 'tis hop'd also may in time reduce them both

to

to Circumstances more proportioned to the Nature of the Trade, and to their own Interest.

Nor that I believe 'twould be best for *England* to have no *East-India-Company* neither; many parts of that Trade are certainly beneficial to the *English* Trade in general; but to carry it on to such a Magnitude as is palpably destructive to the *English* Manufactures, and Impoverishing to the Nation by Exporting such quantities of *Bullion* in Specie, must certainly make it a Publick nusance, a burthen to Trade, and a damage to the Nation.

Add to this the strife between them, their Emulation in Sales must certainly destroy their own Designs, and ruin them both. For cheapness of any Goods Imported which vye with our Manufacture, must be prejudicial to that Manufacture; and when two of a Trade strive to ruin one another by under-selling, it generally ruins the Trade, and both Parties too.

So that from the Contention between these two Companies, Trade in General is Injur'd, our Manufactures discouraged, both Companies will in the end be ruin'd, and the *East-India* Trade spoil'd if not lost.

For it does not follow, That because Eight or Ten Ships a Year from *India*, may be a necessary and pro-

profitable Trade; That therefore Twenty or Thirty must be so too; and 'tis easie to demonstrate, That whereas we may want Eight or Ten Ships a Year in that Trade, Twenty or Thirty would ruin the Trade it self, and be a General prejudice to the Nation.

Trade is in no respect tollerable, but as 'tis Profitable; and the profit consists, or at least depends upon proportion of Circumstances; if the Import exceeds the Demand, Goods must fall, and if the Goods fall, the Profit sinks.

The Companies cannot expect, especially now their Silk-Trade is limited (as by Act of Parliament it is) That this Trade can vent the Import of about Sixty Sail of Ships now abroad; if they come to under-selling one another, they are gone, and their Stock is not worth 20 *per Cent.* from the first Day they begin it.

In the mean Time, if they do find a vent for so great a quanity of Goods as all those Ships must Import, the *English* Manufacture must suffer.

On the whole matter,

Whether we consider the injury to the Publick Credit by the villany of Stock-Jobbers,

The

The expoſing the Eſſentials of the Nations, Proſperiry, to the Management of mercenary Brokers and Parties; who upon every occaſion they are pleaſed to take, when ſuch as they think fit to approve of, are not choſen Lord Mayors or Parliament-Men, ſhall take the Liberty to ſhew their Reſentments by Affronting the Government, ruining Banks and Goldſmiths, and ſinking the Stocks of all the Companies in Town:

Or, the Powerful influence they have by their Money on the current Caſh of the Nation.

Whether any of theſe things are conſidered, I leave it to the Wiſe Heads of the Nation, now concerned to reflect and examine, whether it be conſiſtent with the Safety of the *Engliſh* Nation, with the Honour of the *Engliſh* Government, or with the Nature of the *Engliſh* Trade, to ſuffer ſuch a ſort of People to go on unpreſcrib'd and unlimited, or indeed unpuniſh'd.

What ſafety can we have at home, while our Peace is at the mercy of ſuch Men, and 'tis in their Power to *Jobb* the Nation into Feuds among our ſelves, and to declare a new ſort of Civil War among us when they pleaſe?

Nay, the War they manage is carried on with worſe Weapons than Swords and Muſquets; Bombs may

may Fire our Towns, and Troops over run and Plunder usr But these People can ruin Men silently, undermine and impoverish by a sort of impenetrable Artifice, like Poison that works at a distance, can wheedle Men to ruin themselves, and *Fiddle them out of their Money*, by the strange and unheard of Engines of *Interests*, *Discounts*, *Transfers*, *Tallies*, *Debentures*, *Shares*, *Projects*, and the *Devil and all* of Figures and hard Names. They can draw up their Armies and levy Troops, set *Stock* against *Stock*, *Company* against *Company*, *Alderman* against *Alderman*; and the poor Passive Trades men, like the Peasant in *Flanders*, are Plundered by both sides, and hardly knows who hurts them.

What will become of the Honour of the English Nation, if the principal Affairs relating to the Credit both of the publick and private Funds is dependant upon such vile People, who care not who they ruin, nor who they advance, tho one be the Nation's Friends, and the other its Enemies, and expos'd to their particular Resentments?

He is a worthy Patriot, and fitly qualified for a Representative, who wou'd join his strength to overthrow the Credit of the City, and ruin Trade only to shew his private Resentment for not being chosen as he thought fit to expect.

Lastly,

Lastly, What Condition must the Trade of *England* be soon reduc'd too, when Banks and Paper-Credit, which must be own'd to be a material part of its subsistance, are become so precarious as to be liable to a general Interruption from the breath of mercenary, malitious, and revengeful Men.

It might be said here, *You are very high against Stock-jobbing and Stock-jobbers, no Man ought to complain of an* Evil *he cannot Remedy*. Can you propose how to remove the grievance, and free us from the Inconveniencies you have discovered?

For answer, I might say 'tis not always to be expected that he which finds a Fault shou'd mend it: If an Enemy have laid an Ambuscade to surprise a Town, he who first Discovers it is as instrumental to save the Place as he who defends the Works; and the Wisdom of the Parliament, their present Session being upon us, together with the consequence of the thing it self, methinks might turn the Eyes of all Men from a single Person to that great Assembly, and expect the Remedy where the Power of redress more particularly is lodg'd.

But that I may also let the Reader know that this Disease is not incurable, nor the men unpunishable, I will lay down a few Generals, which if put into execution by the Authority of Parliament, may be effectual to suppress such People as we complain of, off, and alſo to prevent the Conſequences.

*Firſt*, To impeach the Perſons of ſuch Miſdemeanors as on a fair Hearing may be prov'd on them, and among ſuch other Puniſhments as the Authority of Parliament ſhall judg they deſerve: let them be made uncapable of buying, ſelling, transfering, or poſſeſſing, either in their own Names, or the Names of any Perſon in truſt for them, any Shares, or parts of or in any of the Publick Stocks, Banks, or Companies now in being, or ſhall hereafter be form'd or eſtabliſhed, either publick or private.

*Secondly*, Reduce the two Companies into one limited, and reſtrain'd to ſuch Conditions and Articles, as ſhou'd make the Stocks and Shares ſo Transferable, as to Circumſtances of Time and Perſons, as may render alienating the Property more difficult and chargeable; at the ſame time all Stock to be Forfeited to the Informer, which ſhall be Alieniated, Pawn'd, Mortgag'd, Given or Sold, without it be immediately Transfer'd.

*Thirdly*, Charge a Duty of 10 *per Cent.* to be paid the King by the Seller, upon all Stock Transfer'd, as often as it is Alieniated or Transfer'd.

*Fourthly*, Oblige every Perſon to whom any Stock is to be Transfer'd, to ſwear that he will not Buy, Sell, Alieninate or otherwiſe Mortgage or or pledge the ſaid Stock without a legal Entry of the ſame, in the Books of the ſaid Companies, and Transfering the ſame according to *Act of Parliament.*

*Fifthly*, Limit the *Eaſt-India* Company to ſuch Conditions both to Stock and Trade, as may be conſiſtent with the preſerving the Trade to *India* to the *Engliſh* Nation, and yet preventing the ſaid Trade, from interfereing with, encroaching upon, or otherwiſe being detrimental to our own Manufactures; that it may be carried on without *Factions* among the Rich, or *Clamours* from the Poor; *oblige them* to import proper Quantities of ſuch Commodities as ſerve to help forward our own Trade, and ſuch as the Nation wants, as *Saltpetre*, *Raw Silk*, *Spices*, *Drugs*, *Canes* and *Callicoes*, and *limit them* from importing too great quantities of ſuch Goods as leſſen the Conſumption of our own Manufacture.

Theſe methods, with the Additions of ſuch as the Wiſdom of the Nation will find out, wou'd effectually ſuppreſs this pernicious, growing Party, whoſe dangerous Practices, are of ſuch a Nature, that no Man can ſay where they will end.

Then we ſhall Trade upon the ſquare; Honeſty and Induſtry will be the method of Thriving, and plain Trade be the General buſineſs of the Exchange.

Bank-

Bankrupts and Beggars have advanced the mistery of Stock-jobbing, and we can now reckon up a black List of 57 Persons, who within this ten years past have rais'd themselves to vast Estates, most of them from mechanick, and some of them from broken and desperate Fortunes, by the sharping, tricking, intreagueing, scandalous Employment of Stock-jobbing, who have been the Losers, or what the General Stock of the Nation has been better'd by them is, a Mystery too hard to be explain'd.

Now they ride in their Coaches, keep splendid Equipages, and thrust themselves into business, set up for Deputies, Aldermen, Sheriffs, or Mayors; but above all, for Parliament-men, of which (with the mischievous Consequences that are like to attend it) enough is said in a late Pamphlet, intituled, *The Freeholders Plea*; which I noted before, and to which I refer and shall conclude with this short note.

*That I think, with submission, all honest men ought to know their Names in order to shun their dangerous Acquaintance; and the Government has nothing before them, but effectually to suppress and ease the Nation of so intolerable a Grievance.*

FINIS.

4, 1705. John Law, *Money and Trade Considered*, Chaps III and IV, London.

# CHAP. III.

*Of the different Measurs have been used to Preserve and Increase Money. And of Banks.*

THE Measures have been used to preserve and Increase Money, have in some Countries been opposite to what has been used in others: And opposite Measures have been us'd in the same Countries, without any differing Circumstances to occasion them.

Some Countries have rais'd Money in the Denomination, when others have lower'd it; Some have allay'd it, when others who had allay'd it have rectified it; Some have prohibit the Export of Money under the severest Penalties, when others have by Law allowed it to be exported · Some thinking to add to the Money, have obliged Traders to bring home Bullion, in proportion to the Goods they imported. Most

Moſt Countries have try'd ſome or all of theſe Meaſures, and others of the ſame Nature, and have tryed contrary Meaſures at one time, from what they us'd immediatly before, from the Opinion, that ſince the Method uſed had not the effect deſign'd, a contrary would: Yet it has not been found, that any of them have preſerv'd or increaſed Money; but on the contrair.

The uſe of *Banks* has been the beſt Method yet practis'd for the increaſe of Money. *Banks* have been long us'd in *Italy*, but as I'm inform'd the Invention of them was owing to *Sweedland*. Their Money was Copper, which was inconvenient, by reaſon of its Weight and Bulk; To remedy this Inconveniency, a *Bank* was ſet up where the Money might be pledg'd, and Credit given to the Value, which paſt in Payments, and facilitat Trade.

The *Dutch* for the ſame reaſon ſet up the Bank of *Amſterdam*. Their Money was Silver, but their Trade was ſo great as to find payments even in Silver inconvenient. This Bank like that of *Sweedland*, is a ſecure Place, where Merchants may give in Money, and have credit to trade with. Beſides the convenience of eaſier and quicker Payments, theſe Banks ſaves the Expenſe of Caſheers, the Expenſe of Bags and Carriage, loſſes by bad Money, and the Money is ſafer than in the Merchants Houſes, for 'tis leſs lyable to Fire or Robbery, the neceſſary Meaſures being taken to prevent them.

Mer-

Merchants who have Money in the Bank of *Amſterdam*, and People of other Countries who deal with them, are not lyable to the Changes in the Money, by its being allay'd or alter'd in the Denomination : For, the Bank receives no Money but what's of Value, and is therefore call'd Bank-money ; and tho rais'd in current payments, it goes for the Value it was pledg'd for in Bank-payments. The *Agio* of the Bank changes a Quarter or a half *p. Cent*, as current Money is more or leſs ſcarce.

Banks where the Money is pledg'd equal to the Credit given, are ſure ; For, tho Demands are made of the whole, the Bank does not fail in payment.

By the Conſtitution of this Bank, the whole Sum for which Credit is given, ought to remain there, to be ready at demand ; Yet a Sum is lent by the Managers for a Stock to the Lumbar, and 'tis thought they lend great Sums on other occaſions. So far as they lend they add to the Money, which brings a Profit to the Country, by imploying more People, and extending Trade ; They add to the Money to be lent, whereby it is eaſier borrowed, and at leſs uſe ; and the Bank has a benefit : But the Bank is leſs ſure, and tho none ſuffer by it, or are apprehenſive of Danger, its Credit being good ; Yet if the whole Demands were made, or Demands greater than the remaining Money, they could not all be ſatisfied, till the Bank had called in what Sums were lent.

The certain good it does, will more than ballance the

the hazard, tho once in two or three years it failed in payment; providing the Sums lent be well secured: Merchants who had Money there, might be disapointed of it at demand, but the Security being good, and Interest allowed; Money would be had on a small Discompt, perhaps at the *Par*.

Last War, *England* set up a Bank to have the Conveniencies of that at *Amsterdam*, and by their Constitution to encrease Money. This Bank was made up of Subscribers, who lent the King 1200000 *lib.* at 8 and a Third *per Cent*, for 11 years, on a Parliamentary Fund; And were priviledg'd Bankers for that time. The Sum due by the Government was a Security to the People, to make good any Losses the Bank might suffer.

This Bank was safer than the Goldsmiths Notes in use before. It made a great Addition to the Money, having a much greater Sum of Notes out, than Money in Bank. And the Sum lent the King, which was the Fund belong'd to the Subscribers, was negotiat at Profit, and had the same Effect in Trade as Money. I don't know how their Notes came to be at discount, whether from the Circumstances of the Nation, or from ill Management.

The Fund of the Bank of *Scotland* was a 100000 *l.* of which a Tenth was pay'd in. This Bank was safer than that of *England*, there being a Register whereby most Sums lent were secured. Its Notes went for 4 or 5 times the value of the Money in Bank, and by so much as these Notes went for more than the Money

Money in Bank; So much was added to the Money of the Nation.

This Bank was more useful than that of *Amsterdam*, or *England*; Its Notes passing in most payments, and through the whole Country: The Bank of *Amsterdam* being only for that Town, and that of *England* of little use but at *London*.

The stop of Payments which hapned to the Bank of *Scotland*, was foreseen, and might have been prevented. The Consumption of Forreign Goods, and Expense in *England*, being more than the Export of Goods did pay; the Ballance sent out in Money lessen'd the Credit of the Bank. For as Credit is voluntary, it depends on the Quantity of Money in the Country, and Increases or Decreases with it. Coyning Notes of one *Pound* supported the Bank, by furnishing Paper for small payments, and thereby preventing a part of the Demand for Money: By these Notes the Bank might have kept its Credit, till other Methods had been taken to supply the Country with Money; had not a Report of raising the Money occasion'd an extraordinary Demand, which in few days exhaust the Money in Bank, and put a stop to payments.

It would not have been easie in that scarcity of Money to have got enough to support the Bank, tho Men of the best Credit had undertaken it; That Report of raising the Money having only occasioned a Demand from the People in *Edinburgh*. In a short time

time Notes would have come in ſo faſt from the Country, that what Money could have been got, would not have anſwer'd the Demand.

If the Privy Council had lower'd the Money, the *Engliſh* Crown to 5 *ſh.* and the other Money in proportion, to take place 2 pence *p.* Crown in 3 days, and the other 3 pence in a Month; the occaſion of the Demand being remov'd, in all appearance Money would have been return'd to the Bank.

If the ſtate of the Bank had been known, or ſuſpected by the People; ſuch a Proclamation would have had the ſame effect, tho the ſtop of payment had then happen'd. In that caſe, the ſupport of the Bank might have been the Narrative of the Proclamation; The ſecurity being good, few or none would have kept their *M*oney to loſs, rather than return it to the Bank. And if in 3 days *M*oney had not come in ſo faſt as expected, their Lordſhips by a 2*d.* Proclamation might have lower'd the Crown to 5 *ſh.* to take place then, and 6 pence more in 3 days. When the Credit of the *B*ank had been re-eſtabliſh'd, the *M*oney might have been cry'd up, if that had been neceſſary, the Crown to 5 *ſh.* and 5 *pence*, and the other money in proportion as it was before.

*Some are againſt all* Banks *where the Money does not lie pledg'd equal to the Credit.* 1. *They ſay the Demand may be greater than the Money in* Bank. Secondly, *If we are declining in our Trade, or Money, we are not at all,*

*all, or are less sensible of it: And if the* Bank *fail, we are in a worse condition than before.*

To the first it's Answered, Tho the Nation had no Benefit by the addition the *Bank* makes to the Money; Nor the People by being supply'd with Money when otherwise they could not, and at less Interest; And tho the Proprietors had no gain by it: The other Conveniencies, as quicker and easier Payments, *&c.* are more than equal to that hazard; Or Bank Notes, Gold-smiths and Bankers Notes, would not be prefer'd to Money, every Body knowing such a stop may happen to the *Bank*, and that Gold-smiths and Bankers may fail.

The other Objection is the same as to say, a Merchant who had a small Stock, and was capable of imploying a greater; If a Sum were offer'd him without Interest, equal to what he had, and more as his own encreas'd, should refuse it, because he might fancy himself Richer than he was, and if his own Stock decreas'd, that Sum lent would be taken from him.

If 15000 is suppos'd the Money in *Bank*, and 75000 *lib.* of Notes out; 60000 *lib.* is added to the Money of the Nation, without Interest: For what is pay'd by the Borrowers, is got by the Proprietors. As the Money of the Nation encreases, the Credit of the *Bank* encreases, and the Sum of Notes out is greater; And so far from making the People less sensible of the condition of the Country, a surer Judgment of the state

ſtate of Trade and Money may be made from the Books of the *Bank*, than any other way.

If Trade can be carried on with a 100000 *lib.* and a Ballance then due by Forreigners; The ſame meaſures, and a greater Quantity of Money, would make the Ballance greater. Nor is that Additional Money the *Bank* furniſhes, to be ſuppos'd will be loſt, if by a Ballance due from Trade the Silver Money encreaſes: That Credit may fail from an accident when Money is plentiful, and would ſoon be recover'd; 'Tis only loſt by a ſcarcity of Money. Such a Credit may ſupport Trade, in caſes where without it Trade would ſink, but cannot do prejudice.

*Another Objection is made againſt the* Bank. *That it encourag'd the Exportation of Money, by furniſhing Sums in ſuch Species as were of moſt value Abroad.* To anſwer this Objection, I ſhall make a Suppoſition. *A. B.* Merchant has occaſion for a 1000 *lib.* in *Holland*, and deſires *C. D.* Banker to give him a Bill for that value; There is no Money due in *Holland* to *Scots* Merchants, ſo *C. D.* muſt Export the Money to pay the Bill he Draws: But, there being no *Bank*, nor any poſſibility of getting a 1000 *lib.* in 40 *Pence Pieces*, he ſends out Money of different Species. This does not hinder the Money to go out, but makes the Exchange dearer by 2 or 3 *per Cent*, than it would have been if 40 *Pence Pieces* could have been got. And tho no other Money were left, but old *Marks*, if a Ballance is due theſe will go out, tho not worth 10 *Pence*: The Exchange will be ſo much higher, the profit of Exporting

porting is the ſame; And ſo far from doing hurt to the Country, the *Bank* by furniſhing ſuch pieces as could be Exported to leaſt loſs, kept the Exchange 2 or 3 *per Cent* lower than otherwiſe it would have been, and ſaved yearly the ſending out a conſiderable Sum to pay a greater Ballance, the higher Exchange would have occaſioned.

---

# CHAP. IV.

*The ſeveral Meaſures now propoſ'd, conſider'd. As, raiſing or allaying the Money. Coyning the Plate. Regulating the Ballance of Trade. Or, Re-eſtabliſhing the Bank.*

WHEN I uſe the Words, *Raiſing the Money*, I deſire to be underſtood raiſing it in the Denomination; For I do not ſuppoſe it adds to the Value.

There is no way Silver can be made more valuable, but by leſſening the Quantity, or encreaſing the Demand for it. If the Export and Conſumption of Silver be greater than the Import, or the Demand be encreas'd; Silver will be of more Value. If the Quantity Imported be greater than the Quantity Exported or Conſumed,

med, or the Demand leſſen'd; Silver will be of leſs Value.

If raiſing or allaying the Money could add to its Value, or have any good Effect on Home or Forreign Trade; Then no Nation would want Money. A 100 *lib.* might be rais'd or allay'd to 2, to 10, to a 100 times the Denomination it had, or more as there were occaſion. But as 'tis unjuſt to raiſe, or allay Money; Becauſe, then all Contracts are payed with a leſſer Value than was Contracted for; And as it has bad effects on Home or Forreign Trade: So no Nation practiſes it, that has regard to Juſtice, or underſtands the nature of Trade and Money. If *A. B.* ſell 12 Chalder of Victual for a 100 *lib.* payable in 6 Months, with which he is to pay Bills of Exchange of that Value, to be drawn on him then from *France* for Wine he has Commiſſion'd; And in that time the Money is rais'd or allay'd to double, the 100 *lib. A. B.* receives will only pay half the Bill he has to pay, being only equal to 50 *lib.* of the Money he Contracted for. Nor will that 100 *lib.* buy the ſame Quantity of Goods of the Country, that a 100 *lib.* bought before: It will pay where Money is due, and ſatisfie paſt Contracts made upon the Faith of the Publick, becauſe the Prince ſays every Man ſhall take half what is owing him in full Payment. But in bargains to be made, the Value of the Money will be conſidered; Goods will riſe, tho perhaps not to the Proportion the Money is rais'd: And ſuch Perſons as do not raiſe their Goods, equal to the Money, are impos'd on.

When

When *6* pence is raiſed to 12 pence, the *6* pence is worth 12 pence; But the value of the pence is lower'd to Half-pence.

To explain this matter better, I ſhall ſuppoſe when Money is rais'd, Goods riſe, or not.

If Goods riſe, then raiſing the Money has not the effect deſign'd. If a piece of Serge is ſold for 40 *ſh.* and the Shilling be raiſed to 18 *Pence*, the piece of Serge will be ſold for 3 *Pound.* This adds to the Tale of the Money, and pays Debts with two Thirds of what is due, but does not add to the Money. This is the natural Conſequence of raiſing the Money; For, it is not the ſound of the higher Denomination, but the value of the Silver is conſider'd.

If, when Money is rais'd, Goods keep the Prices they had before. Then all Goods exported are ſold for a leſſer Value abroad, and all Goods imported are ſold dearer. ( *Ex.* ) A *Half-crown* is rais'd to 40 *Pence*, and that *Half-crown* buys the ſame Quantity of Goods 40 Pence bought before; Then the Merchant who ſends Goods to *Holland*, to the value of 300 *lib.* which are ſold for 390 *lib.* there, would gain 220 *lib.* on the value of 300 *lib.* exported: Becauſe, 390 *lib.* in *Holland*, would be equal to, or worth by Exchange at the *Par*, or ſent in Bullion, 520 *lib.* in *Scotland.* That Trade would bring no more Profit to the Nation, than when the Return of the Goods yielded only 390 *lib*: For, 390 *lib.* before it was rais'd, had the

the ſame Quantity of Silver, that 520 *lib.* rais'd Money would have; and bought als great a Quantity of Forreign Goods. But that Trade would be ſo profitable to the Merchant, that more People would deal in it than could get Goods to buy; and as more Buyers than Sellers would raiſe the Prices here, ſo one Merchant underſelling the other would lower the Prices in *Holland*. But tho the Prices kept low here, and our Merchants kept up the Prices Abroad: The *Dutch* knowing the Goods were ſo cheap in the Country, would buy none from our Merchants, but Commiſſon them in return of Goods they ſent.

Suppoſe the yearly Export firſt Coſt 300000 *lib.* ſold abroad 390000 *lib.* The Import, and Expenſe abroad 410000 *lib.* and 20000 *lib.* ſent in Money, to pay the Ballance. The Money rais'd one Third, and Goods to keep the Prices they had before, 225000 *lib.* ſent to *Scotland* in Forreign Money, or Goods, or by Exchange, would buy what was ſold abroad for 390000 *lib.* The Export, Import, and Expenſe Abroad continuing the ſame, *Scotland* would be due a Ballance of 185000 *lib.* For, tho *Scots* Goods were ſold under the value, yet other Nations would not ſell their Goods for leſs than before; or than they could have in other Places.

*It may be alledg'd, we have more Product and Manufacture, than is conſum'd, or exported; and ſelling cheaper, would occaſion a greater Demand for our Goods Abroad.*

The

The Product and Manufacture might be much encreas'd, if we had Money to imploy the People: But, I'm of Opinion we have not any great Quantity of Goods, more than what is consum'd or exported. Allow Selling cheaper would occasion a greater Demand; that the greater Demand, would occasion an increase in the Product, and Manufacture, to the value of a 100000 *lib.* and allow that the extraordinary cheapness of Goods, did not occasion a greater Consumption in the Country: Yet, we would be in the same Condition as before; 20000 *lib.* would be still due of ballance, and the Improvement would be given to Forreigners for nothing. But this Improvement is imaginary, for tho the Demand encreas'd, yet without more Money more People could not be imployed, so no further Improvement could be made: We would be forc'd to retrench near one half of the ordinary Consumption of Forreign Goods, and Expense Abroad; not having Money to pay the great ballance would be due.

*Some think Forreign Money being rais'd, would bring in Money to* Scotland.

Tho the *Crown* were rais'd to 10 *sh.* yet if a Ballance is due by *Scotland*, the Exchange will be above the *Par*, and, 'tis not to be suppos'd an *English* Merchant will bring *Crowns* to *Scotland*, when for a 100 pay'd in at *London*, he can have 105 or 6 of the same *Crowns* payed him at *Edinburgh*.

If

If the ballance of Trade was equal, Forreign Money rais'd, and *Scots* Money not rais'd in proportion; Forreign Money would be brought in, and a greater value of *Scots* Money would be carried out. 'Tis the ſame loſs to a Country when Money is rais'd, and Goods do not riſe in proportion: ( *Ex.* ) If Forreigners ſend in Money to buy Goods, and this Money when exported is not valued ſo high as here; the Return in Goods will be ſo much leſs, beſides the want of the Profit we would have had on the Export of our Goods.

If all Import, and Forreign Expenſe were diſcharged, *Scotland* would then be ſo much richer, as there was Bullion or Money imported: But, if that Prohibition be ſuppos'd, *Scotland* would be richer by keeping the Money at the value it has; Becauſe, a greater Quantity would be brought in, to buy the ſame Quantity of Goods.

If we could be ſuppos'd to be without any Commerce with other Nations, a 100 *lib.* may be allay'd and rais'd to have the ſame effect in Trade as a Million: But, if a Stranger were ſuffer'd to come to *Scotland*, he might purchaſe a great part of the Land or Goods with a ſmall Sum. And a rich Man here would make a very ſmall Figure Abroad.

Money is the Meaſure by which all Goods are valued; and unleſs Goods riſe to the full proportion the Money is rais'd, the Goods are undervalued. If the

the yearly Value of *Scotland* in Product and Manufacture be 2 Millions, at 20 Years Purchase 40 Millions. The Money a 100000 *lib.* Raising the Money 20 *per Cent*, makes it pass for a 120000 *lib.* Suppose the Goods rise only 10 *per Cent*, then that a 120000 *lib.* is equal in *Scotland* to a 110000 *lib.* of the Money before it was rais'd; and Buys the same Quantity of Goods. So, an addition is made of 20000 *lib.* to the late, and of 10000 *lib.* to the Value of *Scots* or Forreign Money, compar'd with the Value of *Scots* Goods: But the measure by which Goods are valued, being rais'd in the Denomination 20 *per Cent*; And the Goods rising only 10 *per Cent*: *Scotland* is near 4 Million, or one Tenth less valuable than before. And any Man who Sells his Estate, will receive a Tenth less Silver, or of any other Forreign Goods for it, than if he had Sold it before the Money was rais'd.

France *and* Holland *are given as Examples of raising and allaying the Money.* In *France* the Money is higher in the Denomination than in other Countries, but that does not hinder the Money of *France* to be Exported. When the *Lue d'ore* was at 12 *Livres*, the Ballance was against *France*, Exchange 10 *per Cent* above the *Par*: And a 110 *Lue d'ores* at 12 *Livres* were pay'd then at *Paris*, for a 100 *Lue d'ores* of the same Weight and Fineness at *Amsterdam*, and passing there for 9 *Guilders* Bank Money; So 10 *per Cent* was got by Exporting Money from *France*. When the *Lue d'ore* was rais'd to 14 *Livres*, that did not make the Ballance against *France* less; The Exchange continued the same

ſame, 110 *Luc d'ores* tho at 14 *Livres* were payed for a Bill of a 100 at *Amſterdam*, and the ſame Profit was made by Exporting Money. If the Exchange hapned to be lower, it was from the Ballance of Trade due by *France* being leſs, and that would have lower'd the Exchange whether the Money had been rais'd or not. But the raiſing the Money, ſo far from bringing the Ballance to the *French* ſide, keeps the Ballance againſt *France*: For, as their Goods do not riſe to the full proportion the Money is rais'd, ſo *French* Goods are Sold cheaper, and Forreign Goods are Sold dearer, which makes the Ballance greater, occaſions a greater Export of Money, ſets Idle ſo many of the People as that Money employ'd, leſſens the Product or Manufacture, the yearly Value of the Country, and the number of the People.

*It's thought the* Dutch *Coin* Lue d'ores, *and ſend them to* France, *where they paſs at* 14 Livres. *And, that* Guineas *were ſent from* Holland *to* England, *in the time of the Clipt Money, becauſe they paſt there for* 30 ſh. But theſe People are miſinformed. Ever ſince I have known any thing of Exchange, a *Luc d'ore* at *Amſterdam* whether new or old, has been of more Value by Exchange, than a new *Luc d'ore* at *Paris*. And in the time of the Clipt Money, a *Guinea* in *Holland* was worth more by Exchange, than a *Guinea* in *England*. Theſe who were Ignorant of the Exchange, might buy up *Guineas* or *Luc d'ores*, to carry to *England* or *France*, but they would have got more by Bill. There was a Profit then upon Exporting *Guineas* and *Luc d'ores* from *England* and *France* to *Holland*. The Pound *Engliſh* at at that time was given for 8 *Guilders*, or under; and the Exchange from *Amsterdam* to *Paris* has been these 8 or 10 Years for the most part, considerably above the *Par* on the *Dutch* side. I have known the Pound *English* at 7 *Guilders* 13 *Stivers*, and the *French Crown* of 3 *Livres* bought in *Holland* for 37 *Stivers*, in *London* for 39 Pence half Penny.

Raising the Money in *France* is laying a Tax on the People, which is sooner pay'd, and thought to be less felt than a Tax laid on any other way. When the King raises the *Lue d'ore* from 12 *Livres* to 14, they are taken in at the Mint for 13 *Livres*, and given out for 14; So the King gains a *Livre* on the *Lue d'ore*, and this Tax comes to 20 or 25 Million of *Livres*, sometimes more, according to the Quantity of Money in the Country. But so far from adding to the Money, it stops the Circulation: A part being kept up till there is occasion to Export it to *Holland*, from whence a return is made by Bill, of a Sum of *Livres* equal to the same Quantity of new *Lue d'ores* that were Exported of old ones, and 8 or 10 *per Cent* more, according as the Exchange is on the *Dutch* side. Others who won't venture to send the Money out, keep it till the new Money is cry'd down, so save a 13*th* part, which the King would have got if they had carried the Money to the Mint to be Recoin'd. This Tax falls heavy on the poorer sort of the People.

*Its generally thought the* Dutch *Money is not worth half what it passes for.* But it will prove otherwise when Examined. The *Bank* by which most payments are

are made, receive and pay in *Bank Money*, which is better than the *English*: *Ducatdowns* are at 3 *Guilders*, and other *Bank Money* in proportion; And I'm inform'd the current *Money* has Silver in it to the Value or near, except ſome of their *Skellings* which are worſe than others : The making them worſe was not deſign'd, it was an abuſe occaſioned by too many Towns having Power to Coin : Which abuſe was ſtopt ſo ſoon as known, and that *Species* cry'd down to 5 *Stivers* and a half.

*Some propoſe the Money may be rais'd, to give the little we have left a better Circulation, and to bring out hoarded Money.* The lowering it by degrees to take place in 3 or 4 Months, will have the ſame Effect; And other good Conſequences : For, from what has been ſaid, *page* 30 and 31. There is reaſon to think, if the Money were lower'd to the *English Standard*, Exchange would be on our ſide, and a Ballance due us : Providing the Export, the Import, and Expenſe abroad continued as now.

*There is another Argument for raiſing the* Money, *which is, that ſome Goods don't yield Profit enough abroad, ſo are not exported.* ( Ex. ) *If Serges worth in* Scotland *a* 100 lib. *are worth* 120 *in* Holland, *the* Merchant *won't export them for* 20 per Cent *profit: But if the Money is rais'd* 20 per Cent, *and Goods keep at the Prices they had before, the ſame Money that bought* 100 lib. *of Serges, buying now to the value of* 120 lib. *And theſe Goods being worth in* Holland 144 lib: *That Addition to the*

*the Profit by raising the Money, will occasion the Export of them.*

This is the same as if a Merchant who had a 100 different sorts of Goods, and was offer'd 30 *per Cent* Profit upon 90 of them; but no body offering above 20 *per Cent* Profit for the other 10 Sorts, should add a Quarter to the measure by which he measur'd his Goods, and sell all the 100 Sorts for the same Price he sold them before: As this Merchant would find himself a considerable Loser by this Expedient, so will a Nation who raises their Money.

For the same Reason, it would be a great loss to *Scotland* if all Goods were allowed to be exported without duty; some ought to be free of Duty, and some not, according to their Value Abroad.

The true and safe way to encourage the Export of such Goods, as do not yield great enough Profit; is by a Draw-back. ( *Ex.* ) If Serges sent to *Holland* give only 20 *per Cent* profit, 10 *per Cent* given as a Draw-back will encourage their Export: The Draw-back given to the Merchant is not lost to the Nation, and what is got by the Manufacture or Export of the Goods, is gain'd by the Nation.

A Draw-back is the best Method yet known for encouraging Trade, and it may be made appear, that 10 or 15000 applyed that way, will occasion an Addition to the Export to the Value of a 100000 *lib.* Nor is any

any part of that 10 or 15000 *lib.* loſt to the Nation; For, if *A. B.* and *C. Scotſmen* get ſuch Draw-back, it is the ſame thing to the Nation, as if it had not been given. When Draw-backs are payed out of Funds for the ſupport of the Government, little Money is applyed that way; Becauſe, ſo much is taken from the Prince: But, if there was a National Fund for the encouragement of Trade, that Nation might improve Trade, and underſel other Nations that did not follow the ſame Meaſures. But this is ſuppoſing there was Money in the Country to imploy the People.

Coining the Plate were a loſs of the Faſhion, which may be valued one *6th*, and would add little to the Money: The Plate at the Reſtauration was inconſiderable, having been call'd in a little before. Since there may have been wrought one year with another about 60 Stone weight; of that a great part has been melted down, or exported, the Remainder won't be of great value. What Plate has been imported belongs to a few Men of Quality, who will ſend it out of the Country rather than loſe the Faſhion; and in that they do a Service to the Country, providing they don't ſpend it abroad, becauſe wrought Plate will ſell for more Silver at *London*, than it will melt to here.

If 'tis propos'd the Money be allay'd, and the Advantage of the Allay be given to the Owners of the Plate. Suppoſe the new Money with Allay be rais'd to double the Denomination; 5 *ſh.* of Plate with the Faſhion

Fashion worth 6 *sh.* will give at the Mint 10 *sh.* allay'd Money: But even then the Plate will not be brought in voluntarly, for that Plate sold in *England*, and the Value brought back by Bill, will yield from 11 to 12 *sh.* Exchange being above the *Par*, and 6 pence suppo-sed to be got for the Fashion of the Ounce of Plate.

If it be necessary to coin the Plate, such Plate should be allow'd to be exported as can be sold abroad for more than its Weight: Security being given to import Money or Bullion to the value.

*Some propose a Regulation of the Ballance of Trade, by retrenching the Consumption of Forreign Goods, and Expense in* England: *So the Ballance being brought to be on our side, we may become rich by living within our yearly value, as we became poor by spending beyond it.*

Such a Regulation will have its Difficulties. 1. To discharge all or a great part of the Import, will lessen considerably the Revenue of the Crown; and Her Majesty may not think good to give the Royal Assent to such a Regulation, unless an Equivalent be given. 2. Such a Regulation would not be so strictly kept, but a part of what was used to be imported would be stole in. 3. The Residence of our Princes being in *England*, we are under a necessity of having a Ministry there: Imployments being at the disposal of the Prince, and *London* being a Place of more Diversion than *Edinburgh*, the Gentry will continue to go to *London* for Places or Pleasure.

But

But allowing the Royal Aſſent were given to ſuch a Regulation; either with or without an Equivalent; and the Regulation could be ſo ſtrictly kept, that nothing were imported contrair to that Law; and allow 20000 *lib.* could be ſav'd of the Expenſe in *England*, ſo that the Import and Expenſe Abroad ſhould be 60000 *lib.* leſs than laſt year: Yet there are other Difficulties, that I fear will make the Regulation ineffectual.

1. Suppoſe the Ballance laſt year due by us was 20000 *lib.* the Import and Expenſe Abroad leſſen'd 60000 *lib.* Theſe who propoſe this Regulation may think a Ballance will be due to us of 40000 *lib.* But as the Bank may have ſupplyed us with 60000 *lib.* of Notes, more than the Money in Bank: and as 20000 *lib.* is ſuppos'd to have been exported laſt year: So our Money being leſſen'd 80000 *lib.* the next years Export may be ſo much leſs valuable, the want of that Money having ſet idle a part of the People were then imployed: and a greater Ballance be due than laſt year, notwithſtanding of the Regulation.

2. 40000 *lib.* firſt Coſt of Goods Imported, and 20000 *lib.* ſpent Abroad, leſſen'd the Conſumption of the Goods of the Country; and the Export was by ſo much greater, as the Conſumption of the Goods of the Country was leſſen'd. But this Regulation occaſioning a greater Conſumption of the Goods of the Country, the Export will be leſs.

3. Several

3. Several Merchants may have Exported Goods, tho they had not much Profit upon the Export of them; But because of the Profit to be made upon the Import; which being lessen'd, may likewise lessen the Export.

4. If *Scotland* Discharge or put a very high Duty on the Goods of other Nations, other Nations may Discharge *Scots* Goods.

Allowing there were no difficulties in Regulating the Ballance of Trade, and that the same Measures were followed as are followed in *Holland*; We would grow Richer, but their Riches would encrease in the same proportion: And 50 Years hence *Scotland* would be as Poor as now, in comparison with *Holland*.

If two Countries equal in their Product, People, *&c.* the one with a 100000 *lib.* of Money, and Living within its yearly Value; so that the first Year a Ballance is due of 20000 *lib.* the second Year of 25000 *lib.* and so on. The other Country with 20 Millions of Money, and consuming more than the yearly Value; so that a Million is sent out to pay the Ballance, the second Year 1200000 *lib.* and so on. This Country will be soon Poor, and the other be soon Rich: But if that People who has 20 Millions of Money, will retrench in proportion to the other; they will be Rich and Powerful in comparison with the other.

Considering how small a share we have of the Money of *Europe*, and how much Trade depends on Money: It

It will not be found very practicable to better our Condition, but by an addition to our Money. Or if it is practicable without it, it is much more ſo with it.

The *Bank* will add little to the Money; For as Credit is voluntary, it depends on the Quantity of Money in the Country. And tho the *Bank* had never fail'd, yet it could not have kept its Credit much longer. Becauſe, the Quantity of Money in *Scotland* is not ſufficient to give a Circulation to ſuch a Sum of Notes, as will pay the Charges of the *Bank*, and the Intereſt to the Owners.

'Tis thought the Proprietors of the *Bank* deſign to apply to the *Parliament* for further Priviledges: But as their deſign is not yet made publick, I ſhall only ſay in general, that if other Priviledges are to be given, then it is not the ſame *Bank*; at leaſt not on the ſame Eſtabliſhment it was: In either of theſe caſes, every Perſon ſhould be allowed to ſhare in it.

When a *Bank* is Eſtabliſh't every Perſon may have a ſhare, upon the Terms of the Act of *Parliament*; and he that Offers firſt is preferred. Suppoſe upon the ſetting up of the *Bank*, *A. B.* and *C.* did not Subſcribe to it, becauſe they thought the Eſtabliſhment not favourable enough: So long as they who did Subſcribe can ſupport the *Bank* upon the Terms of the Act of *Parliament*, none will pretend to any ſhare in it; unleſs the Subſcribers are pleas'd to ſell. But if other Priviledges are given, *A. B.* and *C.* as any others of of the Country may desire the Books to be open'd, that they be allow'd to share in it; and any other set of Men who offer the same Security, may at the same time be allowed to set up a *Bank* with the same Priviledges: So every Shire in *Scotland* will desire one. And if new Priviledges are given to this *Bank*, it were a hardship to refuse the same to others, who are able and willing to give the same Security, especially when the Nation stands in need of more Money than this *Bank* would be allowed to give out.

5, 1724. Act of Parliament, *11° Georgii, c. 9, A.D. 1724*, London.

## CAP. IX.

An Act for continuing the feveral Annuities of Eighty eight thoufand feven hundred fifty one Pounds Seven Shillings and Ten Pence Halfpenny, and One hundred thoufand Pounds to the Bank of *England*, until *Midfummer* One thoufand feven hundred twenty feven; and from thence, for reducing the fame to Seventy one thoufand and one Pounds Two Shillings and Three Pence Three Farthings, and Eighty thoufand Pounds, redeemable by Parliament; and for preventing the uttering of forged, counterfeited or erafed Bank Bills or Notes.

' Moft gracious Sovereign,

' WHEREAS by an Act of Parliament, made and paffed ' in the Seventh Year of the Reign of Her late Majefty ' Queen *Anne*, (of bleffed Memory) intituled, *An Act for enlarging* ' *the Capital Stock of the Bank of* England; *and for raifing a fur-* ' *ther Supply to Her Majefty, for the Service of the Year One thou-* ' *fand feven hundred and nine*, the Governor and Company of the ' Bank of *England* were obliged, in the manner therein mentioned, ' to deliver up to be cancelled certain Exchequer Bills, which ' had been made forth by a former Act of Parliament in that Be- ' half; which Bills, with Intereft thereupon, were computed to ' amount to Seventeen hundred feventy five thoufand twenty ' feven Pounds, Seventeen Shillings and Ten Pence Halfpenny; ' and to the end the faid Governor and Company of the Bank of ' *England*, and their Succeffors, might have a competent Recom- ' pence and Confideration for fo doing, and for all their De- ' mands relating thereto, it was by the faid Act of the Seventh ' Year of Her faid late Majefty's Reign enacted, that from ' and after the Feaft of *Saint Michael the Archangel* in the Year ' of Our Lord One thoufand feven hundred and ten, the faid ' Governor and Company of the Bank of *England* and their ' Succeffors, fhould have, receive and enjoy One Annuity or ' yearly Sum of One hundred and fix thoufand and five hundred ' and one Pounds Thirteen Shillings and Five Pence, out of ' fuch Duties on Houfes as are therein mentioned: But it was ' thereby provided and enacted, That at any Time, upon One Year's

7 Ann. c. 7.

§ 8.

§ 14.

' Year's Notice to the ſaid Governor and Company of the Bank ' of *England* or their Succeſſors, and upon full Payment to ' them of the ſaid Sum of One million ſeven hundred ſeventy ' five thouſand twenty ſeven Pounds Seventeen Shillings and Ten ' Pence Halfpenny, and of all Arrears of the ſaid Annuity of ' One hundred and ſix thouſand five hundred and one Pounds ' Thirteen Shillings and Five Pence *per Annum* (if any ſhould ' be then due); then, and not till then, the ſaid Annuity of ' One hundred and ſix thouſand five hundred and one Pounds ' Thirteen Shillings and Five Pence *per Annum* ſhould ceaſe and ' determine; and then alſo the ſaid Duties on Houſes ſhould be ' underſtood to be redeemed by Parliament, and ſhould not be iſ- ' ſued, paid or applied to any Uſe or Purpoſe whatſoever, but by ' the Authority of Parliament: And whereas in an Act of Par- ' liament made and paſſed in the Third Year of Your Majeſty's ' Reign, intituled, *An Act for redeeming ſeveral Funds of the Gover-* 3 G. 1. c. 8.
' *nor and Company of the Bank of* England, *purſuant to former Pro-* ' *viſoes of Redemption; and for ſecuring to them ſeveral new Funds* ' *and Allowances redeemable by Parliament; and for obliging them* ' *to advance further Sums not exceeding Two millions five hundred* ' *thouſand Pounds, at Five Pounds* per Centum per Annum, *as ſhall* ' *be found neceſſary to be employed in leſſening the National Debts and* ' *Incumbrances; and for continuing certain Proviſions formerly made* ' *for the Expence of Your Majeſty's Civil Government; and for Pay-* ' *ment of Annuities formerly purchaſed at the Rate of Five Pounds* per ' Centum; *and for other Purpoſes in the ſaid Act mentioned*; reciting, ' that the ſaid Governor and Company of the Bank of *England*, in § 1.
' regard the common Rate of Intereſt Money was very much ' leſſened under Your Majeſty's moſt auſpicious Government, and ' that ſeveral of the Funds of the ſaid Governor and Company ' of the Bank of *England*, in the ſaid Act mentioned, were re- ' deemable at ſuch Times, and in ſuch Manner, as in the ſaid Act ' are particularly ſet forth; and that they the ſaid Governor and ' Company were willing and contented to accept One Annuity of ' Eighty eight thouſand ſeven hundred fifty one Pounds Seven ' Shillings and Ten pence Halfpenny, being after the Rate of ' Five Pounds *per Centum per Annum*, on the ſaid principal Sum ' of One million ſeven hundred ſeventy five thouſand twenty ſeven ' Pounds Seventeen Shillings and Ten pence Halfpenny, in lieu ' of their then preſent Annuity or Sum of One hundred and ſix ' thouſand five hundred and one Pounds Thirteen Shillings and ' Five pence *per Annum*; and that the ſaid Governor and Com- ' pany were alſo willing and contented to diſcharge and deliver up ' to be cancelled, as many of the Exchequer-Bills, formerly ' made forth, as amounted to Two Millions in Principal Money, ' and to accept an Annuity or Sum of One hundred thouſand ' Pounds *per Annum*, being after the Rate of Five Pounds *per* ' *Centum per Annum*, for the ſame: It was in and by the ſaid Act ' of the Third Year of Your Majeſty's Reign enacted, That the § 2.
' ſaid Governor and Company of the Bank of *England*, and their ' Succeſſors, ſhould have, receive and enjoy the ſaid Annuity or ' yearly Sum of Eighty eight thouſand ſeven hundred fifty one ' Pounds Seven Shillings and Ten pence Halfpenny; in reſpect of ' the ſaid principal Sum of One million ſeven hundred ſeventy five ' thouſand twenty ſeven Pounds Seventeen Shillings and Ten ' pence

‘ pence Halfpenny; which annual or yearly Sum of Eighty eight thouſand ſeven hundred fifty one Pounds Seven Shillings and Ten pence Halfpenny, was thereby charged upon, and made payable from time to time, out of all the Monies ariſen or to ariſe, at the Receipt of Your Majeſty's Exchequer, of or for the particular Duties on Houſes therein mentioned, and of or for the ſaid Duties and Revenues, commonly called the Aggregate Fund, and every or any of them, and was to be paid to the ſaid Governor and Company of the Bank of *England*, and their Succeſſors for ever, from the Feaſt of the Nativity of *Saint John Baptiſt* One thouſand ſeven hundred and eighteen, at the Four moſt uſual Feaſts or Days of Payment in the Year, by even and equal Portions; all which Payments were to be made in ſuch Manner and Form, and with ſuch Preference as are in the ſaid Act preſcribed in that Behalf;

Aggregate Fund.

§ 4. But it was thereby alſo provided and enacted, That upon One Year's Notice to be given at the ſaid Feaſt of the Nativity of *Saint John Baptiſt* One thouſand ſeven hundred and eighteen, or any quarterly Feaſt Day after, and upon Repayment by Parliament, to the ſaid Governor and Company of the Bank of *England*, or their Succeſſors, of the ſaid Sum of One million ſeven hundred ſeventy five thouſand twenty ſeven Pounds Seventeen Shillings and Ten pence Halfpenny, and of all Arrears of the ſaid Annuity of Eighty eight thouſand ſeven hundred fifty one Pounds Seven Shillings and Ten pence Halfpenny *per Annum*, (if any ſhould be then due); then and not till then, the ſaid Annuity of Eighty eight thouſand ſeven hundred fifty one Pounds Seven Shillings and Ten pence Halfpenny *per Annum*, ſhould ceaſe and determine; and in and by the ſaid

§ 5. Act it was further provided and enacted, That the ſaid Governor and Company of the Bank of *England*, ſhould, on or before the Twenty fifth Day of *December* One thouſand ſeven hundred and ſeventeen, deliver up as many Exchequer Bills formerly made forth (then being uncancelled and undiſcharged) as amounted to the Sum of Two Millions in principal Money, to ſuch Perſon or Perſons as the Commiſſioners of His Majeſty's Treaſury, or any Three or more of them, or the High Treaſurer for the time being, ſhould nominate, to be diſcharged,

§ 6. cancelled and made void; and that from and after the Feaſt of the Birth of our Lord Chriſt One thouſand ſeven hundred and ſeventeen, the ſaid Governor and Company of the Bank of *England*, and their Succeſſors for ever, ſhould have, receive and enjoy One Annuity or yearly Sum of One hundred thouſand Pounds, being after the Rate of Five Pounds *per Centum per Annum*, computed upon the ſaid principal Sum of Two Millions; which yearly Sum of One hundred thouſand Pounds was thereby charged upon and made payable, from time to time, out of all the Monies ariſing or to ariſe at the Receipt of Your Majeſty's Exchequer, as well of or for the ſaid ſeveral Duties, Revenues and Incomes, called the Aggregate Fund aforeſaid, as of or for the ſaid particular Duties on Houſes, and was to be paid at ſuch Times, and in ſuch Manner and Form, and with ſuch Preference as are in the ſaid Act preſcribed in that Behalf;

§ 7. and it is by the ſaid Act alſo enacted and provided, That at any Time, upon One Year's Notice to be given at the Feaſt of the Birth of our Lord Chriſt One thouſand ſeven hundred and ſeventeen,

'venteen, or any quarterly Feaſt Day after, and not before, and 'upon Repayment by Parliament to the ſaid Governor and Com'pany of the Bank of *England,* or their Succeſſors, of the ſaid 'Sum of Two Millions, and of all Arrearages of the ſaid yearly 'Sum of One hundred thouſand Pounds (if any ſhould be due 'at the Time of ſuch Payments); then, and not till then, the 'ſaid Annuity of One hundred thouſand Pounds *per Annum* 'ſhould ceaſe and determine; as in and by the ſaid Act it doth and 'may more fully and at large appear: And whereas purſuant to 'the ſaid Act, and the Proviſions therein contained, the ſaid Go'vernor and Company of the Bank of *England* did, on or before 'the Twenty fifth Day of *December* One thouſand ſeven hundred 'and ſeventeen, deliver up as many of the ſaid Exchequer Bills 'as amounted to the ſaid Sum of Two Millions in Principal 'Money, and the ſame were diſcharged, cancelled and made 'void; and they the ſaid Governor and Company of the Bank 'of *England,* have, ever ſince the ſaid Feaſt of the Birth of 'our Lord Chriſt, One thouſand ſeven hundred and ſeventeen, 'received and enjoyed the ſaid Annuity or yearly Sum of One 'hundred thouſand Pounds, and are ſtill entitled unto the ſame: 'And whereas in and by one other Act of Parliament made in 'the Fifth Year of Your Majeſty's Reign, intituled, *An Act for* 5 G. 1. c. 3. '*applying certain Overplus Monies, and further Sums to be raiſed, as* '*well by Way of a Lottery, as by Loans, towards paying off and can*'*celling Exchequer Bills, and for leſſening the preſent great Charge* '*in relation to thoſe Bills; and for circulating and exchanging for* '*ready Money the Reſidue of the ſame Bills for the future,* It is, 'amongſt divers other Matters and Things, enacted and declared, § 22. 'That all the ſaid particular Duties on Houſes, and all the ſaid 'other Rates, Duties, Revenues and Incomes, which by the ſaid 'Act of the Third Year of Your Majeſty's Reign were ſettled 'for anſwering the reſpective Payments therein mentioned (and 'which are denominated to be the Aggregate Fund) and every 'of them, ſhould be continued, and be paid and payable to Your 'Majeſty, Your Heirs and Succeſſors for ever, and that all the 'Monies of the ſaid Duties, Revenues and Incomes which 'ſhould or ought to be brought into the Receipt of the Exche'quer, (except the neceſſary Charges of raiſing, collecting, le'vying, iſſuing, paying and accounting for the ſame) ſhould be 'and are thereby appropriated, and ſhould be iſſued and applied to 'and for the Repayment and Satisfaction of ſeveral yearly and 'other Sums in the ſaid Act particularly expreſſed, in the due 'Courſe, and with ſuch Preferences as are thereby appointed; 'amongſt which Payments an expreſs Proviſion is made for Pay'ment of the ſaid ſeveral and reſpective Annuities of Eighty eight 'thouſand ſeven hundred fifty one Pounds Seven Shillings and 'Ten Pence Halfpenny, and One hundred thouſand Pounds *per* '*Annum*; and it was thereby enacted, That the ſaid ſeveral Annui- § 32. 'ties, and either of them, ſhould ſeverally and reſpectively be re'deemable upon ſuch Payments, and in ſuch Manner and Form 'as in and by the reſpective Proviſions contained in the recited Act 'of the Third Year of Your Majeſty's Reign, are preſcribed for 'the Redemption thereof: And whereas due Notice was given by 'the Right Honourable *Spencer Compton* Eſquire, Speaker of the 'Houſe of Commons, to the ſaid Governor and Company of the 'Bank

'Bank of *England*, for paying of the said Principal Sum of One 'million seven hundred seventy five thousand twenty seven Pounds 'Seventeen Shillings and Ten Pence Halfpenny, and for redeeming 'the said Annuity of Eighty eight thousand seven hundred fifty 'one Pounds Seven Shillings and Ten Pence Halfpenny, attend-'ing thereon, at the Feast of the Nativity of *Saint John Baptist* 'which shall be in the Year of our Lord One thousand seven hun-'dred and twenty five, and pursuant to the said Notice, the same 'is redeemable accordingly: And whereas the Governor and 'Company of the Bank of *England* have agreed and consented, 'That in case they may be permitted to enjoy the said Annuities 'of Eighty eight thousand seven hundred fifty one Pounds Seven 'Shillings and Ten Pence Halfpenny and One hundred thousand 'Pounds, until the Feast of the Nativity of *Saint John Baptist* 'which shall be in the Year of our Lord One thousand seven hun-'dred and twenty seven, That from and after the said Feast Day 'not only their said Annuity of Eighty eight thousand seven 'hundred fifty one Pounds Seven Shillings and Ten Pence Half-'penny, but also their Annuity of One hundred thousand Pounds '*per Annum*, upon the respective Sums of One million seven 'hundred seventy five thousand twenty seven Pounds Seventeen 'Shillings and Ten Pence Halfpenny and Two Millions shall 'be actually reduced to Four Pounds *per Centum per Annum*, and 'be likewise from thenceforth redeemable by Parliament (*a*):' Now, we Your Majesty's most dutiful and loyal Subjects, the Commons of *Great Britain* in Parliament assembled, being desirous to have the publick Debts and Incumbrances lessened and discharged as fast as conveniently may be, with regard to Justice and the publick Faith, do humbly beseech Your Majesty that it may be enacted; and be it enacted by the King's most Excellent Majesty, by and with the Advice and Consent of the Lords Spiritual and Temporal, and Commons, in this present Parliament assembled, and by the Authority of the same, That from and after the Feast of the Nativity of *Saint John Baptist* which shall be in the Year of our Lord One thousand seven hundred and twenty seven, the said respective Annuities aforesaid shall cease and determine; and the said Governor and Company of the Bank of *England*, and their Successors (subject nevertheless to the Proviso and Power of Redemption hereafter in this Act contained in that Behalf, and none other) shall have, receive and enjoy, in lieu of the respective Annuities aforesaid, one Annuity or yearly Sum of Seventy one thousand and one Pounds Two Shillings and Three Pence Three Farthings, in respect of the said Principal Sum of One million seven hundred seventy five thousand and twenty seven Pounds Seventeen Shillings and Ten Pence Halfpenny, and one other Annuity or yearly Sum of Eighty thousand Pounds in respect of the said Principal Sum of Two Millions; which said several and respective annual or yearly Sums of Seventy one thousand and one Pounds Two Shillings and Three Pence Three Farthings and Eighty thousand Pounds, shall be and are hereby charged upon and shall be paid and payable, from time to time, out of all the Monies arisen or to arise at the said Receipt of the

Annuities to the Bank of 88,751 l. 7 s. 10 d. and 100,000 l. to be reduced to 71,001 l. 2 s. 3¾ d. and 80,000 l.

(*a*) [*See further*, 1 *G*. 2. *Stat*. 2. *c*. 8. § 22, 23. 2 *G*. 2. *c*. 3. § 15.]

the Exchequer, of or for the said particular Duties on Houses aforesaid, and of and for the Duties and Revenues called the Aggregate Fund, and every or any of them; and shall be paid and payable to the said Governor and Company of the Bank of *England* and their Successors for ever, from the said Feast of the Nativity of *Saint John Baptist* One thousand seven hundred and twenty seven, at the Four most usual Feasts or Days of Payment in the Year, by even and equal Portions; all which Payments shall also be made in such Manner and Form, and on such Conditions, and with such Preference as are in the said Act prescribed and directed, in relation to the said several Annuities of Eighty eight thousand seven hundred fifty one Pounds Seven Shillings and Ten Pence Halfpenny, and One hundred thousand Pounds *per Annum* respectively. Aggregate Fund.

II. Provided always, and it is hereby enacted, That upon Repayment by Parliament to the said Governor and Company of the Bank of *England*, and their Successors, of the said several and respective Principal Sums of One million seven hundred seventy five thousand twenty seven Pounds Seventeen Shillings and Ten Pence Halfpenny and Two Millions, without any Deduction, Discount or Abatement whatsoever to be made out of the same, or any Part thereof, and of all Arrears of the said respective Annuities of Seventy one thousand and one Pounds Two Shillings and Three Pence Three Farthings and Eighty thousand Pounds *per Annum* (if any such shall be then due); then, and not till then, the said several and respective Annuities of Seventy one thousand and one Pounds Two Shillings and Three Pence Three Farthings and Eighty thousand Pounds, or either of them, which shall be so redeemed, shall from thenceforth cease and determine (*a*); any former Act or Acts of Parliament, or any Provisoes, Matters or Things therein contained, or any other Matter or Thing whatsoever to the contrary notwithstanding. (*a*) [*Redeemed*, 2 *G*. 2. *c*. 3.] On Repayment, Annuities to cease.

'III. And in regard it is intended that the said Annuities may 'be satisfied by any Payments not being less than Five hundred 'thousand Pounds of lawful Money of *Great Britain* at a time, 'and that as the said Principal Money shall be paid off, the 'said Debt and Annuities shall proportionally sink and be abated;' Be it therefore provided and enacted, &c.

" In what Case Annuities to be abated. § 3. Annuities Personal " Estates. § 4. Powers of former Acts, &c. continued. § 5.

'VI. And whereas of late divers Frauds and Deceits have been 'put upon the said Governor and Company of the Bank of *England*, and other Persons, by the altering, forging and counter'feiting of the Bank Bills and Bank Notes of the said Governor 'and Company, and by the erasing and altering the said Bills and 'Notes, and the Endorsements thereupon, and by the tendring in 'Payment, uttering, vending, exchanging and bartering, of such 'altered, forged, counterfeited and erased Bills and Notes, and 'the Endorsements thereupon, to the Prejudice of publick Credit, 'and to the great Hurt and Diminution of Trade and Commerce:' For redressing whereof for the future, Be it enacted by the Authority aforesaid, That if any Person or Persons shall alter, forge or counterfeit any Bank Bill or Bank Note, made or given out for Forging, &c. Bank Bills or Notes.

for the Payment of any Sum of Money, by or for the ſaid Governor and Company, or any Bank Note of any Sort whatſoever, or ſhall eraſe or alter any ſuch Bill or Note, or any Endorſement thereupon, or ſhall tender in Payment, utter, vend, exchange or barter, any ſuch altered, forged or counterfeited Bill or Note, or any eraſed or altered Bill or Note, or the Endorſement thereupon, or demand to have the ſame exchanged for ready Money by the ſaid Governor and Company or their Succeſſors, or any other Perſon or Perſons (knowing ſuch Bill or Note, or the Endorſement thereupon, ſo tendred or demanded to be exchanged, vended or bartered, to be altered, forged, counterfeited or eraſed) and with Intention to defraud the ſaid Governor and Company, or their Succeſſors, or any other Perſon or Perſons, Body Politick or Corporate; then every ſuch Perſon or Perſons ſo offending (being thereof lawfully convicted) ſhall be and is hereby declared and adjudged a Felon, and ſhall ſuffer as in Caſes of Felony.

Felony.

6, 1727. Royal Bank of Scotland, *Copy of a Signature for a New Bank*, Edinburgh.

# COPY
## OF A
# SIGNATURE
## FOR A
# New Bank.

OUR SOVEREIGN LORD Conſidering, that by an Act of Parliament made and paſſed in the Fifth Year of his Majeſty's Reign, intituled, *An Act for ſettling certain yearly Funds, payable out of the Revenue of* Scotland, *to ſatisfy publick Debts in* Scotland, *and other Uſes mentioned in the Treaty of Union; and to diſcharge the Equivalents claimed on the Behalf of* Scotland, *in the Terms of the ſame Treaty; and for obviating all future Diſputes, Charges and Expences concerning thoſe Equivalents*, it is enacted, amongſt other things, That yearly and every Year, from the Feaſt of the Nativity of St. *John the Baptiſt* One thouſand ſeven hundred

A and

and nineteen, the full Sum of ten thousand Pounds of lawful Money of *Great Britain*, shall be a yearly Fund for the particular Purposes in that Act, expressed concerning the same, and shall continue and be payable for ever; subject nevertheless to Redemption by Parliament, according to a Proviso in the said Act contained in that Behalf: And that the said Annuity of ten thousand Pounds, during the Continuance thereof, shall be charged and chargeable upon, and be payable and paid out of the Monies arisen and to arise, from Time to Time, of or for any the Customs, Duties, Excises or Revenues, that are or shall be under the Management of the Commissioners of the Customs, and Commissioners of Excise in *Scotland*, or of any Commissioners, Farmers or Managers of those Revenues, or either of them for the Time being; with such Preference as in the said Act is mentioned: Which said Annuity is thereby enacted to be payable quarterly, in the Manner in the said Act mentioned, and to be free from all Taxes and Impositions whatsoever, laid or to be laid thereupon by Authority of Parliament. And it is thereby further enacted, That it should and might be lawful, to and for his Majesty, by Letters Patents under the Great Seal of *Great Britain*, to incorporate all and every the Proprietors of the Debts and Sums of Money, stated to amount to the principal Sum of two hundred and thirty thousand three hundred and eight Pounds, nine Shillings, and ten Pence, five Sixths of a Penny, due to the Creditors of the Publick in *Scotland*, on the twenty fourth Day of *June* One thousand seven hundred and fourteen; and eighteen thousand two hundred and forty one Pounds, ten Shillings, and ten Pence, two Thirds of a Penny, stated due to *William Paterson* Esquire, making together two hundred and forty eight thousand five hundred and fifty Pounds, and nine Pence half-penny, to be one Body politick, and corporate by such Name as his Majesty should think most proper; and that by such Name the said Corporation should have perpetual Succession, subject to such Redemption as in the said Act is appointed: With such Powers, to do and perform

perform all Matters appertaining to them, touching or concerning the ſaid Capital Sums, and the ſaid yearly Fund payable in reſpect thereof, as his Majeſty by the ſame Letters Patents ſhould think fit to grant. And it was thereby enacted, That the ſaid Capital Sum, amounting to Two hundred and forty eight thouſand, five hundred and fifty Pounds, and Nine Pence half-penny, ſhould be, and be deemed to be the Capital or Joint Stock of the ſaid Corporation; and that the Shares of the Members of and in the ſame, ſhould be from Time to Time aſſignable, transferable and diviſible, in ſuch Manner as his Majeſty by ſuch Letters Patents ſhould preſcribe and appoint, until the Redemption thereof; and that the ſame ſhould be deemed to be perſonal or moveable Eſtates, and ſhould go to Executors or Adminiſtrators, and ſhould not be liable to any Arreſtment or Attachment that ſhould be laid thereupon. And it is thereby enacted, That all and every the Members of the ſaid Corporation, ſhould have and be entitled to an Annuity or yearly Sum, in proportion to his or their Share in the ſaid Capital Sum and Stock, of Two hundred and forty eight thouſand, five hundred and fifty Pounds, and Nine Pence halfpenny; and the ſaid Annuity ſhould be paid in the Manner in the ſaid Act mentioned, and to and for no other Uſe, Intent or Purpoſe whatſoever. And it was further enacted, That above the ſaid Annuity of Ten thouſand Pounds *per annum*, there ſhould be paid to the ſaid Corporation and their Succeſſors, until the Redemption of ſuch annual Sum, the further annual Sum of Six hundred Pounds *per annum*, towards the neceſſary Charges of the Management thereof, as in and by the ſaid Act of Parliament, amongſt other Clauſes and Things therein contained, Relation being thereunto had, doth and may more fully and at large appear. *And conſidering* that his Majeſty, by his Letters Patents bearing date at *Weſtminſter* the twenty firſt Day of *November*, in the eleventh Year of his Reign, in purſuance of the ſaid Act of Parliament, and by virtue of his Prerogative Royal, and likewiſe of his ſpecial Grace, certain Knowledge, and

and mere Motion, did give, grant, make, ordain, declare, appoint and establish, That all and every Person or Persons, Natives and Foreigners, Bodies politick and corporate, who then were Proprietors of the Debts and Sums of Money so stated, to amount to Two hundred and forty eight thousand, five hundred and fifty Pounds, and Nine Pence half-penny; or who by any lawful Title, derived or to be derived, from, by or under the said Proprietors at any time thereafter, should have or be entitled to any Part, Share or Interest therein, should be and be called one Body politick and corporate of themselves, in Deed and Name, by the Name of the *Equivalent Company*; and that such Corporation, and their Successors, should have perpetual Succession, subject to such Redemption as is therein mentioned; and should and might have and use a common Seal, and should by that Name be capable to sue and be sued: And that the Sum of Two hundred and forty eight thousand, two hundred and fifty Pounds, and Nine Pence half-penny, should be accepted, deemed and esteemed the Capital or Joint Stock of the said Corporation; and all the Proprietors of such Stock should be Members of the said Corporation: And that the said Annuity of Ten thousand Pounds *per annum* should be paid to the said Company, or to their Cashier, to be divided and distributed to and amongst the several Proprietors, in proportion to their respective Shares in the said Capital or Joint Stock. *And His Majesty* did thereby further order and direct, limit and appoint, That the said Stock should be transferable and assignable; and all Assignments and Transfers of the said Capital Stock, or yearly Fund, or any Part thereof, should be in the Manner, and according to the Method thereby directed: And likewise appointed, That the said annual Sum of Six hundred Pounds, for Charges of Management, should be paid to the said Corporation, or such as they should authorise under their common Seal to receive the same, for the Uses of the said Corporation. And whereas many of the Proprietors of the said Stock resided in *England*, and others in *Scotland*, who might be desirous to have

have their Intereſt in the ſaid annual and Capital Sums paid or ſecured either in *London* or *Edinburgh*, according to the Place of their reſpective Reſidence; His Majeſty did ordain and appoint, that all and every Perſon and Perſons intereſted in the Debentures therein mentioned, ſhould and might at the Time of delivering up the ſaid Debentures to the ſaid Corporation, declare at which of the ſaid Places he or they would have his or their Share or Intereſt in the ſaid annual and Capital Sums paid and ſecured; and according to ſuch Declaration, each reſpective Proprietor ſhould have Credit in diſtinct Books, to be kept at *London* or *Edinburgh* for that Purpoſe, and receive their Shares and Proportions of the ſaid annual and Capital Sums, when redeemed at *London* or *Edinburgh*, according to their reſpective Credits in the ſaid ſeparate and diſtinct Books; and that diſtinct and ſeparate Books ſhould be kept at *London* and *Edinburgh*, for transferring the Shares, Credits and Intereſts of the reſpective Proprietors, according to their reſpective Intereſts therein, in ſuch Manner and Form as is therein directed and appointed. And that for the better Conduct and Management of this Affair at *Edinburgh*, there ſhould be for ever choſen until Redemption as aforeſaid, at leaſt two of the thirteen Directors to reſide and be at *Edinburgh*, who ſhould have the Cuſtody, Care and Management of the ſeveral and reſpective Books at *Edinburgh*, under ſuch Rules, Orders and Directions as they ſhould from Time to Time receive from the ſaid Court of Directors of the ſaid Corporation, provided always, that as often as any of the Share, or Shares, or Intereſt of any Perſon or Perſons who ſhould have Credit in the Books kept at *Edinburgh*, ſhould be purchaſed by any Perſon or Perſons reſiding at *London*, or the Share, or Shares, or Intereſt of any Perſon or Perſons who ſhould have Credit in the Books kept at *London*, ſhould be purchaſed by any Perſon or Perſons reſiding at *Edinburgh*, the ſame might be diſcharged in one Book, and new Credit taken in the other reſpectively, as the Perſon or Perſons entitled to the ſame ſhould deſire or require the ſame.

And

And His Majeſty did thereby for himſelf, his Heirs and Succeſſors, covenant, grant and agree, to and with the ſaid Corporation or Body politick, and their Succeſſors, That He, his Heirs and Succeſſors ſhould from Time to Time, and at all Times thereafter, upon the humble Suit and Requeſt of the ſaid Corporation or Body politick, and their Succeſſors, give and grant unto them all ſuch further and other Powers, Privileges and Authorities, Matters and Things for rendring more effectual their ſaid Grant, according to the true Intent and Meaning of the ſaid Act, and of the ſaid Grant, which he could or might lawfully grant ſubject to the Power of Redemption therein mentioned, as by the ſaid Grant, or Letters Patents paſſed under the Great Seal of *Great Britain*, Relation being thereunto had, doth and may more fully and at large appear: *And conſidering*, that the ſaid Corporation have by their moſt humble Application to His Majeſty, requeſted that he would be graciouſly pleaſed by Letters Patents under the Great Seal of *Scotland*, to enable ſuch of the Proprietors of the ſaid Corporation as ſhould ſubſcribe their Stock for that Purpoſe to have the Power of Banking in *Scotland* only, with Liberty to borrow and lend upon Security there, that the ſaid Corporation may be, for that Purpoſe empowered to take Subſcriptions at *Edinburgh* from their Members, for ſuch Share of the Stock as they ſhall encline to ſubject to ſuch Trade or Banking, under ſuch Regulations as they by By-laws ſhall appoint; and that ſuch ſubſcribed Stock only ſhall be affected by the Tranſactions relating to Banking, and ſhall after being ſo ſubſcribed, become transferable from the other Stock of the Company, and at *Edinburgh* only, and would erect ſuch Subſcribers into a Corporation for that Purpoſe, and that ſuch Power of Banking ſo eſtabliſhed, would manifeſtly tend to the great Benefit and Advantage of that Part of his Kingdom; and that His Majeſty being willing to give all proper Encouragements to ſuch an Undertaking; *therefore* His Majeſty, in Compliance with the ſaid Requeſt, and by Virtue of His Prerogative Royal, and of His

His especial Grace, certain Knowledge, and meer Motion, and for the Benefit of his Subjects in that Part of His united Kingdom, *Ordains* a Charter to be made and passed under the Seal appointed by the Treaty of Union to be kept in *Scotland* in Place of the Great Seal thereof, nominating, authorizing and appointing, as His Majesty by these Presents, nominates authorises and appoints *James Campbell*, *Paul Daranda*, *John Drummond*, *Edward Harrison*, *Daniel Hayes*, *Benjamin Longwet*, *John Merril*, *Bulstrode Peachy* Knight, *Christopher Jilson*, *Robert Williamson* Esquires Sir *Hugh Dalrymple* Baronet, Lord President of the Session, *Patrick Campbell* of *Monzie*, and *Patrick Crawford* Esquires, or any three of them, in such Way and Manner as they, or the Majority of them shall direct to take and receive at *Edinburgh*, all such voluntary Subscriptions as shall be made on or before the Twenty ninth Day of *September*, One thousand seven hundred and twenty seven, by any Person or Persons, Members or Proprietors of the said Equivalent Company, who have, or shall have Credit for Stock in the Books of the said Company at *Edinburgh* at the Time of such Subscription, of all or any of such Part or Share of the Stock of the said Equivalent Company, as he or they shall think proper, for, and towards raising a Fund for the more effectual carrying on the Trade and Business of Banking there, and the Uses herein aftermentioned; which said Subscriptions, the said Proprietors are hereby impowered to make, and the same shall be fairly entred in Books to be kept for that Purpose, and the present Stock of the said Equivalent Company so to be subscribed as aforesaid, shall from and after the Time of such Subscription be under the Order, Management and Direction of the Company hereby established. And His Majesty, by Virtue of His said Prerogative, and likeways of His especial Grace, certain Knowledge and meer Motion, hath given, granted, made, ordained, constituted, declared, appointed and established; and by these Presents, for himself, His Heirs and Successors, gives, grants, makes, ordains, constitutes, declares, appoints

appoints and eſtabliſhes, That all and every Perſon or Perſons, Natives and Forreigners, Bodies politick and corporate Proprietors of the ſaid Stock, who ſhall ſubſcribe any Share or Shares of the ſaid Stock, and who as Executors, Adminiſtrators, Succeſſors or Aſſignies, or by any other lawful Title, to be derived from, by or under the ſaid Subſcribers, at any Time or Times hereafter, ſhall have or be entitled to any Part, Share or Intereſt of, or in the ſaid Stock, ſo to be ſubſubſcribed as aforeſaid, ſhall be and be called one Body politick and corporate of themſelves, in Deed and Name, by the Name of, *The Royal Bank of SCOTLAND*; and that ſuch Corporation and their Succeſſors by the ſaid Name, ſhall have perpetual Succeſſion, and ſhall and may have, and uſe a common Seal, and that they and their Succeſſors by the ſame Name ſhall be able and capable in Law to ſue and implead, purſue and defend, be ſued and impleaded, purſued and impleaded, purſued and defended, anſwer and be anſwered, in all or any of His Majeſty's Courts within *Scotland*; and that they and their Succeſſors, by the Name aforeſaid, ſhall and may be able and capable in Law to have, purchaſe, receive, poſſeſs, enjoy and retain to them and their Succeſſors, Lands, Rents, Tenements, and Hereditaments of whatever Kind, Nature or Quality ſoever in *Scotland* only: And alſo to ſell, grant, demiſe, analzie or diſpone the ſame. And His Majeſty doth hereby for himſelf, His Heirs and Succeſſors, grant unto the ſaid Company of the Royal Bank of *Scotland* and their Succeſſors for ever, full Power and Liberty to exerciſe the Rights and Powers of Banking in that Part of his united Kingdom called *Scotland* only, and in particular to lend to any Perſon or Perſons, Bodies politick or corporate, ſuch Sum and Sums of Money as they ſhall think fit at any Intereſt not exceeding lawful Intereſt, on real or perſonal Security, and particularly on Pledges of any Kind whatſoever of any Goods, Wares, Merchandizes or other Effects whatſoever, in ſuch Way or Manner as to the ſaid Company ſhall ſeem proper and convenient, and that the ſaid Com-

Company may keep the Money or Cash of any Person or Persons, Bodies politick and corporate whatsoever, and may borrow, owe, or take up in *Scotland* on their Bills or Notes, payable on Demand, to be signed in such Manner, and by such Persons as the Court of Directors herein after mentioned shall direct and appoint, or in such other Manner as the said Court of Directors shall think fit, any Sum or Sums of Money whatsoever. And His Majesty doth hereby declare, direct and appoint, that the said Company shall not at any Time or Times deal or trade, or permit or suffer any Person or Persons whatsoever, either in Trust, or for the Benefit of the same, to deal or trade with any of the Stock, Money or Effects of, or any Ways belonging to the said Corporation, in the buying or selling of any Goods, Wares or Merchandizes whatsoever; provided that nothing herein contained, shall any Ways be construed to extend to hinder the said Corporation from dealing in Bills of Exchange, or in buying or selling Bullion, Gold or Silver in *Scotland* only, or extend to hinder the said Corporation from selling any Goods, Wares, Merchandizes, or Effects whatsoever, which shall really and *bona fide* be pledged, left or depositated with the said Corporation for Money lent and advanced thereon, and which shall not be redeemed at the Time agreed on, or from selling such Lands, Rents, Tenements, or Hereditaments as they shall purchase in Virtue of the Power aforesaid, or from selling such Goods as shall, or may be the Produce of the Lands purchased by the said Corporation, and for the better Accomplishment of the Ends and Intentions proposed by erecting the said Corporation, and for making and establishing a continual Succession of fit Persons to be Managers and Directors of the said Corporation, *His Majesty* doth by these Presents, for Himself, His Heirs and Successors, grant unto the said Royal Bank of *Scotland*, and to their Successors; and doth hereby Ordain and appoint, That there shall be from Time to Time a Governor, Deputy-Governor, Nine ordinary Directors, and Nine extraordinary Directors, to be chosen out of of the Members of the ſaid Company; which ſaid Governor, Deputy-Governor, and Nine ordinary Directors, or any five or more of them, ſhall be, and be called a Court of Directors, for ordering, managing and directing all the Affairs of the ſaid Corporation in Manner by theſe Preſents mentioned: And that Our Right Truſty, and Right beloved Couſin and Counſellor, *Archbald* Earl of *Iſlay*, ſhall be the preſent and firſt Governor, and Sir *Hugh Dalrymple*, Lord Preſident of Our Seſſion, the preſent and firſt Deputy-Governor; And *Andrew Fletcher* Eſquire, one of the Senators of the College of Juſtice, *George Drummond* Eſquire, Lord Provoſt of *Edinburgh*, *Patrick Campbell* of *Munzie* Eſquire, *Richard Dodſwell* Eſquire, *John Philip* Eſquire, *James Paterſon* Eſquire, one of the Commiſſaries of *Edinburgh*, *Hugh Somervell* Writer to the Signet Eſquire, *Patrick Crawford Senior* Eſquire, and *George Irvine* of *Newton* Eſquire, the preſent and firſt Nine ordinary Directors; and *Matthew Lant*, Chief Baron of Our Court of Exchequer in *Scotland*, *James Erskine* Eſquire, one of the Senators of the College of Juſtice, Sir *John Clark*, one of the Barons of Our ſaid Court of Exchequer, *Hugh Dalrymple* Eſquire, One of the Senators of the College of Juſtice, *George Baillie* of *Jerviſwood* Eſquire, *Charles Cathcart* Eſquire, Our Receiver-General for *Scotland*, *George Roſs* Eſquire, one of Our Commiſſioners of Exciſe in *Scotland*, *Charles Erskine*, Our Solicitor-General for *Scotland*, and *James Nimmo* Eſquire, Caſhier to Our Commiſſioners of Exciſe in *Scotland*, the preſent and firſt Nine extraordinary Directors, and ſhall continue in their reſpective Offices, until the Twenty fourth Day of *December*, which ſhall be in the Year One thouſand ſeven hundred and twenty eight, and till others ſhall be duly choſen into their reſpective Offices, and ſworn into the ſame, unleſs they or any of them ſhall ſooner die, or be removed, as is herein after mentioned: And His Majeſty doth hereby for Himſelf, His Heirs and Succeſſors, give and Grant unto the ſaid Incorporation hereby eſtabliſhed, and their Succeſſors; and he doth hereby will and appoint, that it ſhall and may

may be lawful to, and for all and every the Members of the ſaid Incorporation, or Body politick, hereby eſtabliſhed from Time to Time, to aſſemble and meet together at any convenient Place or Places at *Edinburgh*, for the Choice of their Governor, Deputy-Governor and Directors, and for making of By-Laws, Ordinances, Rules, Orders and Directions for the Government of the ſaid Corporation, publick Notice thereof being firſt given in the *Edinburgh Courant*, and in Writing to be affixed on the Market-croſs of *Edinburgh*, Thirty Days at leaſt before the Time appointed for ſuch Meeting; and that all the Members of the ſaid Corporation, hereby eſtabliſhed, or ſo many of them as ſhall be aſſembled, ſhall be, and be called a General Court of the ſaid Corporation; which Court ſhall meet and aſſemble at ſuch Time, and in ſuch Manner as are herein after directed. *And His Majeſty* doth hereby direct, That there ſhall be held four general Courts of the Proprietors of the ſaid Company in every Year, on the Days, and at the Times following; that is to ſay, on the laſt *Tueſday* of the Month of *November*, on the firſt *Tueſday* of the Month of *March*, on the firſt *Tueſday* in the Month of *June*, and the firſt *Tueſday* in the Month of *September* every Year, and that all ſucceeding Governors, Deputy-Governors, and Directors of the ſaid Corporation, ſhall from and after the ſaid Twenty fourth Day of *December* One thouſand ſeven hundred and twenty eight, be every Year choſen for ever out of the Members of the ſaid Corporation, the ſaid Governor then having in his own Right Two thouſand Pounds or more of the capital Stock of the ſaid Company; the ſaid Deputy-Governor then having in his own Right Fifteen hundred Pounds or more of the capital Stock of the ſaid Company; the ſaid Nine ordinary Directors then having each of them reſpectively, One thouſand Pounds or more of the capital Stock of the ſaid Company, and the ſaid Nine extraordinary Directors then having each of them reſpectively Five hundred Pounds or more of the capital Stock of the ſaid Company, on the firſt *Tueſday* in

*March*

*March* every Year, by the Majority of Votes of all and every the Members of the said Corporation present at such general Court. *Provided*, That no Person shall be capable to vote in such or any other general Court, who shall not at the Time of such Voting appear to have Three hundred Pounds or more of the capital Stock of the said Corporation, in his, her, or their own Name or Names, and that every Member shall have one Vote for Three hundred Pounds; two Votes for Six hundred Pounds; three for Twelve hundred Pounds, and four for Two thousand Pounds of such capital Stock as he, she, or they shall have in the said Book or Books in his, her, or their own Name or Names; but no Person shall have above Four Votes; for, or in Respect of any Sum whatsoever, as he, she, or they shall have as aforesaid; and in case of the Absence of any of the said Proprietors, it shall and may be lawful for every such Proprietor being absent by Writing under his Hand, attested by two or more credible Witnesses, to authorise and appoint any one of the Members of the said Corporation, having Three hundred Pounds Stock at the least in his Name, in the Book, or Books of the said Corporation, to be his Proxie, and give a Vote or Votes for him; and in his Name, at any such General Court and Courts in the Election of Governor, Deputy-Governor and Directors. And His Majesty doth hereby further direct, order and appoint, that every Person claiming a Right to vote in any general Court or Courts of the said Company, shall, if desired and required by any other of the Propritors duly qualified to vote at such general Court, be obliged, and is hereby directed to take the corporeal Oath following, *viz. I* A. B. *do swear, That the Sum of*

*of the capital Stock of the Body politick, called*, The Royal Bank of *Scotland, doth at this Time belong to me in my own Right, and not in Trust for any Person or Persons whatsoever.* Which said Oath, shall and may be administred by the Governor or Deputy-Governor of the said Company for the Time being, or in Absence of the said Governor and Deputyputy Governor, then by any two of the Directors then present; and they are hereby respectively authorised to administer such Oath to all and every Person, and Persons, claiming a Right to vote in such general Courts, from Time to Time, accordingly upon such Desire and request as aforesaid; and that no Person refusing to take such Oath, after being desired as aforesaid, shall be capable to vote at such general Courts of the said Company. *Provided* always, That all and every the Proprietors of the said Company, who shall at any Time or Times, authorise any other Proprietor, to vote as a Proxie for him in such general Courts as aforesaid, shall make Oath before one of His Majesty's Justices of the Peace, or the chief Magistrate of any City or Burgh where such Person resides, that the Sum of

of the capital Stock of the Body politick, called, *The Royal Bank of Scotland*, doth at the Time of his signing such Authority, belong to him in his own Right, and not in Trust for any Person or Persons whatsoever. Which said Affidavit shall be produced by every Person claiming a Right to vote by Proxy as aforesaid. And no Person or Persons shall be allowed to vote as a Proxy as aforesaid, unless they not only produce the Authority impowering him to vote as Proxy as aforesaid, but also such Affidavit so sworn by the Person authorising him to vote as his Proxy as aforesaid. And His Majesty doth hereby further direct and appoint, That all succeeding Governors, Deputy-Governors and Directors so chosen as aforesaid, shall severally and respectively continue their respective Offices, to which they shall be severally elected for one Year, and till others shall be duly chosen and sworn into their Places respectively. Provided nevertheless, That in case of Death, Avoidance or Removal of the said Governor, Deputy-Governor, or any of the said Directors for the Time being, the Survivers of them, or the Majority of those remaining in their Offices, shall and may at any Time, upon such Notice given as aforesaid, assemble together the Members of the said Corporation

tion at *Edinburgh*, in order to elect other Persons by Members qualified to vote in Manner as aforesaid, in the Room of those dead, removed, or whose Places shall become void. *Provided also*, That no Person shall be capable of being chosen Governor, Deputy-governor or Director of the said Corporation, who shall not at the Time of such Choice be a natural born Subject of *Great Britain*, or naturalized; and such Governor shall then also have in his own Name, and for his own Use, Two thousand Pounds or more of the said Capital Stock; and such Deputy-governor shall also have in his own Name, and for his own Use, One thousand five hundred Pounds or more of the said Capital Stock; and such Ordinary Directors having each of them respectively in their own Names, and for their own Use, One thousand Pounds or more of the said Capital Stock; and such Extraordinary Directors having each of them respectively, and in their own Names, and for their own Use, Five hundred Pounds or more of the said Capital Stock: And that the said Governor, Deputy-governor or Directors, shall not continue in his or their respective Offices longer than the Continuance of such their respective Interests and Stocks, in their own Names and Rights, and to their own Uses respectively, but upon parting with, or reducing his or their respective Share or Interest in the said Capital Stock, to any lesser Sum than as aforesaid, the said respective Offices, or Places of such Governor, Deputy-governor or Director so parting with, or reducing or diminishing their said Interests as aforesaid, shall cease, determine and become vacant, and others may be chosen in their Rooms by a general Court of the said Corporation as aforesaid. *Provided also*, And His Majesty doth by these Presents for himself, his Heirs and Successors, will, ordain and appoint, That none of the said Persons hereby mentioned to be the first Governor, Deputy-governor and Directors of the said Corporation, or any other Person or Persons hereafter to be chosen to the Office or Trust of a Governor, Deputy-Governor or Director of the said Corporation, shall be capable to execute or act in the

the ſaid Office and Truſt of a Governor, Deputy or Director at any Time or Times hereafter, until he or they ſhall reſpectively take the Corporeal Oath following, *viz. I* A. B. *Do ſwear that the Sum of* *of the Capital Stock of the Body politick, call'd* The Royal Bank of Scotland, *whereof I am elected or appointed to be a* *doth at this Time belong to me in my own Right, and not in Truſt for any Perſon or Perſons whatſoever.* And likewiſe another Oath in the Form, and to the Effect following, *I* A. B. *Do ſwear that in the Office of* *of the Royal Bank of* Scotland, *I will be indifferent and equal to all manner of Perſons, and I will give my beſt Advice and Aſſiſtance for the Support and good Government of the ſaid Corporation; and in the Execution of the ſaid Office of* *I will faithfully and honeſtly demean my ſelf according to the beſt of my Skill and Underſtanding. So help me, GOD.* Which ſaid Oaths, to the ſaid preſent and future Governor, Deputy-governor and Directors, ſhall and may be adminiſtred by the Lord Chief Baron, or any of the Barons of the Court of Exchequer in *Scotland*, of his Majeſty, his Heirs and Succeſſors for the Time being, or by any two of the Directors who ſhall have taken the Oaths in Manner aforeſaid; and they are hereby reſpectively authorized to adminiſter the ſaid Oaths to all and every ſuch Governor, Deputy-governor, Director and Directors from Time to Time accordingly. *And furthermore,* His Majeſty's Will and Pleaſure is, and he doth hereby for himſelf, his Heirs and Succeſſors, ordain and appoint, That the ſaid Governor, Deputy-governor and Court of Directors, or any two of them, ſhall have Power and Authority to adminiſter an Oath to the Caſhier, and all other the inferior Agents or Servants, that ſhall be employed in the Service of the ſaid Company, for the faithful and due Execution of the ſeveral Places and Truſts in them repoſed: And it is hereby further provided and declared, that no Perſon nominated, or that ſhall hereafter be nominated or elected to the Office of Governor, De-

Deputy-governor or Director, or into the Office of Cashier, or into any other inferior Office in the Service of the said Company, shall be capable to sit, vote or act, or to exercise and discharge any such Office, until he shall first have produced before the Lord Chief Baron, or any other of the Barons of the Court of Exchequer in *Scotland*, or before the Court of Directors of the said Company, Certificates from the proper Offices, of his having taken and subscribed the several Oaths that now are, or by any subsequent Law shall be directed to be taken by all Persons bearing and holding any Office, Civil or Military under his Majesty, his Heirs and Successors: And it is hereby further provided and declared, that in Case any Person hereby nominated, or hereafter to be elected a Governor, a Deputy-governor or Director as aforesaid, shall for the Space of forty Days after such Nomination or Election, if in *Scotland*, or for the Space of forty Days after they come into *Scotland*, neglect or refuse to take the said Oaths hereby appointed to be by him taken as aforesaid, or shall refuse or neglect to take upon him his Office, that then, and in every such Case, the Office or Place of every such Person so neglecting or refusing, shall become vacant, and others may be chosen in their Places by a general Court of the said Corporation as aforesaid. And His Majesty doth by these Presents, will, direct and appoint, That the said Governor, Deputy governor and Court of Directors for the Time being, or the major Part of them which shall be present at any Court of Directors for the Time being, may as they shall see Occasion, upon thirty Days Notice to be given as aforesaid, summon and call a general Court of the said Company; and likewise shall from Time to Time, upon Demand to be made by any Nine or more of the said Members, having each One thousand Pounds or more Interest or Share in the said Capital Stock, within thirty Days after such Demand, summon and call such a general Court, to be held at *Edinburgh*, of the Members of the said Corporation, qualified as aforesaid; and in default of the said Governor, Deputy-Governor, and Court of of Directors, or the major Part of them which shall be present at any such Court for the Time being, to summon and call such Court, it shall and may be lawful, to and for the said Nine or more Members, having each one thousand Pounds Stock, as aforesaid, or more, upon thirty Days Notice, to be given in the *Edinburgh* Courant, and in Writing to be affixed upon the Market-cross of *Edinburgh*, to summon and hold a general Court, and there to dispatch any Business relating to the Government or Affairs of the said Corporation, and to remove or displace the said Governor, Deputy-Governor, and any of the said Directors, for any Misdemeanour, or Abuse of his or their Offices; and elect and chuse another or others in his or their Rooms, in the same Manner as the said Election on the first *Tuesday* in *March* yearly, as are herein before directed to be made: And in every Case where the Governor, Deputy-Governor, or any Director or Directors, shall happen to die or be removed, or whose Office shall otherwise become void before the Expiration of the Time for which he shall have been elected, the major Part of the Members of the said Corporation, to be assembled in a general Court at *Edinburgh*, being qualified as aforesaid, shall and may elect and chuse any other Member or Members of the said Corporation, qualified for a Governor, Deputy-Governor or Directors, as aforesaid, into the Office of such Governor, Deputy-Governor, Director or Directors, that shall so die or be removed, or whose Office shall so become void; which Person so to be chosen, shall continue in the said Office or Offices, until the next usual Time hereby appointed for Election, and till others shall be duly chosen and sworn. And for the better managing and ordering the Affairs of the said Corporation, His Majesty doth by these Presents, for Himself, his Heirs and Successors, grant unto the said Body politick and their Successors, for ever; and he doth by these Presents will and appoint, That the said Governor, Deputy-Governor, and ordinary Directors for the Time being, or any five or more of them, shall and may from Time to Time,

and

and at all Times, affemble and meet together, at any Place or Places in *Edinburgh*, for the Direction and Management of the Affairs of the faid Corporation, and then and there to hold Courts for the Purpofes aforefaid, and fummon general Courts to meet as aforefaid, as they fhall fee Caufe. And the faid Governor, Deputy-Governor, and Directors, or the Majority of them fo affembled, fhall and may act according to fuch By-laws, Conftitutions, Orders, Rules and Directions, as fhall from Time to Time be lawfully made and given unto them by the General Court of the faid Corporation, in purfuance of this His Majefty's Charter: And in all Cafes where fuch By-laws, Conftitutions, Orders, Rules or Directions, by or from the General Court, fhall be wanting; the faid Governor, Deputy-Governor, or Directors, or major Part of them fo affembled, fhall and may direct and manage all the Affairs and Bufinefs of the faid Corporation; and fhall and may appoint a Cafhier or Secretary, and all other Agents and Servants, which fhall from Time to Time be neceffary to be employed in the Affairs and Bufinefs of the faid Corporation; and allow and pay reafonable Salaries and Allowances to the faid Agents or Servants refpectively, and them or any of them from Time to Time remove or difplace, as they fhall fee Caufe; and generally to act and do, in all Matters and Things whatfoever, which they fhall judge neceffary, and may lawfully be done, for the well ordering and managing the faid Corporation, and the Affairs thereof; and do enjoy, perform and execute, all the Powers, Authorities, Privileges, Acts, Matters and Things, in relation to the faid Corporation, as fully, to all Intents and Purpofes, as if the fame were done by the faid Body politick hereby eftablifhed, or by a General Court of the fame, according to the true Intent and Meaning of thefe Prefents. *Provided always*, That the Governor, Deputy Governor, nor any of the Directors of the faid Company, either Ordinary or Extraordinary, fhall be capable to be named or chofen into the Office of Cafhier, or any other the Offices of the faid Company. *And* for the better carrying on the Affairs of of the ſaid Company, and the more regular keeping juſt and exact Accounts thereof, His Majeſty doth by theſe Preſents will, direct and appoint, That five at leaſt of the Extraordinary Directors, and four at leaſt of the Ordinary Directors, ſhall and may, and they are hereby directed and required, to meet together, at ſuch Time and Times as ſhall by the ſaid Company, in their General Courts, by their By-laws to be made, purſuant to the Powers hereby given, be directed, limited and appointed; and inſpect, ſtate and audit the Accounts of the ſaid Company; and the ſaid Accounts, when ſo ſtated, ſhall be ſigned and approved of by the ſaid Extraordinary and Ordinary Directors: Provided always, That it ſhall and may be lawful, to and for the ſaid Company, in their General Courts from Time to Time, by their By-laws to be by them made purſuant, to the Powers to them hereby given, to alter, limit and appoint the Powers and Authorities of the Extraordinary Directors; and that they ſhall not have or enjoy any other Powers, except ſuch as ſhall be given to them, and allowed of by the ſaid General Courts, as aforeſaid. And His Majeſty doth, for Himſelf, his Heirs and Succeſſors, give full Power to all and every the ſaid Members, qualified as aforeſaid, in their General Courts or Aſſemblies, by Majority of their Votes, as aforeſaid, to make and conſtitute ſuch By-laws and Ordinances, for, and relating to the Affairs and Government of the ſaid Corporation, and impoſing Mulcts and Amerciaments upon Offenders againſt the ſame, as to them ſhall ſeem meet; ſo that ſuch By-laws be not contrary to the Intent and Meaning of theſe Preſents, or repugnant to the Laws of His Majeſty's Realm; all which Mulcts and Amerciaments ſhall and may be received and recovered to the only Uſe and Behoof of the ſaid Corporation and their Succeſſors, without any Account, or other Matter or Thing to be therefore rendred to His Majeſty, his Heirs and Succeſſors. *And in caſe* any Perſon or Perſons ſhall refuſe or neglect to pay ſuch Mulcts and Amerciaments, ſo impoſed upon him, her or them, upon the Time limited for that Purpoſe, it ſhall and may

may be lawful to the said Court of Directors, and they are hereby authorised to retain the same, out of all or any Dividend or Dividends, that shall become payable to such Person or Persons, so refusing or neglecting as aforesaid. And His Majesty doth hereby further, for Himself, his Heirs and Successors, give full Power to all and every the said Members, qualified as aforesaid, in their General Courts or Assemblies from Time to Time, by Majority of Votes as aforesaid, to make such Calls upon all and every the Proprietors of the capital Stock of the said Corporation hereby erected, as to the Majority of such Members, so qualified as aforesaid, in their General Courts shall seem proper; so as such Calls, so to be made, do not in the whole exceed Fifty Pounds upon every Hundred Pounds of the subscribed Capital of the said Stock, and so as not above Ten Pounds upon every Hundred Pounds of the said subscribed Capital of the said Stock be called at one Time; and that such Calls, so to be made as aforesaid, shall be paid in by the respective Proprietors, within the Time or Times so to be limited by the Order of such General Court for that Purpose, as aforesaid. And that no Person or Persons, who shall refuse or neglect to pay in such Calls at the Time or Times for that Purpose limited, shall be allowed to transfer or part with any Share they respectively have in the said Stock, nor receive any Dividends or Profits on account thereof, till such Calls shall be by them respectively paid: And that all and every Person or Persons, refusing or neglecting to pay the said Call or Calls, shall from and after the respective Times such Calls ought to have been paid, be charged and chargeable with Interest for the said Calls, till the same are respectively paid: And that it shall and may be lawful, to and for the said Governor, Deputy-Governor, and Court of Directors, or the Maiority of them so present, to detain all such Dividends or Profits, as such Person or Persons, so neglecting or refusing to pay their Calls, would otherwise be entitled to, and apply the same for and towards Payment of the said Calls, which should have been respectively paid

paid by them, with Intereſt from ſuch Times as the ſame ought reſpectively to have been paid. *Provided always*, and for aſcertaining and limiting in what Manner, and under what Rules the ſaid capital Stock ſhall and may be aſſignable and aſſigned, transferable and transferred, by ſuch Perſon or Perſons as ſhall from Time to Time have any Intereſt or Share in the ſame, His Majeſty doth hereby direct and appoint, That there ſhall be forthwith provided, and conſtantly kept in the publick Office or Offices of the ſaid Corporation at *Edinburgh*, a Book or Books, wherein all Aſſignments or Transfers ſhall be entred. *And* His Majeſty doth hereby, for Himſelf, his Heirs and Succeſſors, by virtue of his Prerogative Royal, order, direct, limit and appoint, That the Method and Manner of making all Aſſignments and Transfers of the ſaid capital Stock, or any Part thereof, ſhall be by an Entry in ſuch Book or Books, to be kept as aforeſaid, ſigned by the Parties aſſigning or transferring in the Words, or to the Effect following, *viz. I* A. B. *This Day of in the Year of our Lord do aſſign and transfer being all my Intereſt or Share, or (as the Caſe may be) Part of my Intereſt or Share, in the Capital Stock or Fund of the Royal Bank of* Scotland, *and all Benefit ariſing thereby, unto* C. D. *his Executors, Adminiſtrators and Aſſignies, witneſs my Hand,* A. B. Or in caſe the Party aſſigning be not perſonally preſent, then by an Entry in the Book or Books, ſigned by ſome Perſon thereunto lawfully authorized by a Letter of Attorney or Factory under Hand and Seal, atteſted by two or more Witneſſes, in the Words, or to the Effect following, *viz. I* A. B. *This Day of in the Year of our Lord by virtue of a Letter of Attorney or Authority under the Hand and Seal of dated the Day of in the ſaid Year do in the Name, and on the Behalf of the ſaid aſſign*

*assign and transfer*

*being all the Interest or Share, or (as the Case may be) Part of the Interest or Share of the said in the Capital Stock or Fund of the Royal Bank of* Scotland, *and all Benefit arising thereby, unto his Executors, Administrators and Assignies, witness my Hand.* Under which Transfer, the Person or Persons, Bodies politick or corporate, to whom such Assignment or Transfer shall be made, or some other Person by him or them lawfully authorized thereunto, shall sign his or their Name or Names, attesting that he or they do freely and voluntarly accept of the same; and that the Entry signed as aforesaid, and no other Way or Method shall be the Manner and Method used in the passing, assigning and transferring the Interest or Share in the said Capital Stock or Fund, and every such Transfer and Assignment shall be good and valid, and convey the Estate and Interest of the Party assigning of, and in the Stock or Fund so assigned, to the Assignee thereof: And for the better preventing any Frauds in making of Transfers by Letters of Attorney or Factory, His Majesty doth hereby will and and direct, that every such Letter of Attorney or Factory so to be given as aforesaid, shall contain the Names and Designations of the Writers thereof, and the Witnesses to the Execution thereof; and the same shall be attested to have been duly executed by the Person giving such Letter of Attorney or Factory, either by a Notary-publick, or by a Justice of the Peace, or the Minister of the Parish where the Person giving such Letter of Attorney or Factory resides. Provided always, that any Person having any Share or Interest in the said Capital Stock or Fund, may dispose and devise the same by his or her last Will and Testament; but however, that the Executor or Administrator shall not transfer the same, or be entitled to receive any Dividend, until an Extract of the Testament be delivered to the Company, and until an Entry or Memorandum of so much of the said Will, as relates to the said Stock

Stock or Fund, be made in the Book or Books to be kept by, or by Order of the said Corporation for that Purpose. Provided also, that the Shares or Interests of the several Proprietors in the said Company, are and shall be deemed and taken to be personal or moveable Estates, and upon Death, shall go to Executors or Administrators, and not be descendable to Heirs; and the same shall not be liable to any Arrestment or Attachment that shall be laid thereupon, any Law, Usage or Custom to the contrary notwithstanding. *Provided also*, and His Majesty doth hereby for Himself, His Heirs and Successors, will, direct and appoint, That in every Meeting of the said Governor, Deputy-Governor, and Court of Directors, the said Court to consist of the said Governor, Deputy-Governor, or five of the ordinary Directors at least; and in case the said Governor or Deputy-Governor be present, such Governor, or, in his Absence, such Deputy-Governor, to preside: And in case of the Absence of the Governor and Deputy-Governor, the major Part of the Directors then present, shall, and may choose and appoint one of the said Directors then present, to be President of that Court for the Time being, and shall from Time to Time, in the Absence of the Governor and Deputy, appoint one of the said Directors present, to preside in every general Court of such Corporation; and in Default of such Appointment, the general Court when met, shall and may appoint a President of the same general Court; which President when nominated by the Court of Directors, or general Court for the Time being respectively, shall in all Cases of Equality have the casting Vote, but shall have no Vote, except in Cases of Equality of Votes. Provided also, That all Matters and Things which the Governor, Deputy-Governor, and Directors of the said Corparation, shall in Manner aforesaid order and direct to be done by Sub-committees, or other Persons appointed under them, shall and may, by virtue of such Orders be done by the said Sub-committees, and other Persons so appointed. And His Majesty doth likewise hereby for Himself

ſelf, His Heirs and Succeſſors, will, appoint and direct, that the Caſhier of the Corporation hereby erected, or any other Perſon by them lawfully authoriſed, ſhall and may from Time to Time receive from the ſaid Equivalent Company, or any Perſon by them lawfully authoriſed, the Share and Proportion of the ſaid annual Sum of Ten thouſand Pounds, payable by virtue of the ſaid Act of Parliament as aforeſaid, and Dividends in reſpect of ſuch of the Stock of the ſaid preſent equivalent Company, ſo to be ſubſcribed as aforeſaid, and that the ſame ſhall be paid to ſuch Perſon ſo impowered without any Fee or Reward whatſoever. And His Majeſty doth hereby further for Himſelf, His Heirs and Succeſſors, will, direct and appoint, that the ſaid general Courts of the ſaid Corporation hereby erected, ſhall, and are hereby required at two Times in every Year to make and declare ſuch Dividend as they ſhall think proper to be paid and payable to the reſpective Proprietors of the ſaid Stock, at ſuch two of the ſaid quarterly Courts hereby appointed and directed to be kept as they ſhall think proper. *Provided* always, That no Dividend ſhall be made to the Proprietors of the ſaid Stock of the Company hereby erected, but out of the Share and Intereſt of the yearly Annuity or Sum of Ten thouſand Pounds payable to them as aforeſaid, and out of the Profits ariſing and to ariſe, by borrowing and lending of Money, and dealing in the Trade and Buſineſs of Banking, as aforeſaid. *Provided* always, That it ſhall and may be lawful to and for the Company hereby erected in their general Courts, from Time to Time, and as they ſhall think proper, and for the Advantage of the ſaid Corporation, and the Proprietors thereof, to repay all or any Part of the ſaid Sum of Fifty Pounds *per Cent.* that ſhall at any Time have been called by them, upon the Stock of the ſaid Company. Provided always, That it ſhall and may be lawful to, and for the Proprietors of the ſaid Corporation hereby erected, or the Majority of them, in any general Court of the ſaid Company, to be held as aforeſaid, within the ſpace of two Years after the Date hereof, to allow the

Proprietors of all or any part of the Stock of the present Equivalent Company, who shall not have subscribed their said Stock on or before the said Twenty ninth of *September*, One thousand seven hundred and twenty seven, being the Term hereby limited for subscribing the same, to subscribe all or such further and other Part of the said Stock of the said Company into the Stock of the Corporation hereby erected, upon such Terms and Condition, and at such Times as the Majority of the Proprietors of the said first subscribed Stock in such general Courts shall limit, direct and appoint. And His Majesty doth hereby declare and direct, That such Stock of the present Equivalent Company, so to be subscribed in the Terms aforesaid, shall from and after such Subscription be under the Management, Care and Direction of the Corporation hereby erected from the Time of such Subscription, in the same Way and Manner as the Stock to be subscribed on or before the said Twenty ninth Day of *September* One thousand seven hundred and twenty seven, is hereby directed and appointed, and shall and may upon the Terms and Conditions so to be limited and appointed from the Time of such Subscription as aforesaid, enjoy and have all the same Privileges and Liberties, as the Proprietors of the first subscribed Stock shall have and enjoy. And His Majesty doth for Himself, His Heirs and Successors, grant and declare, that these his Letters Patents, shall be in and by all Things valid and effectual in the Law, according to the true Intent and Meaning of the same, and shall be taken, construed and adjudged in the most favourable and beneficial Sense, for the best Advantage of the said Corporation, notwithstanding any Misrecital, Defects, Uncertainty or Impefections in these His Majesty's Letters Patents. And His Majesty doth hereby for Himself, His Heirs and Successors, covenant, grant and agree to, and with the said Corporation or Body politick, and their Successors, that He, His Heirs and Successors, shall, and will from Time to Time, and at all Times hereafter, upon the humble Suit and Request of the said Corporati-

on,

on, or Body politick, and their Succeſſors, give and grant unto them all ſuch further and other Privileges, Authorities, Matters and Things for rendring more effectual this His Grant, according to the true Intent and Meaning of theſe Preſents, which he or they can or may lawfully grant, and as ſhall be reaſonably adviſed and deviſed by the Council learned of the ſaid Corporation or Body politick for the Time being, and ſhall be approved of by the Lord Advocate or Solicitor-General in *Scotland*, for His Majeſty, His Heirs and Succeſſors, on his or their Behalf. And His Majeſty doth further will and command, That this Charter do paſs the ſaid Great Seal *per ſaltum*, without paſſing any other Seal or Regiſter, for doing whereof this ſhall be, as well to the Director of Our Chancellary for writing the ſame as to the Keeper of the ſaid Seal, for cauſing the ſaid Seal to be appended thereto, a ſufficient Warrant. Given at Our Court at *St. James's* the Thirty first Day of *May* One thouſand ſeven hundred and twenty ſeven, in the thirteenth Year of Our Reign. By His Majeſty's command,

R. WALPOLE. WILL. YONGE. GEO. DODINTON.

*This paſſed the Great Seal upon the 8th* July 1727, *by a Warrant from the King.*

Part

# Part of a Clause in His Majesty's Patent for improving Fisheries and Manufactures in *Scotland*, No. 21.

AND We hereby Will and Ordain, That so soon as the said Sum of *L.* 14000, intended for the Improvement of coarse Wool, and the said Sum of *L.* 6000, part of the Arrears of the Annuity of *L.* 2000, shall be paid over to the said Receiver-General of the Crown-Rents and Casualities in *Scotland*, the saids Commissioners and Trustees, or their *Quorum* shall enter into Agreements with any Person or Persons, Bodies politick or corporate, other than the said Trustees, or any Person or Persons in Trust *for them, or either of them, for lending out to them upon sufficient Security the said Sum of L.* 14000 and *L.* 6000 at Interest as above-mentioned; and shall direct their Precepts under their Hands and Seals, to the said Receiver-general, to pay over the particular Sum or Sums of Money therein-mentioned, to such Person or Persons, Bodies politick or coporate, as the saids Commissioners and Trustees shall have agreed with, and to take from such Person or Persons, Bodies politick or coporate, such Security or Securities for Repayment thereof, with Interest to the said Receiver-General, and his Successors in Office for the Use of the Manufactures and Improvements in *Scotland*, as the said Precept shall direct; and upon Receipt of such Precept, the said Receiver-General is hereby authorised and required to pay over such Money, and to take Securities for Repayment thereof, with Interest in such Manner as he shall be therein directed, *&c.*

*The*

## *The Commissioners and Trustees in the said Letters Patents are,*

* 1 CHarles Cathcart Esquire, Master of Cathcart.
* 2 George Ross Esquire, Master of Ross.
* 3 Sir Hugh Dalrymple of Northberwick, Lord President of the Session.

| | |
|---|---|
| 4 Sir James Mackenzie of Royston,<br>* 5 Andrew Fletcher of Milton Esq;<br>* 6 Patrick Campbell of Munzie Esq; | Senators of the College of Justice. |

* 7 Sir John Clark of Pennycuik, one of the Barons of Exchequer.
8 Duncan Forbes Esquire, His Majesty's Advocate.
9 Charles Erskine Esquire, His Majesty's Sollicitor.
* 10 Mr. James Paterson of Kirktoun Advocate.
11 Thomas Hope of Rankiller Esquire.
12 Mungo Graham of Gorthie Esquire.
* 13 George Drummond Esquire Lord Provost of Edinburgh.

| | |
|---|---|
| 14 Archbald Macaulay<br>15 Robert Wightman,<br>16 Alexander Arbuthnot,<br>17 Gilbert Stewart,<br>18 Patrick Lindsay, | Merchants in Edinburgh. |

19 William Jamison Merchant in Leith.
20 James Fall Merchant in Dunbar.
* 21 George Irvine of Newton, Writer to the Signet.

☞ *Those marked *, are Directors of the Royal Bank.*

*To*

*To the KING's Most Excellent Majesty,*

# The humble PETITION of *DAVID* Earl of *Leven*, Governor, and Company of the *Bank* of *SCOTLAND*,

SHEWETH,

THAT the Bank of *Scotland* was erected by Act of Parliament in the Year 1695, for the common Benefit of that Part of your Majesty's united Kingdom; and it seems to have been intended that the same should continue for ever as the National Bank of *Scotland*, subject to the Directions given in that Act.

That since that Time the Company have executed their Trust with the strictest Regard to the Directions of the said Act, without attempting to interfere with the Rights of any other Society or private Person, to the general Satisfaction of all the Nation; and have on all Occasions that offered given Testimony of their Readiness to contribute towards the Service of the present happy Establishment to which they owe their first Erection.

That they have made the Bank as universally useful to the Country, as the State and Circumstances of this Part of your Majesty's united Kingdom will allow, by affording a suitable Credit.

That your Petitioners having been informed, that the Equivalent Society did apply to Your Majesty's Royal Father for a Charter, giving them Powers of Banking in *Scotland*; we addressed His Majesty by humble Petition and Memorial, to prevent the giving thereof, which were most graciously received; and

and we were in Hopes of a Hearing on the Merits of the Caufe.

But the Charter was figned by His Majefty among other Papers, immediately before His Majefty's going Abroad, and directed to pafs the Seal of *Scotland*, by which we were difappointed of a Hearing upon it.

That before the Charter paft the Seals, Your Majefty's Royal Father's Demife interveened; and of Courfe it muft ftop, unlefs Your Majefty's Royal Warrant be given for paffing thereof; which afford us this Opportunity of addreffing your Majefty againft it, for the Reafons contained in a humble Memorial hereunto annexed.

*YOUR Petitioners therefore humbly hope, That Your Majefty may be gracioufly pleafed to ftop the granting any Powers of Banking to the faid Equivalent Company, as tending to the Prejudice of Your Petitioners Old and Legal Eftablifhment, and the general Detriment of this Part of Your Majefty's united Kingdom.*

And Your Petitioners fhall ever pray.

MEMO-

# MEMORIAL

FOR

## *The Governor and Company of the Bank of* Scotland.

THE Bank of *Scotland* was erected by Act of Parliament *Anno* 1695, under the Name of THE GOVERNOR AND COMPANY OF THE BANK OF SCOTLAND, and appointed to have a GOVERNOR, DEPUTY-GOVERNOR, and twenty four DIRECTORS, annually to be elected and chosen for ever, and in all Time thereafter. Which Governor, Deputy-Governor and Directors, are required, at their Entry to their Office, to swear an Oath as in that Act contained; and several Privileges and Advantages are by it given them, for the better supporting and carrying on a Bank for the Benefit of that Part of the Kingdom.

That by the said Act, it is declared unlawful for any other Persons to set up a distinct Company of Bank within that Kingdom, for the Space of Twenty one Years: And tho' it was not thought proper to extend this general seclusive Privilege to any longer Term, at that Time, when it was uncertain, whether the Company would succeed in the Undertaking, or how they would manage their Trust; yet it seems plain, from their being erected in a perpetual Succession, under the Name aforesaid, from an Oath being imposed upon the Directors, which no other Authority than that of the Parliament could impose; and from the Methods appointed as to their suing and being sued at Law, which likewise required a Legislative Authority, that it was intended, in case the Uundertaking should succeed, they should continue THE NATIONAL BANK OF SCOT-

SCOTLAND; and that there was no Thought, any other Bank could be erected, but by the same Legislative Authority.

That the said Company have since that Time, executed their Trust with a very moderate Advantage to the Adventurers, and to the universal Satisfaction of that Part of the Nation. And as the Company was intended to be National, the Door hath been open to all Persons to become Adventurers, so far as the Extent of the Company's Stock goes: And accordingly, most of the Persons of best Account, and of the firmest Affection to the Revolution Interest, to which the Company owed its Being, have been Adventurers in this Society.

The Bank of *Scotland*, upon Advice that Application had been made to His late sacred Majesty by the Equivalent Company, for a new Charter, giving them Powers to carry on a Banking Trade in *Scotland*, in manifest Emulation of, and which must necessarily prejudge the said Bank, Did apply to His Majesty by humble Petition and Memorial, to prevent the granting of the said Charter; which were most graciously received, and those in the Bank were in Hopes of a Hearing on the Merits of the Cause.

But the Charter was signed by His Majesty amongst other Papers, immediately before His Majesty's going abroad; and being directed to pass the Seal of *Scotland*, those of the Bank were disappointed of a Hearing upon it.

That before the Charter pass'd the Seal, His Royal Majesty's Demise interveened; and of Course it must stop, unless His present Sacred Majesty grant Warrant for passing thereof.

'Tis most humbly submitted to His Majesty's Royal Wisdom, since the said Equivalent Company have, in Pursuance of an Act of Parliament made in their Behalf, already obtained a Charter, with such Powers as the Parliament thought proper to give them, if there be any sufficient Reason to extend these Powers to that of Banking, beyond the Intention of the Act of Parliament, for the Advantage of a few private Men, without any publick Benefit, to the Prejudice of the National Bank of *Scotland*,

*Scotland*, already by Law eſtabliſhed; while nothing in the leaſt blameable can, with Truth or Juſtice, be laid to the Charge of that National Company.

That tho' the Memorialiſts will not preſume to judge, how far Powers of Banking, by the Laws and Conſtitution of *Scotland*, might have been granted, notwithſtanding the Eſtabliſhment of the ſaid Bank; yet they humbly ſuggeſt, that no ſuch Powers, nor Powers of the ſame Nature, have at any Time been granted in *Scotland*, otherwiſe than with Conſent of Parliament; much leſs to the Prejudice of a Parliamentary Company before eſtabliſhed.

That as the Bank of *Scotland* have executed their Truſt to the univerſal Benefit and Satisfaction of that Part of the Nation, ſo they have never been wanting to give their Aid for carrying on the publick Service, on every proper Occaſion; as particularly, by undertaking the Re-coinage in *Scotland* immediately after the Union, when the Privy Council were under no ſmall Difficulty how to get it effectuate: And as often as Invaſions have been attempted, or publick Diſturbances or Rebellions raiſed, have taken Care timeouſly to diſpoſe of what Money was in the Bank, in ſuch Manner, as ſecured it from the Power of the Enemy, and in the Hands of Friends to the Government.

That the Sphere of Action by way of Banking in *Scotland*, is ſo narrow, if not puſh'd beyond Bounds, to the Diſadvantage and Danger of that Part of the Nation, that there is no Foundation for the Actions and Support of two Banking Companies; and therefore, if two be erected, this muſt occaſion a continual Juſtling and Attempt to undermine one another, probably to the Ruin of both.

That without the Aſſiſtance of the Credit of the ſaid Bank in *Scotland* at preſent, 'tis well known, that Perſons of the beſt Condition, by Reaſon of the Scarcity of Specie, could not have Money wherewith to go to Market, or Supply their Family

Exi-

Exigencies, far lefs to anfwer thefe neceffary Purpofes, and at the fame Time, to pay their publick Taxes.

That the doing any Thing, efpecially at this Time, to the Prejudice of the Bank, will undoubtedly be attended with the worft Confequences to that Part of the Nation, as it muft occafion a general Convulfion in Matter of Credit, if not put an entire ftop to it; for that the Bank of Neceffity muft ftop further Loans, and muft, to prevent the Attempts of a new created Rival Company, make a general Demand upon their Debitors and Proprietors; and of Confequence, thefe make the like Demand upon the private Perfons adebted to them: And as a great Part of *Scotland* are engaged with the Bank, it is obvious what Confufion this muft produce, and a general Difquiet. And therefore it is humbly fubmitted, if there would not be more Danger than Advantage to the Nation, by gratifying the Equivalent Company in their prefent Demand.

That the granting the Power of Banking to the Equivalent Company, will be highly prejudicial to *Scotland*, and muft be very ungrateful to that Part of the Nation, being that 'tis well known, Two hundred and ten Shares of the Equivalent Company's Stock is in the Hands of other than *Scotfmen*, and only about Thirty eight in the Hands of Perfons refiding in *Scotland*; and fo in Confequence, Two hundred and ten Shares, for Thirty eight of their Profits, by Banking muft be drawn out of *Scotland*; which muft in fo far drain it of Cafh, and muft contribute to difable the Inhabitants there from paying the Taxes, as well as maintaining their private Credit.

The Bank of *Scotland* have been informed, that the Equivalent Company have endeavoured to afperfe their Society, as Perfons difaffected to the prefent happy Eftablifhment. But as by the Nature of their Conftitution, 'tis in the Power of every Man to become Adventurer, and of every Adventurer who purchafes a fufficient Qualification, to be chofen into the Office of Governor, Deputy-Governor and Directors, as thefe Offices are annually filled by the Voice of the whole Adventurers; that Ca-

lumny

lumny is fully refuted by the repeted Proofs given by the Directors of the Bank, of their Readiness to serve and accommodate the Government, on every Occasion that has offered, ever since the first Erection of the Bank.

That the said Equivalent Company, or their Doers, have advanced some very groundless Complaints against the Bank, and Administration thereof, to make way for granting their new Charter with Banking Powers. But this being done at *London*, and in private; those of the Bank have had no Opportunity to vindicate themselves, and justify their Management; as they are very confident they can, if an Occasion is given to do it, and that it shall be thought needful.

The Memorialists would not have appeared against the giving of this Charter to the Equivalent Company, if they did not foresee the bad Consequences to this Country that will attend it, and that the Directors of the Bank would justly deserve Censure for their Silence, when these Consequences should happen, and that they had not in due Time given notice thereof.

Therefore they humbly hope, that no Power of Banking will be granted to the Equivalent Company, to the prejudice of the Bank of *Scotland* established by Act of Parliament, and to the Danger of the Credit of that Part of the Nation, which stands so much engaged with the present Bank, either in Way of Borrowing, or as Adventurers; especially since the granting such Power seems to be of no publick Utility, but is emulously grasped at by a very few of the Equivalent Proprietors who reside in *Scotland*, for their own private Profit, and very probably designed by some as a Subject for Stock-jobbing, the pernicious Consequences of which was some few Years ago very sensibly felt by the whole Nation.

# Observations

UPON THE

# Present State of our Gold and Silver Coins, 1730.

By the late JOHN CONDUITT, Esq.;
Member ſor Southampton, and Master oſ
His Majesty's Mint.

From an Original Manuscript,
Formerly in the Possession of the late
Dr. JONATHAN SWIFT.

---

*LONDON*,

Printed for *T. Becket*, Corner of the
Adelphi, in the Strand. MDCCLXXIV.

7, 1774. John Conduitt, *Observations upon the Present State of our Gold and Siver Coins*, London: Printed for T. Becket.

## OBSERVATIONS UPON THE PRESENT STATE OF OUR GOLD AND SILVER COINS.

WHEN we cannot pay in goods, what we owe abroad, on account of the balance of trade, or for the sale or interest of stocks belonging to foreigners, or for foreign national services, our debts must be paid in gold or silver, coined or uncoined; and when bullion is more scarce or more dear than *English* coin, *English* coin will be exported, either melted or in specie, in spite of any laws to the contrary. All that can be done in such cases is, to take care from time to time, that a pound weight of fine silver be worth as much fine gold in our monies, as it is in the good coins of the neighbouring nations, with whom we have the greatest dealings, that it may turn equally to the merchant's account to pay any balance he owes abroad, or to have any balance that is due to him, sent hither, either in gold or silver; for if gold be valued here higher than in other parts, and silver lower, any debts due to us from abroad, will be paid only in gold, and any debts we owe abroad, will be paid only in silver; and over and above the balance to be paid or received, it will be a profitable trade to import gold, which is over valued, and export silver, which is under valued. The value of gold and silver in respect of each other, has constantly varied in all nations, and must vary according to the plenty or scarcity of either. In *Europe*, for many years, 12 pounds weight of fine silver were equal to one pound weight of fine gold. By the discovery of the silver mines in America, silver fell gradually, from the proportion of 12 to 1, to 16 to 1. In *England*, by the high price of guineas, it has been at all rates, from 12 to above 21 to 1. By the discovery of the new gold mines in Brasil, and an increase of the demand for silver, gold has for some years been falling, and silver rising all over *Europe*. If the importation of gold should still increase, and that of silver decrease, or a greater demand arise for it, a pound of gold may again be worth no more than 12 pounds of silver, as it was formerly in *Europe*, or than 9, as it is now in *China*; and whatever nation will not alter the proportion between gold and silver, according to the general want or abundance of either, only exposes itself to be the dupe of those who do, and to be bought and sold with its own money. In *England*, reckoning the guinea at 1 l. 1s., 15 lb. 2 oz. 10 dwt. 7 grs. of fine silver are equal to one pound weight of fine gold. In *Portugal*, a mark of gold of 22 carrats fine, and two carrats allay, is coined into 102,400 rees, and a mark of silver 11 ounces fine, and one ounce allay, into 6,400 rees; so that at the mint price, one pound weight of fine gold is equal to 16 pounds of fine silver; by reason of which high valuation of gold, and low valuation of silver, there has been no silver coined or current there for several years last past, though but twenty years ago it was in greater plenty than gold. To supply the want of it, they coin pieces of gold of several denominations, from pieces of five moedas, as low as the tenth of a moeda, and a great quantity of copper money; but notwithstanding these helps, they are obliged to open books of debtor and creditor for small sums, and the retailers often refuse to sell their goods, unless the buyers bring change with them: which are difficulties, that would be insupportable in a nation that subsists by trade, carried on chiefly by multitudes of labourers and manufacturers. Though a mark of silver at *Lisbon* produces at the mint only 6,400 rees, yet without considering the high price it bears, when the *Portugueze East-India* ships are going out, it is not to be bought at a medium, one time with another, under 7,200 rees, which reduces the real proportion between silver and gold in *Portugal* as 14 lb. 2 oz. 13 dwt. 8 grs. of fine silver, is to one pound weight of fine gold, at which rate a guinea is worth 19s. 7d.½. In *Spain*, till lately, one pound weight of fine gold was equal to 16 lb. of fine silver at the mint; but weighty silver had always a premium upon it, sometimes as high as 15 *per cent.* Two years ago, pistoles, that used to go for 32 ryals, were made current for 36; and weighty dollars, which used to go for 8 ryals, were raised to 9½, to put them upon a par with the base silver money current in *Spain:* which is an augmentation of 12½ *per cent.* on gold, and 18¾ on silver, and reduces the proportion between silver and gold, at the mint in *Spain*, as 15 lb. 17 dwt. 21 grs. to one pound weight, at which rate a guinea is worth 20s. 11d. But besides the additional augmentation of 6¼ *per cent.* more on silver than on gold, there is still a further premium upon weighty silver; and notwithstanding both the augmentation and the premium, silver only continues to be exported, and only gold and base silver is left in *Spain*. As *Spain* is the country in *Europe* to which the greatest quantities of silver must be brought, and it cannot be transported elsewhere without new charge and risque, it must be cheapest there, and consequently, ought to have a higher value set upon it in other countries than it has in *Spain*. In *France*, when Sir *Isaac Newton* made his table of assays on foreign coins, silver was to gold as 15 to 1; but at present 88 *French* ounces of fine gold, and 8 ounces of allay, are coined into 360 louis-d'ors, which at 24 livres each, make 8640 livres; and 88 ounces of fine silver and 8 ounces of allay, are coined into 99 crowns and three-fifths of a crown, which at 6 livres each, make 597 livres and 12 sols. So that silver to gold in *France* is as 14 lb. 5 oz. 9 dwt. 21 grs. to 1 lb., at which rate a guinea is worth 19s. 11d.¼. In *Holland*, five silver ducatons are generally equal to three gold ducats. The ducatons weigh generally one ounce and twenty-one grains. I have made several assays of the year 1727, and find. they are only 11 oz. 4 dwt.½ fine; whereas they were formerly, like the ducatons of *Flanders*, 11 oz. 7 dwt. fine, and they go still in payment for as much as the *Flanders* ducatons. The gold ducats weigh generally 2 dwt. and 6 grs.; and according to several assays I have made of some of the year 1727, they are 23 carrats 2½ grains fine; at which rate, silver to gold is as 14 lb. 8 oz. 16 dwt. 14 grs. to 1 lb., and a guinea is worth 1 l. 0s. 4d. Sir *Isaac Newton*, in his table of assays, makes the ducat only 23 carrats and two grains fine, and the ducatons 11 oz. 5 dwt. fine, at which rate silver to gold is in *Holland* as 14 lb. 10 oz. 6 dwt. 13 grs. to 1 lb., and a guinea is worth 20s. 6d. As the several provinces differ somewhat in the fineness of their ducats and ducatons, I shall take the medium of these two computations, which is 14 lb. 9 oz. 11 dwt. 13 grs. to 1 lb., at which rate a guinea is worth 20s. 5d. These are the nations with whom we have the greatest dealings. I have not yet been able to inform myself thoroughly of the proportion between gold and silver in the variety of coins in *Germany* and *Italy*; but according to Sir *Isaac Newton's* table of assays, silver is higher in proportion to gold in these countries than in Holland. It appears from hence that gold is at present much higher, and silver lower in *England*, than it is even in Spain, in any other part of *Europe*, or in any mint, except that of *Lisbon*. According to the foregoing computations, the number of grains of fine gold contained in one pound sterling, or in $\frac{20}{21}$ of a guinea, will produce in *France* only 23 livres and 9 sols., and in *Holland* only 35 schellings and 7 grosche in ducats or ducatons: Whereas the number of grains of fine silver contained in 20 shillings will produce in *France* 24 livres 14 sols., and in *Holland* in ducats or ducatons 36 schellings and 7 grosche: so that, it is a profit of above 5 *per cent.* to import gold from *France*, and of near 3 *per cent.* to import gold from *Holland*, and export our weighty silver coin in lieu of it, and a greater advantage in proportion to bring gold hither, rather than silver, to buy goods or pay debts. Anyone who considers how often this exchange of silver for gold may be made in a year, will easily account for the small quantities of silver current now, in proportion to what they were formerly, and see that nothing could prevent a total exportation of our silver coin but the lightness of the greater part of what is remaining; there is still a considerable profit to be made, by culling out the weightiest pieces, and picking up those that are new coined. Whoever melts down any new silver coin, and carries it to market where standard silver in bars now sells for 5s. 6d. per ounce, will make a profit of 6 l. 8s. on each 100 l. sterling, and proportionally for any greater or lesser part. As great quantities of our gold coins are likewise considerably too light, foreigners who take our guineas in quantities only by weight, may melt down the heavy ones, and have 21s. here in silver for the lightest, which will make it turn in some measure to account to exchange them for light silver; but even allowing that it is not worth while to export any silver that is not weighty, it is but an uncomfortable reflection that we shall have no silver coin left among us but what is light, and that every ounce of new silver (which at a medium is a loss of 2d.½ an ounce to those who are obliged to coin it) will very probably be either exported or melted down the moment it becomes current, without which it is useless. Since December 1701, when the great re-coinage was entirely ended, the only quantities of silver sent to the mint were what was taken at *Vigo*, or bought by the publick in the year 1709 at 2d.½ per ounce loss, and in 1711 at 4d. per ounce loss, or sent by the *South-Sea* Company in 1723, when the two millions were remitted, or annually by the *Welsh* Copper Company, and Company for smelting lead with pit-coal, pursuant to an act of parliament: So that in 26 years, no silver has been imported to the mint but what was forced thither, though above 11 millions of pounds sterling have been coined there in gold within the same time. This total cessation of any free coinage of silver for so many years, has not been owing to any want of silver in the nation: for it appears by the custom-house books, that within that time, many millions of pounds weight of silver in bullion and foreign coin have been exported; and by the entries at *Goldsmiths Hall*, that immense quantities have been wrought into plate. If gold and silver had been these last 26 years of the same value in proportion to each other here as in other countries, it is very probable that a great deal of that part of the 11 millions of gold, as was a balance of trade in our favour, would have come to the mint in silver, as it used to do formerly. In the 26 years next after the Restoration, near four millions sterling were coined in silver, though the guinea was then valued as high or higher than it is now.

To bring the silver and gold to the same proportion here as they bear to each other in the neighbouring nations, either the value of the guineas must be lowered in respect of the silver, or the value of the silver raised in respect of the gold. The reasons given for lowering the gold are, that gold is only to be looked upon as a commodity, and so should rise or fall as occasion requires; that it either is not, or ought not to be a legal tender at any certain rate, but go only according to its intrinsic value; and therefore no person will have any reason to complain of any necessary reduction; that if the guinea be 6d. too high, the landlord, who receives his rents in gold, receives 6d. less in a guinea from his tenant than he ought to have, and is defrauded so much; and that if you lower the gold, that will sink the price of the silver, and bring it equally with gold to the mint, and that the exchange will alter to your advantage in the proportion you lower the gold. The objections made to the lowering the gold are, the immediate loss that will accrue upon all the cash in the Exchequer and publick offices, and in the Bank, and in the hands of bankers and private persons, and in the payments to be made to foreigners, at least for debts now due to them; for though when you buy anything of foreigners they will take your gold and silver only according to the intrinsic value, they must receive their debts according to the denomination you put upon them. Thus, all those who lent money in *Spain* upon the flota and galleons, when pistoles went at 32 ryals, and dollars at 8, were by the intermediate augmentation of the money obliged to receive it back again in pistoles at 36 ryals, and dollars at 9½; and *è contra*, if a foreigner orders his correspondent here to sell for him 100 l. *South-Sea* stock, and to remit him the produce of it, which we will suppose to be 105 l. if guineas go here at 21s., the foreigner is paid with 100 guineas; but if they are reduced to 20s. 6d. his correspondent must remit him 102 guineas and nine shillings for what he bought perhaps with guineas at 1 l. 1s. 6d. The objections to the raising the silver are, that where leases have been made or goods sold, or money lent for a certain number of pounds sterling, upon a presumption that a pound weight of standard silver should be paid for 3 l. 2s., if you cut it into 3 l. 4s. the lessor and vendor are defrauded of the additional 2s. That an ounce of fine silver is, and always has been, and ought to be the standing and invariable measure between nation and nation; and that if you once alter the silver, which is your bushel, no nation will know how to deal with you hereafter, and that the exchange will alter to your disadvantage in proportion to the extrinsic augmentation of your silver. In answer to these objections it may be said, that it is worth considering, whether the person who pays ought not to be regarded as well as he who receives; and whether it would not be as hard to hurt the first by lowering the guinea, as the other by raising the silver. That nine parts in ten, or more, of all payments in *England*, are now made in gold, and if so, they will be very little affected by any alteration in the silver. But supposing, for argument sake, that all payments in *England* are paid in silver, the receiver, in that case, loses more at present than he would do if a pound weight of standard silver was cut into 3 l. 4s., for the species of silver in which payments are chiefly made, are now, by wearing, considerably lighter than new coin made after that rate would be. I received from the bank a 10 l. bag of sixpences, another of shillings, another of half-crowns, and another of crowns: and weighed at the mint three single pound-weights out of each bag, and found, that at a medium, 3 l. 10s. in sixpences made but a pound weight, 3 l. 6s. in shillings, 3 l. 4s. 2d. in half-crowns, and 3 l. 3s. 10d. in crowns. The greatest part of silver now remaining in the nation, and most likely to remain, is in sixpences and shillings, and a pound weight of standard silver coined into 3 l. 8. would be equal to them: but allowing there is an equal quantity remaining of each species, a pound weight of silver coined into 3 l. 6s. would be of equal intrinsic value with the present silver. The 6d. was taken off from the guinea, by a proclamation, bearing date the 22d of December, 1717. The exchange was, according to *Castaigne's* papers—

| | 20 Dec. | 24 Dec. | 27 Dec. | 31 Dec. |
|---|---|---|---|---|
| Ansterdam | 34 2 *a* 3 | 34 7 *a* 6 | 34 6 *a* 5 | 34 4 *a* 3 |
| Paris . . | 47 ½ *a* ⅜ | 47 | 47 0 *a* ¼ | 47 ⅜ *a* ½ |
| Cadiz . . | 52½ | 52 *a* 51¼ | 51 ¼ *a* ½ | 51 ¾ *a* 52 |
| Lisbon . | 57 | 55¾ | 55¾ | 55 ¾ |

By this account it appears, that though the several exchanges altered in our favour the 24th of *December*, which was the next post after the reduction of the 6d., yet almost all of them returned to the same course again in two more, except that of *Lisbon*, in which 5s. 7d. is so much beyond the usual course, that it would have been no wonder if it had not kept long there, though no reduction had been made in the guinea. According to the best information I have been able to get, out of the books of those who buy and sell silver, the price of silver of the old standard was, at a medium, in 1713, at 5s. 3d. the ounce; in 1714, at 5s. 4d.; in 1715 and 1716, to

*February*, 1716–17, 5s. 3d.; from the first of *February*, 1716–17, to *July*, 1717, 5s. 3d.½; from *July* to *August*, 1717, 5s. 4d.; from *August*, 1717, to *March*, 1717–18, (during which time the 6d. was taken off the guinea) 5s. 5d.; and from *March* to *April*, 1718, 5s. 6d. By this account, silver was cheaper in the year 1717, and some years before than it was in the year 1718, after the lowering the guinea; nor has it been cheaper any year since than it was in the year 1717, so that the reduction of the 6d. upon the guinea had no lasting effect upon the exchange; did not apparently lower the price of the silver; nor bring one ounce of silver to the mint. When both gold and silver are raised in any country, beyond their intrinsic value, as now in *France*, the exchange will fall in proportion; but as nine parts in ten, or more, of all payments in *England*, are made in gold, and, for want of large parcels of weighty silver, great quantities of guineas are exported, it is to be doubted, whether the raising the silver will alter the exchange even so long to our disadvantage, as the lowering gold did to our advantage. It is certain that the giving silver here the same value, in respect of gold, as it has in other countries, is no reason for falling the exchange; and, in money matters, what is not grounded on a solid foundation, cannot have any durable effect; and the fear of giving foreigners only a groundless pretence for falling the exchange, ought not to deter or divert us from preventing the real advantages they make at present, or may make, at our expense. Necessity and convenience will make that coin the measure which is in greatest plenty: It was for this reason, that silver, and not gold, was the first measure. Wherever the silver coin of any country is bought at a premium, with the gold coin of the same country, there gold is the measure, and silver is the merchandize; and wherever gold is a legal tender, at a certain rate, it is as much a measure as silver. In *Denmark* and *Sweden* the good silver coins are not to be had without a premium: In *Portugal* gold is now the only measure, and in *Spain* too; for no payments are made there in any silver, but what is base, without a premium, even for bills that run payable in dollars.

Gold in *France* is as much a measure as silver; and, whatever it was formerly, is at present as much a measure as silver here, and as legal a tender; being so established by his late Majesty's proclamation, bearing date the 22d of December, 1717, which was grounded on an address from the House of Commons; the title of which is, "A proclamation, declaring the rates at which gold shall be current in payment"; and in the body of it, after specifying that a guinea shall be current for no more than 21s. and broad pieces for no more than 25s. and 23s., there are these words, "at which rates and values we do hereby declare the said respective pieces of coined gold to be current." In *France*, *Spain*, *Portugal*, and *Holland*, the mark of silver, as well as the mark of gold, has, from time to time, been cut into more pieces in tale; and the silver, as well as gold coins of *England*, have been raised and lowered, sometimes by altering the standard, but oftener, and almost constantly, for several centuries together, by cutting a pound weight into more or fewer pieces. In the

20th of *Edward* the Third, a pound weight of silver, of the present standard, was coined into 1 l. 2s. 6d., and afterwards, not gradually, but sometimes falling, and sometimes rising, into 1 l. 5s., 1 l. 10s., 1 l. 17s. 6d., 2 l. 5s., 2 l. 8s., 3 l. (I do not take into this consideration the great debasement of the silver coin, in the reigns of *Henry* the Eighth, and *Edward* the Sixth, in the 5th of whose reign a pound weight of silver, 3 ounces fine, and 9 ounces allay, was coined into 3 l. 12s., at which rate fine silver was raised to 1 l. 4s. per ounce.) In the 2d of Queen *Elizabeth*, the antient standard of 11 oz. 2 dwt. fine, and 18 dwt. allay, (which has been observed ever since) was restored, and a pound weight was coined into 3 l. from that year till the 43d of her reign, when the silver was raised 2s. in the pound weight, which was then coined, for the first time, into 3 l. 2s., at which rate it has continued ever since. In the 20th of *Edward* the Third, a pound weight of gold, of 23 carrats, 3½ grains fine, and ½ grain of allay, was coined into 14 l., and afterwards, not gradually, but sometimes rising, and sometimes falling, a pound weight of the same standard, or of 22 carrats fine, and 2 carrats allay, was cut into 15 l., 16 l. 13s. 4d., 22 l. 10s., 25 l. 2s. 6d., 27 l., 28 l. 16s., 30 l. In the 2d of *Elizabeth* a pound weight, 22 carrats fine, was cut into 33 l. and so continued till the 43d of her reign, when it was cut into 33 l. 10s., and afterwards into 36 l., 36 l. 10s., 37 l. 10s., 40 l. 10s., 40 l. 18s. 4d., 41 l., 44 l., till the 12th of *Charles* the Second, when a pound weight, of 22 carrats fine, and 2 carrats allay, (which has been the standard of gold ever since) was, for the first time, cut into 44 guineas and a half, which, at 1 l. 1s. per guinea, is 46 l. 14s. 6d. If it were a fundamental and unalterable maxim, that silver should be the bushel, and the only and invariable measure always; and a pound weight never cut into more or less pieces, it would not have been raised in other countries, gradually with the gold, nor here from 1 l. 2s. 6d. which it was coined into in *Edward* the Third's time, to 3 l. 2s., nor would such frequent, and almost constant alterations have been made in the silver coin, from the time of *Edward* the Third, to the reign of queen *Elizabeth*. I have searched the council books of the 43d of Elizabeth; but cannot find there the reasons for raising, at that time, the gold coin 10s. in the pound weight, and the silver 2s. In *Townshend's* Collections, mention is made of a bill, brought that year into the House of Commons, to restrain the transportation of money, and to reform certain abuses in the foreign exchanges; and notice is taken, that one of the members for the city, who spoke to the bill, complained, that the *Netherlanders* exported the money out of the realm, and did not coin their money of due standard, as *England* and *France* and *Germany* did; and so gained by all the three. The bill did not pass; but a proclamation was issued, commanding the execution of the old laws against exporting gold or silver, in coin or bullion. From these circumstances, it is not improbable that the cutting the pound weight of gold into 10s. more, and the pound weight of silver in 2s. more, that year, was to put a stop to the carrying out of our money; and that the raising the silver one thirtieth part, and the gold only one sixty-sixth part, was in regard to the proportion they bore to each other in the neighbouring countries: Whatever the reasons were, it is plain, that great queen, who thought the reforming the coin one of the glories of her reign, and valued herself to her people, for conquering that monster, as she called it, after she had restored it to its antient purity and value, and had continued it upon the same foot, without any alteration, for 41 years, found it necessary to alter the measure, and to raise the silver, as well as the gold, and in above a double proportion. I must observe, that in the 43rd of *Elizabeth*, when a pound weight of silver was first fixed at 3 l. 2s., a pound weight of gold, of 22 carrats fine, which is now coined into 46 l. 14s. 6d., was coined into no more than 33 l. 10s., so that, since that time, gold has been raised almost one third, according to the present rate, and much more, according to the former rate of guineas; whilst the silver (which, in other countries, has been raised gradually with the gold, and in *France*, since the 43rd of *Elizabeth*, has been raised from 20 livres, 5 sols., 4 deniers per mark, to 49 livres, 16 sols.) has not been raised here at all, though, since that time, the importation of gold into *Europe* has been much increased, by the discovery of the new mines in *Brasil*, and, consequently, it is less valuable; and the real intrinsic value of silver is much enhanced, by the great demand of silver for the several *East India* Companies set up in *Europe*, and a much greater consumption of it in wrought plate and gold and silver laces, and must still increase; for silver is of much more general use than gold in manufactures, and the demand of it for *China* and the *East Indies* is not likely to lessen:

Whereas gold is imported from the *East*, as well as the *West Indies*; nor is there any particular demand for it out of *Europe*. These considerations have raised the silver 12½ *per cent.* in *Portugal*, and probably induced the *Dutch* to make their ducatons 2½ dwt. worse than they used to be, and the *French* to bring their silver from 15 to 1, to under 14½ to 1, and the *Spaniards* to raise the silver 6¼ *per cent.* more than the gold. In *England*, where the silver has not been raised in so many years, the coinage of silver has sunk gradually: In the first six years after the Restoration, four times more money was coined in silver than in gold; in the next 14 years, more gold than silver; in the next 8 years, above three times more gold than silver; in the next 13 years, out of foreign bullion, above 15 times more gold than silver; and in the remaining 26 years, above 11 millions of gold, and no silver, but what was forced into the mint in the manner already mentioned.

Gold and silver, on account of the workmanship, and the certainty of the standard, ought to be worth more in money than in ingots. Laws have been made here, and in other countries, to compel goldsmiths to sell them at a lower rate in bullion than they were worth in coin. It is a policy in several countries, and turns to a good account in *Holland*, to make base silver monies current for much more than the intrinsic value; but no where, except in *England*, any metal is worth less in coin than in bullion; and wherever it is so, there can be no coinage but what is forced, and the public is at the charge of coinage, only to encourage and supply the unlawful trade of exporting and melting it down. Whilst an ounce of standard silver sells at market here for 5s. 4d.$\frac{1}{2}$ at a medium, one time with another, and will yield as much, or more abroad, and will produce but 5s. 2d. at the mint, it is beyond dispute a profit of 2d.$\frac{1}{2}$ per oz. to melt the weighty coin into bullion, or to export it, and a loss of 2d.$\frac{1}{2}$ per oz. to send it to the mint; and, consequently, it is in vain to expect silver should come to the mint, or the coin not be melted down and exported. This is clear in reason, and is confirmed by the fatal experience of many years: There may be variety of opinions about the cause, but the fact is undeniable. Some think it is owing to the high price of gold, and low price of silver, at the mint; and others attribute it to the prohibiting the exportation of our own coin, and allowing that of bullion and foreign coin. The real value of silver is not to be taken from the price it bears, at any particular or extraordinary occasion; but from a medium of the rate it has been at for several years. The proper period to compute from seems to be, from the time of the reduction of the 6d. upon the guinea, that the effect the lowering the gold had on the silver, whatever it was, may enter into the computation. Silver which yields at the mint only 5s. 2d. per ounce, is worth, at a medium, taken from the price it has been at, according to Castaigne's papers, from *December*, 1717, to *August*, 1728, 5s. 4d.$\frac{1}{2}$ in bars, and 5s. 5d.$\frac{1}{4}$ in foreign coin; to which last article $\frac{3}{4}$d. per oz. more must be added, because pieces of 8 are, one with another, at least the value of $\frac{1}{2}$d. per oz. worse than standard; so that an ounce of standard silver, in pieces of 8, costs at least 5s. 5d.$\frac{3}{4}$. Gold, which yields at the mint 3 l. 18s. per oz., is worth at a medium, taken from the price it has been at for the same time, according to Castaigne's papers, 3 l. 18s. 3d. in bars, and 3 l. 18s. 6d.$\frac{3}{4}$ in foreign coin. Though the allowing the exportation of bullion and foreign coin only, certainly gives them a value over and above our coin; yet the difference between the price of silver, in the mint and at market, cannot be wholly owing to that; for we have not, during 26 years, been always under a necessity of exporting gold and silver to pay debts abroad: At several times all the foreign exchanges have been to our advantage, and silver, in foreign coin, which, on account of the certainty of the standard, and the conveniency of the tale and distribution, is, at a medium, worth 1d.$\frac{1}{2}$ per oz. more than in bars, has been many times as cheap as in bars, and sometimes cheaper, as it was for several months in the years 1719, and 1722. If the prohibition of the exportation of our coin, and the allowing that of bullion, was singly the cause of the stoppage of the coinage of silver, it would have the same effect on the gold, which lies under the same disadvantage of being legally inexportable, and yet that has been coined in great plenty; and if silver and gold bore the same proportion here to each other, as in the neighbouring countries, it would turn to a better account to export gold than silver, it being more easily transported, and often paying less freight; but the difference between the premium upon gold in bars and gold in foreign coin, is, according to the foregoing computation, only 3d.$\frac{3}{4}$ in 3 l. 18s., and upon silver 1d.$\frac{1}{4}$ in 5s. 4d.$\frac{1}{2}$, which is near five times as much, and yet more silver is exported than gold, which is a plain indication that gold has a better market here than silver, and in other countries silver than gold; and that consequently is one great reason of the cessation of any free coinage of silver. It is certain that the prohibition of the exportation of *English* coin, and the allowing that of bullion in England, which concerns us only, can have no effect upon the price of silver in other countries: and all over *Europe*, silver is dearer, in proportion to gold, than at the mint in *England*.

It is a very great misfortune for any nation, especially a trading one, to be under the necessity of prohibiting the exportation of their coin; and a loss whenever it is put in practice. If the balance of trade be in our favour, laws for that purpose are needless; and if it be against us, they are in a great measure ineffectual; and only put the honest and the timorous to the necessity of buying gold at 3 l. 18s. 3d. an ounce, and silver at 5s. 4d.$\frac{1}{2}$ an ounce, perhaps of those who have it at 3 l. 18s. and 5s. 2d. by melting down the coin. The prohibiting the exportation of our coin does not save us from paying our debts abroad, nor keep more gold or silver in the nation; on the contrary, it obliges us to pay our debts at a dearer rate, and carries out a greater quantity of gold and silver than would be sufficient in our own money. When we oblige a merchant to give 3 l. 18s. 6d.$\frac{3}{4}$ for the same quantity of fine gold in moedas, as he may have for 3 l. 18s. in the guineas, with which he pays for those moedas;

and 5s. 6d.$\frac{3}{4}$ per ounce for the same quantity of silver in pieces of 8, as he may have in weighty *English* money for 5s. 2d., we raise the coin of the King of *Portugal* and King of *Spain* here so much, and pay for the extrinsic value we ourselves put upon it. According to the accounts laid before the House of Commons, from *December*, 1722, to *December*, 1727, 490,805 ounces of gold, and 14,316,424 ounces of silver, were exported in foreign coin; and 39,377 ounces of gold, and 1,076,046 ounces of silver in bullion. Allowing the premium, on account of the exportability, only to be 4d.$\frac{3}{4}$ per oz. on gold in foreign coin, and 1d. per oz. on gold in bullion; and 1d.$\frac{3}{4}$ per oz. on silver in foreign coin, and $\frac{1}{2}$d. per oz. on silver in bullion; the loss to the nation, within those 5 years, by prohibiting the exportation of our own money, and allowing that of bullion and foreign coin, was 116,510 l. 5s. 5d.$\frac{3}{4}$, without reckoning the loss on the great quantities which are exported unentered, by private traders to the *East Indies*, and other places. In those 5 years, above 13 times as much silver, and above 12 times as much gold, was exported in foreign coin as in bullion; and if gold be worth 3d.$\frac{3}{4}$ more in moedas, and silver 1d.$\frac{1}{4}$ in pieces of 8, than in bars, the *English* coin, if exportable, would be better worth that additional value, as being better coined, more equally sized, and less varying from the known standard. The Merchant is at present unwilling to import bullion into *England*, because the re-exportation of it, when the court of aldermen is not sitting, is impracticable, and, at best, is attended with difficulties. Whereas *Holland*, by giving credit at the bank for gold and silver, at ½ *per cent. per annum*, and by allowing the free exportation of their money, is become the great mart and repository of gold and silver, whilst *Portugal* and *Spain*, which are the fountains of both, can keep neither, though the exportation of them be capital by law. The *Hollander* is never under the necessity of giving 1½ *per cent.* more for gold, and above 7 *per cent.* more for silver, in moedas and pieces of 8, than in the coin of his own country, as the *English* merchant does at this time; and whenever the exchange is against him, remits the coin of his own country, instead of drawing at loss, by which means the exchange, which is often, for many months together, 5 *per cent.* or more against us, can never be long above ½ *per cent.* to the disadvantage of *Holland*.

I have been informed, that in the year 1718, a bill was prepared at the Treasury, for allowing the exportation of *English* coin, and prohibiting that of bullion and foreign coin, but was never brought into the house; in lieu of it, quarter guineas were ordered to be coined, to supply the want of silver, which were soon discontinued, as being of no service. The objections to such a bill are, that where paper credit is carried to a great height, a free exportation of money, without any restraint, in case of any shock to credit, might be of ill consequence; that the *East India* Company will always want great quantities of silver; that all the wine, brandy, brocades, toys, lace, and cambrick, from *France* and *Flanders*, and the iron, and naval stores and timber, from *Denmark* and *Sweden*, are paid for with gold and silver; and that foreigners have great sums in our stocks, the interest of which goes constantly out of the kingdom, and often the principal; all which articles will occasion a constant exportation of money. On the other hand, it is to be considered, that *Holland* and several other countries are great gainers by allowing the exportation of their coin, and have never found any inconveniency by it; that since gold and silver are, and must be exported, to answer foreign demands, it is best to let them go out in such a shape as will cost the nation least, and produce the most in foreign markets. Most of our silver coin (especially the shillings and sixpences, which are of the greatest use) and much of our gold coin is at present so light, that the greater part of it is likely to remain with us, without some very urgent necessity, though the exportation of it should be allowed. It, therefore, seems advisable to make a temporary law, by way of trial, to allow any persons to export, within a certain time, the same quantity in weight of gold and silver, *English* money, as they import in bullion to the mint, upon paying the charge of coinage when they export it; and to lay, at the same time, a duty, much greater than the charge of the coinage, upon the exportation of bullion, to prevent the melting down the coin into bullion for exportation; and a duty, at least equal to the charge of the coinage, upon foreign coin, when exported, that silver and gold may not, as at present, be worth more in foreign than in *English* coin. Such a law would not be entirely new and unprecedented; for in an act of the 27th of *Edward* the Third, c. 14, entitled, "An Act allowing merchants to bring in gold or silver to the King's exchanges, and carry out as much," there is the following clause: "That none carry out of our said realm and lands the old sterling, nor other money but our new money of gold and silver," (both which were raised that year, the gold one fifteenth, and the silver one tenth), "except the merchants strangers that bring to our said realm and lands any manner of money, and there will employ this money within our realm and lands; whom we will, that they may re-carry into their country all this money, or as much as shall remain thereof not employed, without impeachment, so always that good and lawful search be thereof made, in the ports and other places, where any arrival is; and that all the money that every merchant stranger shall bring within our said realm and lands, shall be put in writing by the searchers, to the intent that no merchant shall carry more beyond the sea than he brought into the same realm and lands." A law of this nature would very much encourage the importation of bullion, and lessen the necessity and temptation of exporting money clandestinely; none could be exported publickly, by virtue of it, but what was first coined at the expense of the exporter, which he would be enabled to bear, by saving the premium he now pays for bullion and foreign coin, on account of its being exportable, and the interest he pays for money borrowed upon bullion; for, by carrying the mint bills to the bank, he would have the immediate use of the bullion, as soon as it was imported to the mint, and the nation the benefit of it whilst it circulated amongst us, which it would be more apt to do in the useful form of money, than in the useless form of bullion; and it is highly probable, that when so much would be coined, some of it would stick and remain in the nation. The height of paper credit is the strongest argument for trying this, and all other methods that are likely to encrease the coinage; for whilst paper credit does, in a great measure, the business of money at home, merchants and bankers are not under the necessity, as they were formerly, of coining a quantity of specie for their home trade; and as paper credit brings money to the merchant to be exported, the money may go away insensibly, and not be missed till it be too late; and where paper credit is large and encreasing, if the money be exported, and the coinage decrease, that credit may sink at once, for want of a proportionable quantity of specie, which alone can support it in time of distress. A liberty of exportation of money would probably encrease the trade of picking out the heaviest pieces, and perhaps, in time, create a premium upon weighty gold and silver, as in *Spain*, unless prevented by rigorous laws, as in *France*, where the culling out the weightiest pieces, and selling them for a premium, (as well as many other undue practices relating to the money, not taken notice of by our laws) is a capital crime. This leads to the consideration of the lightness of our present money, which is a matter of so great consequence, and deserves so particular an attention, that I have taken all possible methods to come at as true a state of it as the nature of the affair will admit. Were the lightness of the money no more than what must happen by wearing, the mischief would not be so grievous; but some persons have been convicted, several prosecuted, and more suspected, of filing, washing, and otherwise diminishing it; and what is still worse, there is too much reason to fear, that foreigners, who are out of the reach of our laws, and have the command of great quantities of our coin, are guilty of the same practices. If the unavoidable lightness, occasioned by wearing, should be carried to any great height, by illegal methods, the money may, in a shorter time than is imagined, be in as bad a condition as it was formerly by clipping, and put the nation hereafter to the great inconvenience, and immense expense of another re-coinage. The lightness of the broad pieces has already, in a manner, cried them down; for though they pass currently among private persons, especially in the country, the officers of the revenue and the bank have, for some years, refused to take even weighty ones, to the great detriment of trade, and in direct contradiction to his late Majesty's proclamation, by which they are as current at 25s. and 23s. as the guineas are at 21s. This shews, that whenever the other gold and silver monies shall be reduced by wearing, or otherwise, to want as much of their just weight, in proportion, as broad pieces do now, the same fate may attend them, and is a warning to take due and timely care to obviate, as far as possible, so great an evil. If proper methods had been taken, from time to time, before the clipt silver monies were reduced to the condition they were in 1695, the great inconvenience and expense of the re-coinage, which became then unavoidable, might have been prevented. I have already observed, that of the several parcels of silver I weighed at the mint,

3 l. 10s. in sixpences, 3 l. 6s. in shillings, 3 l. 4s. 2d. in half crowns, and 3 l. 3s. 10d. in crowns, made but one pound weight; so that, at an average, all the species together were 4s. too light in 3 l. 2s. Upon four 100 l. bags of crowns, weighed at the bank, after deducting 1 oz. 5 dwt. for the weight of each bag, there were wanting, at an average, upon each 100 l., 11 oz. 9 dwt. 10 grs., which is 7 dwt. 2 grs. or 1s. 9d.$\frac{3}{4}$ on one pound weight, or 3 l. 2s. Upon four 100 l. bags of half crowns, at an average, 1 lb. 2 oz. 4 dwt. 10 grs. upon each 100 l., which is 8 dwt. 19 grs. or 2s. 3d.$\frac{1}{4}$ on 3 l. 2s. Upon four 100 l. bags of shillings, at an average, 1 lb. 11 oz. 10 dwt. 16 grs. on each 100 l., which is 14 dwt. 14 grs. or 3s. 9d. on 3 l. 2s. Upon 4 100 l. bags of sixpences, at an average, 3 lb. 4 oz. 18 dwt. 4 grs. on each 100 l., which is 1 oz. 5 dwt. 8 grs. or 6s. 6d.$\frac{1}{2}$ on 3 l. 2s. The lightness upon these crowns, half crowns, shillings, and sixpences together, is, at an average, 1 lb. 10 oz. 10 dwt. 16 grs. on 100 l., which is 13 dwt. 22 grs. or 3s. 7d. on 3 l. 2s. Twenty-five 100 l. bags of promiscuous silver at the bank weighed each, at an average, exclusive of the bags, 3 lb. 2 oz. 9 dwt., which is 2 lb. 0 oz. 12 dwt. 22 grs. below the standard weight of 100 l., and 15 dwt. 6 grs. or 3s. 11d.$\frac{1}{4}$ upon 3 l. 2s. Taking the medium of the weight of the several parcels of crowns, half crowns, shillings, and sixpences, weighed separately at the mint, and at the bank, and of the 25 100 l. bags of promiscuous silver, weighed at the bank, the lightness upon the silver coin is at present 3s. 10d. upon 3 l. 2s., which is 6 l. 3s. 7d.$\frac{3}{4}$ *per cent.* According to an account laid before the treasury, by

the officers of the mint, in February, 1712, there were then wanting, by wearing and unlawful diminishing together, on a 100 l. bag of sixpences, from 14 oz. to 15 oz.; upon a 100 l. bag of shillings, 7 oz. ½; upon a 100 l. bag of crowns or half crowns, 4 oz.; so that in the last 16 years, from 1712 to 1728, 100 l. in crowns is diminished from 4 oz. to 11 oz. 9 dwt. 10 grs., 100 l. in half crowns, from 4 oz. to 1 lb. 2 oz. 4 dwt. 10 grs., 100 l. in shillings, from 7 oz. ½ to 1 lb. 11 oz. 10 dwt. 16 grs., 100 l. in sixpences, from 14 oz. ½ to 3 lb. 4 oz. 18 dwt. 4 grs., which is, upon the whole, above two-thirds more than in the preceding 16 years, from the great re-coinage in 1696, to 1712; and this is the more extraordinary, because any want of weight there was in the single pieces, when first coined, was included in the computation upon the first 16 years; and complaints were made, at the time of the re-coinage, that some of the country mints made the money too light. Though, perhaps, old silver, worn so smooth that the whole superficies is rubbed, may wear faster than the new, where only those parts that rise are touched, that alone could not occasion such a disproportionate decrease of the weight, which must be owing to the exportation or melting down of the weightiest pieces, or more illegal diminutions than were practised formerly.

I weighed at the mint three times 44½ guineas, in guineas and half guineas, separately, of all reigns but the present, and found, at an average, 3 dwt. 15 grs. wanting on 44 guineas and one half, which is 1 gr. 85–89ths on a guinea, and 6 dwt. 6 grs.

on 89 half guineas, which is 3 grs. 33–89ths on two half guineas. As the number of half guineas bear no proportion to the number of guineas, I weighed likewise three times 44½ guineas, in guineas and half guineas promiscuously, as they came from the bank, and found them, at an average, 4 dwt. 10 grs. too light, which is 2 grs. 34–89ths on a guinea. At the bank, 25 bags of 1000 l., containing 952 guineas and 8 shillings, weighed, at an average, (exclusive of 1 oz. 5 dwt. for the bag, and 1 oz. 9 dwt. 2 grs. for the 8s.) 21 lb. 0 oz. 11 dwt. 5 grs., which is 4 oz. 3 dwt. 4 grs. below the standard weight of 952 guineas, and is 2 grs. 23–238ths on a guinea. Taking the medium of the weight of these several parcels of guineas and half guineas, weighed at the mint and at the bank, the lightness at present is 2 grs. 40–89ths on a guinea, which is near 2 *per cent.;* but as it is not probable that the lightest guineas are carried to the bank, which is the only place where they are weighed, and where light ones are often rejected; it is to be feared that the lightness upon all the half guineas and guineas which are current in the nation, is much greater. It is difficult to make any exact computation of the lightness of the broad pieces; for, since the exchequer and bank refuse taking them, no information can be had from thence; and they differ much more, in respect of each other, than the guineas. I have weighed several singly, and in parcels, and find, at a medium, that the whole 25s. and 23s. pieces are about ten grs. too light, one with another; it is to be feared that the halves and quarters are much lighter, in proportion. There were several proclamations, in the reigns of Queen *Elizabeth*, *James* the First, and *Charles* the First, ordaining, that upon account of the wear of the gold monies, a 20s. piece that wanted but 3 grains should be current, without any abatement; and that any that wanted above 3, and not more than 6 grains, should be current, upon paying after the rate of 2d. for every grain wanting; and that any that wanted more than 6 should be punched, and current only by weight. It might not be, perhaps, improper to make some regulation of this nature concerning the broad pieces, making a proportionable allowance for the further diminution by wearing, since the reign of *Charles* the First. As they are liable to be clipped, which guineas are not, and equally liable to be filed and washed, and we find, by daily experience, that they are illegally diminished, the evil will encrease, and the sooner a remedy is applied, the less the loss will be, wherever it is to fall; and it is a great inconvenience to trade, and some reproach to the government, to have the coin of the country current between man and man, and yet not taken in the public receipts. Though the other gold and silver monies be not yet so light as to require a remedy of this kind, private orders may be given to the officers of the revenue to weigh constantly all large parcels of gold, as well as silver money, and to refuse such as are so light as to give a suspicion of their being unlawfully diminished; which rules would of consequence be followed by the bank and goldsmiths, and would make it more difficult to put off light money, and might, in some measure, prevent further illegal diminutions. New rewards may likewise be given, to encourage the discovery of those who are guilty of such practices, and the conviction of them made more practicable. The wear upon the gold and silver monies would be much greater, but for the general use of bank bills; and as it is a dead loss to the nation, and a very considerable one, it might not be improper to oblige the officers of the revenue and the bank, and all bankers, to cover the counters where they tell their money, with cloth or leather; for, the telling money on wood, especially with a mixture of sand, very much encreases the wear. As foreigners receive our gold and silver monies in large parcels, only by weight, it is highly reasonable to prevent there imposing light money upon us, by enacting severe penalties against any who shall import any quantity of gold monies, above 40 grains too light upon the pound weight; or silver, being above two pennyweight too light upon the pound weight; and by making all single pieces, light in proportion, forfeited to the searchers and collectors, and any others who shall discover them; and the examining and weighing the gold and silver monies, when imported, may be a means of discovering such as are counterfeited abroad. If foreigners, who take our money in large parcels only by weight, are suffered to pour in light money upon us, at the same rate as if it was weighty, we may happen to pay them over and over again, for a diminution of their own making; and it is to be feared, so large a profit, without any danger of punishment even if discovered, is too great a temptation to be resisted.

These are the observations which have occurred

to me upon the present state of our gold and silver monies, in regard to the lightness of them, the making them exportable, and the present disproportion between gold and silver, which I have put together, because it is proper to have them all under consideration at once; for, any regulations that shall be thought proper to be made, about the lightness of the silver monies, must be governed by the number of pieces into which the pound weight shall be coined for the future; and it will be necessary, before any exportation of money be allowed, to bring the gold and silver coin nearer a par to one another, in proportion to the value set upon each by the neighbouring nations.

According to the foregoing computations, silver to gold is

| | | Lb. | Oz. | Dwt. | Gr. | |
|---|---|---|---|---|---|---|
| In | Portugal . . . | 14 | 2 | 13 | 8 | Lb. to 1 of gold |
| | Spain . . . . | 15 | 1 | 17 | 21 | |
| | France . . . | 14 | 5 | 9 | 21 | |
| | Holland . . . | 14 | 9 | 11 | 13 | |

At a medium, 14 lb. 07 oz. 18 dwt. 3 grs. of fine silver is equal to one pound weight of fine gold.

According to the foregoing proportions, a guinea is worth

| | | s. | d. |
|---|---|---|---|
| In | Portugal . . . . . . . | 19 | 7½ |
| | Spain . . . . . . . . | 20 | 11 |
| | France . . . . . . | 19 | 11¼ |
| | Holland . . . . . . . | 20 | 5 |
| | | 80 | 10¾ |
| | At a medium, | 20 | 2¾ |

The real value of silver is still encreasing, as has been already observed; silver money is, at all times, of more general use than gold; less liable to illegal diminutions; and of particular service in any distress of credit: Very great quantities of it have been melted down and exported, and very little coined for many years; for which reasons the coinage of silver money ought at present at least to be encouraged preferably to that of gold. If a pound weight of silver be cut into 3 l. 4s. and a guinea remain at 1 l. 1s., the proportion between gold and silver will be 14 lb. 8 oz. 16 dwt. 4 grs. of silver to 1 lb. of gold; at which rate silver will be lower here than it is at a medium of the proportions in the countries above-mentioned, though *Spain* be taken into the computation; and ½d. per oz. cheaper than it has been sold for, at a medium, at market in bars, these last ten years, ½d. per oz. cheaper than what the public gave for it in 1709, and 2d. cheaper than what the public gave in 1711, to encourage the coinage. It will not introduce any necessity of re-coining the old silver monies; for the sixpences, shillings, and half crowns, coined after that rate, will be heavier than the old ones, and the crown pieces so very inconsiderably lighter, that it is not worth taking notice of. If the prohibition of the exportation of money should be continued, and, in order to make some amends for that disadvantage upon our coin, it should be thought proper to raise the silver higher, by cutting a pound weight into 3 l. 4s. 6d., the proportion between gold and silver will then be as 14 lb. 7 oz. 8 dwt. 20 grs. to 1 lb., which is about the medium of the proportions observed in the above-mentioned countries; 5s. 4½d. per ounce is the medium of the market price for these last ten years, which the money ought rather to exceed. Shillings and sixpences so coined will not be so light as the old ones, and the crowns and half crowns so little lighter, that they will not be in so much danger of being melted down, for the sake of so small a profit at the mint, as they are at present, when they produce 5s. 6d. per oz. at market. If anything shall be thought proper to be done on this head, it cannot be put in practice more seasonably than at a time when the great quantities of silver, which have been so long locked up in the *West Indies*, are about to be distributed, and so great a portion of them is likely to come to *England*. If nothing be done, it is in vain to expect any silver should come to the mint freely, or that what is new coined, or weightiest of the old money, should not be melted down or exported. The effects of the *Flotilla*, which have been distributed some time, and of which large quantities have been sent to *England*, have not brought any silver to the mint, nor lowered the price of silver at market; nor is there any reason to hope, that whilst the present mint price of silver continues, and the money is inexportable, the silver in the galleons, when sent home, will bring more silver to the mint than has been brought hither by the many *Spanish* fleets that have come to *Europe* these last 26 years. The raising the silver to 3 l. 4s. or 3 l. 4s. 6d. cannot bring any silver to the mint, whilst it bears so much higher a price at market as it does at present; but it will certainly prevent the importing gold to the mint, only for the sake of exchanging it for silver, which is such a coinage as is only advantageous to private persons, but highly detrimental to the public, and therefore ought to be discouraged. When gold and silver bear the same proportion to each other here, as in the neighbouring countries, the mint is the pulse of the trade of the nation in general, as the constant course of exchange is of that with any particular country. If our imports exceed our exports, we spend more than our income, and must consequently grow poorer; and whatever expedients may be thought of, neither gold nor silver can naturally come to the mint; but what is already in the nation, near the just weight, must, by degrees, be exported, in spite of any laws to the contrary. The only effectual methods to increase the coinage, and keep what is coined in the nation, is to follow the examples of other nations, in encouraging our own manufactures, and retrenching our luxury, especially such part of it as is bought of foreigners, who take nothing of us in exchange but Gold and Silver.

All which is most humbly submitted.

JOHN CONDUITT.

FINIS.

# BANKS

AND

# PAPER-MONEY;

FROM

# ESSAYS,

MORAL, POLITICAL, &c.,

BY

DAVID HUME, Esq.

PUBLISHED IN

1752.

8, 1752. David Hume, 'Banks and Paper-Money' from *Essays, Moral, Political &c*, London.

* * * THIS has made me entertain a doubt concerning the benefit of *banks* and *paper-credit,* which are so generally esteemed advantageous to every nation. That provisions and labour should become dear by the encrease of trade and money, is, in many respects, an inconvenience; but an inconvenience that is unavoidable, and the effect of that public wealth and prosperity which are the end of all our wishes. It is compensated by the advantages, which we reap from the possession of these precious metals, and the weight, which they give the nation in all foreign wars and negociations. But there appears no reason for encreasing that inconvenience by a counterfeit money, which foreigners will not accept of in any payment, and which any great disorder in the state will reduce to nothing. There are, it is true, many people in every rich state who having large sums of money, would prefer paper with good security; as being of more easy transport and more safe custody. If the public provide not a bank, private bankers will take advantage of this circumstance; as the goldsmiths formerly did in LONDON, or as the bankers do at present in DUBLIN: And therefore it is better, it may be thought, that a public company should enjoy the benefit of that paper-credit, which always will have place in every opulent kingdom. But to endeavour artificially to encrease such a credit, can never be the interest of any trading nation; but must lay them under disadvantages, by encreasing money beyond its natural proportion to labour and commodities, and thereby heightening their price to the merchant and manufacturer. And in this view, it must be allowed, that no bank could be more advantageous, than such a one as locked up all the money it received,* and never augmented the circulating coin, as is

* This is the case with the bank of AMSTERDAM.

usual, by returning part of its treasure into commerce. A public bank, by this expedient, might cut off much of the dealings of private bankers and money-jobbers; and though the state bore the charge of salaries to the directors and tellers of this bank (for, according to the preceding supposition, it would have no profit from its dealings), the national advantage, resulting from the low price of labour and the destruction of paper-credit, would be a sufficient compensation. Not to mention, that so large a sum, lying ready at command, would be a convenience in times of great public danger and distress; and what part of it was used might be replaced at leisure, when peace and tranquillity was restored to the nation.

* * * * *

I scarcely know any method of sinking money below its level, but those institutions of banks, funds, and paper-credit, which are so much practised in this kingdom. These render paper equivalent to money, circulate it throughout the whole state, make it supply the place of gold and silver, raise proportionably the price of labour and commodities, and by that means either banish a great part of those precious metals, or prevent their farther encrease. What can be more short-sighted than our reasonings on this head? We fancy, because an individual would be much richer, were his stock of money doubled, that the same good effect would follow were the money of every one encreased; not considering, that this would raise as much the price of every commodity, and reduce every man in time to the same condition as before. It is only in our public negociations and transactions with foreigners, that a greater stock of money is advantageous; and as our paper is there absolutely insignificant, we feel, by its means, all the ill effects arising from a great abundance of money, without reaping any of the advantages.*

---

* We observed in Essay III. that money, when encreasing, gives encouragement to industry, during the interval between the encrease of money and rise of the prices. A good effect of this nature may

Suppose that there are 12 millions of paper, which circulate in the kingdom as money (for we are not to imagine that all our enormous funds are employed in that shape), and suppose the real cash of the kingdom to be 18 millions: Here is a state which is found by experience to be able to hold a stock of 30 millions. I say, if it be able to hold it, it must of necessity have acquired it in gold and silver, had we not obstructed the entrance of these metals by this new invention of paper. *Whence would it have acquired that sum?* From all the kingdoms of the world. *But why?* Because, if you remove these 12 millions, money in this state is below its level, compared with our neighbours; and we must immediately draw from all of them, till we be full and saturate, so to speak, and can hold no more. By our present politics we are as careful to stuff the nation with this fine commodity of bank-bills and chequer-notes, as if we were afraid of being overburthened with the precious metals.

It is not to be doubted, but the great plenty of bullion in FRANCE is, in a great measure, owing to the want of paper-credit. The FRENCH have no banks: Merchants bills do not there circulate as with us: Usury or lending on interest is not directly permitted; so that many have large sums in their coffers: Great quantities of plate are used in private houses; and all the churches are full of it. By this means, provisions and labour still remain cheaper among them, than in nations that are not half so rich in gold and silver. The advantages of this situation, in point of trade as well as in great public emergencies, are too evident to be disputed.

The same fashion a few years ago prevailed in GENOA, which still has place in ENGLAND and HOLLAND, of using services of CHINA-ware instead of plate; but the senate, foreseeing the consequence, prohibited the use of that brittle

---

follow too from paper-credit; but it is dangerous to precipitate matters, at the risk of losing all by the failing of that credit, as must happen upon any violent shock in public affairs.

commodity beyond a certain extent; while the use of silver-plate was left unlimited. And I suppose, in their late distresses, they felt the good effect of this ordinance. Our tax on plate is, perhaps, in this view, somewhat impolitic.

Before the introduction of paper money into our colonies, they had gold and silver sufficient for their circulation. Since the introduction of that commodity, the least inconveniency that has followed is the total banishment of the precious metals. And after the abolition of paper, can it be doubted but money will return, while these colonies possess manufactures and commodities, the only thing valuable in commerce, and for whose sake alone all men desire money?

What pity LYCURGUS did not think of paper-credit, when he wanted to banish gold and silver from SPARTA! It would have served his purpose better than the lumps of iron he made use of as money; and would also have prevented more effectually all commerce with strangers, as being of so much less real and intrinsic value.

It must, however, be confessed, that, as all these questions of trade and money are extremely complicated, there are certain lights in which this subject may be placed, so as to represent the advantages of paper-credit and banks to be superior to their disadvantages. That they banish specie and bullion from a state is undoubtedly true; and whoever looks no farther than this circumstance does well to condemn them; but specie and bullion are not of so great consequence as not to admit of a compensation, and even an overbalance from the encrease of industry and of credit, which may be promoted by the right use of paper-money. It is well known of what advantage it is to a merchant to be able to discount his bills upon occasion; and every thing that facilitates this species of traffic is favourable to the general commerce of a state. But private bankers are enabled to give such credit by the credit they receive from the depositing of money in their shops; and the bank of ENGLAND in the same manner, from the liberty it has to issue its notes in all payments. There was an invention of this kind, which was fallen upon some years ago by the banks of EDINBURGH; and which, as it is one of the most ingenious ideas that has been executed in commerce, has also been thought advantageous to SCOTLAND. It is there called a BANK-CREDIT; and is of this nature. A man goes to the bank and finds surety to the amount, we shall suppose, of a thousand pounds. This money, or any part of it, he has the liberty of drawing out whenever he pleases, and he pays only the ordinary interest for it, while it is in his hands. He may, when he pleases, repay any sum so small as twenty pounds, and the interest is discounted from the very day of the repayment. The advantages, resulting from this contrivance, are manifold. As a man may find surety nearly to the amount of his substance, and his bank-credit is equivalent to ready money, a merchant does hereby in a manner coin his houses, his household furniture, the goods in his warehouse, the foreign debts due to him, his ships at sea; and can, upon occasion, employ them in all payments, as if they were the current money of the country. If a man borrow a thousand pounds from a private hand, besides that it is not always to be found when required, he pays interest for it whether he be using it or not; His bank-credit costs him nothing except during the very moment in which it is of service to him: and this circumstance is of equal advantage as if he had borrowed money at a much lower interest. Merchants, likewise, from this invention, acquire a great facility in supporting each other's credit, which is a considerable security against bankruptcies. A man, when his own bank-credit is exhausted, goes to any of his neighbours who is not in the same condition; and he gets the money, which he replaces at his convenience.

After this practice had taken place during some years at EDINBURGH, several companies of merchants at GLASGOW carried the matter farther. They associated themselves into different banks, and issued notes so low as ten shillings, which they used in all payments for goods, manufactures, tradesmen's labour of all kinds; and these notes, from the established credit of the companies, passed as money in all payments throughout the country. By this means, a stock of five thousand pounds was able to perform the same operations as if it were six or seven; and merchants were thereby enabled to trade to a greater extent, and to require less profit in all their transactions. But whatever other advantages result from these inventions, it must still be allowed that, besides giving too great facility to credit, which is dangerous, they banish the precious metals; and nothing can be a more evident proof of it, than a comparison of the past and present condition of SCOTLAND in that particular. It was found, upon the recoinage made after the union, that there was near a million of specie in that country: But notwithstanding the great encrease of riches, commerce, and manufactures of all kinds, it is thought, that, even where there is no extraordinary drain made by ENGLAND, the current specie will not now amount to a third of that sum.

*FINIS.*

# ESSAY

## On PAPER-MONEY and BANKING;

FROM ESSAYS ON THE

PUBLIC DEBT, FRUGALITY, &c.

*Publiſhed in*

M.DCC.LV.

9, 1755. Lord Elibank, 'Essay on Paper-Money and Banking' from *Essays on the Public Debt, Frugality &c*, London.

## PAPER-MONEY, BANKING, &c.

IT is with the greatest concern I have heard, for some years past, the daily complaints made by all ranks of people in this part of the country, in common with the rest of the kingdom, upon the scarcity of gold and silver money; the decay of trade and manufactures; the slow progress of husbandry; and lastly, (what one would scarcely believe could be a concomitant evil with those just mentioned) the increase of luxury, and expence of living. And it is with no less astonishment, that I have so long observed the supine sloth and careless indifference of my countrymen about the causes or cure of this complicated mischief, which threatens poverty and ruin to themselves and their posterity for some generations. It might have been expected, at least, that some one of public spirit, endowed with sufficient abilities, would have drawn his pen in such a national cause, and, in that belief, I had no inclination to undertake a task, for which I found myself very unequal; but when I reflected that the greatest events have been brought to pass, and taken their rise from the smallest beginnings,—that the *Roman* empire was saved by the cackling of a goose,—I was not without hopes that my own weak endeavours might be successful, in some measure, to awaken my countrymen to a sense of their present misery, and perhaps be assistant to them in finding a remedy: if what I now write can have that effect, I shall be well pleased.

Frugality and industry are the two great sources of riches; and when we consider that a desire of gain and an application to the means by which it is to be attained are inseparable from the common principle of self-preservation, one would think there would be little occasion to recommend the practice of these virtues to mankind; but if we reflect, that among such a number as that of mankind, all pursuing the same end, of providing for themselves, and, as it were, running to one common goal, the more active, cunning and vigilant will soon over-reach those of less abilities, it must follow, that the views and interests of individuals thus interfering, will beget a sort of universal war among mankind, and in proportion, as one set of men prevail in their pursuits, the opposite interests must be sunk and discouraged; thus industry and frugality may be swallowed up by rapine and violence.

Now, I take this to be the case with agriculture, trade and manufactures in this country: every one is sensible of the slow progress of the first, and of the stagnation and decay of the other two; and, I imagine, it is no less obvious, that this effect cannot have been produced by any cause flowing from the nature of the things themselves; for industry sets no bounds to itself, and 'tis but a foolish pretence to say that trade can be overstocked, so long as the numbers of mankind and their wants are in proportion, the cause therefore must be extraneous; our industry must be borne down and oppressed by the superior industry, weight or interest of those whose pursuits after gain are inconsistent with the good of trade and manufactures.

The arts by which industry may be oppressed, are as various as those whereby it is promoted; every quality in nature hath its contrary; but we need not search very deep to find out the cause of our present misery, one presents itself, which will solve the whole phænomena and symptoms of it, and that is, the currency of PAPER-MONEY or BANK-NOTES, which by increasing the quantity, has sunk the intrinsic value of our money, and introduced all the real inconveniencies of plenty of money, without the smallest advantage to any individual but the bankers themselves.

I may venture to affirm that there is, at least, twice the value of bank-notes as there is of real money circulating in *Scotland*, (if I had said six times the value, perhaps I had spoke within bounds) and these notes have equal currency with the money itself, which they represent; so that here is the whole cash of the kingdom tripled by a fiction, without any addition to our riches: let us attend to its operation, and the inconvenience will be obvious.

It is a maxim, that the price of labour and commodities is always regulated by the quantity of money circulating in a state; increase or diminish the money, and prices must rise or fall in a certain proportion: the consequence to agriculture, trade and manufactures, is apparent; when money is augmented, the farmer and handy-craftsman must pay higher wages to his servants, and must raise the price of his grain or commodity, to indemnify himself. The merchant buying these at a high price, must sell accordingly, if he can, but will soon find himself undersold at foreign markets, where the same goods manufactured or produced in other states, which have less money, can be sold, perhaps, a half or a third cheaper, and to more profit; this obliges the merchant to give over his trade, or be ruined; and the industry of the merchant being thus stopt, the stagnation must operate backwards from one trade to another, till it affects agriculture, where it begun.

These inconveniencies, when arising from a plenty of real money, are fully compensated by the riches which occasioned them, and the above stagnation of trade will last no longer than other states continue to undersell us, which cannot be very long; for the trade of any state will be an inlet to riches, and money will flow in upon it till that state be likewise full, and its entrance be stopt by the same repletion: from that state it will go to another, and so on, till it becomes on a perfect level and equality throughout the whole.

But what must be the miserable situation of trade and manufactures, in a state, where the policy and interested motives of individuals have so contrived it, that the entrance of money, which would be the necessary consequence of its trade, is debarred by a kind of stratagem or illusion, *viz.* by creating an imaginary money of paper, which the substance, credit or interest of the projectors makes to supply the place of real money?

Now, such is our own situation, an immense value of bank-notes hath been poured in upon us, and increaseth daily. Every body takes them for money, without the smallest scruple, and believes himself as rich when possessed of them, as if he had the value in gold and silver; with this imagination, the price of labour and every commodity, and consequently the expence of living is raised, industry, arts, and trade overwhelmed and discouraged, and every other inconveniency felt, that can be produced by the plenty of real gold and silver. Under such a pressure, it must add greatly to our mortification, when we consider that all the real specie, which these notes falsely represent, would have actually entered into the country, by the means of trade, before prices could have been raised, or trade sunk to such a degree as they are at present; and when that inconveniency happened, we should, at least have had the consolation to think that we had got our fill before we removed from the feast, and might then have said:

*———Edisti satis atque bibisti*
*tempus abire tibi est————————*

whereas all we gain by our present œconomy, is to look fat and fair while we consume away with a dropsy. But this public calamity, however destructive of the general good of the society, hath been contrived and brought upon us, as I have said, by the policy and interested motives of individuals, whose fortunes are thus built upon the ruins of their fellow-subjects; the certainty of which may be easily demonstrated; for it is apparent, that the value of all the immense quantity of notes circulating in the kingdom, must have been paid to these bankers, when they were first issued, either in money, labour, or commodities; and if we shall suppose the quantity of those circulating notes to be double to the real circulating specie, it follows that two-thirds of the substance and trade of the nation have got into the hands of the bankers; for as the whole money in a state represents, and is the value of the whole stock of labour and commodities which it produces, so two-thirds of the one must be equal to two-thirds of the other.

And altho' these bankers by the creation of so much money, have raised the price of labour and commodities to such an excessive height, as must be the destruction of trade and manufactures, yet they are the only individuals in the state who do not suffer by it; for by continually increasing their imaginary money, they balance the increase of the price, and so are no poorer by buying dearer than they were before.

One may be apt to wonder how these pernicious practices of bankers should remain so long unchecked in a well regulated society; and it must be confessed, that such an imposture could never have been palmed upon us, but under favour, and by the assistance of a spirit of blindness and delusion, which has thrown, as it were, a mist before our eyes, to lead us astray: no man, with his eyes open, would tamely behold another picking his pocket; and is it to be supposed, that a thinking people would give away two-third parts of their stock for a bit of paper which a foreigner would not take for a farthing, and which any commotion in the state may reduce to as little value at home?

But here it may be asked, Is there then no national advantage arising from this institution of banks and paper-credit, in a state? Is there no plausible plea, at least founded either on reason or experience, for a practice so universal? For answer, I beg leave to refer to the following verses of Mr. *Pope:*

*Blest paper credit! last and best supply!*
*That lends corruption lighter wings to fly!*
*Gold, imp'd by thee, can compass hardest things,*
*Can pocket states, can fetch or carry Kings;*
*A single leaf shall waft an Army o'er,*
*Or ship off senates to some distant shore;*
*A leaf, like Sybil's, scatter to and fro*
*Our fates and fortunes as the winds shall blow;*
*Pregnant with thousands flits the scrap unseen,*
*And silent sells a King, or buys a Queen.*

But after all, it must be confessed that banks, if under due regulations, might be of use to facilitate commerce in a state; such for instance, as a bank, constituted on the model of that of *Amsterdam,* (where all the money that comes into it is lockt up, and never again sees the light, no payments being there made again in money, but by way of transfers of stock), or such a bank, where no more notes should be issued than exactly corresponded to the money given in; in which case, the notes would be much more convenient than the money itself, as being of more easy transport, and safe custody; and the bankers would become a very usefel and harmless part of the society, as being a sort of public servants for keeping and telling out our money: but as for our present scheme, which leaveth an unlimited dictatorial power to bankers to send abroad notes to what value they please, tho' perhaps twenty times as much as the value of all the money in the kingdom, and impose the same upon us for gold and silver, I make no hesitation to pronounce it absolutely pernicious, and destructive of all trade, industry, and manufactures. I cannot represent this our mismanagement, or the advantage of a contrary scheme, in better words than those of the ingenious Mr. *Hume,* in his Political Essays, from which I have borrowed some of the foregoing arguments: after taking notice that the practices of bankers will introduce paper-credit into every opulent kingdom, he adds: "But to endeavour artificially to increase such a "credit, can never be the interest of any trading nation; "but must lay them under disadvantages, by increasing money "beyond its natural proportion to labour and commodities, "and thereby heightening their price to the merchant and "manufacturer. And in this view it must be allowed, that "no bank could be more advantageous than such a one as "lockt up all the money it received, and never augmented the "circulating coin, as is usual, by returning part of its trea-"sure into commerce. A public bank, by this expedient, "might cut off much of the dealings of private bankers and "money jobbers; and tho' the state bore the charge of "salaries to the directors and tellers of this bank, (for "according to the preceding supposition, it would have no "profit from its dealings) the national advantage, resulting "from the low price of labour and destruction of paper-

"credit, would be a sufficient compensation. Not to men- "tion, that so large a sum, lying ready at command, would "be a great convenience in times of public danger and "distress; and what part of it was used might be replaced "at leisure, when peace and tranquillity were restored to the "nation."

As I would be loath to ominate bad things, I shall not take upon me to foretel the evil consequences of this implicit faith, this unlimited trust, this lethargic carelessness of my countrymen, with regard to paper-credit;—I need only say, that it is a maxim, that security is always dangerous, and often the fore-runner of destruction.

But I hope that the evil consequences to trade, industry and arts, which have been already produced and so heavily felt, by the means of this paper-money, will be sufficient to awaken the spirit of every one who wishes well to the country, and to make him stand up in self-defence, to oppose this torrent which threatens to swallow up our trade and industry, to close up the sluices by which it has entered, and endeavour to force it back to the fountains from whence it proceeded.

I am sensible how difficult a matter it will be to remedy this evil of so long standing, which like an inveterate malady hath become part of our constitution, and is not to be conquered by sudden or violent applications. It is not to be supposed, that the bankers, who are possessed of such a share of the riches, trade, and consequently the power of the nation, will submit to be spoiled of all by those who are weaker than themselves: a very considerable part of our merchants are furnished with credit by those bankers, to near the full extent of their trade, and so have become obliged, thro' necessity, to circulate their notes, or lose the credit which supports their trade; the reformation therefore cannot be expected to begin from them, though it is they who must give it the finishing stroke: it must therefore proceed from those who are not immediately dependent on the bankers, that is, the landed gentlemen, farmers, and manufacturers, who have the command of all the labour and native commodities in the kingdom. There is no law that obligeth us to take bank-notes for money; and if these three classes would make a vigorous resolution not to circulate any such, or receive them in payment for their grain, labour, or manufactures, unless at an advanced price, we should very soon see these notes shrink into a narrow compass, and, with the same pace as they retire, we shall see trade, industry and arts advance, and assume new life and vigour; for by this vast diminution of our circulating money, the prices of labour and every thing must soon fall in a certain proportion; the farmer will soon get servants at reasonable wages, which will be a spur to his industry, and enable him to cultivate his ground, produce more grain, and to pay a higher rent to his landlord; the cheapness of all the necessaries of life will enable the landlord to sell his grain, and every artizan his commodity, at a lower price, without diminution of his profit; the merchant buying all these at a lower price, can afford to carry them to foreign markets, where he is sure of a ready sale and profitable returns. This will encourage him to enlarge his trade, arts and industry will flourish, and money will flow in upon us, till its entrance is checked again by its plenty and high prices.

All these good effects, which I have mentioned, will be the necessary consequence of the diminution of the quantity of our circulating money. Add to this, the pleasure and satisfaction which it must be to every one's mind, when he reflects that the money he acquires by his industry or good fortune is his own, and will afford him the necessaries or pleasures of life, at home or abroad, independent of any commotions or credit of bankers: this consideration alone, I say, ought to banish paper-money for ever.

*FINIS.*

10, 1775. Act of Parliament, *15° Georgii III, c. 51, A.D. 1775*, London: House of Commons.

ANNO DECIMO QUINTO

# Georgii III. Regis.

---

## CAP. LI.

An Act to reſtrain the Negotiation of Promiſſory Notes and Inland Bills of Exchange under a limited Sum, within that Part of *Great Britain* called *England*.

WHEREAS various Notes, Bills of Exchange, and Draughts for Money for very small Sums, have for some Time past been circulated or negotiated in lieu of Cash within that Part of Great Britain called England, to the great Prejudice of Trade and Publick Credit; and many of such Bills and Draughts being payable under certain Terms and Restrictions, which the poorer Sort of Manufacturers, Artificers, Labourers, and others, cannot comply with otherwise than by being subject to great Extortion and Abuse; be it therefore enacted by the King's most Preamble.

most Excellent Majesty, by and with the Advice and Consent of the Lords Spiritual and Temporal, and Commons, in this present Parliament assembled, and by the Authority of the same, That all Promissory or other Notes, Bills of Exchange, or Draughts, or Undertakings, in Writing, being negotiable or transferrable, for the Payment of any Sum or Sums of Money less than the Sum of Twenty Shillings in the Whole, which shall be made or issued at any Time from and after the Twenty-fourth Day of June, One thousand seven hundred and seventy-five, shall be, and the same are hereby declared to be, absolutely void and of no Effect, any Law, Statute, Usage, or Custom, to the contrary thereof in any-wise notwithstanding.

After *June* 24, 1775, all Promissory Notes, *&c.* for less than 20 *s.* to be of no Effect.

And be it further enacted by the Authority aforesaid, That if any Person or Persons shall at any Time or Times, from and after the Twenty-fourth Day of June, One thousand seven hundred and seventy-five, by any Art, Device, or Means whatsoever, publish or utter any such Notes, Bills, Draughts, or Engagements, as aforesaid, for a less Sum than Twenty Shillings, or on which less than the Sum of Twenty Shillings shall be due, and which shall be in any-wise negotiable, or shall negotiate the same; every such Person shall forfeit and pay, for every such Offence, any Sum not exceeding Twenty Pounds, nor less than Five Pounds.

Persons uttering such Notes or Bills for less than 20 *s.* *&c.* shall forfeit not exceeding 20 *l.* nor less than 5 *l.*

A

# TREATISE

ON THE

# COINS OF THE REALM;

IN A

# LETTER

TO

# THE KING.

---

BY

CHARLES EARL OF LIVERPOOL.

---

OXFORD,

AT THE UNIVERSITY PRESS, FOR CADELL AND DAVIES,

STRAND, LONDON.

1805.

11, 1805. Charles Earl of Liverpool, *A Treatise on the Coins of this Realm; in a Letter to the King*, pp. 69–86, Oxford: Printed at the University Press for Cadell & Davies.

In the reigns of Charles II. and James II. the Silver Coins, of which the old hammered Money conſtituted a conſiderable part, had been gradually diminiſhed, by clipping, and other frauds. In the beginning of the reign of King William III. theſe practices increaſed rapidly; and the Silver Coins were in general become ſo very defective, that it was found, upon experiments made by the Officers of the Exchequer, in the year 1695, that they wanted, upon the whole, nearly one half of their weight. The great evils, to which the people, as well as the Government, were thereby expoſed, are fully deſcribed by Mr. Lowndes, who was then Secretary of the Treaſury, in a Report made by him on the 12th September of that year, to the Lords Commiſſioners of his Majeſty's Treaſury. He informs their Lordſhips, "that in conſequence "of the defective ſtate of the Silver Coin, great contentions "daily aroſe among the King's ſubjects, in fairs, markets, "ſhops, and other places throughout the kingdom, to the "diſturbance of the public peace;—that many bargains and "dealings were totally prevented and laid aſide, which leſ-"ſened trade in general;—that perſons, before they con-"cluded any bargain, were neceſſitated firſt to ſettle the price or

See a Table at the end of Mr. Lowndes's Report on the Silver Coins, in which theſe experiments are accurately ſtated.

" or value of the very Money they were to receive for their " goods; and that they ſet a price on their goods accordingly; " —that theſe practices had been one great cauſe of the raiſing " the price, not only of all merchandiſes, but of every article " neceſſary for the ſuſtenance of the common people, to their " great grievance [a];—that the receipt and collection of the " public taxes, revenues, and debts, were extremely retarded, " to the damage of his Majeſty, and to the prejudice of a " vigorous proſecution of the war; ſo that there never were " in his remembrance ſo many bonds given and lying unſatiſ- " fied at the Cuſtom Houſe, or ſo vaſt an arrear of exciſes;— " that, from the ſame cauſe, many complaints were daily tranſ- " mitted from the Commiſſioners, Receivers, and Collectors " of the land-tax." And in proof of the degree to which the receipt of that tax had been affected, by the defective ſtate of the Coin, Mr. Lowndes referred the Lords of the Treaſury to the account of the ſum brought into the Exchequer in the courſe of that year, compared with the timely payments of the like tax in preceding years. With reſpect to the foreign commerce, Mr. Lowndes obſerves, " that the exchange with " the Low Countries was fallen ſo very low, that the public " loſt about four Shillings in the Pound upon all Monies re- " mitted thither;—that the exchange to Hamburgh and the " Eaſt countries for all naval ſtores and other goods was ſtill " lower; and to all places in the Mediterranean, the ex- " change was yet more to the prejudice of this country; and

[a] Mr. Locke, in his Anſwer to Mr. Lowndes, confirms this account of Mr. Lowndes, that all ſorts of proviſions and commodities had riſen exceſſively.

that

" that there were very great loſſes, on that account, in remit- " ting Money for the payment of our fleets and armies :" and he further obſerves, " that the price of Silver in Bullion " was riſen to 6s 5d per ounce, and that the Guinea having " riſen to 30s, paſſed in currency at a much higher value than " the price of Silver in Bullion would then juſtify [a]." The conſequence was, that all the Silver Bullion in the kingdom, that could be collected, inſtead of being brought to the Mint, was exported in return for Gold Bullion, in which foreigners made their payments to their own advantage, and to the great detriment of the merchants and manufacturers of this country, who had any commercial intercourſe with them.

Such was the alarming ſituation of the kingdom at a period when it was engaged in a foreign war, on the ſucceſs of which depended the preſervation of our liberties, and all the benefits derived from the Revolution. Among the various parties, into which the kingdom was at that time divided, there was not one, which did not think that ſome remedy was abſolutely neceſſary. Many propoſitions were made. Two of theſe moſt attracted the attention of the public ; one, offered by Mr. Lowndes, who had long been Secretary of the Treaſury ; the other, by Mr. John Locke. The conduct of this difficult buſineſs fell to the lot of Mr. Charles Montague, then Chancellor of the Exchequer. He followed principally the plan propoſed by Mr. Locke, and called to his aſſiſtance Mr. Newton, afterwards Sir Iſaac Newton, whom he then made

[a] Silver Bullion had riſen in price $24\frac{1}{5}$ per cent. The Gold Coin in tale had riſen about $36\frac{1}{3}$ per cent.

Warden

Warden of the Mint, and Dr. Halley. The kingdom was then divided chiefly into two great factions ; ſo that from political motives Mr. Montague met with oppoſition in every meaſure he propoſed. He loſt, in the Houſe of Commons, at firſt, many queſtions, eſſential to the ſucceſs of his meaſures ; but by bringing the ſame propoſitions repeatedly under the conſideration of the Houſe, he at laſt carried them, though with very ſmall majorities.

The old hammered Coins, which had been moſt reduced, began at this time to be exchanged for ſuch of the remaining Silver Coins as were more perfect, and leſs clipped, at a premium. The firſt meaſure therefore, which the Parliament adopted, was to paſs an Act, forbidding the receiving or paying of any *broad Silver Money*, or Silver Money unclipped, of the Coin of this kingdom, for more than its nominal value in tale. But this meaſure produced another evil ; for, in conſequence of it, all the perfect and unclipped Silver Coins began to be hoarded, ſo that they appeared no longer in circulation; and as the Parliament had not forbidden the exchange of the deficient or clipped Silver Coins for Guineas, or other Gold Coins, the former were then exchanged for the Gold Coin ; and the Guinea, which had paſſed before generally for 21s 6d, or 22s, began now to paſs for 30s ; and it would have riſen to a greater value, if the Officers of the Exchequer, and the Receivers of the public revenue, had not refuſed to receive it in payment, at a higher rate. To remedy this laſt evil, the Parliament paſſed two Acts, mentioned in a former part of this Letter, forbidding firſt the currency of Guineas at any higher rate than 26s each ; and afterwards, at any higher rate than

6th and 7th William III. ch. 17. ſec. 2.

See Mr. Lowndes's Report, p. 114. See alſo Mr. Locke's Eſſay.

7th and 8th William III. ch. 10. ſec. 18.

than 22s each. They alſo paſſed an Act, ſuſpending, for a limited time, the coining of Guineas; and as it was foreſeen, that Guineas, either ſuch as had been formerly remitted to foreign countries, or had been counterfeited abroad, would be imported in great quantities, the Parliament at the ſame time prohibited the importation of Guineas.

7th and 8th William III. ch. 19. ſec. 12.

7th and 8th William III. ch. 13.

To ſupport the currency of the clipped and deficient Silver Coins, the Parliament enacted, that all taxes and debts due to the Crown, for exciſe, cuſtoms, &c. and the whole year's land-tax, might be paid to the collectors, at any time before the 4th May 1696, in the clipped Coins; and that all loans of Money, borrowed on the authority of Parliament, might alſo be paid in the clipped Coins, as if the ſame were good and lawful Money, unleſs otherwiſe ſpecially directed. And in ſubſequent Acts the remainder of the clipped Coins was ordered to be received at the Mint, and by the Receivers of the public revenue for a limited time, by weight, but at a value exceeding the Mint price of Bullion.

7th and 8th William III. ch. 1.

8th William III. ch. 2.

8th and 9th William III. ch. 6.

To give additional credit to the new Silver Coins, as ſoon as they ſhould be iſſued, the Parliament enacted, that the clipped Money "ſhould be recoined by the Mill and Preſs into "current Money of this realm, to hold ſuch weight and fine-"neſs as are preſcribed by the preſent Indenture of the Mint, "which weight and fineneſs are declared to be, and ſhall re-"main to be, the ſtandard of, and for the lawful Silver Coin "of this realm."

7th William III. ch. 1. ſec. 2.—This clauſe of the Act is not printed in the common edition of the Statutes.

Encouragements were at the ſame time given for bringing Plate

7th and 8th William III. ch. 19. sec. 2.

Plate to the Mint, and 6d for every ounce of ſtandard Silver ſo brought in was to be paid as a premium: and all perſons keeping inns, or other public houſes, were forbidden to have any Silver Plate in their houſes, except ſpoons. It was further enacted, that no Bullion, either of Gold or Silver, in Ingots, or otherwiſe, ſhould be exported, except upon proof before the Lord Mayor of London, that the ſame was not made of the Coins of this realm, or clippings thereof, or of Plate wrought within the kingdom. They permitted, however, Bullion, equal in value to 200,000l ſterling, to be exported by licence from the King, for the payment of his Majeſty's forces in foreign countries.

As it was of great importance to bring the new Silver Money into currency as ſpeedily as poſſible, the Recoinage was carried on not only at the Tower, but Mints were eſtabliſhed for this purpoſe in different parts of the country, and perſons of ſcience were ſent to theſe Mints, to ſuperintend and control the operations there carried on.

This important buſineſs was very far advanced in the firſt two years; but it appears by accounts received from the Officers of the Mint, that four years were neceſſary for the completion of this Recoinage. The quantity of Silver Coins made on this occaſion amounted in tale to 6,812,908l 19s 7d; of which, 5,091,121l 7s 7d was coined at the Tower, and 1,791,787l 12s was coined at the country Mints.

I have not been able to find, in any public office, an account of the whole charge and loſs, which the public incurred

curred by this Recoinage. The Officers of the Mint have indeed furnished an account of the charges for the making or fabrication of the new Money, or what may properly be called the Mint charges. They amounted to 179,431l 6s; but the losses sustained by the receipt of the principal part of the clipped and deficient Coins, at their nominal value, as well as the charge for premiums paid to induce persons to bring in the remainder, and to bring Plate and Bullion to be coined, are no where stated with any certainty. It is presumed however, that these charges and losses could not amount in the whole to less than 2,700,000l.*

* It appears, that the actual quantity of Silver Money either recoined or made of Plate, brought to the Mint, was 6,882,908l 19s 7d. If we suppose, that only two thirds of this sum, that is, 4,588,605l 19s 8⅔d, were worn and clipped Coins, which were diminished nearly one half, and received at the Exchequer in payment of the public revenues, and of loans, at their nominal value, the loss to the public on this account would amount to 2,294,302l 19s 10⅓. If again we suppose that the remaining third being 2,294,302l 19s 10⅓d, cost the public no more than 6d per ounce, or about 10 per cent., this is a further loss to the public of 229,430l. Add to this the charges of coining, or Mint charges, amounting to 179,431l 6s. These three sums make together 2,703,164l 5s 10⅓d. This is a very moderate estimate of the whole loss incurred by the public by this Recoinage. Mr. Lowndes, in his Report to the Lords of the Treasury, estimated the quantity of the worn and clipped Silver Money, then current, at 4,000,000l; and the loss, which the public would incur by recoining it according to the old standard, at 2,000,000l. Anderson, in his History of Commerce, says, that the Recoinage cost near 3,000,000l. The common histories estimate it at 2,200,000l. It does not appear from the Journals, that the Parliament ever voted so large a sum, expressly for this purpose; but it is probable, that a considerable part of this loss shewed itself only in deficiencies of several branches of the revenue; and that the House of Commons, in making it good, did no more than vote sums to supply these deficiencies. It is extraordinary, however, that no account should

Great as this charge was, the loffes which the Government, as well as the people of this kingdom, continued daily to fuffer, till the Recoinage was completed, juftified almoft any expence, which might be incurred for their relief. To the great loffes already ftated, as occafioned by the defective ftate of the Silver Coin, it may be proper to add, that in every contract made by Government, or individuals, the deficiency of the Coin muft have been taken into confideration, and the price of every article augmented, probably in a much greater proportion, than this deficiency would juftify.

Mr. Locke, whofe advice on this occafion was principally followed, as before obferved, had confidered the fubject with that depth of thought, by which all his writings are diftinguifhed; and he had treated of it in a philofophical and fpeculative view, with great ability; but he appears not to have adverted to many circumftances of a practical nature, neceffarily connected with this fubject; and it is probable that he was not well informed of the hiftory of our Coins, which would have pointed out thefe circumftances to him. He afferted as a certain fact, "that Silver Coins made the Money "of Account, or Meafure of Commerce, in England and the "neighbouring countries." How far this affertion is well founded, we fhall have occafion to fhew hereafter. He then laid it down as a principle which could not be controverted, that "an ounce of Silver, whether in Pence, Groats, or Crown

See Mr. Locke's Letter to a Member of Parliament in 1691.

fhould have been made out at that time, of the actual lofs occafioned by the Recoinage; or if any fuch account was made out, that it fhould not have been preferved in fome of the public offices.

"Pieces,

" Pieces, Stivers or Ducatoons, or in Bullion, is, and always " eternally will be, of equal value to any other ounce of Sil- " ver, under what ſtamp or denomination ſoever." Of this principle there can be no doubt: but from theſe two premiſes he drew the following concluſions:

Firſt, That the high price of Silver Bullion at that time was to be aſcribed to the defective ſtate of the Silver Coins then in currency; and that whenever the Silver Coins were reſtored to their due weight, the price of Silver Bullion would fall, ſo as to be nearly the ſame as that, at which it was valued at the Mint. Secondly, that the Gold Coins, if their value in currency was not fixed by public authority, would paſs in payment, with reference to the Silver Coins, *according to the current rate;* that is, according to the relative value of Gold to Silver at the market.

If the concluſions reſulting from the foregoing premiſes were univerſally true, and had operated on the preſent occaſion to their full extent, it is certain, that as the Silver Coins then wanted nearly one half of their weight, the price of Silver in Bullion ſhould have riſen in the ſame proportion; that is, to about 10s per ounce: and that the Guinea ſhould have riſen to nearly twice the value, at which it had hitherto paſſed in currency, that is, to about 44s; but neither of theſe conſequences happened. The price of Silver in Bullion roſe to no more than 6s 5d per ounce; and the Guinea roſe only to the value of 30s. It is true, that the further riſe of the Guinea was prevented, by orders given to the Officers of the Exchequer, and to the Receivers of the public revenue, not to to receive it in payment at a higher rate; and ſome time afterwards the value of the Guinea was ſtill further limited, by the two Acts of Parliament, as before mentioned.

As the Silver Coin was ſo very defective, before the general Recoinage was undertaken, and as during this Recoinage there could have been very little of it in currency, it is certain, that the Silver Bullion, which was then purchaſed, muſt have been paid for principally in the Gold Coin. It was natural therefore to expect, that Silver Bullion would have taken its price in due proportion, with reference to the current value of the Gold Coin. But it is ſingular, that as the Gold Coin had not taken its value in a due proportion with reference to the deficient Silver Coins, ſo Silver Bullion did not take its price in a due proportion with reference to the current value of the Gold Coins. The Gold Coins, though they had riſen $36\frac{4}{11}$ per cent. paſſed in currency at $46\frac{2}{3}$ per cent. leſs than their true value, compared with the deficient ſtate of the Silver Coins; and Silver Bullion, though it had riſen $24\frac{6}{31}$ per cent. was then ſold at $9\frac{677}{847}$ per cent. leſs than its true value, compared with the current value of the Gold Coins.

Mr. Lowndes ſays, that the Guinea then paſſed at 30s, *with the almoſt unanimous conſent and agreement of the common people;* and he adds, that there was *no other viſible reaſon* for this extraordinary riſe in the value of the Gold Coins above the price at which Silver Bullion then ſold, except the *danger and vexation,* which the people had experienced from every Money tranſaction in the clipped and deficient Silver Coins.

Whatever

Whatever may have been the cauſes of theſe ſtrange incongruities in the value of the Gold and Silver Coins, and of the price of Bullion with reference to theſe Coins, as before ſtated, they ſerve at leaſt to prove, that the events, which then happened, by no means correſponded with the concluſions, which, in Mr. Locke's opinion, reſulted from the principles laid down by him, and on which he ſo much relied. They afford alſo ſtrong reaſon to infer, that there are other cauſes, which may ſometimes influence the value of Coins, while they are current only within the realm; as well as the price of the precious metals in reference to them, beſides the intrinſic value of the metal in ſuch Coins[a].

It may however be ſaid, that thoſe were times of confuſion, and that no principles, however true, were likely in ſuch times to produce their full effect. Let us ſee then what effect theſe principles produced, when the Recoinage was completed, and when all the clipped and deficient Silver Coins were driven out of circulation, and ſuch only as were thought to be perfect were permitted to be current.

When the Recoinage of the Silver Coin was completed, the price of Silver Bullion did not even then fall, ſo as to be nearly[b] the ſame as the Mint price; and the Guinea, the

[a] There cannot be a ſtronger proof of the truth of this obſervation, than that which is afforded by the currency of the preſent deficient Silver Coins, which now circulate at their nominal value, and even ſometimes bear a premium, though they are deficient, to the degree that will be ſtated hereafter.

[b] Whenever the balance of commerce is againſt this country, and there is a want of Bullion to be exported, Bullion will always ſell at a ſmall advance above

value of which in currency had been reduced by an Act of Parliament to 22s, became current, without any interposition of public authority, at 21s 6d; but it did not fall in so great a degree as it ought to have fallen, according to the relative value of Gold to Silver at the market. The consequence was, that the new Silver Coins were immediately melted down and exported; and though 6,882,908l 19s 7d in tale had been lately coined, the most considerable part of this great sum, in the course of eighteen years, disappeared, and the public were deprived of the use of it; so that Sir Isaac Newton, in his Report of the 21st September 1717, says, "that if Silver "Money should become a little scarcer, people would in a "little time refuse to make payments in Silver, without a "premium." Another consequence resulted from the same cause; very little Silver Bullion was brought to the Mint to be coined. From the year 1699, when the general Recoinage was completed, to the end of the year 1717, no more than 674,831l 15s 9¼d in tale was coined; and of this sum 320,372l 12s were ancient Scottish Silver Coins, or foreign Coins permitted to be current in Scotland before the Union, which were recoined at Edinburgh into Coins of the English

above the price at which it is valued at the Mint, in consequence of the laws prohibiting the exportation of Coin. This advance must always be sufficient to compensate the risk of melting down or exporting the Coin, and this compensation is generally estimated at about 1 per cent. And whenever the demand for Bullion to be exported is very great, the price of it will rise still higher, and it is probable that the value of the Coin would in such case rise in a like proportion, if that value was not limited by public authority. In such case however there will be always a greater temptation to melt down and export the Coin.

standard.

ſtandard, by virtue of the Treaty of Union. Two other parts of this ſum, that is, 78,811l 6s, coined in the year 1709, and 76,780l 16s, coined in the year 1711, were principally made of Plate, brought to the Mint in conſequence of ſpecial encouragements then given. From the Plate ſo brought in 144,000l was converted into Coin, and only 11,592l 2s was coined from Silver Bullion brought into the Mint in the uſual courſe, during theſe two years: ſo that the natural or ordinary coinage of Silver, during this period of eighteen years, amounted to no more than 210,459l 3s 9¼d.

Martin Folkes, Table of Engliſh Silver Coins, p. 131. Note.

The exportation of the Silver Coins was at that time occaſioned by the high price of Silver Bullion at the market, and by the high rate, at which the Gold Coins continued to be current, compared with that of the Silver Coins. The high rate of the Gold Coins, to which the people then voluntarily ſubmitted, can only be aſcribed to the preference, which at that time began to be given to the uſe of Gold Coins in all payments, at leaſt of conſiderable amount. It is evident, that during the late Recoinage the common people had become accuſtomed to the uſe of the Gold Coins; and the reaſon, which induced them ſtill to prefer them, was perhaps the convenience of making large payments in Coins of that metal. This change, from what had been the caſe in the reign of Charles II. was probably owing to the great increaſe in the commerce of the country, and to an augmentation in the price of every commodity, ſo that payments in general required Coins made of the moſt valuable metal. The fact certainly is, that from this period the Gold Coins began to take the aſcendency, and to become the more uſual inſtrument of com-

commerce and meaſure of property, in preference to the Silver Coins. In the reign of King William, when the Silver Coins were ſo very deficient, Mr. Locke had ſaid, *It is no wonder, if the prices and value of things be confounded and uncertain, when the Meaſure itſelf is loſt.* To reſtore this Meaſure the public had expended 2,700,000l. But notwithſtanding ſo great an expence, this Meaſure of Property, in the lapſe of a very few years, was a ſecond time loſt, and had again no exiſtence, unleſs it had paſſed into the Gold Coin.

In this ſtate were the Coins of this kingdom in the year 1717, when the miniſters of George I. alarmed at the great diminution of the Silver Coins, which had been made in ſuch great quantities not twenty years before, took the ſubject into conſideration. They applied to Sir Iſaac Newton, then Maſter of the Mint, for his advice. The ſubject was referred to him, and he reported, "that the principal cauſe of the exportation "of the Silver Coin was, that a Guinea, which then paſſed "for 21s 6d, was generally worth no more than 20s 8d, according to the relative value of Gold to Silver at the market, "though its value occaſionally varied, and it might be worth "ſomething leſs, whenever there was a great demand for the "export of Silver, particularly to the Eaſt Indies, and perhaps "ſomething more, whenever a Plate fleet was juſt arrived "from Spaniſh America." He then ſuggeſted, that 6d *ſhould be taken off from the value of the Guinea, in order to diminiſh the temptation to export and melt down the Silver Coin; acknowledging however that* 10d *or* 12d *ought to be taken from the Guinea, in order that Gold may bear the ſame proportion with the Silver Money in England, which it ought to do by the courſe*

*course of trade and exchange in Europe.* This proposal of the Master of the Mint may be considered as a second attempt to restore to the Silver Coin the quality of a measure. But it is evident, that Sir Isaac Newton, who was no less distinguished for modesty, candour, and caution, in every opinion which he advanced, than for the accuracy and strength of his understanding, and for the large and extensive view which he took of every subject that came under his consideration, offered this proposal only *as an experiment;* and he adds, that the effects of this measure *would shew hereafter, better than can appear at present, what further reduction would be most convenient for the public.* This great man appears to have been apprised of the fluctuation which frequently happens in the relative value of the two precious metals; and he was probably apprehensive, that if the rate, at which the Gold Coins were to pass, had then been reduced, in full proportion, compared with the value of the Silver Coins, there would be the greatest danger[a] that these Gold Coins, which were at that time almost the only instrument of commerce remaining in the kingdom, might in their turn be melted down and exported; and yet, if they were not lowered still further, the Silver Coins would, in a degree, be subject to the same evils as before.

In pursuance of the advice of Sir Isaac Newton, the Lords of the Privy Council recommended to His Majesty, King

[a] When the value of the Gold Coins is in exact proportion with that of the Silver Coins, the Gold Coins will certainly be exported before the Silver Coins, because the bulk of the Gold Coins is less than that of the Silver Coins, and consequently there is less risk, trouble, and charge, in exporting them.

George

George I. to lower, by proclamation[a], the value of the Guinea to 21s; and the other Gold Coins in proportion. By this meaſure, which gave in effect the legal value of 21s to a Piece originally intended to be current at 20s, the value of fine Gold, compared with that of fine Silver, was eſtimated, in the Coins of this country, as $15\frac{2859}{13640}$ to 1; and this laſt riſe in the value of fine Gold compared with fine Silver was 5 per cent.; and the whole riſe in the value of Gold from the 1ſt James I. that is, in a ſpace of 115 years, was $39\frac{12}{67}$ per cent.; conſiderably more than one third.

But the Lords of the Privy Council, in executing this meaſure, did not conform to the principle adopted by Parliament, in the 7th and 8th of William III. of leaving the Guinea and other Gold Coins to be paid or received at any value under the rates by them limited. In the proclamation iſſued on this occaſion, it was not ſimply ſaid, that each Guinea *ſhould not paſs for more than* 21s, and the other Gold Coins in proportion; but it is expreſsly declared, *that the ſaid reſpective Pieces of coined Gold ſhall be current at the rates and values then ſet upon them.* By this injunction, the Guinea and all the other Gold Coins became legal tender, at the rates therein declared. They could no longer vary in their value, according to the relative value of Gold to Silver, as they had varied ſince the year 1663.

But though the Guinea was then reduced to 21s, from

[a] In all the Mint indentures from the 15th of Charles II. the Guinea had been called a Twenty Shilling Piece; and it was ordered to paſs at that rate. But on this occaſion a new indenture was made, dated 6th May 1718, in which this Piece of Gold Coin was called a Guinea, or a Twenty-one Shilling Piece; and it was ordered to paſs for twenty-one Shillings Sterling.

21s 6d,

21s 6d, it was ſtill rated at a higher value than it ought to be, compared with the Silver Coins, by at leaſt 4d, or $1\frac{10}{31}$ per cent. Experience has proved, that when Coins of two metals are made legal tender at given rates, thoſe who have any payments to make, will prefer to diſcharge their debts or obligations, by paying in that Coin which is over-rated. From that period, therefore, all conſiderable payments have been made in the Gold Coin; and the Silver Coins have generally ſerved only in making ſmall payments, or in exchange for the fractional parts of the Gold Coins. It has before been obſerved, that, previous to this proclamation, the people were diſpoſed to make their payments in the Gold Coins, in preference to thoſe of Silver. This laſt meaſure tended to confirm what was before the diſpoſition of the people, and gave the Gold Coins a complete aſcendency in the currency of the kingdom; and the Silver Coins have ſince become a mere repreſentative of the Gold Coins, for the purpoſes before ſtated. The greateſt part of the good and weighty Silver Coins, which then remained, have ſince been melted down and exported. And it appears by the accounts preſented by the Officers of the Mint, that from the year 1717 to the end of the laſt century, that is, in a period of eighty-three years, no more than [a] 584,764l 17s 5½d in tale of Silver has been coined: and from the year 1760 to the end of the ſame century, that is, in a period of forty years, no more than 63,983l 15s 5d in tale has been coined; and the Silver currency has gradually fallen into its preſent ſtate of imperfection.

[a] A conſiderable part of this Silver Coin was made from the Silver brought into the kingdom by Lord Anſon, taken in the Acapulco ſhip. Other parts were produced from Silver taken in other prizes.

I have

I have now completed the account of the alterations and debaſements made in the Coins of the realm, under the two firſt heads; and will therefore proceed to treat of them under a third head, that is, by lowering the ſtandard or fineneſs of the metal, of which the Coins were made; or, in other words, by diminiſhing the quantity of pure metal, and proportionally increaſing the quantity of alloy. The reaſons for treating this part of the ſubject under a ſeparate head have already been aſſigned. The whole of theſe extraordinary tranſactions were indeed a convulſion in the monetary ſyſtem, which never happened in this kingdom, except in the ſhort period from the 34th Henry VIII. to the 6th Edward VI. But this mode of debaſing Coins has been frequently practiſed in other countries, particularly in France, during the reigns of Philip de Valois, of his ſon John, who was ſome time a priſoner in England, of Charles VI. and of his ſon Charles VII. During a great part of the reign of theſe Sovereigns, the kingdom of France was diſtracted by internal factions, and by the invaſions of the Engliſh under thoſe great Monarchs Edward III. and Henry V; and the French Kings before mentioned were in great want of revenue to reſiſt the wars, that were then ſucceſsfully waged againſt them.

# Three Letters

on

# The Price of Gold

Contributed to

*The Morning Chronicle* (London)

in

August–November, 1809

by

David Ricardo

12, 1809. David Ricardo, Three letters on 'The Price of Gold', *The Morning Chronicle* (London), August–November 1809, London.

## I

[*The Morning Chronicle*, August 29, 1809]

## *THE PRICE OF GOLD.*

The present high market price above the mint price of gold, appears to have engrossed a great portion of the attention of the public; but they do not seem to be sufficiently impressed with the importance of the subject, nor of the disastrous consequences which may attend the further depreciation of paper. I am anxious, whilst there is yet time, that we should retrace our steps and restore the currency to that healthful state which so long existed in this country, and the departure from which is pregnant with present evil and future ruin.

The mint price of gold is 3l. 17s. 10½d. and the market price has been gradually increasing, and was within these two or three weeks as high as 4l. 13s. per ounce, not much less than 20 per cent. advance.

It is remarkable that between the years 1777 and 1797 the average price of gold was not higher than 3l. 17s. 7d. During that period, our currency was one of acknowledged purity. It is only since 1797, since the year that the Bank has been restricted from paying its notes in specie, that gold has risen to 4l., 4l. 10s., and latterly to 4l. 13s. per ounce. Whilst the Bank pays its notes in specie, there can never be any great difference between the mint and market-prices of gold. It is well known that, detection being difficult, notwithstanding the most severe, and, perhaps, absurd laws, when it becomes greatly the interest of individuals from a high market price of gold, the coin will be melted and sold as bullion, or exported, as it best suits the views of those who engage in such traffic. If, then, whilst the Bank paid in specie gold rose to 4l. or more per ounce, these dealers would exchange their notes at the

Bank, obtaining an ounce of gold for every 3l. 17s. 10½d. in bank notes. This gold would be melted and sold, or exported for 4l. or more in bank-notes per ounce; and as this operation might be repeated daily, or indeed hourly, it would be continued till the Bank had withdrawn the superfluous quantity of their notes from circulation, and had thereby brought the market and mint prices of gold to a level. This is the only check which can exist to an over issue from the Bank, and was so well known that the Bank never ventured on it with impunity.

No efforts of the Bank could keep more than a certain quantity of notes in circulation, and if that quantity was exceeded, its effects on the price of gold always brought the excess back to the Bank for specie. Under such regulations the market price of gold could never rise much above the mint price, for who would give 4l. or more, in bank-notes, for an ounce of gold, when he might obtain the same at the Bank for 3l. 17s. 10½d. It would be the same thing as offering an ounce of gold and 2s. 1½ d. for an ounce of gold.—When we talk of a high price of gold, it can have no meaning, if estimated in gold, or in notes which are immediately exchangeable for gold. It may be high, estimated in silver, or in goods of all kinds, and it is only when gold is high compared with goods, or in other words that goods are cheap, that any temptation is offered for its importation. When it is said that we may obtain 1l. 5s. for a guinea by sending it to Hamburg, what is meant but that we may get for it a bill on London for 1l. 5s. in bank-notes? Could this be the case if the bank paid in specie? Would any one be so blind to his interest as to offer me one guinea in specie and four shillings, for a guinea, when he might obtain the same at Hamburgh at par, paying only the expences of freight, &c.? It is only because he cannot get a guinea at the Bank for notes, that he consents to pay it with notes at the best price he can, or in other words he sells 1l. 5s. of his bank-notes for a guinea in specie.

When the Act restricting the Bank from paying in specie

took place, all checks to the over issue of notes were removed, excepting that which the Bank voluntarily placed on itself, knowing that if they were not guided by moderation, the effects which would follow would be so notoriously imputable to their monopoly, that the Legislature would be obliged to repeal the Restriction Act.

Whilst the Bank is willing to lend, borrowers will always exist, so that there can be no limit to their over-issues, but that which I have just mentioned, and gold might rise to 8l. or 10l. or any other sum per ounce.—The same effect would be produced in the price of provisions and on all other commodities, and there would be no other remedy for the depreciation of paper, than the Bank withdrawing the superabundant quantity from circulation, by insisting on the merchants paying their bills as they became due, and refusing to renew their loans until the scarcity of circulating medium should so raise its value that it would be at par with gold. It could rise but little above that price, for from that moment importation of gold would commence, and if the Bank were gradually to withdraw all their notes from circulation, the place of those notes would as gradually be supplied by imported gold, which the high price—I mean the high price in goods, would infallibly draw to this country.

If my view of this subject has been correct, we are enabled to ascertain the amount of depreciation at which Bank notes at any time may be, and when gold was at 4l. 13s. per ounce, they appear to have arrived at the enormous discount of 20 per Cent. I may be asked if Bank notes are at so great a discount, how comes it that no shopkeeper will sell more goods for twenty guineas than for 21l. in Bank notes. For this I can only account by supposing that the trade of purchasing guineas at a premium, or in other words selling Bank notes at a discount, is one which would expose the man who openly undertook it to so much obloquy and suspicion, that notwithstanding the profit, no one is hardy enough to encounter the risk, particularly as the law is very severe against melting the coin or exporting it. But that it is practised secretly there can be no doubt, as the profit attending it is enormous, and the number of guineas in circulation, considering that nearly 60 millions have been coined in the present reign, is diminished to a very small amount.

It is sufficient for my argument if I prove that it is a trade which can advantageously be carried on—that if tradesmen could openly and readily sell guineas for twenty-three shillings each, or more in Bank notes, they could afford to sell their goods cheaper for gold than for Bank notes;—and it is sufficiently evident that buying guineas at twenty-three shillings is between 9 and 10 per cent. premium, and selling gold at 4l. 13s. or nearly 20 per cent. premium, is a trade much more advantageous than many carried on in the city of London.

If further proofs of the depreciation of Bank notes were wanting, and that it was caused by an over-issue, it would be found in the present rate of exchange with foreign countries. To make this apparent may require us to consider what is meant by the rate of exchange, and the rules and limits to which it is subject.

If I purchase from a resident in Holland goods of that country, the bargain is made in the money there current. I have consequently contracted to pay him a certain number of ounces of silver of a given purity. As the comparative value of silver and gold is nearly equal all over the world, my debt may be either estimated in silver or in the number of ounces of gold for which it would exchange. And if a merchant in Holland has purchased from a resident in London goods which are valued in English money, he has contracted to pay a certain number of ounces of gold of known purity or fineness.

To save the expence of the freight and insurance attending the exporting and importing of a quantity of gold to liquidate these debts, it suits the convenience of both the parties, after agreeing how much money of the one country is equivalent, considering its weight, purity, &c., to that of the other, and which is called the par of exchange, to make a transfer by means of a bill, which is done by my paying to the English merchant the sum which I am indebted to my Correspondent in Holland, the English merchant ordering his Correspondent in Holland to pay to mine the same amount, estimated at the rate of exchange agreed on, in Dutch money. The advantage to both parties is saving freight and insurance. Now if two or more parties had been indebted to merchants in Holland, there would have been a competition between them for the purchase of this bill, and the seller would no longer have been satisfied with saving the freight and insurance on the importation of his gold, but would have exported, and would have obtained a premium for his bill, which it would have been the interest of either of the other parties to have given him, provided such premium did not exceed the expence of the transport of the metals. It is necessarily kept within that limit, for either would say, "the number of ounces of gold which I owe in Holland are ready to pay my debt. I am willing to give them to you to pay it for me, and to add to it the expences which would attend the sending it; but nothing can induce me to give more, as if you do not accept my offer, I shall suffer no further disadvantage by sending the gold!"—This is therefore the natural limit to the fall of the exchange, it can never fall more below par than these expences; nor can it ever rise more above par than the same amount.

But since the restriction on the Bank paying in specie, the fall of the exchange has kept pace with the rise in gold, and is now considerably lower than the limits which I have pointed out, and which may be accounted for in the following manner:—

A merchant can no longer say, that he is possessed of a sufficient number of ounces of gold to send abroad to pay his debt; he may say, indeed, that he has a sufficient number of bank notes, which if he could sell at par, or exchange at the Bank for what they profess to be, viz. an ounce of gold for every 3l. 17s. 10½d. he would have sufficient gold to pay his debt; but as things are, he must either sell his bank notes and be contented to obtain an ounce of gold, or 3l. 17s. 10½d. for every 4l. 13s. of notes, or agree to make an allowance at that rate to the person with whom he negociates his bill. Thus then it appears, that the exchange may not only fall to the limits which I have before mentioned, but also in an inverse proportion to the rise of gold, or rather the discount of bank notes. But these are the limits within which it is even now confined. It cannot on the one hand rise more above par than the expence of freight, &c. on the importation of gold, nor on the other fall more than the expences of freight, &c. on its exportation, added to the discount on bank notes.

If bills of exchange were payable in gold and not in bank notes, the restriction on the Bank from paying in specie, could not in any way affect the exchange beyond the limits which I before specified.

What becomes then of the argument which has so often been urged in Parliament, that whilst the rate of exchange continued against us, it would not be safe for the Bank to pay in specie, when it is evident that their not paying in specie is the cause of the present low exchange.

Let the Bank be enjoined by Parliament gradually to withdraw to the amount of two or three millions of their notes from circulation, without obliging them, in the first instance, to pay in specie, and we should very soon find that the market price of gold would fall to its mint price of 3l. 17s. 10½d. that every commodity would experience a similar reduction; and that the exchange with foreign countries would be confined within the limits above mentioned.

It would then be evident that all the evils in our currency were owing to the over-issues of the Bank, to the dangerous power with which it was entrusted of diminishing at its will, the value of every monied man's property, and by enhancing the price of provisions, and every necessary of life, injuring the public annuitant, and all those persons whose incomes were fixed, and who were consequently not enabled to shift any part of the burden from their own shoulders.

---

## II [1]

[*The Morning Chronicle*, September 20, 1809]

To the EDITOR of the MORNING CHRONICLE.

*SIR,*

In the observations which I made on the high price of gold in the *Morning Chronicle* of the 29th ultimo, I expressed my apprehensions of the serious consequences which might attend the increasing depreciation of paper. By lessening the value of the property of so many persons, and that in any degree they pleased, it appeared to me that the Bank might involve many thousands in ruin. I wished, therefore, to call the attention of the public to the very dangerous power with which that body was entrusted; but I did not apprehend, any more than your Correspondent, under the signature of "A Friend to Bank Notes," that the issues of the Bank would involve us in the dangers of a national bankruptcy.

Allowing to this writer, that the demand for gold has increased, whilst the usual supplies have been withheld, I am not convinced by any arguments which he has advanced, that the market price of gold could have been thereby affected, unless the medium in which the price was estimated was depreciated. That the scarcity of gold should increase its value cannot be doubted; that it would in consequence, when exchanged for other commodities, command an increased quantity of them, is as certain; but no scarcity, however great, can raise the market price much above the mint price, unless it be measured by a depreciated currency.

A pound of gold is coined into forty-four guineas and a half, or 46l. 14s. 6d. This is, therefore, the mint price, and cannot be called, as your Correspondent calls it, an arbitrary value. It is the simple declaration of a fact, that forty-four guineas and a half are of the same weight as a pound of gold, and one-twelfth of that quantity or 3l. 17s. 10½d. of an ounce.

Experience has proved to us, and particularly that of the twenty years preceding 1797, during the vicissitudes of war and peace, of favorable and unfavorable trade, that 46l. 14s. 6d. or a mint pound, would purchase sometimes a little more, and sometimes a little less than a pound of uncoined gold; and whilst an equal amount of bank notes would do the same, they would not be said to be depreciated. This they always did previous to the restriction on the Bank paying in specie, and for some time after it. Will this writer explain to us why any demand, however great, should induce any one to give, as has been lately done, 55l. 16s. in bank notes, for a pound of gold, if they are of equal value with 55l. 16s. in coin? Does he reflect that the gold actually contained in 55l. 16s. weighs one pound and a fifth of a pound? Is it seriously believed that he would give this for a pound? If it is agreed that he would not, then is the fact of the depreciation of bank notes fully established. If for the purchase of gold a greater quantity of corn, hardware, or any other commodity, were given than usual, it might justly be said that the scarcity of gold had increased in value. But what is the fact? If I go to market with corn or hardware, I can purchase 55l. 16s. in bank notes with precisely the same quantity that I am obliged to give to procure a pound of gold, or 46l. 14s. 6d.

I do not dispute with this writer but that it may be advantageous to a foreigner to send his goods to London, and after selling them for 25s. give that sum for the purchase of a guinea. He may possibly be doing it now with profit to himself. But he would not give twenty-five shillings for a guinea, if he did not pay for it in a depreciated medium. Again, I ask, does he think it possible that he would give a guinea and four shillings for a guinea, or bank notes to that amount, if they were exchangeable for that sum?

From the observations of this writer we should be led to suppose, that gold being at a higher price on the Continent than it is here, we might obtain there for it 4l. 15s. or more per ounce; but we should be mistaken in forming such a conclusion. It is paid for there in a medium not depreciated, and is probably somewhere about 4l. per ounce. But a purchaser here at 4l. 10s. can afford to sell it there at that price; because by means of the low exchange, (caused by the depreciation), he can reimburse himself for the depreciation of 15 or 20 per cent. to which our currency has arrived.

It is contended, too, that all the effects on the Exchange, "which I attribute to the issue of bank notes, would equally be felt if there were not a single bank note in circulation."

If our circulation were wholly carried on by specie, I believe it would be difficult for this writer to convince us, that the exchange might be 20 per cent. against us. What could induce any person owing 100l. in Hamburgh, to buy a bill here for that sum, giving 120l. for it, when the charges attending the exportation of the 100l. to pay his debt could not exceed 4l. or 5l.?

The severity of the law against the exportation of gold coin, prevents *any* one from openly selling bank-notes at a discount, not from any delicacy, as your correspondent supposes me to say, against doing an immoral or an unlawful act, but from the fear that as it is known that no one can purchase guineas but with a view to exportation, he would become an object of suspicion,—he would be watched and unable to effect his purpose. Repeal the law, and what can prevent an ounce of standard gold in guineas from selling at as good a price as an ounce of Portugal coin, when it is known to be rather superior to it in purity? And if an ounce of standard gold, in guineas, would sell in the market (as Portugal coin has lately done) at 4l. 13s. per oz. how long would a shopkeeper sell his goods at the same price either for gold or bank-notes indifferently? The penalties of the law, therefore, have degraded the few guineas in circulation to the value of the bank-notes, but send them abroad and they will purchase exactly what an equal quantity of Portugal coin will.

This is the temptation to their exportation, and operates the same as a demand from abroad. Our currency is already superfluous, and it is worse than useless to retain the guineas here. But diminish the currency by calling in the excess of bank-notes:—Make a partial void, as your correspondent justly observes was done in France and other countries, from the annihilation of their paper-credit, and what can prevent the effectual demand which would thereby be immediately created, from producing an importation of gold, and consequently a favorable exchange?

If our circulating medium has been augmented a fifth, till that fifth be withdrawn the prices of gold and commodities will remain as they are. Increase the quantity of notes, they will rise still higher; but withdraw the fifth, as I earnestly recommend, and gold and every other commodity will find its just level, and whilst the Bank continues to possess the confidence of the public, the representative of an ounce of gold, or 3l. 17s. 10½d. in bank-notes will always purchase an ounce of gold.

The hint thrown out of altering the mint price to the market price of gold, or, in other words, declaring that 3l. 17s. 10½d. in coin, shall pass for 4l. 13s. besides its shocking injustice would only aggravate the evil of which I complain. This violent remedy would raise the market price of gold 20 per cent. above the new mint price, and would further lower the value of bank-notes in the same proportion.

It has been shewn incontrovertibly by that able Writer, Dr. Adam Smith,* that the rate of interest for money is regulated by the rate of profits on that part of capital only which does not consist of circulating medium, and that those profits are not regulated but are wholly independent of the greater or lesser quantity of money which may be employed for the purposes of circulation; that the increase of circulating medium will increase the prices of all commodities, but will not lower the rate of interest.

We must not, therefore, depend upon the criterion, namely, the rate of interest so strongly recommended by your correspondent, by which to judge of the issues of the Bank; because, if Dr. Smith's reasoning be correct, if our circulating medium were ten times as great as it is, the rate of interest would not be permanently affected.

I think, Sir, I have succeeded in proving that my alarms are not altogether groundless, and that there does exist a great depreciation in our currency, affecting the interests of the public annuitant, and of those whose property consists in money, without any corresponding advantages. The evils attending a variable medium, as it affects all contracts, are too obvious to require to be noticed. The permanency of the value of the precious metals first recommended them as the general medium of exchange. That advantage is now lost to us, and we cannot consider our currency on a solid foundation till it be restored to the value of that of other countries.

By withdrawing a certain quantity of Bank of England notes from circulation it is supposed, by Mr. Cobbett, that their place would be immediately supplied by country bank-notes.[4] No such effect would, in my opinion, take place; on the contrary, I think such a measure would oblige the country-banks to call in at least as many, if not considerably more, of *their* notes.

A Bank of England note and a country bank note are now of equal value, and their quantities are proportioned to the business which they have to perform. By withdrawing Bank of England notes from circulation you increase their value and lower the prices of commodities in those places where they are current. A Bank of England note will then be more valuable than a country bank-note, because it will be wanted to purchase in the cheaper market; and as the country bank is obliged to give Bank of England notes in exchange for their own, they would be called upon for them till the quantity of country paper should be reduced to the same proportion which it before bore to the London paper, producing a corresponding fall of the prices of all commodities for which it was exchangeable.

A writer in *The Pilot* newspaper has been pleased to suppose, that a gentleman who has written in your paper under the signature of "Mercator," has done so "in aid or in imitation of, or in conjunction and conspiracy with me." The fact can of itself be of little importance. If his arguments or mine or weak, let him shew them to be so; but "No Trafficker" is mistaken.—The sentiments of "Mercator" are only known to me as they are to him, through the medium of *The Morning Chronicle*.[5] I am Sir, &c.

R.

## III [6]

[*The Morning Chronicle*, November 23, 1809]

To the EDITOR of the MORNING CHRONICLE.

*SIR,*

Had your Correspondent, "A Friend to Bank-notes," when he first did me the honour to notice my observations on the high price of Gold, contended, as he now does, that Bank-notes were the representatives of Silver, but not of Gold Coin, we should sooner have discovered from whence the difference of our opinions on the subject in dispute between us arose. I should then, Sir, have spared him the trouble of giving so many proofs of that which is indisputable; namely—*that if Silver be the sole measure of value, Gold being at 4l. 13s. per oz. is not, of itself, evidence of Bank notes being at a discount.* Indeed, I thought that in the following observations I had admitted that position [7]—"When we talk of a high price of Gold, it can have no meaning if estimated in Gold, or in Notes which are immediately exchangeable for Gold. It might be high estimated in Silver, or in goods of all kinds." It was evident from the tenor of that and the subsequent paper, that I considered Gold Coin as the standard of commerce, and by it estimated the depreciation of Bank-notes. I had no reason to suppose that it was otherwise considered by your Correspondent. In one place he called Bank-notes a "substitute for Gold;" in another he observes, that "Had not this restriction been imposed, the great and growing demand for Gold upon the Continent would have drawn every Guinea out of the Country, and would have left us without resource in any emergency which might arise, by which its credit would be shaken." The restriction could only have enabled the Directors of the Bank, if they had been so disposed, to prevent the Guineas locked up in the Bank from being exported. Those in circulation have been as liable to be sent out by the Country since, as before that measure. But, if Silver only be the standard of currency, as is now asserted, the Bank might have paid their Notes in our present debased Silver Coin; in Shillings, for example, debased 24 per cent. below their standard weight and value, the Guinea, therefore, would not have needed that protection. The Silver would not have been demanded, because it could not have been either melted or exported, but at a loss of 24 per cent. If Silver be the standard of currency, Bank-notes were, in 1797, at a premium of 24 per cent. and are now at a premium of 14 per cent.

But if, as I shall attempt to prove, Gold be the standard of value, and consequently, Bank Notes the representatives of the Gold-coin, I do expect that this writer will agree with me that Bank Notes are at a discount, and that the excess of the market above the mint price of Gold measures the depreciation.

The price of standard Silver bullion was on Tuesday last 5s. 9½d. per oz. On the same day, the price of standard Gold bullion was 4l. 10s. per oz. An ounce of Gold was therefore equal to about 15½ oz. and not 18 oz. of Silver.

If, then, we estimate the value of Bank Notes by the price of Gold bullion, they will be found to be 15½ per cent. discount. If by the price of Silver bullion 12 per cent. discount. But your Correspondent would no doubt observe, that this conclusion from the price of Silver bullion would be correct, if our Silver currency were not degraded by wearing and clipping, but as it was known to be depreciated by being deficient in standard weight, the high price of Gold bullion might in a great measure, and that of Silver bullion wholly, be caused by that deficiency. Bank Notes are, according to this argument, the representatives, not of our standard Silver currency, but of our debased Silver Coins.

It is observed by Lord Liverpool, in his letter to the King on the state of the coins,[3] that the law now is, and has been since the year 1774, "That no tender in payment of money made in the Silver Coin of this realm, of any sum exceeding the sum of 25l. at any time, shall be reputed in law or allowed to be legal tender, within Great Britain or Ireland, for more than according to its value by weight, after the rate of 5s. 2d. for each ounce of silver."

Bank-notes are not then the representatives of the debased silver coins. A holder of a Bank-note of 1000l. might refuse to take more than 25l. in the present debased Silver currency. If the remaining 975 l. were paid him in shillings, he would receive them by weight, at their Mint value of 5s. 2d. per oz. which, with the 25l. of debased Silver, when sold at the present price of 5s. 9½d. per oz. would yield 1110l. in Bank-notes. Here then it is proved, on this writer's own principles, that if Silver be the standard currency, Bank-notes are at a discount of 11 per cent.

For the following reasons given by Lord Liverpool, in the work before mentioned, I consider Gold as the standard measure of value. He observes,[9] "that the Silver Coins are no longer the principal measure of property: all commodities now take their price or value in reference to the Gold Coin, in like manner as they took their value in a former period in reference to the Silver Coins. On this account the present deficiency of the Silver Coins, great as it is, is not taken into consideration, in paying the price of any commodity, to the extent in which they are legal tenders. It is clear, therefore, that the Gold Coins are now become, in the practice and opinion of the people, the principal measure of property."

He then states,[10] that in the reign of William the Third, the Guinea was current at even so high a value as 30s.; that the Gold Coins rose or fell as the Silver Coins were more or less perfect. "No such increase or variation in the value of Gold Coin has taken place since the year 1717, when the rate or value of the Guinea was determined by proclamation, and the Mint indenture, to be 21s. and the other Gold Coins in proportion; though the Silver Coins now current have long been, and are still, at least as deficient as they were at the beginning of the reign of King William. The Guinea and other Gold Coins have, notwithstanding, constantly passed since 1717, at the rate or value given them by the Mint indentures."

"The two foregoing reasons clearly prove the opinion of the people of Great Britain on this subject, in their interior commerce and domestic concerns. I will in the next place shew what has been the opinion of foreign nations concerning it." In the reign of King William the exchanges rose or fell according to the perfection or defect of our silver coins. Before the recoinage in 1695, the exchanges with all foreign countries were 4s. in the pound against England, and with some of them considerably more. "The same evil, however, has never existed since the year 1717, though our silver coins have, during all this interval, been very defective. But, on the other hand, our exchanges with foreign countries were very much influenced to our disadvantage, when our gold coins were defective, that is, previous to the reformation of our Gold Coins in the year 1774." Lord Liverpool considers this as a proof that foreigners consider our Gold Coins as the principal measure of property. Another argument is drawn from the prices of gold and silver bullion. When our Gold Coin was defective previous to the re-coinage in 1774, gold bullion advanced considerably above its mint value, but immediately on its being brought to its present state of perfection, gold bullion fell to something under the mint price, and has continued so for twenty years previous to 1797. "It is evident, therefore, from these facts, that the price of gold bullion was affected by the state of our gold coins, though the price of this bullion had not since the year 1717, been so affected by the defective state or condition of our silver coins." The price of silver bullion has, since the year 1717, been affected by the perfection or defect of our Gold Coins, but has not been so by the defective state of our Silver Coins.—"From all which it is evident, that the value of Gold or Silver Bullion has, for 40 years at least, been estimated according to the state of our Gold Coin solely, and not according to that of Silver Coin. The price of both these metals rose when our Gold Coin was defective; it fell when our Gold Coin was brought to its present state of perfection; and it may, therefore, justly be inferred, that, in the opinion of the dealers in the precious metals (who may be considered as the best judges on a subject of this nature), the gold coin has in this respect become the principal measure of property, and consequently the instrument of commerce." In another passage, Lord Liverpool considers a pound sterling to be 20-21 of a guinea.[11] The same opinion is advanced by Sir J. Stewart[12]—"At present (says he) there are no sterling pounds in silver money; there is no silver in England in any proportion to the circulation of trade; and, therefore, the only currency by which a pound can be valued is the guinea."

The Bank-Directors must have been of the same opinion, when they stated in their evidence before Parliament, that it was their usual practice to limit the amount of their notes when the market price of gold exceeded the mint price.[13]

In the Report of the Committee of the House of Lords in 1797, it is observed, that "Gold is the mercantile coin of Great Britain, and silver has for many years been only a commodity, which has no fixed price, and is very rarely carried to the Mint to be coined, but varies according to the demand for it at the market."[14]

I am, Sir, your obedient Servant,

R.

Nov. 4

[1](page 4) "INTRODUCTION.—The writer of the following pages has already submitted some reflections to the attention of the public, on the subject of paper-currency, through the medium of the Morning Chronicle. He has thought proper to republish his sentiments on this question in a form more calculated to bring it to fair discussion; and his reasons for so doing, are, that he has seen, with the greatest alarm, the progressive depreciation of the paper-currency. His fears have been augmented by observing, that by a great part of the public this depreciation is altogether denied, and that by others, who admit the fact, it is imputed to any cause but to that which to him appears the real one. Before any remedy can be successfully applied to an evil of such magnitude, it is essential that there should be no doubt as to its cause. The writer proposes, from the admitted principles of political economy, to advance reasons, which, in his opinion, prove, that the paper currency of this country has long been, and now is, at a considerable discount, proceeding from a superabundance in its quantity, and not from any want of confidence in the Bank of England, or from any doubts of their ability to fulfil their engagements. He does this without reluctance, being fully persuaded that the country is yet in possession of the means of restoring the paper currency to its professed value, viz. the value of the coins, for the payment of which it purports to be a pledge.

He is aware that he can add but little to the arguments which have been so ably urged by Lord King, and which ought long before this to have carried conviction to every mind; but he trusts, that as the evil has become more glaring, the public will not continue to view, without interest, a subject which yields to no other in importance, and in which the general welfare is so materially concerned.

*Dec. 1, 1809.*"

See "The High Price of Bullion, a Proof of the Depreciation of Bank Notes" (Second edition, corrected. London: 1810), iii, iv.

[2](page 15) Ricardo's first communication (August 29) was followed by a letter from "Mercator," dated September 4 and published in *The Morning Chronicle* of September 7, in which Ricardo's views were warmly and somewhat sophomorically defended. As remedial measures, the partial resumption of specie payments and the limitation of the Bank's note-issuing power were urged. In *The Pilot*, also a London newspaper, of September 7, "F." explained the high price of gold as due to extraordinary demand. In the same paper of September 8, "Mercator" charged that the high price of gold was due to the extensive purchase of guineas for export, in which illicit traffic "Mercator" was doubtless a participant! "Mercator" replied to these two critics with some vigor in the *Chronicle* of September 12, and dwelt upon the injury done the "public annuitant or person of fixed stipend" by the rise in prices. "No Trafficker"

retorted in *The Pilot* of September 13 in a rambling, unpleasant letter which added nothing to his first statement.

A more important contribution appeared in the *Chronicle* of September 14, over the signature "A Friend to Bank Notes but no Bank Director"—from the pen, as we now know, of Hutches Trower. Trower protested against the alarmist note which he found in Ricardo's communication. He ascribed the high price of gold to increased demand, consequent upon the collapse of the French assignats and to diminished supply, resultant from interrupted trade with America. The Bank's issues, instead of heightening the price of bullion, had actually checked it by serving to that extent as a substitute for gold. Ricardo's brief explanation of the failure of guineas to command more goods in ordinary purchases than bank notes was sharply criticised. The possibility was considered of reducing the standard price of gold to a price nearer its market price so as to prevent an otherwise inevitable efflux of gold whenever specie payment should be resumed. Finally, it was asserted that the rate of interest was to be regarded as the real index of the redundancy or otherwise of the money supply.

This communication was the immediate occasion of Ricardo's *Chronicle* letter of September 20. Cf. "Letters of David Ricardo to Hutches Trower and others, 1811-1823" (ed. Bonar and Hollander. Oxford: 1899), vi-vii.

[3](page 18) "Wealth of Nations," bk. II, ch. iv; in Thorold Rogers' edition, vol. I, pp. 357-359.

[4](page 19) Cf. Cobbett's *Political Register* of September 16, 1809. In a paper on "Jacobin Guineas," Cobbett refers to "The philosopher who writes in the Chronicle," and asks, "Besides does this writer imagine, that the country-bankers would not make money to supply the place of any reduction at the Bank of England?"

[5](page 19) The opening phrase of the letter of "No Trafficker," published in *The Pilot* of September 13 is, "A gentleman who has written in *The Morning Chronicle* under the signature of MERCATOR, in aid or imitation of, or in conjunction or conspiracy with another writer in the same paper upon the subject of the present high price of gold," etc. Cf. note 2, above.

[6](page 21) The publication of Ricardo's second contribution stimulated further controversy in the columns of the *Chronicle*. On September 23 "A Lover of Cash" invited an expression of opinion from "A Friend to Bank Notes" (Hutches Trower) as to whether general prices had risen proportionately with the increased note circulation. In the same issue "T." praised the "clear and convincing statement from your intelligent correspondent R.," described the attempt to account for the high price of gold by any other cause than the depreciation of paper as "downright nonsense and infatuation," and agreed with Ricardo, as against Cobbett, that the increased issues of the country banks resulted from the conduct of the Bank of England. On September 26, "A. Z." denied that notes were at a discount, emphasized

the absence of dual prices, asserted that gold coin and not gold bullion was the standard of value, and explained the excess of the market above the mint price of gold as the measure of unwillingness to violate the law by melting down guineas. "Mercator" was heard from again on September 29, with a repetition of earlier arguments and an even more emphatic support of Ricardo's views: "I cannot help reverting to the statements of your *original* correspondent on 29th last, considering his alarms not imaginary but real, his positions well founded, his arguments unanswered, and his deductions incontrovertible." On October 10 appeared a well-written reply, signed "L.," to the communication of "A. Z." (September 26), in which the striking fact that as many commodities could be bought for 21 shillings in paper as for a guinea in gold was explained as due partly to the illegality of melting guineas (Ricardo's argument) and partly to the legal tender quality of the notes. Attention was called to the increasing profits of the Bank and to the rise in the value of Bank stock during the Restriction.

On October 30 Hutches Trower, writing under the same pseudonym, "A Friend to Bank Notes but no Bank Director," made lengthy but unfortunate reply to Ricardo's letter of September 20. He withdrew his proposal of an alteration in the standard and did not press his earlier suggestion that the rate of interest was an index of the value of money, but practically rested his entire case on the contention that silver was the standard measure of value: "It now, therefore, either remains for this writer [Ricardo] either to show that silver is not the medium *in which the value of gold is estimated* (that is to say, that *it is not the only measure of value*), or, that being that medium, it is not depreciated; or to admit, that the *high* market price of gold is the effect of an increased demand. From which admission it will necessarily follow that that high price is no proof that Bank notes are at a discount. Should he find himself obliged to embrace this latter alternative, then will there be an end of the question between us."

On November 3, "L." urged that the Bank circulation be reduced to the amount of notes outstanding in 1797, and on November 22 "W. S." called attention to attempts then being made to force inconvertible county bank notes into circulation in London. Ricardo's third contribution appeared on November 23 and terminated this phase of the controversy.

[7] (page 21) See page 10, above.

[8] (page 22) "A Treatise on the Coins of the Realm; in a Letter to the King" (Oxford, 1805), p. 129. This and other passages cited contain minor verbal and typographical inaccuracies.

[9] (page 23) *Ibid.*, p. 141. In Lord Liverpool's text, after the words "in reference to the Gold Coins," follows a clause here omitted, viz., "that is, in reference to the quantity of Gold Coins, for which they could be exchanged;"

[10] (page 23) *Ibid.*, pp. 141-145.

[11] (page 25) *Ibid.*, p. 153.

[12](page 25) "An Inquiry into the Principles of Political Oeconomy" (London, 1767), vol. II, p. 89; in the collected "Works, Political, Metaphysical and Chronological" (London, 1805), vol. III, p. 120.

[13](page 25) Doubtless based upon the statement of Henry Thornton in "An Enquiry into the Nature and Effects of the Paper Credit of Great Britain" (London, 1802), p. 231-232: "For, if at any time the exchanges of the country became so unfavorable as to produce a material excess of the market price above the mint price of gold; the directors of the bank, as appears by the evidence of some of their body given to parliament, were disposed to resort to a reduction of their paper as a means of diminishing or removing the excess, and of thus providing for the security of their establishment." Cf. Ricardo's "High Price of Bullion" (in McCulloch's edition of "Works," p. 276), wherein this passage is cited in full.

[14](page 25) "Report of the Lords Committees appointed a Secret Committee to enquire into the Causes which produced the Order of Council of the 26th of February 1797," p. 261. It is of curious interest that the copy of the "Report" by which the above citation has been verified (in the Library of Congress in Washington, D. C.) was the property of John Pearse, deputy governor of the Bank of England at the very time Ricardo was writing, and soon after its governor.

# REMARKS

UPON SOME PREVALENT ERRORS,

WITH RESPECT TO

# CURRENCY AND BANKING,

AND

SUGGESTIONS TO THE LEGISLATURE AND THE PUBLIC AS TO THE IMPROVEMENT OF

# THE MONETARY SYSTEM.

BY GEORGE WARDE NORMAN, ESQ.

LONDON:
PELHAM RICHARDSON, 23, CORNHILL.

1838.

13, 1838. George Warde Norman, *Remarks upon some Prevalent Errors with respect to Currency and Banking, and Suggestions to the Legislator and the Public as to the Improvement of the Monetary System*, London: Pelham Richardson.

In the autumn of 1832 the Author of the following pages wrote a pamphlet containing a short exposition of what he considered the true principles of Currency, and their application to the state of our monetary system as it existed before the renewal of the Bank Charter. He was prevented from publishing it at that time by circumstances unnecessary to be detailed; but having since reflected on the subject, and finding reason to imagine that the events of the last four years confirm the correctness of the general views he had previously entertained, he has reprinted that portion of his production which contained them with a few trifling alterations. He has added suggestions for the improvement of our paper circulation, as it exists at present, and a few observations on some opinions brought forward in the recent publications of Colonel Torrens and Mr. S. J. Loyd, whose kindly feelings towards him will not, he is sure, be diminished by a little criticism, intended solely to further the progress of a science which has been so greatly benefited by their devotion to it. With respect to the opinions of the latter gentleman, it must be remarked, that what is said, applies solely to his first pamphlet—the last having appeared while the present publication was in the press.

# SECTION I.

PRINCIPLES OF CURRENCY—ERRONEOUS CRITERIA USUALLY APPLIED TO DECIDE UPON ITS PROPER AMOUNT—PLAN OF AN IMPROVED PAPER CURRENCY.

Of all the great questions that have for many years occupied the public attention, there is not one on which opinions have prevailed more discordant, or less reconcilable for the most part, to sound principles than the important subject of Currency and Banking. The discussions in the periodical press which, on other matters, have so greatly tended to enlighten and instruct, upon these seem calculated almost universally to darken and mislead, and the consequence is, that with respect to the Currency, a future is now opened to us, upon which even a bold man, alive to the dangers that environ us, can hardly look without dread.

It is with this feeling that the Author of the

following pages sits down to the task of investigating shortly the general questions of Currency and Banking, with a particular application to the situation of the country at present. He purposes to treat the subject as divided into four distinct heads. The first will contain his exposition of the principles on which a paper circulation should be regulated, and a plan for carrying them into practical effect, supposing the legislature to be perfectly unshackled; together with a refutation of various erroneous opinions entertained by different persons whose authority influences extensive classes. The second will examine the nature and effect of the different remedies which have been suggested, in order to cure the evils in the existing system of circulation. The third will furnish a few remarks on the late and previous periods of commercial suffering, connected with derangement in the Currency in this and other countries, intended to elucidate by a practical application the correctness of the principles previously laid down. The fourth will exhibit the writer's view of the best course to be pursued in the actual state of affairs.

In executing this task it will not be attempted to trace every principle that may be adduced to the foundation on which it rests: such as have been already proved by writers of the greatest authority in economical science, or which are in themselves sufficiently evident, will be assumed without discussion—while illustration and argument will be employed, when they appear necessary, to establish truths less apparent or less generally acknowledged. By such means alone the advantage of brevity can be attained, without a too heavy sacrifice in point of clearness and precision. The present moment appears peculiarly propitious for such an undertaking as that now proposed; the public attention is awake to the important matters to be treated of, while the current of affairs has become sufficiently clear and tranquil to enable us to look calmly on our late disasters, and consider the possibility of finding some plan which may either altogether prevent a repetition of them, or at any rate render the periodical hurricanes in the commercial world less frequent and destructive. The recent publications of Col. Torrens, Mr. S. J. Loyd, and Mr. J. H. Palmer, the first so justly distinguished for scientific acquirements, while the two latter add to a knowledge of general principles an acquaintance with facts surpassed by none, have afforded the Author great assistance, of which he has availed himself without scruple; for such authorities he cannot but feel the highest respect, and they will not imagine that he evinces any want of it when he presumes to differ from their views, or considers their arguments inconclusive.

All civilized countries, in all ages, have adopted the precious metals as the medium of exchange. The want of some such medium is discovered at the earliest advance from barbarism. We hear occasionally of salt, cowries, or cocoa-nuts being used for this purpose; but these imperfect instruments are speedily abandoned: and the first point to be considered is, whether or not any better general measure and standard of value can be employed than gold and silver. Upon this question a negative may safely be pronounced. No other commodities possess in so high a degree the required qualities. These qualities have been enumerated by several authors; it is only necessary to mention a few:—

DIVISIBILITY,
DURABILITY,
BEAUTY,
UNIVERSALITY OF DEMAND,
CONSTANCY OF VALUE.

The last is the most important of all, and deserves particular observation, as it renders the precious metals pre-eminently fitted for the most delicate part of their functions, that of being used as a measure of the value of other commodities.

That commodity upon the whole will possess the greatest uniformity of value, the production of which demands the greatest uniformity of sacrifice on the part of those who obtain it; the supply of, and demand for, which are subject to the least degree of sudden and considerable increase and diminution, and which at the same time is the most durable. In all these respects, or at least in a combination or majority of them, gold and silver possess incontestable superiority—as an instance or two will best evince.

Corn has sometimes been proposed as a measure of value, but we see that a good or bad harvest will alter its price in the proportion of one half or more. Labour, a favourite standard with some authors, and the best in a philosophical point of view, is unfit for practical reference, and occasionally subject to great temporary variations when compared with commodities, dependent upon the changes in demand and supply; while there is every reason to believe that during a long course of years, no considerable change has occurred in the cost of producing the precious metals, so as permanently to affect their price; or any alteration in the supply and demand, capable of producing even a temporary effect to any considerable extent. Experience shews that the precious metals, though furnished by different countries, and under varied circumstances, bear nearly the same relation to each other for a long course of years: and, on the whole, we may generally feel assured that when the price of other commodities, measured in them, varies within short periods, the cause is to be sought for in circumstances affecting the former.

The value of the precious metals depends, as has been already observed, on the cost of producing them, on the expenditure of capital and labour employed to extract them from the earth and fit them for use: but the principles according to which they are distributed among the different nations employing them either in manufactures or as money, have not been sufficiently considered by economists, and merit a few observations.

Only a few countries produce gold and silver in any considerable quantities; other countries must obtain the stock which they may require either from the former directly, or from those which have subsequently purchased them, by exchanging a certain quantity of their produce for them. The price which they must pay for them will be that which the producers, or prior purchasers, are willing to accept as an equivalent. That country, then, which can produce, with the least sacrifice, a given quantity of commodities of general utility, fitted for foreign use, will be enabled to obtain, with the least sacrifice, a given quantity of the precious metals. It arises from this circumstance, that in what may be called unproductive countries, like Sweden and Poland, commodities of home growth or manufacture are cheap, or, in other words, gold and silver are dear; a great deal of Swedish or Polish labour being necessary to produce an article which other nations will purchase; while in productive countries, like England, gold and silver are cheap, on account of our greater means of purchasing them; of course there are some other causes affecting the relation which the money prices of different countries bear to each other, of which the chief is taxation, but they do not directly affect the present inquiry.

The price of the precious metals measured in commodities, or, what is the same thing, the price of other commodities measured in them, being thus fixed in each particular country, the whole mass of coin and bullion is distributed, according to the respective wants of the several countries upon the principle of competition. A has a certain quantity of products of a certain money value to exchange a certain number of times, and requires, therefore, a certain amount of coin to perform these exchanges; B has commodities of only half the money value, or half the number of exchanges to be performed; half the coin will, therefore, satisfy its wants, and so on to the end of the alphabet.

We must here remark, that, as above explained, the value of gold and silver in different countries does not at all depend upon the quantities which each country may possess, but solely upon the cost of producing or of purchasing them. They may be cheap as in the United States, or in England during the last war, when compared with other commodities, where there is little of them, or dear as in Hindostan, where they are supposed to be abundant: indeed, one of the effects which flow from the increased knowledge and civilization that accompany augmented wealth, is the introduction of more economy in the use of the circulating medium. It is probable that at this moment France possesses less of the precious metals than before the Revolution, and England less than it did fifty years ago.

It must also be remarked, that although the cost of production ultimately regulates the value of the precious metals by limiting their quantity, the price which can be obtained for them at any given moment, depends upon the demand and supply; in this they resemble all other commodities.

It is upon the principle above described that at any particular period the precious metals are distributed through the general markets of the world; but the circumstances which affect this distribution are numerous, important, and constantly in operation, so that the currency of each particular country is in a perpetual state of oscillation.

The most important of the above circumstances are good and bad harvests, the improvements in machinery, the imposition or removal of taxes, the enactment or abrogation of prohibitive or restrictive laws, and the introduction or extinction of paper money. Events of this nature affect the circulation not merely of the country where they occur, but those of all other countries connected with it, either directly or indirectly. We will take an instance for the purpose of explanation, under the head of taxation. Suppose a duty to be levied on an article of merchandise usually exported from

A to B, the effect of such duty will be to increase the price of that commodity in B: this increased price will of course cause a diminished demand. Let us then further suppose that this diminished demand is carried to such an extent, that the aggregate value of the article in question sold to B after the imposition of the duty, is only one half of what it was before, say half a million instead of one million. A still requires the same quantity of goods from B as before, but it has only half the previously existing means of paying for them in its own goods. A will then be obliged to export treasure in payment until the value of its currency has been so much appreciated, and that of B so much depreciated, that it will become once more advantageous to export goods instead of money in discharge of any balance still due. The altered distribution of the precious metals as respects A and B will become permanent, until some fresh occurrence arises of the nature of those above enumerated to affect it anew; but it must be here remarked that, although for the sake of simplifying the case, only two countries have been supposed as affected by the change in the distribution of the precious metals; yet, practically, all countries having commercial transactions with them will be affected in a nearly equal degree. B, whose currency has been augmented, and whose commodities have consequently been raised in price above the level of those of C, will part with a portion of its lately acquired treasure to the latter country—a similar process will follow between C and D, and so on. Supposing again, a certain quantity of the precious metals to be released from the circulation of England by the substitution of Bank notes,—the amount of gold and silver no longer wanted here will be exported, and finally divided among the rest of the world, other things remaining unaltered, in proportion to the currency which each country previously held.

The process above described requires from its great practical importance to be maturely considered, and the following inference that directly flows from it should be firmly fixed in the reader's mind. No change in the value of a currency, either purely metallic, or of convertible paper, arising merely from a change in its amount, and leaving the standard unaltered, can take place in any given country without ultimately affecting, in an almost equal degree, the currencies of all other countries. The value of this principle will be seen particularly hereafter, when we have to criticise certain prevailing opinions.

Some persons might hesitate to subscribe to this principle who would readily allow its validity with relation to commodities other than the precious metals. Thus, let us suppose cotton goods to be in general demand, like gold and silver, and the trade in them to be perfectly free as that in gold and silver must practically be,—is it not plain that a fall in the cost of producing them in any one country, occasioning an equivalent fall of price there, would infallibly cause a fall of price in all other couutries, to nearly the same extent, minus the expense of transport?

It must not be imagined that changes in the distribution of the precious metals take place only occasionally, and after considerable intervals, or that they are usually accompanied by any violent alteration of prices. The latter can never much exceed a small per-centage above the cost of freight, carriage, and insurance on the coin and bullion transported; the profit remaining to those individuals who engage in this branch of trade, owing to their competition with each other being necessarily very small, while their operations are of weekly, and indeed almost daily, occurrence. This class of traders is guided by the course of exchange, or the price which can be obtained for the currency of one country in that of another—the par of exchange expressing that relation between them, at which a certain quantity of gold or silver employed in the purchase of a bill, drawn from one country on another, will produce, when the bill is paid, an equal quantity of gold or silver in that other country. The par is usually the medium of the variation in price between the currencies of the two countries; the difference on either side of it being limited to an amount a little exceeding the cost of transmitting coin or bullion.

It is unfortunate that no precise and neutral terms have been employed to designate the state of the exchanges. The epithets high and low are equivocal, as when we say the Paris Exchange is high, it may be supposed either that a given sum of French money will command a large sum of English money, or that a given sum of English money will command a large amount of French money, while the epithets favourable and unfavourable are still more objectionable; for the former being applied to a state of commercial relations which involves an import of treasure, the latter to one which occasions an export of it, they necessarily imply that the former is to be desired, and denotes a prosperous condition of the trading world, the latter the contrary; the truth being that both states of the Bullion Market are advantageous, gold and silver being always sent out or brought into the country when they answer better than other commodities, and never when they answer worse. It is true that under our faulty system of Currency we occasionally suffer from a want or an over supply of them, but these are artificial evils of our own creating. The author must content himself with pointing out the mischief arising from the absence of an appropriate phraseology, without pretending to supply the deficiency.

So far we have chiefly considered currency as composed of the precious metals alone. It is now necessary to direct our attention to some effects arising from the employment of paper in a greater or less degree.

Convertible paper implies on the part of the issuer, whether the government itself, a company, or an individual, a promise to discharge each note in a certain quantity of gold or silver of a certain fineness. As the holder has the right of exchanging notes for coin or bullion at his pleasure, and will certainly do so, whenever the operation is attended with a profit, convertible paper, setting insolvency aside, must be identical in value with the coin it represents—there can be no appreciable difference, except under very extraordinary circumstances, and for short periods, such as those which accompany political discredit. The evil, should it exist, would be speedily cured, unless insolvency on the part of the issuers supervened.

An issue of paper money produces precisely the same effect on general prices as would follow from an augmentation in the quantity of the precious metals—it raises them; first in the country where the paper is issued; then in those countries which have the most immediate connexion with the former country; and, finally, in the general market of the world; on the contrary, a calling in of paper-money has a directly opposite tendency. Gold and silver become appreciated, first in the country requiring an additional stock of them, and subsequently in all others. The effects thus described are produced very speedily upon two or more countries, between which there subsists an intimate mercantile connexion, and would be felt after a short interval, wherever the precious metals were produced, or used as the medium of exchange, or for any other purpose. Merchants immediately discover the places where they are most wanted, where they will purchase the greatest quantity of other goods, and to those places they are sent until the equilibrium has been restored.

It is impossible to calculate exactly, in any given circumstances, the maximum of time which might be required to produce the effects here described; but, taking the past oscillations in the amount of our own currency as a fair ground of estimate, we may safely assume that, in a few years after a derangement in the value of the precious metals in any one European country had taken place, its effects would be definitively distributed throughout the remainder of that quarter of the world, and the equilibrium of their several currencies be restored.

The following short statement, without pretending to perfect accuracy, will give a sufficiently clear view of the changes in the equilibrium of the whole currency of this country, compared with those of foreign countries, during the last few years:

| | | | | | | |
|---|---|---|---|---|---|---|
| Gold came in from | about | June, | 1819, | to | about | Oct. 1824. |
| went out from | .. | Nov. | 1824, | to | .. | Nov. 1825. |
| came in from | .. | Jan. | 1826, | to | .. | Aug. 1828. |
| went out from | .. | Sept. | 1828, | to | .. | Feb. 1829. |
| came in from | .. | Mar. | 1829, | to | .. | Aug. 1830. |
| went out from | .. | Aug. | 1830, | to | .. | Mar. 1832. |
| came in from | .. | Mar. | 1832, | to | .. | Oct. 1833. |
| went out from | .. | Oct. | 1833, | to | .. | Apr. 1835. |
| came in from | .. | April, | 1835, | to | .. | Apr. 1836. |
| went out from | .. | April, | 1836, | to | .. | Feb. 1837. |
| came in from | .. | Feb. | 1837.* | | | |

It must be again remarked, that the above observations, explanatory of the law which governs the value of the precious metals in all countries and keeps them in equilibrium, are of the greatest practical importance, on account of the numerous errors to which an opposite opinion has led: they will be frequently adverted to hereafter, and merit the constant recollection of those who wish to form clear notions on the subjects now under discussion.

It has been already observed that the rate of exchange marks the price which the money of one country bears in that of another—it is indeed our sole guide, and affords the only rule by which we can judge whether the currency is superabun-

* The above epochs are nearly those of the commencement of increase or decrease in the treasure of the Bank, which, being frequently influenced by internal causes, do not exactly coincide with the indications presented by the foreign exchanges; these last as noted would not have exhibited more certain results.

dant, deficient, or of the proper amount. Here again we have a principle apparently both clear and undeniable, which is yet little understood by the public at large, and even neglected by not a few persons who are looked up to as authorities in such matters. The common form which its denial assumes, is an assertion that the currency is in excess or deficient, because the prices of certain articles of merchandise are high or low, or the rate of interest low or high, or because the circulation has been augmented or diminished; or, lastly, because the amount of deposits in the hands of bankers is large or small, increasing or diminishing. A few observations upon each of these mistakes which abound in the City articles of newspapers, and are to be found even in the evidence of persons called before the last Bank Committee, may not be inappropriate here.

One, two, twenty, nay, it is possible, though highly improbable, that all the commodities in England might fall in money price, without any appreciation of the currency, that is to say, without the occurrence of any change affecting the precious metals themselves. If such an event should take place, without any derangement in the exchanges, or should continue when, after a derangement, the equilibrium had been restored, we might be almost sure that the cause was to be sought in some circumstance extrinsic to the currency, unless at the same period a corresponding fall, of nearly similar amount, could be traced in the money prices of all other countries. Then, indeed, it might be fairly assumed, though not with absolute certainty, that the phenomenon was referable to some alteration in the value of the precious metals themselves. Past experience has shewn only one instance in the history of the world, when an alteration in the real value of gold and silver within a short period could have produced any sudden and considerable effect upon prices in general. It took place during the period which succeeded the discovery of America. The evil then was a rapid depreciation; it is now supposed that a real enhancement of value is taking place to a certain small degree. The supposition, owing chiefly to the suspension of mining operations in the Spanish colonies, may be correct; but the effect must have been counteracted to some extent by the general improvements in banking; and there is every reason to imagine, that no considerable effect will have been produced in this way, before a restoration of tranquillity, and accumulation of capital in those parts of the globe most rich in the precious metals, will increase their production to its former amount, and perhaps far beyond. Even at present it is chiefly in silver that any great defalcation exists; for the gold received within a few years from the Ural mountains, and still more lately from the United States, is a supply of recent origin, and must tend in some degree to fill up the vacuum caused by the political troubles in Spanish America.

Thus, then, even a general fall of money prices might not render what is called an equitable adjustment consistent with any sound principles of justice or policy. Such a circumstance, should it occur, would probably be traceable to some causes acting on commodities other than gold and silver, and we may affirm such to be the case, with very little chance of error, when the supposed fall can only be traced in one particular country.

The above reasoning will enable us to appreciate the true value of the arguments which attribute to Peel's Bill, or to the recal of £1 and £2 notes, an effect upon money prices in England equal to 50 or 60 per cent. Those who adduce them in order to produce even a colour of reason in their favour, must shew, 1st, That the fall has been nearly equal, and has applied to all commodities whatever at home; 2nd, That it has taken place in a degree almost similar both as to extent and intensity abroad. An attentive examination of Price Currents since 1819 will shew a total failure in both points, which is confirmed as to foreign countries by a complete absence of any general complaint of a fall of prices referable to the currency, of a similar kind to what has so long prevailed here.

The second prevailing error which influences many persons in the judgment they form of the proper amount of currency at any given time, is that which consists in regarding the current rate of interest as a criterion. The phrase "interest of money" has had, perhaps, much influence in bringing this opinion into vogue, and it is fostered by the circumstance, that Bank notes are usually issued upon securities bearing interest. Yet both sound economical principles and experience concur in shewing that it is perfectly unfounded and can only lead to delusion, as the following considerations will evince.

Interest is the price which the borrower pays to the lender for the use, not of money, but of capital. The loan is, indeed, usually made in money in the first instance, but that is a mere matter of convenience, arising from its being an universal medium of exchange. A cotton and a woollen manufacturer require a quantity of the raw material employed in their respective trades; in order to obtain it they each borrow £1000 from their banker, and pay it away immediately to the merchants who have imported the Spanish wool and the Brazilian cotton, which thus constitute the real loans to them. Or, if provided with the raw material, they may want the means of furnishing the wages of their workmen, in which case the same result is finally obtained, although after one additional step, beyond what appears in the example last supposed. The money is now paid to labourers, who distribute it among the different shopkeepers by whom their wants are supplied. The meat, bread, clothing, &c., really constitute in this instance the capital borrowed, for which interest is paid. It is true that a certain portion of money being, under present circumstances, one of the instruments of production, thus forms a part, though generally a very inconsiderable part, of capital; but this is not the circumstance to which those who maintain the doctrine now impugned allude. Interest would continue to exist was there no such thing as money in the world, and were all exchanges performed by barter. It is not of course meant to be denied that, especially under present circumstances, while the greater part of the currency is advanced by the issuers upon securities bearing interest, the increase or diminution of the currency will have no effect whatever upon the rate of interest, but merely that the effect will be transient, and—excepting as to the small extent in which money enters into capital, and there is a specific demand for it—that it arises chiefly from circumstances peculiar to our monetary system. Suppose the Bank at any given period to throw £1,000,000 in paper upon the money market of London by a purchase of Exchequer-bills to that amount, the immediate consequence will be, that those who want to borrow Bank-notes will be able to obtain them at a lower interest than before; but the excess will in all probability be speedily absorbed, the capital obtained for it will be employed in the production or distribution of commodities, and the permanent effect of the augmented circulation will be seen in higher prices and a fall in the exchanges.

The following facts will confirm the views here maintained of the absence of any necessary connexion between an extended or contracted currency, and a low or high rate of interest.

During the operation of the Bank-restriction Act, when an excess of issue had depreciated the currency from 5 to 30 per cent., the rate of interest was always much higher than it has ever been since the return to cash payments; occasionally it reached 8 and perhaps 10 per cent., while, when the Bank issues were subsequently reduced, and the exchanges rose, it rapidly fell. In 1822, 1823, and 1832, the general circulation was low, and the rate of interest was low also, and the same circumstance has occurred in the last few months, and exists at present. Towards the end of 1824, and the beginning of 1825, and again in 1836, anterior to any contraction, and when, confessedly, the circulation was very high, the rate of interest rose. In all these instances the fact is exactly opposite to what is assumed by those who maintain the opinion now animadverted on. In the summer of

1830, and perhaps on some other occasions, we had a high currency, and a low rate of interest. It appears, then, on the whole, that there is no fixed and necessary connexion between them; although, while the process of contraction is going on there is a tendency in the rate of interest to rise, and the reverse while the currency is expanding. It is greatly to be wished that no part of the paper circulation were to be issued in loans at all, but on this point more will be said hereafter.

Another mistake, somewhat analogous to the last, is that which decides upon the sufficiency of the currency exclusively by a comparison of its amount at different periods. This mode of viewing the subject assumes that the demand for currency, that is to say, the value of the commodities to be exchanged, the number of exchanges, and the velocity of the circulation, shall be always equal; but as these must manifestly vary from year to year, and even from month to month, it follows that the amount of currency, instead of being fixed, must constantly change in order to suit the wants of the community. The exclusive appeal to this criterion, and not a proper attention to the amount of the currency at given periods, is here objected to; for although the demand for it is not fixed, yet it seldom alters rapidly or extensively within short intervals, and thus useful inferences may often be drawn from attention to this point. It is greatly to be wished, in order to render our knowledge more accurate and complete, that all Banks whatever, issuing paper, including those in Scotland and Ireland, were compelled to publish the amount of their issues at regular and stated times. The separate returns should be methodized, and inserted in the London Gazette, or some other authentic source of official information.

The fourth in the list of errors now commented upon is that which proposes to regulate the amount of currency by attention to the deposits in the hands of the Bank of England and private bankers, thus assuming that there is some fixed and necessary connexion between the state of the currency and the balances left unemployed by the public. Persons agreeing in the main point are still diametrically opposed to each other as to the inference which ought to be drawn from it, some affirming that deposits being so much taken from the circulation must tend to reduce its amount, and that when they increase, the Bank ought greatly to extend its issues, in order to fill up the vacuum; while others regard large deposits as a proof of a superabundant circulation, and as calling on the Bank, without reference to the exchanges, for a reduction in its issues. The fact is, that the amount of deposits affords not the supposed criterion. It is even more removed from the truth than that which is taken from the rate of interest, for it depends mainly upon the rate of interest, though many other circumstances also influence the unemployed balances. They may be either high or low, with either a high or low currency. It is quite true, that inconvenience may in some cases arise from an union of the business of issuing paper with that of receiving deposits. The currency and deposits may both be large, the latter may be drawn out, and the circulation be thus augmented, when the amount of Bank notes is already too high, and when it may be difficult to realize securities; or the former being low, may be still further diminished by an augmentation of the latter—great skill and management are required on such occasions to reconcile, as far as may be, duties to a certain degree incompatible. This can only be effected, and that in part, by a strict attention on the part of the Banks to the state of the exchanges, and by an employment of the deposits, in rigid accordance with, and subserviency to, the inferences derived from it.

Having thus shewn that neither the range of money prices, the rate of interest, the absolute and comparative amount of the circulation, and the quantity, and increase or diminution of deposits, so commonly referred to as infallible criteria of the sufficiency or insufficiency of the currency, can be at all relied on, we are naturally carried back to the exchanges as the only sure and certain guide upon which a thorough and complete reliance can be placed, at almost all times and under all circumstances.

In the foregoing observations we have treated of the currency, without any peculiar attention to the substance of which it may be composed. We must now revert particularly to a paper circulation. It has been shewn that the precious metals afford the best, and indeed the only safe, standard of value; but they are very costly and so cumbrous, that their exclusive use in a country like England would oppose great and almost insurmountable obstacles to the transactions of commerce upon their present scale. The separate advantages of fixity of value, cheapness and convenience, are obtained by employing Bank notes, pieces of paper containing promises to pay on demand certain weights of gold or silver, as the case may be, of a certain fineness.

The amount of Bank notes and coin taken together, if the former be convertible, cannot, except perhaps for a short period, exceed or fall short of the money that would circulate were the currency purely metallic. They can never remain at the same amount long together, but will vary in consequence of the numerous circumstances which influence prices both at home and abroad. The process of variation consists in the return of notes to the Banks for gold or silver when the currency is high, and the demand for notes in exchange for gold or silver when the currency is low. The maximum and minimum of the whole circulation, in any given oscillation, will be nearly the same, whether it be purely metallic or mixed: the utmost that can result from error on the part of the issuers is, perhaps for a short time during a progressive increase or diminution, to keep it a little too high or too low, and to prolong more or less the period at which the maximum or minimum will be attained by, on one side, re-issuing notes as fast as they are paid off in coin or bullion, on the other, by recalling notes issued against coin or bullion.

A paper currency will be more or less perfect in proportion as its contractions and expansions resemble those which would take place in the amount of a purely metallic currency under similar circumstances. It might be considered practically perfect if, in addition to being thoroughly convertible and unexposed to discredit, except perhaps in times of very great political excitement, it were at every moment to be of precisely the same value as the metallic medium which might supply its place, being increased and diminished under the same circumstances, at similar periods, and to a like extent. To attain this perfect equality of value on the whole, its amount would usually be somewhat less than a similar value in coin, owing to its superior convenience and power of performing a somewhat greater number of exchanges.

We have seen that neither the range of general prices, the rate of interest, the relative amount of currency at different times, nor that of deposits, afford any fixed or certain rules for the guidance of the issuers of paper money, and that such are to be sought for in the state of the exchanges alone. What then is to be thought of our present system, wherein one mass of issuers, the Joint-Stock Banks and Country Bankers, look almost exclusively to these fallacious criteria; while the Bank of England, which alone even pretends to adhere to correct principles, is thwarted by the injudicious conduct of its associates, and frequently embarrassed by the difficulties of its own position in the twofold capacity of money issuer and agent for ordinary banking business! No correct notions can ever be formed upon the subject of currency, unless the business of issue be clearly separated in the reader's mind from the other transactions which form the real and legitimate employments of the banker. They are, in fact, not merely distinguishable, but dissimilar, and, perhaps, irreconcilable. The rule of utility would place the former exclusively in the hands of the government, to be exercised by it directly, or through the medium of some delegated body as peculiar circumstances might render most convenient, while the latter would be left perfectly free. In barbarous ages powerful subjects were occasionally permitted to possess mints of their own; but since political knowledge has increased, these pernicious privileges have been abolished, and at present, in all civilized countries, the sovereign power, of whatever nature it may be, retains the coinage in its own hands. If it were now to be proposed that private persons should be allowed to strike money, most people would at once perceive that nothing but mischief could result from such a measure,—that under such a system, the currency would either be the same as before, and no good would arise, or different, in which case evil would have been produced. Yet is it not undeniable that all the arguments which apply to the Mint are strictly applicable to the issue of paper money; and that their force is increased by others strictly peculiar to the latter? A sovereign carries its own value with it, and cannot be subject to discredit or insolvency on the part of the issuer, while the very small profit that could be derived from a private mint would afford a sufficient guarantee against the risk of over-issue.

The cuckoo cry we so often hear, as to the dangers and abuses of a monopoly, is a pregnant instance of the argument "ad ignorantiam." Monopolies are usually unpopular because pernicious, and when pernicious, ought to be abolished; but when, in one case out of a hundred, advantage arises from them, the common good requires that they should be maintained. Let it be assumed, then, that the issue of paper should be confined to the state; what seems the best plan on which the wants of the country could be supplied? We must here suppose that the field is open, that no set of persons have acquired a sort of vested interest which it may be difficult to deal with, that no established habits or prejudices interfere with the free agency of the legislature, and the course to be pursued seems sufficiently clear.

The ordinary business of banking would be left perfectly open, to be carried on by single persons, by ordinary partnerships, or by joint-stock companies, as the freest competition shewed to be most advantageous. The issue would be managed as follows.—Let us suppose a paper circulation of thirty millions to be required; of this sum a certain amount, say one-third in the first instance, would be invested in coin and bullion, though experience might subsequently prove that proportion to be unnecessarily large, and the remainder in profitable securities or the discharge of public debts. An establishment would then be formed, whose simple and exclusive business it would be to issue notes for gold and silver, and gold and silver for notes. The former operation would be required when the exchanges were high, the latter when they were low; the contractions and expansions of the currency would be perfectly natural, and it would differ no otherwise from one purely metallic than by its superior cheapness and convenience; all ordinary banking business would be strictly forbidden to the issuing body, the expenses of management would be small, and the profit, reckoning the gain both of the government and the public, considerable; the notes of course would be a legal tender from every body but the Bank itself, and the most perfect publicity would be enforced.

The danger of forgery, particularly applicable to small notes, seems to afford the only good ground for rejecting Mr. Ricardo's plan of making the notes payable in bullion instead of coin, and thus saving the expense of a mint, except for silver.

Some persons might prefer mint notes,—simple receipts for coin or bullion,—for every one of which a corresponding amount of gold should be retained; but this plan, though more cheap and convenient than a metallic circulation, would cut off a source of considerable saving to the state, without any corresponding advantage.

It would certainly be desirable in many points of view that the paper money should be only exchangeable for coin in the metropolis, but against this plan it might be urged that inconvenience would occasionally exist in the provinces from a want of coin, which there would be no legal obligation on any body to supply. It is certain, however, that bankers would be compelled to provide a sufficient stock of coin for the accommodation of their customers, perhaps at a considerable expense to themselves, if obliged frequently to bring it from London. To meet this expense, they would either charge a premium on payments in gold, or incur a loss. The way to meet this evil, should it be deemed of sufficient importance, would be to establish branches of the metropolitan establishment in different parts of the country. These, if not too much multiplied, and under proper regulations, would not occasion any very heavy expense.

## SECTION II.

EXAMINATION OF THE VARIOUS SCHEMES PROPOSED TO REMEDY THE EVILS OF THE CURRENCY—LOWERING THE STANDARD—AN EQUITABLE ADJUSTMENT—UNLIMITED FREEDOM OF ISSUE—AN INCONVERTIBLE GOVERNMENT PAPER—TEMPORARY ISSUES BY GOVERNMENT—A SILVER STANDARD—A DOUBLE STANDARD.

THE object of the last section has been to point out the true principles on which a paper currency ought to be regulated, and to expose the unsoundness of the false criteria by which its sufficiency or insufficiency are frequently estimated.

It has been shewn that the precious metals afford the best and only safe standard, and that a mixed circulation, consisting of coin and paper, will be more or less perfect, in proportion as at every moment it approaches in a greater or less degree to what would be the amount of coin (allowing for the greater convenience of Bank notes) in case there was no paper. We have farther seen that the exchanges afford the only test by which a correct opinion can be formed as to the state of the circulation in point of extent—that the Bank of England is the only body issuing notes which even pretends, in an imperfect degree, to regulate its amount according to the dictates of this safe monitor; while the private and joint-stock banks, acting upon a principle of competition, and diminishing and increasing their issues in consequence of changes in the money-market, or in the prices of commodities, must necessarily, under certain circumstances, do much mischief.

The public in general attribute much greater importance to the fluctuations and other evils of our system of currency than they fairly deserve. According to some authors of great repute, and the almost concurrent opinion of the newspapers, all the misfortunes which have afflicted trade during the last fifty years are traceable to them alone. This opinion is an immense exaggeration of the truth. Mr. Loyd well observes, "that in "examining what we are in the habit of calling "the state of trade, we find it subject to certain "conditions which are periodically returning; "it revolves apparently in an established cycle. "First we find it in a state of quiescence—next "improvement — growing confidence — prosperity—excitement—over-trading—convulsion—"pressure—stagnation—distress—ending again "in quiescence." Now this established cycle will be found in countries, like France or Holland, before the revolution, in both of which the currency for practical purposes may be considered as metallic, with its conditions as plainly, if not as strongly marked as in England or America. Experience shews us, that in such countries, and during periods when no variation in the value of gold and silver was suspected, mercantile excitement and a spirit of wild speculation have nevertheless appeared occasionally with all their attendant mischiefs; and there were so many causes pointing this way in operation previously to the panic of 1825 and our late disaster, that no rational doubt can be entertained, but that had no such thing as a Bank-note then existed in England, the years 1825, 1826, and 1837 would still have brought with them a numerous train of mercantile disasters. At the time of the South Sea Bubble the Bank of England circulation was very small, and increased slowly, and that of other issuers was in its infancy, yet the infatuation which then prevailed far surpassed what has been seen in our days.

Nevertheless, although sober reason denies the unfounded assumption, that all great commercial convulsions may be traced to a faulty system of currency, there can be no doubt but that this country has suffered greatly of late years, from the nature of its paper circulation, which, viewed as a whole, presents the following exceptionable points :—

1. A tendency to vary in amount both as to excess or deficiency in an unnecessary degree, and at unsuitable periods.

2. A liability to discredit, both mercantile and political, in a large portion, if not the whole of it.

3. Insolvency on the part of many of the issuers.

Insolvency shews itself in two forms, which it is necessary to distinguish, as they are frequently separated in fact, and are in some degree characteristic of two classes of issuing bodies. The first is a simple inability to discharge notes on demand, while their ultimate liquidation is certain, and is frequently not even doubted of by the holder. The second form of insolvency is that which involves loss on the part of creditors.

All the objections usually urged against our present currency, however varied in terms, in so far as they are well founded, may be conveniently ranged under these heads. The object of the present section will be to examine the various popular remedies which have been proposed for the purpose of placing our monetary system on a secure foundation, and to decide upon their advisableness according to the principles proposed in the present publication.

It would be a waste of time and labour to hunt out every nostrum proposed by the merest political quack. Those suggestions which have emanated from persons considered to be of high authority in such matters, and which have obtained a certain weight in public opinion, alone deserve a serious attention. Among the most important, from the popularity it has acquired, and from the tremendous evils which would flow from its adoption, is that which proposes in effect, though not always in words, a lowering of the standard by an increase of paper. To this then our attention shall be first directed.

The supporters of this scheme consider that since the return to specie payments, and especially since 1825, the currency has been insufficient in point of amount—that the precious metals have been enhanced in value, and that prosperity can never return until a large increase of the circulation has taken place. Some of them do not appear to know that such an increase is impossible, unless the standard is lowered, so as to create a depreciation; while others seem to be aware that depreciation and increase of paper must go hand in hand, and that if we are to have twenty-five millions of Bank-notes instead of eighteen, they can only be paid, if convertible at all, in what they call " little sovereigns."

We have already seen that the value of the precious metals, if raised in any one country, from causes specially affecting them, must speedily be raised in all, and in a nearly equal degree; and that without appealing to the difficult test of Price Currents in England, the absence of all suspicion of such an occurrence, to any considerable extent, on the continent, is a sufficient proof that it has had no existence there, or consequently here. If this be the case, it is clear that the fall in certain commodities and classes of commodities so constantly and confidently referred to, when it has taken place, is referable to some of the other elements which influence prices—of which by far the most important is a diminution in the cost of production, arising from improved machinery, greater scientific skill, cheaper and more rapid communication, &c.

It may here be useful, by a short illustration, to show that producers do not usually suffer from a fall of money prices, arising from a diminished cost of production,—that they are as well off in such a case as the public creditor, or the receiver of any kind of fixed income. Let us suppose a community composed of a certain number of shoe-makers, a certain number of hat-makers, and a certain number of fundholders; that the first produced annually 300 pair of boots, worth £300, the second 300 hats, worth also £300, and that the last received the produce of a tax, raised in equal proportions from the other two classes, to the amount of £200;—this revenue they would employ in the purchase of 100 pair of boots, and 100 hats,—while the shoe-makers and hat-makers exchanged with each other one half of the stocks that respectively remained to them. Each of the three classes would then possess 100 pair of boots and 100 hats. Now let us imagine some great improvement in the manufacturing process, which should enable the productive classes, with the same capital as before, to obtain a double return—600 pair of boots and 600 hats, the money-tax remaining unaltered—the price of each would fall 50 per cent., from £1 to 10*s*.—the fund-holders would be enabled to purchase 200 pair of boots and 200 hats—their power of consuming would be doubled, but that of the producers would be augmented in an exactly equal proportion—they would retain 400 pair of boots, and 400 hats, instead of half that quantity, as in the former instance.

Having thus shewn that the evil complained of does not really exist, it may be well to cast a glance over the effects of the proposed remedy: it is plain, that, considered as a mere numerator, it matters not to the nation whether a sovereign exchanges for one sheep or two, provided that in the latter case all other commodities measured in gold are depressed in an equal proportion: it is plain also that the current expenses of the government, other than the fixed sums payable to the public creditor, would be augmented, should the standard be lowered; all this will probably be granted; but then, it is said, that the public creditor gets more than he bargained for, and that mortgagees, lessors, and annuitants, are in a similar situation. To this it can only be replied, that when these parties entered upon their engagements, a clear understanding existed on both sides, that they were to be paid in the legal currency of the country, and that no deliberate attempt should be made to reduce its value; that most of them derive their rights from transactions anterior to 1797, or to the period when Bank notes became depreciated, and posterior to 1819, and that even as to those which accrued, during the period of depreciation, their peculiarity of character arose from the joint ignorance of government and people, that the persons in question always looked forward to a restoration of the standard, (which a formal act of the legislature declared should take place at a fixed period,) if they ever thought about it at all, and that to fine them now, because they or their predecessors made a good bargain thirty years ago, would be the height of injustice.

It is farther to be considered, that even allowing the truth of the unfounded assumption that an enormous appreciation of the currency has taken place, and that it would be desirable to place what has been quaintly termed the debtor interest in the situation it would have occupied, had this appreciation never existed,—the plan of lowering the standard would still attain the object very imperfectly. In assuming any fixed rate of depreciation in the currency, we could only relieve those accurately who had previously suffered from a fall in commodities to the same extent; many others would still have the same reason to complain as they have now, and demands for a repetition of an operation, so convenient for those who dislike paying their debts at twenty shillings in the pound, would be endless. Besides this, it may be remarked, that whatever allowance could be claimed on a principle of justice for the losses of the "debtor interest" since 1819, must be admitted in favour of the "creditor interest," during the depreciation. As far as the public debt is concerned, the effect of such an adjustment has been accurately shewn by the calculations of Mr. Mushet, from which it appears, that the public gained almost as much by paying in a depreciated currency, between 1797 and 1819, as they had lost up to the time when his work was published.

It has been supposed hitherto, that although the standard should be reduced, the paper money was to be still convertible; but an inconvertible paper appears sometimes to be preferred; in that case we should have all the evils hitherto alluded to, and constant variations in the value of the currency besides.

The truth is, that the whole scheme is a plan of robbery, propounded with much circumlocution, and wrapped in many mystic phrases. It is a plan calculated to plunder all persons possessed of funded property, mortgages, annuities, deposits in the savings' banks, or with bankers, or who have insured their lives, and the members of all benefit societies; that is to say, those persons who, considered as a whole, form the most moral and intelligent part of the community: it would transfer to their neighbours a certain portion of their wealth, without adding a farthing to that of the nation at large. Its effect upon the condition of the working class would be peculiarly deplorable. A great stagnation in most branches of industry would take place in the first instance, from the shock given to the confidence of capitalists by so flagrant a violation of national faith. But even supposing this evil to be surmounted, *it would be long before* wages attained the same level compared with the objects on which they were expended as existed previously to the depreciation. This interval might, indeed, under certain circumstances, be prolonged for many years, during all which time the poor would suffer severe privations, deliberately inflicted upon them by the legislature. The supporters of the scheme declare, indeed, that this view of the case is incorrect, and that it would, if adopted, fill every body's pocket with money, and greatly elevate the condition of the poor; but this is a mere gratuitous assertion, utterly unsupported by argument, and opposed alike to sound principles and the unerring voice of experience.

It must be remarked that the plan in question has nothing of novelty belonging to it—it has been a great favourite with bad governments in all ages, but has usually been abandoned so soon as the public became sufficiently enlightened to measure the acts of their rulers by even a rude standard of public utility; thus Henry VIII. was almost the last debaser of the coin in England, and Louis XIV. in France. There is still one country in Europe where the scheme is so frequently resorted to, that assuming the doctrines of the Birmingham Political Union on this subject to be well-founded, we might expect to find it a perfect paradise, replete with whatever can make existence desirable, and presenting wealth and profitable employment for the whole population. Alas for the theory of the depreciators! the country in question is Turkey, and the wise legislator whom they require the ruling powers here to imitate is Soldan Mahmoud.

Enough has been said upon the depreciation of the standard as a remedy for national distress. The next recommendation to be examined is what has been called an equitable adjustment: it proposes to send commissioners all through the country with power to regulate every contract entered into since 1790, with reference to the average prices of wheat, mutton, and wool, during periods of about five years each.

Here again we have an assumption that the precious metals are an improper standard, and that we ought to resort to another instead of them; it is clear, however, that the one proposed wants almost every quality required for that purpose; in fact, notwithstanding the dispute between the late Mr. Cobbett and Mr. Attwood, the schemes they respectively advocate differ from each other but little in point of principle; considered practically, that of the latter is sufficiently easy of execution, whereas that of the former would meet with such insurmountable obstacles, that it is truly wonderful that its acute and able supporter should have ever contemplated its being carried into effect, as an event within the range of possibility; an attempt, indeed, might be made, immense confusion might be created, and a great deal of cruelty and injustice might be perpetrated, but a bonâ fide accomplishment of the so-called equitable adjustment extending over all transactions through a space of forty years is a mere theoretic dream.

Mr. Cobbett sometimes included in the plan now examined, the application of a sponge to the national debt; but this, whether expedient or inexpedient, a point which may be safely left to the plain sense and honest principles of the reader, has no necessary connexion with it. Considered as a measure of finance, it does not possess the merit of novelty, having been resorted to by tyrants and oppressors at all times. The non-payment of debts is a very plain and easy method of relieving an embarrassed Exchequer.

The next scheme for the improvement of our monetary system is that which proposes to establish what has been called a free trade in banking; its first requisite, of course, is the abolition of the partial monopoly now possessed by the Bank of England, and its supporters usually contemplate the gradual extinction of the country bankers as issuers of paper, and desire to see the currency supplied by joint-stock banks acting on a principle of competition.

The unfavourable notions associated with the term monopoly have greatly contributed to confer popularity on the permission of unlimited competition among the issuers of paper money; it is necessary, then, once more to recollect that monopolies are only inexpedient when opposed to the common interest, as happens in a vast majority of cases; if coinciding with the common interest, they of course merit our approbation. The usual objection to monopolies is, that they furnish a commodity dearer or worse, or both, than would be supplied under a system of free trade; but this objection does not apply to the case of a body which possesses peculiar privileges in the issue of paper money. A paper currency is more or less perfect in proportion as it possesses the three properties enumerated in the first Section, viz. equality in amount at every moment with the coin that might circulate in its place—freedom from discredit—convertibility. The following considerations will shew that these qualities, on the whole, are more likely to belong to the issues of one body than of many—cheapness and fitness, in the highest degree, to perform the required functions are included in them.

It has been seen that the exchanges are the only real criterion of the state of the currency, and that all others are fallacious. The managers of one issuing establishment, supposing all their proceedings to be made public, would be placed under a feeling of responsibility, which would render it almost impossible for them wholly to forget even for a moment this great truth; but supposing, instead of one, we have ten or a hundred banks, the responsibility is so divided as to become completely inefficient—the loss and inconvenience of over issues does not always fall upon the peccant bank, but upon its neighbours, and thus at periods of advancing prices, which ought, in a natural state of things, to be checked by a currency little if at all expansive, we find invariably a large increase in the issues of small banks, which foster a morbid spirit of speculation, and thus lead to immense evil when the recoil takes place.

It is imagined that the plan of exchanging notes between the banks at certain fixed periods is sufficient to prevent over-issue on the part of any one of them; but let us suppose, as is usually the case, that the tendency to over-issue is simultaneous and common to all or to a majority, it is plain that this measure can afford no sufficient protection; even should the error be confined to a single bank, and that bank be considered by the public to deserve confidence, the over-issue, though restrained, will not be prevented—the check can, of course, only apply to those notes which pass into the hands of other banks; but besides these there is a great quantity in the tills of tradesmen, and the pockets of the public at large, on which it has no effect whatever. It is thus that some years ago a new bank at Edinburgh is said to have established, within two years, a very extensive circulation, in spite of the united and most determined opposition of all those previously existing.

Colonel Torrens in his Letter to Lord Melbourne maintains, somewhat in opposition to these views, that the Bank of England at present has the immediate power of preventing over-issues on the part of its provincial brethren; those who agree with him are referred to the opposing testimony contained in the tabular statements of the issues of the Bank of England and joint-stock and country banks, presented at p. 77. Even this statement affords a result far short of the truth, taking the three kingdoms into account. We may be certain that Scotland contributed largely to swell the excess, although unfortunately we are deprived of the means of ascertaining to what amount. The truth appears to be that, Colonel Torrens's general principles are correct, but their operation is far less immediate than he imagines. He does not allow enough for friction; in other words, a considerable period may elapse before the check arising from the exportation of the precious metals, and the consequent return of notes, is felt. When indeed there are many issuing banks, this check can never be felt immediately by more than a few. In England it is only felt by one, which is *de facto* charged with providing a metallic basis for the whole currency.

It is difficult to explain fully and satisfactorily the nature of the friction above alluded to. The great increase of auxiliary currency during periods of high prices and commercial excitement, will afford, in a great degree, a solution of the difficulty. Thus, let us suppose an over-issue on the part of the provincial banks, that of the Bank of England remaining at the proper amount. Bills of exchange in large quantities, payable in London, will be drawn by sellers on purchasers at Liverpool, Manchester, &c. &c. These, to a certain extent, will balance and discharge each other, and will at any rate prolong the time at which the state of prices out of London is to be tested by the state of the metropolitan currency, to which, however, these must finally adjust themselves.

Again, the prices of many articles of indispensable necessity, under ordinary circumstances, will be a little higher in a vast city than in smaller towns or the country, owing to the expense of transport; an obstacle is thus opposed to the ordinary course of equalizing the currency under the circumstances supposed, viz. a transmission of goods from the former to the latter. It must be left to the reader to decide if the above remarks help to explain what he will hereafter find to be an indubitable fact. Any further discussion would occupy too much space here. But to return to the point from which the remarks on Colonel Torrens's arguments have led us.

Even assuming that a number of banks could be found, all of them disposed to conduct their business perfectly well; that there should not exist even one among the number, which, allured by the prospects of immediate gain, or the desire of under working a rival, should increase its issues imprudently; supposing all this, still the effect would merely be, that we should be as well off as with a single issuer, but no better. Now is the chance of our attaining so very improbable a result sufficient to induce us to incur the enormous risk of a failure?

It must never be forgotten that all the objections here made to the principle of competition apply merely to the issuing of paper. Any thing like interference on the part of the government by exclusive privileges or otherwise in the true and legitimate objects of banking is equally injurious and unjust.

All the arguments hitherto urged against the scheme of unlimited competition, suppose it to be rendered as perfect as possible, by compelling all issuers of paper to give security for their circulation, and to publish their accounts, which might render their notes almost, if not quite, as free from objection on the score of freedom from discredit, and ultimate convertibility, or at least solvency, as those of a single establishment would be. But if we suppose, as is the case at present in England, that neither security nor effective publicity should be enforced, the evil would be increased prodigiously. These regulations would do away with even the shadow of a reason for making any difference between the business of banking and any other commercial undertakings, with respect to the limited or unlimited liability of partners. Under any circumstances, indeed, it seems inexpedient, as regards the public, and unjust as regards private bankers, to favour especially joint-stock banks, by making a particular law in their behalf. Partnerships "en common-dite," and " sociétés anonymes," to use the language of the French law, should be allowed universally or not at all.

" Competition in the issue of paper money
" has never been tried to an unlimited extent
" except in one instance, that of the United
" States, and the able publication of Mr. Gal-
" latin will inform us of the success with which
" the experiment was attended. It is to be ob-
" served, that in America the publicity of ac-
" counts is generally enforced, and although no
" security is taken, yet all the banks, with one
" exception, to which Mr. Gallatin alludes, were
" chartered, and their paid-up capitals were
" considered sufficient to guard against any
" danger of insolvency; in most instances the
" responsibility of shareholders seems to have
" been unlimited. Yet in the period more par-
" ticularly adverted to, viz. between 1811, when
" the first bank of the United States was dis-
" solved, and 1816, when the existing bank
" was established, nothing could be less satis-
" factory than the state of the circulation. In
" August and September, 1814, all the banks,
" south and west of New England, stopped pay-
" ment in consequence of excessive issues,
" which brought the notes, or a large proportion
" of them, to a discount; and an undue spirit
" of speculation was fostered, subsequently
" productive of great calamity, when specie
" payments were restored; — at length these

" evils became so monstrous, that a wish to re-
" establish one general centre of circulation was
" forced on the public mind, and produced the
" existing bank of the United States, chartered
" in April, 1816, which has amply fulfilled all
" that was expected from it, having served as a
" check to the proceedings of other companies,
" equalized and given solidity to the currencies
" of the several States, and afforded by means
" of its branches secure places of deposit, and
" cheap and rapid means of transmitting money
" between every part of the Union, as well as
" between America and Europe. The charter
" of this bank will expire in 1836, and the
" President, Jackson, has put his veto on a bill
" which had passed both Houses of Congress
" for its renewal. It may be safely predicted,
" that should this renewal finally be refused, a
" state of things will return similar in kind to
" what occurred between 1811 and 1816, though
" not perhaps in degree, because the evil was
" then doubtless aggravated by the war with
" Great Britain, and by a less general enforce-
" ment than at present of publicity of accounts.
" Mr. Gallatin mentions, that in all the New-
" England States, in Virginia, Georgia, and
" some others, publicity of accounts is now
" prescribed by law, and that it had never in-
" jured any institution properly conducted. Be-
" tween the 1st July, 1811, and the 1st July, 1830,

" 165 banks failed in the United States; their " joint capital was about thirty millions of dol- " lars; that belonging to the state banks now " in existence being about 110 millions. The " amount of loss incurred by the creditors in " general was very large, but has not been as- " certained—that of the government alone was " about four millions. So great have been the " evils arising from the bank issues in the Union, " that they seem to make Mr. Gallatin wish, on " the whole, that no paper circulation whatever " had been allowed, though he is well aware of " the advantages which belong to it."

The above paragraph has been left in the state in which it was originally printed, although not published, as explained in the prefatory notice, in the early part of 1833, and is now inserted—not to gratify the vanity of the Author by presenting him in the character of a prophet, but as shewing that the disastrous phænomena which have lately occurred on the other side the Atlantic, are no more than might have been anticipated from the principles he has endeavoured to explain. The evidence they afford is particularly valuable in a point of view hitherto little adverted to by writers on currency. Alarmed by the losses sustained by the creditors of the Banks which failed between 1811 and 1816, the Americans have generally compelled the chartered banks since established to furnish large paid-up capitals, and have made almost unlimited publicity a condition of their existence. These precautions will probably secure in a great majority of instances, the discharge of their liabilities some time or other. There will be but little ultimate insolvency, yet almost absolute certainty on this point, even such a degree of certainty as in the case of the United States Bank at Philadelphia with its eight millions sterling of capital, it would be madness to deny, did not at the hour of trial secure the immediate convertibility of their issues.

It may here be remarked as a curious fact, that at the instant when the stoppage of the American Banks took place in 1837, a depreciation of the paper-currency appeared exceeding 10 per cent, and that in cases where ultimate loss was not to be feared by the most timid. From this it may be inferred, that, in spite of the check arising from the foreign exchanges, a mixed currency may be depreciated to that extent under certain circumstances, when issued and regulated on erroneous principles.

It is impossible to abandon this subject without a passing observation on the remedial measures lately under the consideration of Congress, if not already sanctioned by it. These were alike unworthy of the government that proposed and of the legislature that debated upon them. It is really monstrous to look only to the possible loss of a few millions of dollars, by a government which has a surplus revenue so large as to be a heavy incumbrance; while no measures are even proposed for a radical improvement in the currency, the state of which has lately produced such mighty disasters. Such is the effect of ignorance and party spirit combined. Supposing the cabinet of Washington to be sustained in its views by the representatives of the American people, and that the Union is left to be supplied with a paper currency by an unlimited number of banks, acting in competition, and without any controul from the action of one powerful central body, we may anticipate with certainty a succession of catastrophes such as we have lately seen, occurring at intervals more or less distant, according to circumstances — but perhaps one more example may suffice, to convince the most obdurate Jacksonian.

Had the year 1825 or 1836 found the United Kingdom with a currency furnished by three or four hundred joint-stock and private banks, a large number of them in operation in London, and without the controul of one great body like the Bank of England, it is the Author's firm conviction, which his love of truth makes it his duty to state, in spite of the delicacy of his position, that in both cases a large majority, if not the whole, however ultimately solvent, would have been found wanting in the hour of need, in other words would have stopped payment; but to return from this digression.

The example of Scotland is one which produces a great effect on the public mind with reference to the question now under discussion. The general solidity of the Banks in that country is an admirable feature, and they fairly deserve all the admiration that has been lavished on them as secure places of deposit, and much praise for the way in which they perform the proper business of Banking; the only fair exception under this head being, perhaps, the so much lauded cash credits, which seem very nearly analogous to the discount of accommodation-bills, and calculated to produce the same results. In periods of excitement and rising prices they stimulate speculation unduly, and afford a spectacle of specious and factitious prosperity; while, when the recoil takes place they sweep the solvent and comparatively prudent trader into the same net with the rash adventurer, and lead to awful and wide-spread ruin. Perhaps it is chiefly owing to them that, in periods of commercial difficulty, no country is said to suffer from insolvency more severely than Scotland. Manchester, where banks of issue have never existed, until recently and then to a small extent, furnishes, in this respect, an interesting and instructive contrast. It is, however, as issuers of paper money that the Scotch Banks are chiefly open to criticism. They do not keep any considerable reserves of gold, relying always on the Bank of England for a supply. It is plain that this mode of operation would be considerably modified, were they exposed to the immediate test of specie payments; but in other respects their conduct is highly exceptionable. In times of prosperity they push out their notes and credits to an undue extent, and are consequently compelled to diminish them as violently, when circumstances alter, thus inflicting on the public oscillations in the currency much more violent than could occur with a metallic circulation, or with paper regulated on sound principles. Supposing such banks to be acting in London and exposed to the direct operation of the foreign exchanges, we might certainly expect greater prudence on their part. Still the inherent vice of issues made in competition and upon securities bearing interest, would exist. The paper would have a tendency to increase when the rate of interest or when prices rose, and to be unduly contracted, when prices and the rate of interest had fallen; the country could not be better off than with a single source of issue in the capital, and, there is every reason to believe, would be much worse off.

The next proposed improvement which demands our consideration is one which has often been suggested. It consists in the extinction of the Bank of England and all other banks of issue and proposes to fill up the vacancy occasioned by the withdrawal of their notes by an inconvertible Government paper, without any reduction of the standard.

Against this scheme it may be objected, that it could yield no greater profit to the community than a well-regulated convertible currency, and would be exposed to some peculiar inconveniences.

The transactions of individuals, guided by the exchanges, test exactly the quantity of the paper circulation, under a good system ; at every moment they keep it to the proper amount. Under the supposed scheme we should, indeed, have the exchanges for our guide, but they would not of themselves, and by their own action, regulate the issues ; that delicate operation would be left to the Government Commissioners, and would necessarily be more imperfectly performed. If an attempt were made at all times to circulate the greatest possible quantity of inconvertible paper, and to vary its amount according to circumstances, it cannot be doubted but that occasionally the notes would be depreciated more or less from excess ; at other periods they might be deficient, and thus the public be exposed to the evils of a currency and standard unnecessarily subject to fluctuation. In order to avoid this evil, it would be prudent to fix the amount of inconvertible paper within the minimum of the convertible paper which might otherwise circulate; in which case it is clear that nothing would be gained in the way of profit by the employment of the former beyond what would be yielded by the latter. In times of political discredit, an inability to pay in specie on the part of the best-regulated Bank of Issue, making a profit of its circulation, is always possible. Under similar circumstances, an inconvertible circulation would be depreciated—there would be two prices, one in paper, the other in coin. Altogether, though founded in a great degree on correct principles, this plan seems to present many, great, and almost insuperable inconveniences.

Another suggestion made for the improvement of the currency has been, that the Government should be authorized on certain special occasions to issue securities in the nature of Exchequer-bills, which might possess the public confidence in a higher degree than any part of the existing circulation, and thus alleviate an accidental panic. It is sufficiently plain that an issue of such a nature would be eminently inconvenient, inasmuch as it would involve the necessity of calculating the interest every time that a bill changed hands. And it seems inconceivable that it could be less liable to discredit than Bank of England notes, which, in consequence of the large debt always due from the Government to the Bank, must be considered Government paper so far as regards security. Thus, then, since the Charter has been renewed, it may be safely affirmed that this scheme would prove useless, and of course inexpedient; but should a perfectly free competition in the supply of paper money be allowed, it is very probable that some measure of this kind would occasionally be found desirable. Under such circumstances we might expect, from time to time, periods of mercantile discredit, which would apply to the whole or the majority of the existing Banks; their notes would be returned to them and a vacuum created, similar to what occurred in December 1825, which an issue of paper bearing the guarantee of the Government might to a certain degree fill up, though not with such facility or advantage as Bank of England notes. It must not be forgotten that, during the panic, Exchequer-bills were at a discount.

A re-issue of £1 and £2 notes is with some persons a sure remedy for all commercial distress. The reason given for their efficiency in this way is, that they would raise prices, or render it more easy to borrow. On the first point, it must be remarked, that, being by the supposition convertible, they could never fall below the value of the gold for which they might be exchanged at the will of the holder, and that the sole effect on prices which the largest issue of them could produce, would arise from the letting loose the sovereigns they might displace, and allowing them to swell the disposable stock of bullion in the world. It must be allowed that in this way a certain fall in the value of gold would be produced; but it is equally certain, looking to the variations of the agio at Paris during the last twenty years, that in point of extent it would be hardly appreciable. So much for the influence of £1 and £2 notes on general prices. In respect to the facilities which they might offer in the obtaining of loans, it must be recollected that, where people borrow, it is not usually money, but capital, they want,—that the issuer of paper creates no capital whatever, but merely lends his credit, upon which the holder of his notes is enabled to obtain the capital of other people, or whatever commodities he may require,—that thus, no greater amount on the whole is disposable in consequence of his operations. Some difference, however, in the distribution there will probably be, and it need not be disputed but that certain persons did formerly, and, perhaps, should small notes be re-issued, would again obtain accommodation, which they are now deprived of. It may, however, be greatly doubted whether, at the present moment, any considerable number of people are to be found, who deserve credit and cannot readily obtain it. The rate of interest is surely sufficiently low, for those who have security to give; those who are in a less fortunate situation ought not to be able to borrow readily, at least not at or under the legal rate of interest.

On the whole, supposing the existence of a perfect system of paper currency, such as has been proposed in the first Section, there appears no sufficient reason, except from the danger of forgery, why £1 and £2 notes should not form a part of it. They would be cheaper and more convenient than gold; but as things now are and probably will be, it seems, on the whole, inexpedient to restore the small notes. They are peculiarly liable to excess and to discredit, and are thus very dangerous to the issuers, while the continuance of a large stock of gold in the general mass of our currency seems, under present circumstances, highly desirable.

The next schemes which demand attention are those for changing the standard from gold to silver, or for creating a double standard, as has been so strongly urged by Lord Ashburton. Some of the persons who advocate them really mean to produce a depreciation, though they do not always say so. Enough has been already remarked upon the injustice and impolicy of that measure, and in the following observations it will therefore be assumed, that no such object is in contemplation, that it is only meant to alter the nature of the standard, without lowering it.

The great and indeed only benefit arising from a silver standard is one of convenience,—

that metal being adopted as the basis of circulation in every country except England, we are now deprived of the advantage of a fixed par of exchange with any, and a certain degree of difficulty and uncertainty is thus imposed on persons engaged in mercantile transactions, as well as on the Bank of England, and the other issuers of currency. This inconvenience might have rendered it desirable, when cash payments were resumed, to have made Bank-notes payable in silver instead of gold, but is not of sufficient importance to make an alteration at present advisable, especially as that measure would render it necessary to re-coin all the silver now in circulation, at a loss to the Government of many hundred thousand pounds, or to enact that a greater weight of metal than twenty of the current shillings should form the new pound sterling, in which case the holders would suffer a loss of the difference between the current and the real value, and great difficulty be felt from the introduction of inconvenient fractions into every account. It may be farther remarked that, in consequence of the immense transactions of the Bank, gold in all probability would still be usually employed as at present, and that the calculations of an agio, constantly varying, would open a new source of perplexity to the public.

The introduction of silver as a joint standard with gold appears to be recommended chiefly because it is supposed that, in times of pressure, the Bank might derive facilities from being enabled to pay in either, and might be the better enabled to combat the efforts of great capitalists and speculators on the exchanges, whose interest might lead them to embarrass it by intercepting or withholding supplies of gold. Upon this it may be remarked, in the first place, that the supplies of bullion are derived from so many sources and attainable with so much facility, that it would be out of the power of any particular individuals, even if so disposed, to effect their object, except momentarily, and to an inconsiderable extent, and that even at present, the silver in the hands of the Bank is almost as useful in correcting an unfavourable exchange as gold would be, the only difference being, that occasionally, and for a short period, a specific demand arises for the latter usually connected with political causes. In case of an internal demand for sovereigns, silver can always be employed to purchase the metal from which they are to be coined, and in case of need, the operation could be completed with great rapidity. The above are chiefly objections to the plan for a mixed standard, considered in point of detail; but there are others which shew it to be inconsistent with sound economical principles.

There can never be at any one time more than one real standard, because the debtor will of course pay in the cheapest medium which the law allows him. The effect of a double standard would in all probability be to depreciate the currency. Whenever the metal newly introduced, silver for instance, was dearer than gold, payments would still be made in the latter, and the new regulation would produce no real effect. But if in the course of time silver became a cheaper medium of payment than gold, it would instantly be adopted as such, and so continue, until gold perhaps once more fell below silver, and resumed its former place as the medium of payment; in both cases debts would be discharged upon lower terms, than if they had been paid in currency of the previous standard.

Thus it appears that a double standard, by giving two chances of a fall in value to the debtor instead of one, must tend in the long run to enable him to discharge his obligations on lower terms than a single one, in other words will probably depreciate the standard: but it would also tend from the counteracting agency of the second metal, to check the effect of any rise in the first metal, and thus give the standard a greater degree of steadiness, though at a lower range of value. On the whole it would seem that the advantage of the plan is not sufficient to render a change desirable.

# SECTION III.

REMARKS ON THE LATE AND PREVIOUS PERIODS OF COMMERCIAL DISTRESS CONNECTED WITH DERANGEMENTS IN THE CURRENCY.

THE most remarkable periods of commercial distress connected with derangement of the currency, in recent times, have been those of 1792, 1810, 1816, 1825, and 1836. The earliest of these seems to have been considered at the time as a sort of natural visitation, without provoking any deep inquiry into its causes; but the second nearly coincided with the celebrated Report of the Bullion Committee, which first directed the public attention to the state of the Currency, and threw a clear and steady light on that before neglected subject. It does not, however, appear that any body imagined the abortive speculations and bankruptcies of that year to have arisen from the over-issue, and consequent depreciation, of Bank-notes; nor did such an opinion prevail with respect to the disasters of 1816. The discussions, however, on Peel's Bill gave new importance to the Currency, and in 1825 bank-notes had become the whole and sole agent, upon the right management of which the weal or woe of the trading community mainly depended: this opinion, though not perhaps explicitly adopted by any author of great repute, yet received apparent support from many. From that time it became popular, and is now carried so far that the entire regulation of the Currency, being supposed to rest upon the Bank of England, men are found to throw upon that body alone the blame of originating every ill-directed or exaggerated access of the spirit of speculation.

The reader will recollect, from what was stated at the commencement of the second Section, that the Author does not participate in this opinion. The evils of an imperfect and ill-managed Currency are, indeed, great, but still less overwhelming than many imagine. To suppose that, with a Currency purely metallic, or with a paper-circulation managed on such correctly scientific principles as to be exactly equivalent to it in all its attributes except superior cheapness and convenience, we should have no periods of commercial distress; that the trading world would never have to see their calling pass through the cycle of changes which Mr. Loyd so well describes, is to say, in other words, that a majority of all merchants, manufacturers, farmers, and other traders are always perfectly wise and prudent, or that a well-managed Currency is a sovereign remedy for their errors and mistakes. The first proposition being abandoned as untenable, we will devote a little attention to the second.

Nobody can deny that discredit and insolvency on the part of the issuers of paper-money must inflict a serious injury on commerce, and most persons will allow that a mixed Currency, though, generally speaking, secure and convertible, which at particular periods shall vary in amount from the metallic currency which might supply its place, is a source of very considerable evil. The question is as to the quantum of this evil; and here, unfortunately, we have no experience to guide us. France, indeed, and some other countries possess currencies which may be considered as metallic; and the first has suffered less from the hot and cold fits of the commercial fever than England or America. But then her trade is far less extensive, and its relations less complicated; and, for this and other reasons, a fair parallel between them cannot be drawn. Holland, before the Revolution, might have furnished better evidence; but the Author knows not the source whence it is to be drawn. Such a history of the commerce of the Seven Provinces as would furnish it does not exist, or has never reached him. In default of direct testimony, then, let us examine the periods of commercial distress that have occurred during the last generation, and see if in each of them causes did not exist, wholly independent of the currency, sufficient to account for a large portion of their evils.

In 1810 we had the license trade, the spirit of gambling and demoralization it occasioned, the opening new channels of communication in the place of old, enormous profits for a time:—in 1816, the close of the artificial emporia created by the war, the return of trade to ancient seats, every thing was new, every thing to be re-created, errors and miscalculations of all kinds were inevitable:—in 1825, we had the recoil from the very low prices of 1822, the independence of the Spanish American colonies, with all the exaggerated notions of their vast wealth, and, to omit minor agents, a sort of epidemic vertigo, the origin of which it were vain to assign to a particular cause.

The crisis of 1836 was more partial than any that had preceded it; indeed it presented but little more derangement than may be expected to occur every five or six years, except what the opening the trade with China and our relations with America will fully explain. In all these cases the mismanagement of the paper currency prolonged and intensified the evils which would have existed without it, but did not altogether occasion them. In America itself, this mismanagement was carried to the highest pitch, and there the substratum was to be found in the great and rapid advancement of the giant Republic, and to use Mr. Loyd's phraseology,—"the improvement, the growing confidence, and "the prosperity" long continued and carried to an extent, which to sanguine men exhibited no bounds.

However, after all due limitation, and the correction of the extravagances of public opinion, there can be no doubt that the stream of commerce would run far more smoothly with a good system of paper money than a bad one, and that the evils felt in each of the periods above alluded to were augmented by an imperfect currency; the effect of which appears, in truth, to be, to exaggerate a state of things arising from other causes, but rarely to originate it. The general excitement calls for enlarged issues, and these large issues sustain prices above their proper level, until the bubble bursts; then the nature of the evil changes, issues are too hastily contracted, discredit is extended and prolonged unnecessarily, and prices fall to an undue extent, and continue low longer than they ought before the equilibrium is restored. There is thus a cycle of action and re-action.

It being then allowed that the evils of periods of commercial distress have been augmented, though not wholly occasioned by the nature of the medium of exchange and the conduct of its managers, it may be useful to conclude this section with a short review of the accusations that have been brought against the Bank of England and the Joint Stock and Private Banks for the course pursued by them during the few years ending with 1836.

The following tabular statement will afford the best materials for guiding our judgment.

| Date. | Average Circulation Bank of England. | England. Joint-Stock and Private Banks. Aggregate Circulation. | Ireland. Average Amount of Notes half-yearly, on which Composition is paid by Joint-Stock Banks, and actual circulation, Bank of Ireland. | Total. | Treasure, Bank of England. |
|---|---|---|---|---|---|
| 28th Dec. 1833 | £ 17,469,000 | £ 10,152,000 | £ 5,081,000 | £ 32,702,000 | £ 10,200,000 |
| 29th Mar. 1834 | 18,544,000 | 10,191,000 | .... | .... | 8,753,000 |
| 28th June, ,, | 18,689,000 | 10,518,000 | 5,036,000 | 34,243,000 | 8,885,000 |
| 27th Sept. ,, | 18,437,000 | 10,154,000 | .... | .... | 6,917,000 |
| 28th Dec. ,, | 17,070,000 | 10,659,000 | 5,250,000 | 32,979,000 | 6,978,000 |
| 28th Mar. 1835 | 18,152,000 | 10,420,000 | .... | .... | 6,295,000 |
| 27th June, ,, | 17,637,000 | 10,939,000 | 5,140,000 | 33,716,000 | 6,613,000 |
| 26th Sept. ,, | 17,320,000 | 10,420,000 | .... | .... | 6,284,000 |
| 26th Dec. ,, | 16,564,000 | 11,134,000 | 5,334,000 | 33,032,000 | 7,718,000 |
| 26th Mar. 1836 | 17,669,000 | 11,447,000 | .... | .... | 8,014,000 |
| 25th June, ,, | 17,184,000 | 12,202,000 | 5,629,000 | 35,015,000 | 6,868,000 |
| 20th Sept. ,, | 18,147,000 | 11,733,000 | .... | .... | 5,719,000 |
| 13th Dec. ,, | 17,361,000 | 12,011,000 | 5,864,000 | 35,236,000 | 4,445,000 |

NOTE.—The dates in the returns of the Bank of England Circulation do not exactly agree with those of the other Banks; but the difference in time never exceeds a few days. The Parliamentary papers do not furnish materials for a more accurate comparison.

It must be remarked upon this table, that it does nòt in the latter periods referred to give a correct notion of the diminution in the issues of the Bank of England, because, during 1834, 5, and 6, contracts were successively entered into for the substitution of Bank of England notes for those of private issuers. On this point the reader is referred to page 16 of Mr. Palmer's first pamphlet. The increase in the branch circulation there shewn was the consequence of these contracts, and ought to have diminished the private issues pro tanto.

The low circulation at the close of 1835 was connected with the operation of the West India Loan.

The above table, which it would be most interesting and useful to complete by adding the circulation of the Scotch Banks for the several corresponding periods, if the requisite returns had been laid before Parliament, certainly evinces by a superfluity of evidence that none of the banks whose issues are comprehended in it have conformed to the strict rule; that their issues should be at every moment of precisely the same value as the metallic medium, which might supply their places, being increased and diminished under the same circumstances at similar periods and to a like extent. If not to have attained this degree of perfection subjects them to blame, from blame they cannot escape; but a calm review of the situation in which they have been placed will shew, that their errors are less imputable to ignorance or ill-will, than to their respective positions, or at any rate that they are less flagrant than is commonly imagined.

We will examine the accusations brought forward a little in detail, and first those directed against the Bank of England Setting newspaper critics aside, the most formidable accusers of the Bank Directors are Colonel Torrens and Mr. Loyd, both of whom object generally, that sufficient attention has not been paid to the state of the exchanges, and that the issues have not varied as a metallic currency would have naturally varied. They both of course allege by implication that the Bank Court was pledged to govern its conduct according to the above standard. But such was not the case. The principle laid down by Mr. Palmer and others in their evidence before the committee of 1832, was this, that at a period of full currency the Bank endeavoured to hold an amount of treasure equal to about one-third of its circulation and deposits, and the remaining two-thirds in securities, and to keep this amount of securities unchanged during the efflux of treasure consequent upon a period of low exchanges, so that the diminution of coin and bullion might be accompanied by a corresponding reduction of liabilities, viz. circulation and deposits.

This principle obtained the express or tacit approval of the Government, of Parliament, and the public at large, and with reference to it, and it alone, the authorities of the Bank ought to be judged. They did not imagine, as Colonel Torrens seems to suppose, that a reduction of deposits was equivalent to a reduction of circulation, or that consequently their principle was perfect; they knew its weak point, viz. that it allowed an adverse exchange to be met by a diminution of deposits, a favourable exchange by an increase of deposits, instead of by a diminution or increase of the circulation; but they propounded it because it was the best, the easiest to be explained and acted upon, that they could venture to bring forward or hope to maintain; as such, it was received by those to whose judgment they are bound to conform, and having thus obtained all the sanctions which the circumstances of the case permitted, surely the Directors are not to be blamed for having violated another and different law to which they never pretended to be subject. Those who thus blame them ought to have enforced on them, the public, and the Government, a more perfect system, at the time the present was adopted.

This view of the subject being agreed to, it remains to be seen how much the Bank has really deviated from its principle. It must be premised that under it, reckoning the rest or undivided profit at about three millions, twenty-four millions of securities might fairly be held. Now the average quarterly amount really held as stated by Mr. Horsley Palmer, deducting the investments for the West India loan, and the money belonging to the East India Company, upon which a few words will be said presently, was as follows :—

| | | |
|---|---|---|
| 1833. | 1st October | £24,200,000 |
| | 31st ,, | 23,600,000 |
| 1834. | 1st April | 23,500,000 |
| | 1st July | 22,600,000 |
| | 30th September | 24,900,000 |
| | 30th December | 23,400,000 |
| 1835. | 31st March | 25,100,000 |
| | 30th June | 23,800,000 |
| | 29th September | 22,900,000 |
| | 29th December | 22,000,000 |
| 1836. | 29th March | 22,000,000* |
| | 28th June | 22,600,000 |
| | 27th September | 24,800,000 |
| | 27th December | 25,000,000 |

The largest deviation in more than three years appears then never to have exceeded two millions, or 10 per cent., and that from circumstances connected with the West-India Loan, in the autumn of 1835, which it would take up too much room to explain, but which deprived it of any great degree of culpability; at other periods the devia-

* There was here a clerical error of £2,000,000 in Mr. Palmer's Table.

tion did not exceed 7, and was seldom even 5 per cent.

Most readers will allow that an exact conformity to the principle in question is impossible,—setting aside other disturbing influences, the varying amount of deficiency bills will effect the amount of securities from quarter to quarter, and cannot be conveniently counteracted.

But Mr. Loyd remarks upon the above statement of securities held by the Bank, that it is an arbitrary mode of making up an account to produce a desired result; implying of course that the securities held against the money belonging to the East-India Company, and that paid in on account of the West-India Loan, and subsequently lent by the Bank, ought to be considered as a portion of the securities, to which the recognized principle of management is applicable, and that consequently the whole or published amount of securities, as being irregular, and often much larger than twenty-four millions, evinced on the part of the Bank of England a great deviation from this principle.

Now it must be recollected that the sum of twenty-four millions was assumed as the proper amount to be held in securities upon a view of an amount of circulation and deposits, of which the deposits in question formed no part, and when their existence was not even contemplated. Owing to the realization of the Company's commercial assets, its balance very greatly exceeded the usual amount, and the East-India Directors naturally determined to make the excess productive. The Bank borrowed and employed this excess for fixed periods, taking care that the money-dealers to whom it was lent should be pledged to re-payment at the precise moment when the money was wanted by the authorities in Leadenhall-street. It was considered, and surely with reason, that by taking the entire management of this kind of transaction, the Bank would insure the least possible interference with the currency and money-market, especially as the India Company is unused to such affairs. Had the Bank taken the money, paid interest for it, and not re-loaned it, for the sake of apparently, but not really adhering to its principle of management, and the amount of securities originally fixed in accordance with it, viz. twenty-four millions, a sum amounting sometimes to three or four millions would have been abstracted unnaturally from the currency of the metropolis, to the serious inconvenience of the public.

The reasoning applicable to the employment of the Company's money tells with increased force on that derived from the West-India loan. Had the Bank determined to hold to the fixed amount of securities in the autumn of 1835, the consequence would have been that almost the whole currency of the metropolis would have been found within its coffers. We may be told that this could not have happened; that the notes would have oozed out through the discount-office to a greater or less extent, and the amount of securities been *pro tanto* augmented; this is doubtless true; but would not such a forced action have interfered materially with the natural play of the currency and the ordinary affairs of business, while hardly any inconvenience was felt under the course pursued, viz. an offer of advances at a rate of interest calculated to call for, and which did indeed call for nearly the exact amount of the loan, such advances being repayable at the periods when the compensation was to be disbursed to the proprietors of slaves. The whole transaction thus described appears to be creditable to the Bank, rather than deserving of blame; and it seems equally clear that Mr. Palmer was fully justified in omitting all reference to the West-India loan, as well as to the India Company's extra deposits, in his statement of securities.

We must finally recollect that the sum of twenty-four millions was recognized as the amount to be held in securities, on certain data, say about thirty-one millions in circulation and deposits, and three millions of rest or surplus capital; but it is clear that these data would have required to be reviewed after the lapse of a few years; nobody could imagine that the amount was to be invariable. A complete oscillation in the currency, that is to say, a period commonly of three to five years, would usually be followed by a state of things requiring a re-adjustment. At present it may be doubted if the Bank can properly fix its amount of securities at more than from twenty-two to twenty-three millions, viz. about nineteen millions for two-thirds of twenty-nine millions of circulation, and deposits, and three millions of rest.

The above observations on the conduct of the Bank will, it is hoped, relieve the Directors from a large portion if not the whole of the blame which has been cast upon them for deviating apparently from the principle of holding a fixed amount of securities; and here it may be remarked that Colonel Torrens allows them to have been passably consistent in this respect.

Other accusations of minor importance have been brought against them, which would occupy too much space, and be foreign to a work, the object of which is to explain the principles of currency, and suggest improvements in our existing system of circulation. One or two points, especially the insufficiency of the published accounts of the Bank, animadverted on by Mr. Loyd, will be noticed hereafter—at present it may suffice to say that they are such as the law prescribes.

Let us now examine the conduct of the joint-stock and private banks as issuing bodies. A reference to the table, at page 77, will shew that their deviation from sound principle has been of an extensive kind. To omit other instances of it, between March and June 1836 the private issuers in England, in defiance of a generally adverse exchange, a diminution of treasure in the coffers of the Bank, and of the Bank circulation, augmented their notes £755,000, or about 6½ per cent. viz. from £11,447,000 to £12,202,000. The Irish joint-stock and private banks were still more extravagant; for, comparing the half-years ending June 1835 and June 1836, they increased their circulation from £1,713,000 to ££2,291,000, or about 30 per cent. The Bank of Ireland did not participate in this error.

The public has no means of subjecting the Scotch Banks to the same ordeal which has been applied to their English and Irish brethren; but we may feel perfectly assured that, were their accounts published, they would exhibit equally glaring evidence of a deviation from sound principle.

It is clear then that joint-stock banks and private banks manage the part of their business which consists in issuing notes very badly, so far as the public interest is concerned; but though their errors in this respect are sufficiently manifest, it does not therefore follow that the opprobrium cast upon them is well founded. There has been no legal duty imposed upon them with respect to the mode in which their circulation should be conducted other than that of discharging their obligations in gold or Bank-of-England notes. They have been left to act upon their own views of their own interest; these views, sometimes well, sometimes ill-founded, have indeed led them astray, so far as the good of the country is concerned, but then surely we ought to blame the Legislature, which has forborne to prescribe or enforce any particular line of action, rather than persons, who, left to their free agency, naturally imagined themselves fully justified in following the only principle which seemed applicable to their case, viz. that of obtaining the largest possible profit.

Indeed, when it is considered that during a period of very severe pressure prolonged for many months, only two joint-stock banks, and very few private bankers stopped payment and that the creditors of the former will probably lose nothing, it would seem that the private issuers deserve much praise rather than blame for their conduct during the late hurricane in the money-market.

This view of the subject is strengthened when it is considered that they neither had nor have any easy and correct method of adjusting their circulation, so as to make it vary as a metallic circulation would vary. The accounts published by the Bank may not be sufficiently explicit;

but, even after they had been rendered as complete as the greatest admirer of publicity would ask for or desire, still it appears impossible for a private issuer to devise any practical plan for the regulation of his currency fully calculated to attain the end in view. Even the most expert economists at the head of a joint-stock company could hardly do more than watch the circulation of the Bank and the ingress and egress of treasure into or out of its coffers, and strive to extend or contract their issues accordingly. It is surely visionary to expect even as much as this from a vast majority of the issuing bodies, now established in the three kingdoms, especially when they are wealthy, and holding a large amount of securities always marketable in London, may feel assured of being able at any moment to command the amount of gold or Bank of England notes they may require. While the exchanges are falling and the rate of interest rising, such bodies will almost invariably be led astray, and induced to extend their issues instead of contracting them, and will err in an opposite direction when circumstances change, although in direct defiance of all sound principle. Experience, and *à priori* reasoning, alike confirm this view. The business of issue well conducted can yield but a moderate profit; ill-conducted so far as the public is concerned, it may yield a far more considerable profit: can any reasonable man doubt which course will be pursued?

In concluding this section it may be well to direct the reader's attention once more to the tabular statement at page 77, with a view to point out the conclusive evidence it affords, in refutation of the elaborate reasoning of Colonel Torrens, intended to shew that the Bank of England has always the power of controlling the issues of provincial Banks within a period so short as to prevent any derangement in the whole currency. We there see an almost progressive increase in the latter part of 1835 and the first six months of 1836, in the circulation of the joint-stock and private banks, while that of the Bank of England had on the whole diminished, and this during a period of time quite long enough to influence prices, and cause great mercantile miscalculations. It is very true that convertible paper cannot permanently be depreciated, that it must at length become equivalent to the specie it represents; but under certain circumstances the adjustment may be long deferred, as observed before; the arguments of Colonel Torrens are correct, as shewing the mode in which the controlling principle acts. His error consists in assigning to it a greater rapidity of action than it really possesses.

Colonel Torrens further blames the Bank of England for having established branches and made contracts with joint-stock banks with a view of inducing them to issue Bank of England notes instead of their own. If the table above referred to shews that the Bank of England on the whole has managed its circulation on more correct principles than its rivals, this censure will appear to be misplaced. Indeed, it seems clear that the influence of the controlling currency will be more effective in proportion as it forms a larger part of the whole. Added to this consideration there is another of no small importance. It is agreed on all hands that our money system is defective, that changes in it are required; now in a few years the charter of the Bank may be modified, and its functions and mode of action altered with facility to suit the views of the Legislature, but to interfere with the provincial banks will be found a more difficult task, and the difficulty will increase with every augmentation of their hold on the whole mass of the currency. If then the management of the Bank of England circulation had been worse instead of better than that of private issuers, it might still have been on the whole consistent with the public good to have increased the relative proportion of the former.

In concluding this section it is necessary to call the reader's particular attention to an evil as completely inherent in the present system of paper issues in this country, as the tendency to over-issues, when a spirit of speculation is abroad, prices rising, and the rate of interest high, viz. a directly opposite tendency,—a disposition on the part of all banks to contract their circulation, in periods of stagnation, distress, and quiescence, to adopt once more Mr. Loyd's phraseology, in a greater degree than could occur with a metallic currency, or paper regulated on a metallic basis. The mischief above-mentioned has been often alluded to in this pamphlet, but has not been duly appreciated by the public; yet its effects are perhaps as disastrous, except that they do not involve insolvency on the part of issuers, as its opposite. In a natural state of the currency, any amount of treasure imported, except for the mere purpose of exportation, would occasion an increase of circulation to an equal amount, and the consequence would be that the currency on the whole could never fall quite so much or remain so long below its average amount as at present.

It is probable that an increase will be found in the treasure of the Bank, between its lowest amount last spring, and the highest just previous to the next turn of the exchanges, of from seven to eight millions. Now such an influx of treasure is unnatural, and could never occur with a metallic circulation—its effects, greater or less, in proportion to the extent of the error, will be accompanied in the first instance by a depression of prices, unnecessary in extent and continued too long, and finally by a reaction, which will occasion an equally unnecessary and faulty excess the other way.

Such is the state of things at present; its cause is obvious—all banks look to profit in the issue of their notes; when interest is high and large profits are to be made, they make advances freely; when prices fall, engagements run out, and the demands of borrowers diminish, they are almost irresistibly impelled to limit the supply of paper-money. Thus we see that, under existing circumstances, the state of the money-market and of prices, which have been already shewn to be fallacious criteria, and not that of the exchanges, the only safe one, chiefly regulate the amount of the currency. It is hoped that the above very imperfect observations will suffice to attract the reader's attention to a point of very great importance, which for its complete elucidation would require much more space than can be afforded to it here.

# SECTION IV.

---

REASONS WHY THE SCHEME FOR A PAPER CURRENCY PROPOSED IN THE FIRST SECTION CANNOT NOW BE ADOPTED—MEASURES WHICH THE LEGISLATURE OUGHT TO ADOPT, SO AS GRADUALLY TO INTRODUCE A BETTER SYSTEM.

WE have seen, in the first Section, that, in order to furnish a perfect paper currency to the country, it would be necessary to have a single issuing body, which should be strictly prohibited from engaging in any banking transactions, properly so called, either by receiving deposits, or by making advances in the usual way on securities bearing interest, excepting at its first establishment and to a fixed extent, or subsequently upon due consideration, when it was found that the positive amount or proportion of treasure and securities might safely be altered. The only business of such an establishment would be to issue notes for gold and silver, and gold and silver for notes, and its effect would be, that the currency would exactly and at every moment be equalized by the exchanges, without any interference whatever from other causes. Under present circumstances, however, almost insurmountable obstacles oppose themselves to the execution of this plan; and the object of this section will be to describe a course more practicable though less perfect, which may indeed ultimately lead to the adoption of the former.

It may here be remarked that at the two last periods, when the attention of Parliament has been called to the state of the currency, and measures of legislation have been the result, the great evil against which these have been directed was insolvency on the part of the issuers of notes. The numerous failures among country banks in 1792, 1810, 1816, and 1826, and the wide-spread distress they occasioned, sufficiently account for this; and the example of the Scotch banks, among whom insolvency is almost unknown, led to the establishment of joint-stock banks in England, with a special regard to their superior solidity when compared with private bankers. In this point of view the measures of the Legislature were judicious, and its object has been, to a certain degree, obtained. But we have seen that issuing bodies, although perfectly solid, may derange the circulation and occasion serious evils to the country by violating the principle that a paper currency should vary as a metallic currency would vary. This is a doctrine, if not of recent discovery, at least only pressed upon the public attention in the last few years; yet its importance is great, and without exact attention to it no material improvement in our money system is possible.

The following, it must be recollected, are the chief evils which present themselves in our existing paper circulation.

1. A tendency to vary both as to excess or deficiency in an unnecessary degree and at unsuitable periods.

2. A liability to discredit both mercantile and political in a large portion of it, if not the whole.

3. Temporary or permanent insolvency on the part of many of the issuers.

Viewed on the whole and with reference to these three points, the most objectionable portion of the existing currency is that which is formed by the notes of the country bankers; then come those of the joint-stock banks, while that of the Bank of England is by far the most perfect, being not only quite unobjectionable in point of security, but also issued with a constant although too imperfect reference to the state of the exchanges, and upon the plan of holding a fixed proportion of securities, which has hitherto appeared the best under the circumstances in which that establishment is placed. The first great reform, then, which the legislature should undertake, were its hands free, would be to abolish altogether all provincial issues whatever; but against so sweeping an enactment it would be urged, that some of the issuing bodies are in possession of unexpired charters, which could not be infringed without their consent, and that others have a sort of vested interest in the business they carry on, with which it would be very harsh, if not unjust, to interfere,—that even supposing the plea of injustice could be overruled, great difficulties would still present themselves from the strong opinion which prevails in many parts of the empire of the local advantages which the inhabitants derive from private Bank paper—an opinion which, however erroneous, would render its abolition eminently unpopular, and might lead to an ebullition of public feeling which no Government could withstand. What took place in Scotland, in 1826, respecting small notes, may afford some, though but a faint notion of the state of things that might be expected, should such a measure be pressed; and on the whole, then, it must be allowed, that an issue of provincial paper is an evil which cannot be removed at once, however great may be its extent, and that we must therefore content ourselves with the application of palliatives, some of which will be proposed hereafter.

Assuming that no forcible attempt ought to, or indeed can with any hope of success, be made to put an end at once to the circulation of the private and joint-stock banks, it will probably be granted that during the continuance of the Bank Charter, it would be unjust, even were it expedient to establish a government issue in the metropolis, upon the plan proposed in the first section.

It remains then to be seen what plan could be devised calculated to introduce a better order of things,—a plan which should at the same time be just to existing interests, and efficacious with respect to its objects. It will of course be necessary to divide our proposed alterations into what concerns, 1st, the Bank of England, 2dly, country issuers.

The principle of retaining a fixed amount of securities lately acted upon by the Bank had the merit of being the first, if not the only system at all in accordance with the rules of science which has ever yet guided the conduct of any very important body issuing a paper currrency; yet it is palpably faulty, as mixing together circulation and deposits, things in their nature distinct, and treating an increase or diminution of the former as equivalent to an increase or diminution of the latter; it is besides, as experience has shewn, of extremely difficult application, and requiring, to be understood in practice, much explanation, which may not after all be successful in making it perfectly intelligible to the public. Rendering full justice to the talent of those who devised this scheme, it seems clear that the time is come when it ought to be abandoned, and the plan so ingeniously explained by Colonel Torrens, viz. that of forming two district establishments within the walls of the Bank, of which one should form the banking, the other the circulation department, be substituted for it, provided there are no insuperable difficulties of a practical kind in the way. Upon this point the author's acquaintance with the internal mechanism of the Bank is not sufficiently particular to enable him to pronounce a decided opinion ; he can only say, that although perhaps great, he cannot think them insuperable, and that no minor obstacles in the details of the Corporation should be allowed to stand in the way of a great public good. For an account of Colonel Torrens's plan, the reader might be at once referred to that gentleman's letter to Lord Melbourne, but it will be convenient to state it here, especially with a view to render his sketch more complete, though the frame-work will still be only incompletely filled up.

The circulation department should strictly confine itself to the exchange of gold for notes and notes for gold, with the following exceptions: 1st, That it might be allowed to purchase and sell silver in the market at fixed published prices, and to a certain amount, say two to three millions sterling. 2d, It should be compellable at all times to buy bar gold or foreign gold coin at £3 : 17 : 6 per ounce, and be allowed to sell at

£3 : 17 : 9; but it should not be obliged to pay its notes except in the current coin of the realm: the object of this regulation would be to impose a certain obstacle in the nature of a seignorage to the constant transport of treasure into and out of the country, and thus diminish the expense of coinage. 3d, It might also be permitted to lend notes upon coin or bullion, at a low rate of interest—say one per cent.: this might at times afford facilities to commerce, and furnish a small profit, while it could lead to no derangement in the currency.

The circulation department should commence operations with an amount of treasure equal to from one-third to one-half the notes in circulation, and comprehending both gold and silver; from eight to ten millions would be an ample reserve. This amount of coin and bullion would probably, indeed, be much more than subsequent experience, acquired after two or three revolutions in the currency, would shew to be necessary; still, in commencing a new system, even an excess of caution is wise. The notes in circulation not represented by the precious metals would be invested in securities bearing interest; and the amount of these securities thus handed over to the circulation department would not be allowed to vary, unless at some future period it might be found expedient to diminish the proportion of the treasure reserve, or unless the whole amount of the paper-currency should increase or diminish. Some new arrangements respecting the Branch Banks would be requisite; but to enter upon them here would occupy too much space. Speaking generally, they should be assimilated to private or joint-stock banks, and their notes be only payable where issued. Complete publicity should exist.

The banking department would be left to the management of the Directors, under the superintendence of the Proprietors. Their object, of course, would be to make as large a profit as might be consistent with prudence and good management; and in their attempts to do so they would no longer be thwarted by having to discharge two sets of duties, often inconsistent with each other. Their mistakes, if any, might be injurious to their employers, but could not affect the public interests in the same way as at present.

With a view to increase the disposable banking capital, the Government ought to give its aid, by rendering available a portion of the capital lent to the State. No direct repayment would be necessary, but merely an arrangement by which this portion of the National Debt should be made saleable like the Three per Cent. Consols or Reduced. The new stock might be called the Bank New Three per Cents. The disposable and active capital would thus be the above amount of stock, say, in the first instance, five millions, about three millions and a half paid off and invested in annuities after the last renewal of the charter, and the rest, about three millions, added to these sums, the banking department would have to employ the deposits, both public and private. On the whole, it would seem that the adoption of the above plan would tend to increase rather than diminish the profits of the Corporation.

It would be well if an arrangement could be made by which the Bank of Ireland should be united with that of England, as far as concerned the circulation department, or at any rate that a separation should take place in its business, similar to that here proposed for the latter. This would place the currency of the sister island on a more firm and consistent basis than it has hitherto possessed.

But, supposing the above scheme to be adopted, the important question arises, how are we to deal with the currency of the private issuers? That currency, we may be assured, will and must be issued on erroneous principles: it never can vary as a metallic currency could vary; erring sometimes on the side of excess, sometimes of deficiency, it will be exposed at particular periods to mercantile discredit, and in times of extreme pressure a portion of the issuers will become insolvent, either permanently or for a time.

There can be no doubt but that the complete extinguishment of all private issues, at the earliest practicable period, should be the great object of the Legislature; and it seems clear that a law effecting this object at once, and making compensation to those who suffered under it, if such compensation could be fairly claimed,—a point upon which the writer will not enter,—would be the wisest course that could be adopted. But, supposing that no Ministry could even venture now upon such a measure, and that the country is not ripe for it, at least there could be no objection to pass a law forbidding any persons not now in possession of the privilege to make use of it; and it might be possible also to abolish all private issues prospectively, say in ten or twenty years, and to forbid the establishment of any new branch of an existing bank in the meantime.

The circulation department of the Bank should also be compelled to furnish its notes to any issuing body which might deposit an equivalent amount of treasure and approved securities, in the proportion of one-third of the former to two-thirds of the latter. This arrangement might appear unjust to the proprietors of Bank-stock, who, as above stated, would have to furnish in the first instance coin and bullion equivalent to perhaps half their issues, but as they are now practically obliged to provide a metallic basis for the whole currency, they would not in reality be aggrieved by this apparent want of proportion. The interest on the securities deposited would be paid to the depositing bank, after deducting a small compensation for the expenses of the establishment.

The private issuers would not in this way make as large a profit as they now do, but they would make as much as they ought to make, and would be freed from all anxiety as to discredit and other inconveniences which occasionally, at present, are the sources of great loss to them.

The most ample publicity should be enforced on all issuing bodies in the three kingdoms—not the mere meagre details which now appear quarterly in the Gazette—but the monthly circulation and reserve of bullion and Bank-of-England notes of each bank. These returns should be methodized and averaged, and otherwise be rendered as intelligible and useful to the public as possible. To this regulation should be added an enforcement of adequate security to the public for the amount of the circulation. Several good effects would result—the prevention of loss to holders of notes—a considerable safeguard against discredit, and the creation of a motive for the private and joint-stock banks to abandon a portion of their business, which they cannot carry on for the benefit of the public. They would doubtless struggle against a law which had a tendency to obstruct their freedom of action and somewhat diminish their profit. They might raise a cry of injustice ; the answer to it would be that they have only a permissive right to trench on the prerogatives of sovereignty by coining money, for which privilege they never paid. That even to abolish this right, when its exercise had been found to be pernicious to the common weal, could not be considered unjust,—still less then to modify it,—to subject it to certain conditions which should do no more than prevent its abuse. The securities given would of course bear interest, a lower interest probably than that now yielded by the capital borrowed upon notes, but still as much as a body issuing paper-money, with a due regard to the welfare of the community, can fairly expect.

It is the more necessary to take immediate measures for the reform of the country issues, because, as things now are, the existence of the currency of the Bank of England out of the metropolis hangs upon a thread. Even in Lancashire, which used to be supplied by it exclusively, joint-stock notes are now circulated, and will gradually more and more make their way, until their rivals are entirely expelled. The final result will be to confine the latter to a constantly diminishing circle around the metropolis. It need hardly be remarked that the Bank of England cannot, with propriety, compete at all times with private establishments in the ordinary details of banking, or consequently keep out its circulation in opposition to theirs.

The reader will observe that, in what has preceded, it has not been attempted to exhibit a plan perfect in all its parts, but to furnish a rough sketch which, in its practical application, would require to be carefully considered, so as to meet the existing state and future exigences of the country in a way the most complete, and with the least possible shock to existing interests. No doubt, however, exists in the author's mind, that any apparent difficulties which such a scrutiny might unfold, could be readily overcome should the Legislature, fully impressed with the weighty evils inherent in the present state of the currency, set about their removal with an earnest zeal, proportioned to the magnitude of the occasion.

And here it may be necessary to remark, that, although after summing up and comparing opposing inconveniences, it seems highly desirable, on the whole, that the Bank should be divided without delay into the two departments for circulation and ordinary banking business, yet under the supposition of the country circulation being allowed to remain in its existing state, immense difficulties will occur in maintaining inviolably this separation. Under such circumstances we may anticipate with almost perfect certainty, and within a few years, a period of over-issue and subsequent discredit of provincial paper, attended perhaps by many failures on the part of the issuers, who ordinarily keep a very trifling reserve, relying upon the resources of the Bank in times of pressure. In such a state of things the Bank of England, as it now exists, would freely extend its issues on all sorts of securities, and thus supply the vacuum. The circulation department could not afford aid in this way without a gross violation of its rules. In December 1825 and January 1826 many millions in notes and gold were issued from the Bank, and were all wanted, so enormous was the vacuum, inasmuch as the exchanges rose during that period and long afterwards. Upon the proposed scheme this sum could only be provided by importation of treasure, and notes issued upon it, and would require perhaps a year before it could be put in circulation. The above is doubtless a weighty objection, but not invincible; the difficulty it points out might be met by a temporary deviation from the strict laws of the institution, guarded by the provisos best calculated to prevent their violation in any cases except those of absolute necessity. Thus the Directors of the

Bank might be authorized to make advances on securities from the funds of the circulation department to a limited amount upon an application to that effect from the First Lord of the Treasury, the Chancellor of the Exchequer, and the President of the Board of Trade for the time being, such application, with the reasons for it, being inserted in the Gazette, and laid before Parliament. The difficulty would thus be overcome with perhaps some risk of abuse, in the application of the remedy; and this circumstance should furnish one more argument for a reform of the provincial issues, which are not only imperfect in themselves, but create a serious obstacle to the introduction of a good system in the metropolis.

Some writers, and the high authority of Mr. Loyd may be cited in support of their views, are of opinion that a great good would result from a publication of the accounts of the Bank in more detail than at present. The Author is an avowed enemy of all mystery and concealment, and would readily agree to the greatest publicity being given to all items, which the public may have an interest in knowing; such for instance as actual, along with averaged amounts; but he would not anticipate the removal of any large portion of the evils attending our present system of currency from the change thus proposed. Well-informed and inquisitive persons may learn all that is necessary to form a correct judgment on the state of the currency at present, and speaking practically, a country issuer need only refer to the state of the treasure and circulation, their increase or diminution: average amounts are those from which the most useful inferences are to be drawn.

A yearly or half-yearly report to the Proprietors would be a more instructive document than the most elaborate accounts published without any accompanying remarks. The above paragraph supposes that the plan and division into two departments should not be adopted. Was it to take effect, the greatest publicity would of course be given to the account of the circulation department, while the banking department would become a mere private speculation, and its accounts would be dealt with as the Proprietors might judge best for their own interests.

In conclusion, we may observe that, however desirous the Directors of the Bank of England might be to introduce the proposed system, they cannot be expected to do so on their own responsibility, especially in the existing state of public opinion, which has almost every thing to learn on the subject of currency. They must receive an impulse, or at least a summons from without; they must have the concurrence and support of the government, perhaps of the legislature, of the court of proprietors, and if possible of the community at large, and it is difficult to say who should take the initiative. This is a matter which the author leaves to the consideration of others, satisfied if he has at all contributed to throw light upon the subject of currency, which, though apparently easy and simple, has called forth more conflicting opinions and gained a less firm footing, with reference to its true principles, in the public mind, than any other which has elicited an equal degree of attention and discussion.

THE END.